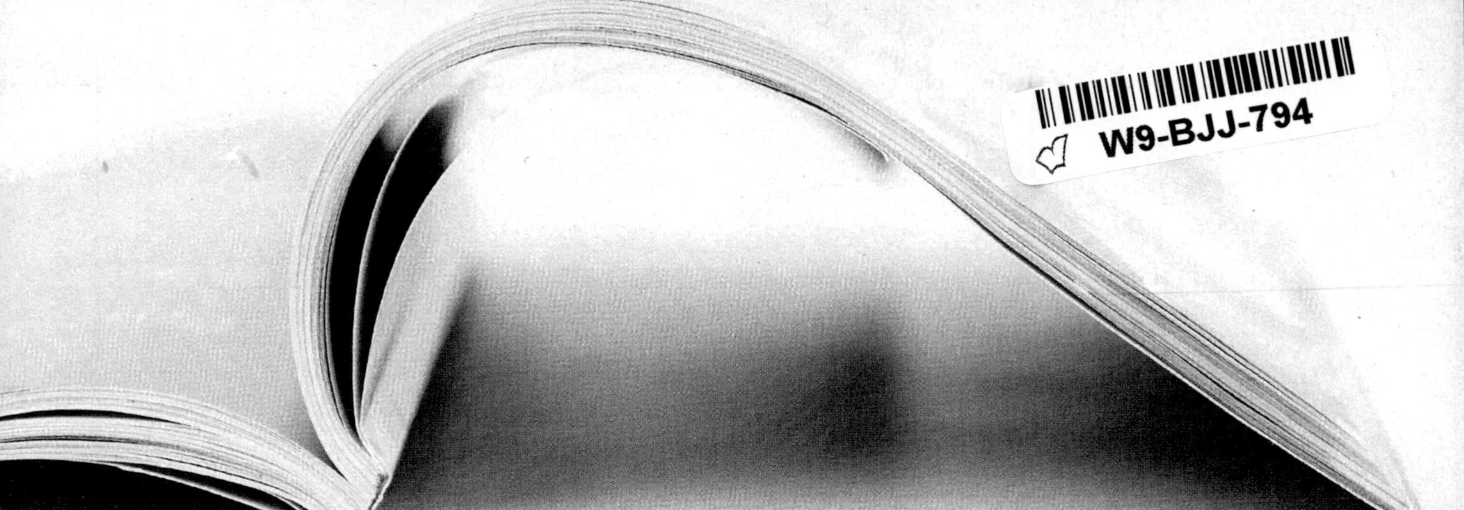

IN THE BOOK

▶ LEARN MORE ABOUT THIS 4LTR PRESS SOLUTION ▶

AN INNOVATIVE CONCEPT IN TEACHING AND LEARNING SOLUTIONS DESIGNED TO BEST REACH TODAY'S STUDENTS

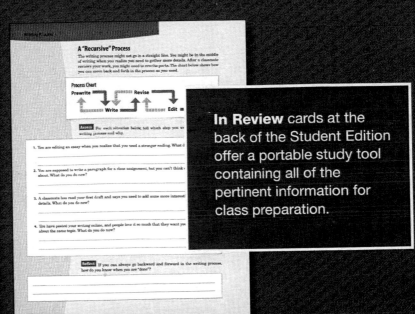

Writing Process | IN REVIEW

The Writing Process

Writing is a process. It is very difficult to write a great paragraph or essay all at once. The process makes writing easy by breaking the job into five steps:

Process	Activities
Prewriting	Start the process by (1) selecting a topic to write about, (2) collecting details about it, and (3) finding your focus, the main idea or thesis.
Writing	Then write your first draft, using your prewriting plan as a general guide. Writing a first draft allows you to connect your thoughts about your topic.
Revising	Carefully review your first draft and have a classmate review it as well. Change any parts that could be clearer and more complete.
Editing	Edit your revised writing by checking for style, grammar, punctuation, and spelling errors.
Publishing	During the final step, prepare your writing to share with your instructor, your peers, or another audience.

Assess Demonstrate your understanding of the writing process by matching the steps in the process with the activities that are appropriate to each step.

1. Prewriting
2. Writing
3. Revising
4. Editing
5. Publishing

- Correcting errors in punctuation and spelling
- Posting your work online or sharing it with your instructor or family members
- Deciding what you want to write about and gathering details about it
- Asking a classmate to read your work and help you figure out the best way to fix it
- Creating a first draft and letting your planning guide the way

Reflect Which part of the writing process is most challenging to you? Why?

Writing Process

A "Recursive" Process

The writing process might not go in a straight line. You might be in the middle of writing when you realize you need to gather more details. After a classmate reviews your work, you might need to rewrite parts. The chart below shows how you can move back and forth in the process as you need.

Process Chart

Prewrite → Write → Revise → Edit

Assess For each situation below, tell which step you w... writing process and why.

1. You are editing an essay when you realize that you need a stronger ending. What d...
2. You are supposed to write a paragraph for a class assignment, but you can't think ... about. What do you do now?
3. A classmate has read your first draft and says you need to add some more interesti... details. What do you do now?
4. You have posted your writing online, and people love it so much that they want you... about the same topic. What do you do now?

Reflect If you can always go backward and forward in the writing process, how do you know when you are "done"?

In Review cards at the back of the Student Edition offer a portable study tool containing all of the pertinent information for class preparation.

THE STATS

WRITE 1
Are you in?

"I like how it is presented, and I like the concept. Just looking at it makes me **want to read it.**"

– **Chas Smith**, Student *James Madison University*

60%

Percentage of students who are multimodal learners

Research on learning styles has consistently shown that the majority of today's students are kinesthetic learners and use all of their modalities (Visual, Aural, Read/Write, and Kinesthetic) to take in new information. Throughout **WRITE 1** and the accompanying online materials, students and instructors will find interactive tools and activities to accommodate any learning style and foster an exciting learning environment.

87%

Percentage of students who believe that 4LTR Press solutions are designed more closely to the way they study

Our complete learning solution delivers content in multiple formats, accessible both online and in print.

92%

Percentage of students who are likely to use the CourseMate website to study for a class or test

Cengage Learning's **CourseMate** brings the concepts of writing to life with interactive learning, study, and exam preparation tools that support **WRITE 1**.

97%

Percentage of students who are likely to use the In Review cards

Unique to **WRITE 1**, our book's In Review cards offer a handy at-a-glance reference for need-to-know material.

STUDENT TESTED, FACULTY APPROVED

THE 4LTR PRESS PROCESS

ARE WE LISTENING?

Reach out to students to understand their learning preferences. Now more than ever, students are visually oriented. **WRITE 1** uses charts, graphs, photos, and illustrations throughout each chapter to help students better understand the writing process.

DID WE DO IT?

Develop learning solutions based on today's students and validate through iterative process to ensure the ideal product mix. WRITE 1 includes *real* student writing samples to illustrate the writing process, as well as clear objectives, explanations, and directions. Designed for the way today's students access information, each two-page spread provides students with a clear start and end point for their work.

DO YOU LIKE IT?

Gain faculty approval to finalize the product and content mix specific to the discipline. Thanks to the 60 instructors who collaborated with us to bring **WRITE 1** to the classroom.

ARE YOU IN?

Publish the student-tested, faculty-approved teaching and learning solution. WRITE 1 teaches students the traits of successful sentences and paragraphs and the inextricable link between reading and writing. Portable study tools and powerful digital resources—including **CourseMate** and the optional **Aplia for Basic Writing** homework solution—combine to help students take their writing to the next level.

ARE YOU KIDDING?

Our research never ends! Continual feedback from students ensures that we keep up with their changing needs.

Dr. Deborah King

WRITE 1

Baltimore City Community College Edition

Dave Kemper | Verne Meyer | John Van Rys | Patrick Sebranek

CENGAGE Learning™

Australia • Brazil • Japan • Korea • Mexico • Singapore • Spain • United Kingdom • United States

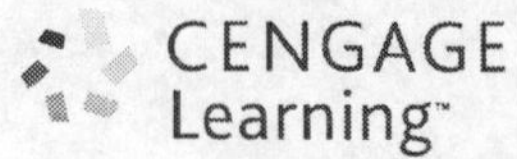

WRITE 1; Baltimore City Community College Edition

Executive Editors:
Maureen Staudt
Michael Stranz

Senior Project Development Manager:
Linda deStefano

Marketing Specialist:
Courtney Sheldon

Senior Production/Manufacturing Manager:
Donna M. Brown

PreMedia Manager:
Joel Brennecke

Sr. Rights Acquisition Account Manager:
Todd Osborne

Cover Image:
Getty Images*

*Unless otherwise noted, all cover images used by Custom Solutions, a part of Cengage Learning, have been supplied courtesy of Getty Images with the exception of the Earthview cover image, which has been supplied by the National Aeronautics and Space Administration (NASA).

WRITE 1
Dave Kemper | Verne Meyer | John Van Rys | Patrick Sebranek

For product information and technology assistance, contact us at
Cengage Learning Customer & Sales Support, 1-800-354-9706
For permission to use material from this text or product,
submit all requests online at **cengage.com/permissions**
Further permissions questions can be emailed to
permissionrequest@cengage.com

ISBN-13: 978-1-133-43992-9

ISBN-10: 1-133-43992-6

Cengage Learning
5191 Natorp Boulevard
Mason, Ohio 45040
USA

Cengage Learning is a leading provider of customized learning solutions with office locations around the globe, including Singapore, the United Kingdom, Australia, Mexico, Brazil, and Japan. Locate your local office at: **international.cengage.com/region.**

Cengage Learning products are represented in Canada by Nelson Education, Ltd.
For your lifelong learning solutions, visit **www.cengage.com/custom.**
Visit our corporate website at **www.cengage.com.**

Printed in the United States of America

READING

Contents

WRITING

WRITE 1:
Sentences and Paragraphs

CONTENTS

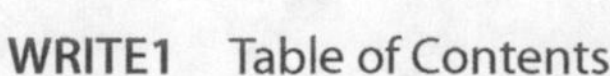

"Easy writing make
hard reading, bu
hard writing make
easy reading.
—Florence Kin

READING

Words for Read/Write Class

1. Approximately
2. Conversion
3. Fraction
4. Percent
5. Equivalent
6. Improper
7. Product
8. Inequality
9. Compare
10. Expanded
11. Prime
12. Median
13. Divide
14. Reciprocals
15. Simplest
16. Perimeter
17. Translating
18. Composite
19. Expression
20. Operations
21. Remainder
22. Estimation
23. Articulate
24. Skeptical
25. Flamboyant
26. Emphasis
27. Belligerent
28. Complacency
29. Augment
30. Tantalize
31. Circumscribe
32. Compatible
33. Synopsis
34. Coherent
35. Communal

Lesson 1

Before You Read or View, Take Four Actions.

Before you read or view, you can quickly take four actions that dramatically improve comprehension (that is, understanding):

1. Survey the reading selection or program to get an overview of what will be coming.
2. Guess the purpose of the reading selection or program.
3. Predict what's going to happen.
4. Think about your prior knowledge of the subject matter.

We will discuss each action one at a time. It will take some time to describe each action. However, you should take just a few moments to apply all four actions before you start reading a selection.

1. Survey to Get an Overview of What's Coming.

Surveying a reading is like watching a preview. When you go to a movie, often you have already seen the preview for it several times. The preview shows you some of the highlights of the movie. You often know who the main characters are (and which actors play them), you've viewed some of the scenery and settings, and you have a sense of the film's genre—whether the movie is going to be a fast-paced action adventure, a romantic comedy, or a horror flick.

Similarly, if you take a few moments to survey or preview a reading selection, you will tremendously improve your chances of comprehending the reading selection. When you preview, you do not read the whole selection, you only examine selected parts. Following are the parts to look at.

Read These Parts Quickly When You Survey.

- **The title:** What do these words reveal about the subject? Some titles also have a subtitle. For example, here is a title from a health book: "Working Out on Campus: Student Bodies in Motion." The main title is "Working Out on Campus," and the subtitle is "Student Bodies in Motion." You should read both parts of the title to gather information when you survey.
- **The headings:** Read each heading and, for a moment, think about how it relates to the title. You can tell the headings from the regular text in different ways:

  1. Headings may sit on their own lines.
  2. Headings may be in **bold** or *italic* type.
  3. Headings may be printed in all capital letters.
  4. Headings may be printed in a different color than the regular text or in a larger size.

- **The first sentence of each paragraph:** Read each first sentence quickly to get a sense of what that paragraph will cover.
- **Words that are in boldface or *italic* type:** These words are likely to be some of the most important ideas the author wants you to remember. In textbooks, words that are in **bold type** are often followed by a definition of that word.
- **Images and their captions:** If photos, graphs, or charts are part of the reading, look at them and read their captions. The caption is the title or sentence that explains the visual. We will talk more about visuals and captions in Lesson 14.

Example of Surveying

In the following reading selection, the parts that are highlighted in yellow are the parts you read when surveying. Take a moment to think about each highlighted piece of text as you read it.

Engage in Your Learning Process

1 Most people have mastered "the look"—with which you stare blankly at someone while trying to act interested. In reality, your mind is wandering more than listening or learning. It could be that the person speaking is not very interesting or that you are just tired or unmotivated that day.

2 No matter the situation, it is your responsibility to understand what the person is saying. In a learning situation, the key is to engage with the speaker. To engage means to get either mentally or physically involved and to participate actively. Active participation (1) increases concentration, (2) improves listening, (3) seems to make the time go quicker, and (4) positively affects overall learning.

3 How can you actively take part in a learning situation? Five key ways to engage in the learning process are discussed in the following sections.

4 **BE THERE AND DO IT.** One obvious way to increase your potential for learning is to be physically and mentally present. Whether you are learning in a classroom or lab or searching the Internet, learning sessions are a very important part of the learning process. Since learning is an individual activity, there is no substitute for being there. In every learning situation, you have the choice of acting like a sponge or a rock. Learners who act like sponges soak up the information through active participation, demonstrate a positive learning attitude, and possess an eagerness to learn. On the other hand, learners who act like rocks generally have a negative learning attitude and are, in effect, just occupying space. It should be no surprise that sponges learn more than rocks.

5 **SIT CLOSE TO THE ACTION.** This is an easy way to ensure your participation in the learning process. Sitting up front limits distractions from others and gives you a clear view of the instructor and the instructor a clear view of you. Learners in front usually sit up taller than those in the back and thus appear more eager and ready to learn. Though you may feel a little uncomfortable at first, try sitting in front in your next class. You just might find yourself concentrating better and learning more.

6 **FEARLESSLY ASK AND ANSWER QUESTIONS.** To ask an intelligent question and to respond intelligently, you have to be listening and concentrating. Too many learners feel that asking questions makes them look stupid. Actually, learners who don't ask questions don't learn nearly as much or as easily as those who do.

7 Remember that you aren't expected to know it all; that's why you are studying—to learn. Your job as a student is to ask questions so you can learn more. Though you may feel a little uncomfortable asking questions in front of others, many times, they are happy the question was asked, as they themselves had the same question in mind but were afraid to ask. In the workplace, active questioning is essential for clarifying work tasks and communicating efficiently with others.

8 Questions can be asked during instruction, after class, during office hours, or in a scheduled appointment. As long as the question is answered, it doesn't matter where or when it is asked. Remember to keep an ongoing list of the questions you have so you don't forget them.

9 Not all questions need to be asked aloud. When you are curious about a topic, write down your questions. Decide which ones someone else can answer and which ones you can research yourself. Asking questions and working to find the answers will help you learn even more.

10 Questions are easy to ask when you use the **5W's and H:** who, what, when, where, why, and how. For example, if you are taking a computer course and the day's topic is "Font Styles and When to Use Them," you might think about the following questions:

1. Who uses the fonts?
2. What are the font styles?
3. When should the font be changed?
4. Where do I get fonts?
5. Why should fonts be used?
6. How many fonts are available?

Think of yourself as a young child, a curious student of the entire world. By learning to ask questions, you will understand the world better while learning more in less time.

11 **TAKE NOTES.** Taking effective notes is like taking a picture for later reference of anything you see, hear, or read. Learners who take notes are more focused, have information to study from, and—most importantly—daydream less. Even if you are not required to take notes, creating your own notes will help you learn more. Knowing how to take good notes will transform the act of reading—which for many is a passive activity—into an active process. Note taking while reading forces you to concentrate because you are actively seeking out important information. *More concentration means less mind wandering. Less mind wandering means more learning in less time.*

12 **GET HELP.** Even the most active learners need some help sometime. Assistance can come from your instructor, boss, or fellow learners. The time to ask for help is not the day of or the day before an exam or a project deadline. Starting to prepare at least a week ahead will ensure that the help you need is available when you want it. Classroom instructors generally do not have a lot of sympathy for students who wait until the last minute to ask for help. Bosses have even less tolerance for employees who wait to ask for help.

—Beale, *Success Skills: Strategies for Study and Lifelong Learning,* 3rd edition

INTERACTION 1–1 Reviewing What You Learned from Your Survey

Using only the information from the parts of the reading highlighted in yellow, answer the following questions on your own or with a partner.

1. What process is being described in this reading? ______________________________

____

2. What are five ways to actively take part in this process?
   - ______________________________
   - ______________________________
   - ______________________________
   - ______________________________
   - ______________________________

3. Aside from the headings, what words or letters are in **bold type** in this reading selection? __________ What does this mean? __________

4. What sentences are in *italics*? ______________________________

____

____

5. Someone once said that the only stupid question is the question you don't ask. Would the author of this selection agree with that statement? Why or why not?

____

____

____

____

Remember: Previewing selected parts of a reading before you start reading it straight through is a tremendous boost to reading comprehension.

INTERACTION 1–2 Surveying a Movie Review

1. Which of the elements that you should read while surveying are in the movie review that follows? Check them.

____ Title

____ Headings

____ First sentences of paragraphs

____ Words in bold or italic type

____ Visuals and captions

2. Highlight or underline the parts of this movie review that you should read while surveying.

New Moon Delivers . . . Six Packs

Suzie Soule

1 The Twilight Saga continues with the *New Moon* movie that arrived in theaters Friday, November 20, 2009. This year's most anticipated film really delivers to the fans of the Twilight Saga. I loved *New Moon* because of its trueness to the book. It will be a harder task for the next installment, *Eclipse*. Even if you are not a Twi-hard (a fan of the Twilight Saga), you can appreciate the movie.

2 *New Moon* correlated with the book by telling the story of why Edward left Bella—because he feared for her life with Vampires. Unless you have read the books, you might be lost as to what is going on with the movie. The camera angles and effects were a little too complicated and took away from the story.

3 The best parts of the movie were the gratuitous shirtless Quileutes. Audible expressions were heard from the female viewers in the theater when Jacob Black (Taylor Lautner) takes off his shirt for the first time in the movie. Costuming for the movie must have been easy because there were a lot of cut off jean shorts. Jacob Black is caring for Bella Swan (Kristen Stewart) and she tells him, "You're kind of beautiful, you know?" Yes, we know. His body was amazing. Especially when you compare [it] to how Jacob looked in *Twilight*.

Photos 12/Alamy

4 *New Moon* also delivers great special effects. The Quileutes' morphing into werewolves was very smooth. The fight scenes with the Volturi

were good as well. Christopher Heyerdahl, as the Volturi Marcus, was very chilling. Dakota Fanning did a great job as Jane. I look forward to seeing more of her in *Breaking Dawn*.

5 Overall the movie was what I expected from the second installment of the Twilight Saga. *New Moon* delivers what women want . . . beautiful men with great bodies. (For the critics, there have been gratuitous topless women in movies for decades. It's about time that women get a chance to see some skin.) *New Moon* also delivers a love story that is so strong it affects the people physically. It is the classic story of star-crossed lovers with [the] twist of a love triangle between a girl-next-door, a vampire and a werewolf.

—"New Moon Delivers ... Six Packs" by Suzie Soule.
Associated Content—Yahoo. November 21, 2009

Using only the material you highlighted or underlined, answer the following questions.

3. What movie is being reviewed? New Moon
4. What series is it a part of? The Twilight Saga
5. What is the writer's favorite part of the movie? Shirtless Quilette, Special effects
6. What are two places in your highlighted material that give you the answer to question 5?
   - P 3
   -
7. What are two other reasons the writer liked the movie?
   -
   -

Lesson 2

While You Read or View, Stay Active and Focused.

As you read, focus your attention on the meaning of the words, sentences, and paragraphs you are reading. You can help yourself stay focused and attentive in the following ways:

- **Picture or hear what the author is saying.** Create a photo, a movie, or a soundtrack in your mind.

  Suppose you read: A US Airways jet was forced to crash land in the Hudson River after it hit a flock of geese.

  You would create a movie in your mind: A jet hit a flock of geese. The jet started falling. The plane landed in a river. (Each person would imagine somewhat different details. People who knew more about the crash would picture it more accurately than others.)

AP Photo/Edouard H. R. Gluck

- **Put ideas into your own words.** See if you can restate what the author is saying.

  Suppose you read: To raise people's awareness about global warming, the World Wildlife Fund has organized Earth Hour, one hour in which major buildings around the world will turn off their lights. Participating buildings in the United States include the Empire State Building, the Golden Gate Bridge, and the St. Louis Gateway Arch.

You might restate these ideas by saying to yourself: Some big buildings all around the world, including three in the United States, are going to turn off their lights for an hour to draw people's attention to the problem of global warming. The World Wildlife Fund has planned this event, which is called Earth Hour. (Some details are missing. If they were important to know, you would go back and reread to find them.)

- **Predict what the author is going to say next.** What is this about, and where is it going?

  Suppose you read: Chuck Faesy thought his fence-building days were over.

  You might predict: He thought they were over? So I guess they weren't. I predict the next sentence will tell how Chuck Faesy had to build another fence.

- **Search for connections to your own life and to other ideas and situations.** How is this information or event like something you already know?

  Suppose you read: Franklin Delano Roosevelt's first Inaugural Address is now known for only one sentence: "The only thing we have to fear is fear itself."

  —From Zakaria, "There's More to Fear Than Fear," *Newsweek*, February 2, 2009

  You could make various connections: You might think of Barack Obama's inauguration and what he said. You might think of other famous speeches and the sentence that is most remembered from them. Or you might think about the quotation and try to connect it to times in your life when you were afraid. Is the quotation true? Is the only thing we have to fear—fear?

- **Be open to learning something new that doesn't fit easily into information you already have.** How is this situation or idea different from something you're familiar with?

  Suppose you read: Harvard psychologist Howard Gardner does not agree with traditional definitions of "intelligence." He argues that there are eight different kinds of intelligence and says that intelligence is not inborn.

  You might consider: Perhaps when you were in elementary school, certain children were considered the "bright" ones. Gardner's idea is different. It suggests that everyone has a certain kind of intelligence. Depending on your experiences, you might need to rethink certain situations that happened earlier in your life.

INTERACTION 1–7 Staying Active and Focused While You Read

Use the strategy shown in parentheses before each of the following sentences to understand the author's meaning. If the strategy helps you understand that sentence, put a √ on the line after it. If it doesn't help you, put an X on the line.

1. (Hear) The world around us is full of sounds. _____
   (Search for connections) All of them are meaningful in some way. _____
   (Hear) Stop for a moment and listen to the sounds around you. _____
   (Learn something new) What do you hear? _____
   (Predict) Why didn't you hear those sounds a moment ago? _____
   (Learn something new) We usually filter out "background noise" for good reason, but in doing so we deaden our sense of hearing. _____
   —Adapted from Titon, et al., *Worlds of Music*, Shorter 3rd Ed. (2009)

2. (Predict) For many Americans, gun ownership provides a comforting feeling of safety. _____
   (Learn something new) In the six-month period following the terrorist attacks of September 11, 2001, for example, handgun sales increased by 455,000 over the same period the year before. _____
   (Put ideas in your own words) The vast majority of Americans who own guns are law-abiding citizens who keep their firearms at home for self-protection. _____
   (Picture) Law enforcement efforts are mostly concerned with keeping guns out of the hands of those—such as children, the mentally ill, and criminals—who might use guns to harm themselves or others. _____
   —Gaines & Miller, *Criminal Justice in Action: The Core*, 5th edition

3. (Predict) A *tamalera* is a mandatory piece of tamale-making equipment that functions as a giant steamer, and I wasn't certain I could buy one in Utah. _____
   (Search for connections) You are toast without one, especially if you are making mass quantities of tamales to give away to family and friends, which is the only reason my mom makes tamales. _____

(Picture) A tamalera resembles an aluminum trash can, including the handles and lid, but it is half the size. _____

(Picture) It is shiny, almost like silver, with a shelf inside. _____

(Search for connections) You fill it with a gallon or two of water, set it to slow boil, and steam your tamales there for a couple of hours. ______

—Huerta, *Educational Foundations*

INTERACTION 1–8 Deciding on a Reading Strategy to Use While Reading

The readings that follow are from a variety of sources. As you begin reading, decide which "during reading" strategy you want to try. Write down the strategy. Try a different strategy for each paragraph.

Strategies to Use While Reading

- Picture or hear.
- Put ideas into your own words.
- Predict.
- Search for connections.
- Learn something new.

1. Strategy you are trying: ________________________________

Last summer, Creigh Deeds, who was then the Democratic candidate for governor of Virginia, killed a 270-pound black bear with his car near the little Appalachian town of Millboro, where the two of us grew up in the 1970s. The bear had lumbered out of the woods and Deeds couldn't brake fast enough. The bear died instantly. The candidate's car didn't fare much better. The news went out over the police scanner, and within a few hours most everyone in rural Bath County knew all about it. It wasn't long before Deeds started receiving urgent phone calls from locals. They weren't worried about him. They wanted to know what he was going to do with the bear. "People kept coming up to me for days," Deeds recalled recently when I traveled around the state with him. "'Can I have your bear, Creigh, can I have your bear?'" They wanted to use it to train their bluetick hounds for hunting, or to make a rug, or to eat.

—Tuttle, "Mr. Deeds Goes to Town," *Newsweek*, October 26, 2009

How well did that strategy work for this paragraph? Very well Okay Not well

2. Strategy you are trying: ______________________________

Bean and Sausage Soup

Sausage lends hearty flavor to this Italian-flavored soup. For best results, add the sausage near the end of the cooking time, as indicated, just long enough to heat it through. For color, you can brown the sausage first in a skillet, if you like, and drain off the excess fat, but it isn't really necessary.

—Haughton, *The Best Slow Cooker Cookbook Ever*

How well did that strategy work for this paragraph? Very well Okay Not well

3. Strategy you are trying: ______________________________

Mummies Revealed

X-rays are perhaps the most important tool used today to examine Egyptian mummies. Before X-rays were possible, no one could see what lay hidden beneath the tightly wrapped mummies without unwrapping them. So, for many years, scientists unwound mummies to study them, but they destroyed them in the process. X-rays gave archaeologists a way to "see" inside the mummies without damaging them.

—McClafferty, *The Head Bone's Connected to the Neck Bone*

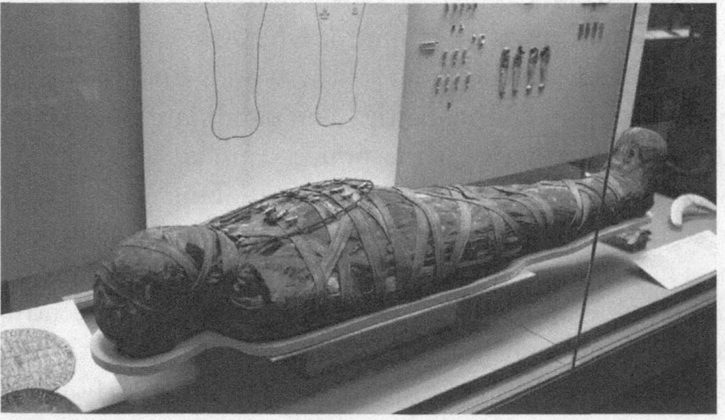

How well did that strategy work for this paragraph? Very well Okay Not well

4. Strategy you are trying: ______________________________

Poverty

We need to remind ourselves why so many children are orphans today: because their parents were not able to get treatment for AIDS, most likely because they could not afford it, or because they lived in a country which was too poor to provide basic health care. We must know that one of the greatest assaults on human dignity is poverty, where you wake up not knowing where you're going to get your next meal. When you cannot have decent accommodation for yourself and your children. When you cannot feed them, and send them to school. That is the greatest assault on human dignity.

—Nelson Mandela, former president of South Africa

How well did that strategy work for this paragraph? Very well Okay Not well

5. Strategy you are trying: ______________________________

The Police Force

For many years, the typical American police officer was white and male. As recently as 1968, African Americans represented only 5 percent of all sworn officers in the United States, and the percentage of "women in blue" was even lower. Only within the past thirty years has this situation been addressed, and only within the past twenty years have many police departments actively tried to recruit women, African Americans, Hispanics, Asian Americans, and other members of minority groups. These efforts have produced steady, though not spectacular, results. Minority representation as a whole in American police departments increased from 14.6 percent in 1987 to 23.6 percent in 2003. During that time, the percentage of female police officers rose from 7.6 to 11.3 percent, the percentage of African American officers grew from 9.3 to 11.7 percent, and the percentage of Hispanic or Latino officers expanded from 4.5 to 13 percent.

—Gaines & Miller, *Criminal Justice in Action: The Core*, 5th edition

How well did that strategy work for this paragraph? Very well Okay Not well

Review: Ways to Stay Active and Focused While Reading

As you read, stay active and focused using the following techniques:

- Picture or hear what the author is saying.
- Put ideas into your own words.
- Predict what the author is going to say next.
- Search for connections to your own life and to other ideas and situations.
- Be open to learning something new that doesn't fit easily into information you already have.

Lesson 3

After You Read or View, Think, Talk, and Write.

What do you do after you watch a TV program, a movie, or a YouTube video? Your action probably depends partly on why you were watching it to begin with.

- **If you were watching to be entertained,** you may think back on a favorite part of the story, or you may think about the movie or program as a whole to decide what you feel about it.
- **If you were watching to be informed,** you may ask yourself what you learned, and why it matters to you.
- **If you were watching to be persuaded,** you might ask yourself if you were convinced, and why.

When you are reading in college, your most likely purpose is to become more informed—to learn something new. You will probably have to be able to show on a test that you have learned the material, too. There are three related tasks that you can do to review the information that you have read:

- **Think about the ideas in the reading selection.** Each time you finish a section of a textbook chapter, a magazine or newspaper article, or a chapter in a nonfiction book, stop and think. Here are three helpful hints:

  1. **5W's and H.** Ask yourself who, what, when, where, why, and how. In other words, review and remember the basic information you read.
  2. **Connect.** Make connections between the ideas in the reading and your own prior knowledge. This will help you understand the reading selection.
  3. **Search for patterns.** You might find repeated words or ideas that help you understand the topic or patterns the author has used to organize the ideas. This will help you analyze the reading selection.

- **Talk about the ideas in the reading selection.** Talking helps people understand ideas in a way that just thinking to yourself does not. First, you and your classmates may have noticed different things about the ideas, so it's good to combine your knowledge. Second, talking is a method of *rehearsing* your knowledge. Just as a dancer or actor needs to rehearse before a performance, college students need to rehearse their knowledge before a class discussion or test. One effective way to rehearse is to have one person ask the other person questions. You can switch back and forth between asking and answering.
- **Write about the ideas in the reading selection.** Writing is another form of rehearsal. It can be even more useful than talking if you are preparing for a test because most tests are written. However, writing is more than a test prep method. When you write, you find out how much you know about a topic. You can also look at what you wrote and think about whether it all makes sense. You can write important terms and their definitions. You can write a summary of a section (we'll teach you how in Lesson 14). You can also write down your questions about what an author has said.

Reviewing and rehearsing your knowledge are important when you need to remember what you read.

Review: Three Ways to Rehearse Information After You Read

- Think about the ideas in the reading selection.
- Talk about the ideas in the reading selection.
- Write about the ideas in the reading selection.

INTERACTION 1–10 Think, Talk, and Write After You Read

Read the selection from a Web site and answer the questions that follow.

How to Survive a Plane Crash

Charles W. Bryant

1 It's every air traveler's nightmare. Sudden turbulence throws you backward. The beverage cart flies by and crashes into the rear of the cabin. You're losing altitude quickly, and your seatbelt is jammed between the seats. Oxygen masks drop from above, but you didn't pay attention to preflight instructions. People scream, pray, and clutch each other as the plane descends downward at an improbable angle. You think you're going to die.

2 The good news is that an airplane crash doesn't necessarily mean certain death. In fact, of the 568 U.S. plane crashes between 1980 and 2000, more than 90 percent of crash victims survived.

3 In the event of an air disaster, there are things you can do that can increase your odds of living. Keeping a calm, cool head amidst panic and disorder isn't easy, but key to your chances. So are the clothes you wear, the luggage you bring, and where you stow it. Some research even indicates that the seat you choose might help.

4 The most common question asked of crash experts is "Is there a safest seat?" Official sources say that it makes no difference because no two plane crashes are alike. *Popular Mechanics* magazine did some exhaustive research that seems to point to the rear of the plane as the safest spot. They studied data of every U.S. commercial jet crash in the last 36 years and found that passengers in the rear of the plane are 40 percent more likely to survive than those in the first few rows. The Federal Aviation Administration's position is that there is no safest seat. The FAA also concluded in a 2005 report that there's no evidence that any one carrier is any safer than the next.

5 In the event of a crash, there are things you can do to give you a better shot at making it out alive. Following are five tips that everyone should know before they get on their next flight:

- After you board, find the two closest exits and count the rows between them and your seat. In the event of darkness or smoke, feel the seats and count until you reach the exit row.
- Ready for the impact. The official FAA crash position is to extend your arms, cross your hands and place them on the seat in front of you, and then place your head against the back of your hands. Tuck your feet under your seat as far as you can. If you have no seat in front of you,

bend your upper body over with your head down and wrap your arms behind your knees. Always stow your carry-on bag under the seat in front of you to block the area.

- Wear long pants, sleeves and closed-toed shoes. This will help protect you from glass, metal and the elements.
- If you're with your family, talk to your children about what to do in the event of an emergency. Divide the responsibility of helping your children between you and your spouse. It's easier for one parent to help a single child than for both to try to keep everyone together.
- Pay attention to the preflight instructions, as all planes are different. When the oxygen mask drops, put it on yourself first before attempting to help someone else. If you fall unconscious, you have no chance of helping your travel mate.

—From http://adventure.howstuffworks.com/how-to-survive-a-plane-crash.htm/printable.

Think About the 5W's and H

1. What is the purpose of this article?

   To persuade To inform To entertain
2. Who is this article about? ____________________
3. What is it about? ____________________
4. When did 568 U.S. plane crashes occur? ____________________
5. Where does *Popular Mechanics* say is the safest place to sit in a plane? ________

   ____
6. Why should you count the seat rows between you and the two closest exits?

   ____
7. Why should you place your carry-on luggage under the seat in front of you?

   ____
8. Why should you put on your own oxygen mask before helping others with theirs?

   ____
9. How can you protect yourself from glass and metal in a crash? ________

   ____

Search for Patterns and Write

10. How many of the tips given in paragraph 5 for having a better chance of survival are things you would have to do before a disaster started to happen? ________

    What are they?

    - ________________________________
    - ________________________________
    - ________________________________
    - ________________________________

Connect and Talk

11. Have you ever been in a plane that was shaking, dropping quickly, or otherwise acting in a way you didn't expect? Yes No
12. What was your reaction—what did you do? Discuss your reactions with your classmates.

    ____

    ____

PART 2

"Intelligence plus character—that is the goal of true education."

These words are from Dr. Martin Luther King Jr., used at the end of the movie *Stomp the Yard.*

He will challenge their traditions.

Their traditions will change his life.

Screen Gems/The Kobal Collection/Picture Desk

Find chapter-specific interactive learning tools for *Activate*, including quizzes, videos, and more, through CengageBrain.com.

Videos Related to Readings

Vocab Words on Audio

Read and Talk on Demand

Paul Mckeown/iStockphoto.com (phone)
bluestocking/iStockphoto.com (pens/pencils)

Vocabulary Development

Whether you are motivated to attend college because you hope to get a better job, your parents are "forcing" you to go, you love to learn, or you want to change the world, a true education changes the way you view and understand the world around you. And at the core of every true education is a good vocabulary.

Having a good vocabulary allows you to express your ideas and feelings in a way that others will understand. It allows you to participate in the life of our culture through understanding what others have to say about government, education, the arts, and the sciences. And it allows you to read the ideas of people from long ago or far away whose thoughts still have something valuable to offer, whether at work, at home, or at school.

This part of the book focuses on developing your vocabulary by using word parts, context clues, and the dictionary, and by understanding the author's tone. All are important skills to develop in your quest to change the world . . . or at least to change **your** world! Good luck!

Share Your Prior Knowledge

Share your educational goal with a classmate. Then discuss what character is, and how you think an education helps build character (or, more specifically, will help build yours). Come up with one or two ideas.

Lesson 4

Before You Read, Use Word Parts to Expand Your Vocabulary.

The single most powerful way to quickly expand your vocabulary is to learn word parts. Learning one word part can increase your understanding of hundreds of unfamiliar words. In this lesson you will learn some of the most productive word parts in the English language. If you learn all the word parts covered in this lesson, you will know the meanings of thousands of words you have never seen before.

Test Your Prior Knowledge.

Before we go on, however, take a little test to see how much you already know about word parts. We think you already know quite a bit.

1. How do you know what **girlfriend** means? ____________________
____
2. What does the -s at the end of **movies** mean? ____________________
3. What does the **un-** at the beginning of **unsafe** mean? ____________________
____
4. If the word **beautiful** is broken into two parts, **beauty + -ful,** which part carries the root meaning of the word? ____________________

As you probably noted when you answered question 1, some words are composed of two different words that each can stand alone and mean something. These are called **compound words.**

Question 2 is a different case. Here, a word that can stand on its own—*movie*—is combined with a letter that cannot stand alone as a word. But the -s still adds meaning to the word. It means "more than one." Some word parts have to be attached to others. When the word part is attached at the end of the word, it's called a **suffix.** Some words have more than one suffix.

The **un-** in *unsafe* (question 3) is similar to the **-s** in *movies:* it can't stand alone as a word. The difference, of course, is that **un-** comes at the beginning of the word, not at the end. These word parts are **prefixes.** In fact, the **pre-** in **prefix** is itself a prefix that means "before." Just as with suffixes, some words have more than one.

Finally, in question 4, *beauty* carries the root meaning of the word. This root comes from a Latin word—as do many English words. Many English words also come from Greek. In this chapter, you'll learn both Latin and Greek roots. Some roots stand alone as words, like *beauty.* But some roots need to be attached to other word parts to suggest a meaning to readers.

Definitions of Word Parts

- **Root:** The root carries the main meaning of a word. A word usually has at least one root. It can have more than one. The root can be found at the beginning, middle, or end of a word.
- **Prefix:** Placed before a root, the prefix changes the meaning of the word. Not all words have prefixes. Some words have one prefix; others have more than one.
- **Suffix:** Placed after a root, the suffix often changes the part of speech (such as noun or verb) and thus changes the way the word acts in the sentence. Not all words have suffixes. Some words have one suffix; others have more than one.

Figure 2.1 Words Composed of Word Parts

As you can see from Figure 2.1, a word has at least one root, but it may or may not have prefixes or suffixes. And it may have more than one of each. Read across each line to put the word parts together to form a whole word.

prefix +	prefix +	root +	root +	suffix +	suffix
			mind		
			mercy	ful	
			beauty	ful	ly
	un		real	ist	ic
	re		mind	er	
re	con	struct		ed	
		demo	graph	y	

When you combine roots with other word parts, sometimes their spelling changes. For example, if you combine *mercy* and *ful*, the resulting word is spelled *merciful.* It has an *i* instead of a *y.* Word parts often have alternative spellings depending on what other word parts they are attached to.

Look for Meaning in Word Parts.

A reference list of roots, prefixes, and suffixes that you can use while you read is provided on pages 105–107. In this section we'll look at a small number of roots and some of the other word parts they can be combined with. You'll see how to analyze the word parts and then how to infer the meaning from the word parts and the reading context.

Roots: Sight, Hearing, and Touch

Let's start with some roots that have to do with using your senses of sight, hearing, and touch.

Study the three roots. (When roots are given with a slash between them, that means they are spelled in different ways.) As you read each root, picture using the sense listed under the heading "Basic meaning."

Root	Basic meaning	Example words
vid/vis	see	video, visible, visionary
aud	hear	audio, audible, audience
tact/tang/tig	touch	contact, tangible, contiguous

Combining Word Parts

Notice that each root can be combined with the suffix **-ible.** This suffix can also be spelled **-able,** and that's what it means: "able to be."

- **Visible** means "able to be seen."
- **Audible** means "able to be heard."
- **Tangible** means "able to be touched."

You can tell from these examples that sometimes you have to put the meaning of the suffix in front of the meaning of the root for the combined meaning of the whole word to make sense.

Spotlight on Inference: Working with Word Parts

When you use word parts to figure out the meaning of a word, you often have to use **inference.** Inference is the process of putting together the bits of information you read to see what they add up to. You do this by using your logic and your prior knowledge. Here is an example using the word **contiguous.**

prefix	+	root	+	suffix
con-		tig		-uous
together		touching		full of

When you put the meanings of the word parts together, you get "full of touching together" or "touching together fully." Now, you could draw any number of conclusions about what this means. So the next step in figuring out the word's meaning is to look at the context. Suppose you read this sentence:

> Canada and the United States are **contiguous** countries.

Given this context, you could infer that **contiguous** means "sharing a boundary" or "neighboring." The two countries share a border—they touch together fully. Notice the border on the map.

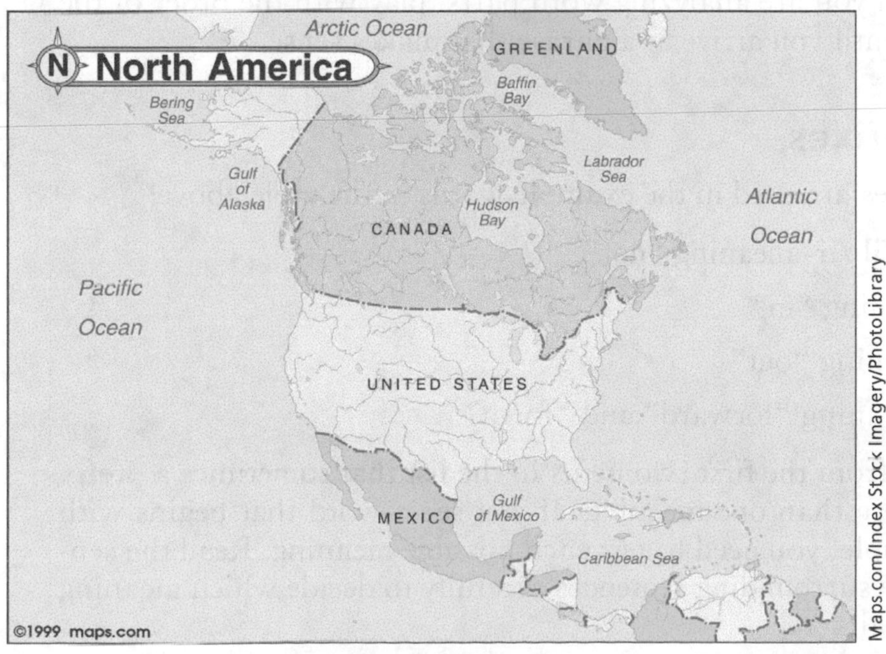

Maps.com/Index Stock Imagery/PhotoLibrary

Roots: Leading, Carrying, and Pulling

Study these three roots. Make a mental movie of each action to help you remember it.

Root	Basic meaning	Example words
duc/duce/duct	lead, bring, take	induction, produce, conduct
port	carry	comport, export, import
tract/trah	pull, drag, draw	contract, extract, protract, retraction

Combining Word Parts

Notice that each root can be combined with the prefix **com-**, which is also spelled **con-**. This prefix means "together," as you saw in the word *contiguous.*

- **Conduct** means "lead together."
- **Comport** means "carry together."
- **Contract** means "draw together."

Notice that in the meaning of these words, the root is put before the prefix. When you are analyzing word parts, play with the order of the word parts until you arrive at a phrase that makes sense.

More Prefixes

Other prefixes are used in the example words in the table above:

- **in-/im-/il-/ir-** meaning "not"
- **in-** meaning "in"
- **ex-** meaning "out"
- **pro-** meaning "forward" and "forth"

You can see from the first two items in the list that sometimes a prefix can have more than one meaning. If you see a word that begins with **in-**, for example, you need to test each possible meaning. Read the sentence and the surrounding sentences carefully to decide which meaning is more logical.

Look at Prefixes for Changes to Meaning.

Roots carry the basic meaning of the word, but prefixes change that meaning. Look at the following table of prefixes. Memorize these five prefixes, and you will gain a partial understanding of more than 60 percent of all English words that have prefixes. Notice that half of them can mean "not."

As you read the example words, divide them into word parts to figure out what they mean. For even better practice, write them on a separate piece of paper and divide them into word parts with plus signs between each part.

Prefix	Basic meaning	Example words
un-	not	unkind, unproductive, unstoppable
re-	again; back	reduce, reproduce, retract
in-/il-/im-/ir-	not	inactive, illegal, impossible, irresistible
dis-	not; apart	disrespect, distrust, distract
en-/em-	cause to	enlarge, enrage, embolden

On pages 105–107 is an alphabetical list of word parts you can refer to as you read.

INTERACTION 2–3 Stating Word Meanings

State the meaning of the following words based on their word parts.

1. **retrain** ______________________________
2. **irreligious** ______________________________
3. **unforgettable** ______________________________

4. **impolite** ______________________________

5. **retract** ______________________________

6. **endanger** ______________________________

7. **disconnect** ______________________________

8. **illogical** ______________________________

9. **reproduce** ______________________________

10. **empower** ______________________________

Review: Prefixes

The root of a word carries the basic meaning, and prefixes change that meaning.

Look at Suffixes to See How Words Act in Sentences.

Suffixes often change the part of speech of words and, thus, how the words act in the sentence.

Suffixes That Can Indicate Actions—Verbs:

- **-s:** plays, ends, happens (-s on a verb indicates actions that happen again and again)

  *But note that -s on a noun means "more than one."

- **-ing:** laughing, remembering, choosing (**-ing** indicates action happening now)

- **-ed:** touched, lighted, described (**-ed** indicates action that happened in the past)

When you see a verb in a sentence, you can ask, "Who or what is doing this? When is this happening?" Figuring out who is doing what in a sentence will improve your reading comprehension.

Suffixes That Indicate Conditions or Processes—Nouns:

- **-ance/-ence:** guidance, dependence, tolerance
- **-hood:** neighborhood, manhood, statehood
- **-ion/-sion/-tion:** suspension, vacation, completion, partition

When you see a noun in a sentence, you can ask, "What is this thing doing? What relationship is there between this noun and other nouns?" To understand sentences fully, you need to understand the relationships between words.

Suffixes That Indicate Characteristics of Something—Adjectives:

- **-ly** (characteristic of): fatherly, miserly, homely
- **-less** (without): motherless, waterless, loveless
- **-ing, -ed:** Also used as verb endings, these endings can indicate adjectives that are describing people, places, things, and ideas: caring brother, expected visitor.

When you find an adjective, you can ask, "Who or what is this word describing?"

Suffixes That Can Indicate How, When, or Where An Action Is Done—Adverbs:

- **-ly** (characteristic of): nicely, instinctively, suddenly
- **-fully** (full of): faithfully, joyfully, fearfully
- **-wise** (in a certain direction or position; with respect to): clockwise; likewise

When you see an adverb in a sentence, ask, "What verb or other words is this describing?"

See pages 105–107 for a list of suffixes that you can consult while you are reading.

INTERACTION 2–4 Selecting the Best Suffix

For each word in *italics*, select a suffix from the list below that helps the word act the way it needs to in the sentence. Notice that in three words, the final letter has been removed because the spelling changes when the suffix is added.

-ance	-ence	-hood	-ing	-less	-ly	-s	-ion	-tion

1. Although they had started their marriage deeply in love, their partnership became *joy*_________ after they lost a child.
2. Her utter *depend*_________ on her mother made her itch for her freedom.
3. He *commute*_________ to his office, 45 minutes each way.
4. The farmer carefully controlled his herd's *reproduc*_________ to make sure that only the cows who gave a lot of milk had calves.
5. She was outwardly patient but *inward*_________ frustrated.
6. The *extract*_________ of every bit of silver from the mine meant that all the miners lost their jobs.
7. She was *laz*_________ around the house on her day off.
8. He was holding his hurt wrist *protective*_________.
9. She asked for the rabbi's spiritual *guid*_________.
10. He spent most of his *child*_________ with his grandmother.

Review: Suffixes

Suffixes often change the part of speech of a word, and thus change how a word acts in a sentence. Suffixes can indicate:

- Actions—these are verbs.
- Conditions or processes—these are nouns.
- Characteristics of things—these are adjectives.
- How, when, or where an action is done—these are adverbs.

Word Parts Glossary

The following 146 commonly used word parts are organized alphabetically so they will be easy to find while you read. Read down the column that describes the word part you are searching for. Remember that sometimes a word starts with a root rather than a prefix.

Prefixes	Roots	Suffixes
ab-/abs-: away	annu: year	-able: able to
ad-: to, toward	anthrop: human	-age: condition or state of
ante-: before	aster/astro: star	-al: characteristic of
anti-: against	aud: hear	-ance: state, condition, action
auto-: self	bio: life	-ate: act upon
bi-: two	cap: take, seize	-ative: adjective form of a noun
circum-: around	cede/ceed/cess: go, yield, surrender	-cracy: government
com-/con-: together; bring together	chron: time	-ed: happened in the past (on a verb), or characteristic of (on an adjective)
counter-: opposite	cog/gnosi: know	-en: made of
de-: reverse, remove, reduce	corp: body	-ence: condition or state of
demi-: half	dem: people	-ent: causing or being in a certain condition
dis-: not; apart	dict: say	-eous: possessing the qualities of
en-/em-: cause to	dorm: sleep	-er: comparative (faster = more fast)
ex-/e-/ec-/ef-: out; up	duc/duce/duct: lead, bring, take	-er: person who
fore-: before	fact: make	-es: noun plural (boxes)
hemi-: half	flu: flow	-est: superlative (happiest = most happy)
hyper-: above, more	geo: earth	-ful: full of

(*Continued*)

Prefixes	Roots	Suffixes
hypo-: under, less	graph: write	-hood: condition or process of (neighborhood)
in-/im-: in, into	gress: walk	-ial: characteristic of
in-/im-/ir-/il-: not	gyny: woman	-ible: able to
inter-: between, among	ject: throw	-ic: characteristic of
intra-: within	junct: join	-ical: characteristic of
macro-: large, long	log/logue: word, thought, speech	-ing: present participle of verb (enjoying)
mal-: bad, wrong	man/manu: by hand	-ion: condition, process of
micro-: small	merc: money received for work; price	-ious: possessing the qualities of
mid-: middle	mit/mitt/miss: send	-ish: characteristic of
mis-: wrongly	morph: form	-ise: verb ()
mis-/miso-: hatred	mors/mori/mort: dead	-ism: state, quality, or condition
mono-: one	nom: name, term	-ist: one who; characterized by
non-: not	path/pat: feeling, suffering	-ity: state of
over-: too much	ped/pedo: children	-ive: adjective form of a noun (massive)
pan-: all	pel: drive	-ize: make
poly-: many	pend: hang	-less: without
post-: after	philo/phil: love	-ly: characteristic of
pre-: before	phobia: irrational fear	-ment: state of
pro-: forward	phon: sound	-ness: state of, condition of
pseudo-: false	plic: fold	-nym: name
re-: again, back	port: carry	-ology: field of study
semi-: half	sat/satis: enough	-or: person who
sub-: under	scrib/script: write	-ous: possessing the qualities of
super-: above	sta: stand	-s: verb (swims); noun plural (trees)
sur-: more, above, over	struct: build	-sion: condition, process of
syn-/sym-: together, with; united	tact/tang/tig: touch	-some: characteristic of

Prefixes	Roots	Suffixes
trans-/tres-: across	theo: God	-tion: condition, process of
tri-: three	tract/trah: pull, drag, draw	-ty: state of
un-: not	trib: pay, bestow	-wise: in a specified direction, manner, or position
under-: too little	ven/veni/vent: come	-worthy: worthy of
ultra-: beyond, exceeding	vert: turn	-yze: verb (analyze)
uni-: one	vis/vid: see	
	viv: life	

- What if a word part is not in the Word Parts Glossary? Look in a college dictionary (see page 151). The word parts are often given toward the beginning or end of an entry. Because word parts show which languages a word comes from, you will often see an abbreviation of the word *Latin* or *Greek* with the word parts. See *Lat.* in the dictionary entry on page 151 for an example.
- What if you don't understand the combination of word parts? First, look at the sentences around the word to see if they can help. We will talk more about context in Lesson 5. Second, look in a dictionary. We will talk about using a dictionary in Lesson 6.

Lesson 5

While You Read, Define Words in Context.

As you work through this lesson, you will learn strategies to help you determine the meanings of words you do not know based on the **context** in which they are used. If you have completed Lesson 4, you have probably noticed that the word *context* is composed of a prefix and a root: **con- + text.** Since *con-* means "together," and *text* means "weave," you can figure out that *context* means "the words woven together with the new word." Words weave together to make meaning, and the meaning of a word changes—a lot or a little—depending on its context. The context is the word's setting or environment.

Find Context Clues While Reading.

Context clues are hints about the meaning of a word that are located in the surrounding words or sentences. When you are trying to figure out what a word means, look in the sentences surrounding the word. Clues to your word's meaning can be found anywhere within a paragraph, but they are often found in one or more of the following three places:

1. The actual sentence in which the unknown word appears.
2. The sentence before the one in which the word appears.
3. The sentence after the one in which the word appears.

Here is an example of a context clue for the word *conceive.*

> Some people should not drink. For example, women who are pregnant or trying to conceive should not drink any alcohol.

If you didn't know what the word *conceive* means, you could figure it out from the sentence it appears in. The words "are pregnant" is a context clue that helps you understand "trying to conceive." Conceive means "get pregnant." Notice that this definition is not very technical.

However, it does the job: it gives you enough understanding so you can keep reading. That is the goal to aim for.

Recognize Four Kinds of Context Clues.

We will focus on four common kinds of context clues: examples, antonyms, synonyms, and your own logic interacting with the words on the page. Context clues are EASY:

Example
Antonym
Synonym
Your Logic

You won't necessarily use the context clues in this order, but the word EASY will help you remember some different strategies to try when you don't know the meaning of a word.

Examples

Look for **examples** that might give you clues to a word's meaning. Examples may describe or explain an unknown word. At times, the author may use signal words like these to let you know an example is coming.

Words that signal examples:
for example, for instance, such as, to illustrate

Laura's "conversations" are more like monologues. For example, the last time I talked with her, she spent half an hour describing her new apartment. I couldn't get in a single word.

As you can see, the word *monologue* has something to do with talking a lot and not letting the other person say anything. You can tell because of the examples given: *she spent half an hour describing her new apartment* and *I couldn't get in a single word.* Based on these examples, you can tell that a monologue is a long speech made by one person.

INTERACTION 2–8 Using Example Context Clues with Signal Words

Each sentence includes a **boldfaced** vocabulary word.

A. Circle the example signal words.
B. Underline the example that provides a clue to the word's meaning.
C. Guess the meaning of the vocabulary word and write it on the line.

1. Some college students major in the **social sciences,** such as communications (the study of how people talk and otherwise communicate with each other) and sociology (the study of how people act when they're together).

   Social sciences are ____

2. A sociologist studies how people act in **social** contexts. For example, some sociologists study how people act in family groups, and others study how people are affected by their religious membership or local community.

   Social means ____

3. Sociologist Mattijs Kalmijn has studied the social **factors** that influence whom people fall in love with and marry. To illustrate, one factor that matters is how large the person's community is. The larger it is, the more likely it is that a person will marry someone from inside the group.

   Factors are ____

4. Other sociologists study what makes a marriage stable, and they find that **economic** factors influence whether a marriage will continue or end in divorce. For instance, the lower the income of a family, the more likely it is that the marriage will be unstable. Also, satisfaction generally increases for both partners when both are working and making money.

   Economic means ____

Antonyms

Antonyms are words that have opposite meanings, such as *high* and *low.* Sometimes you can figure out the meaning of a word by finding its antonym in a context that shows the author means to contrast (show the difference between) the two words.

Words that signal contrast:
on the other hand, in contrast, however, but, yet, instead, even though, although, unlike

Bullies often seem confident, yet they are actually insecure.

The word *yet* signals a contrast between the two parts of the sentence that are divided by the comma. To figure out the meaning of *insecure,* you can use that signal word as a clue. You might also notice that the sentence shows contrast in its wording: *seem confident . . . , are actually insecure.*

The word with an opposing meaning is *confident.* So *insecure* means (roughly) "not confident." This is a **working definition** for the word *insecure.* Notice that we found the opposite word, and then put *not* in front of it. You can also use the word *doesn't* instead of *not* to help you form a working definition.

Suppose you knew the word *insecure* but not the word *confident.* A working definition for *confident* would be "not insecure." The *in-* in *insecure* means "not," and so does the word *not* itself. When you put two *not*'s together in English, they cancel each other out. So, "not insecure" means "secure."

INTERACTION 2–12 Using Antonym Context Clues

Each sentence includes a **boldfaced** vocabulary word.

A. Underline the antonym that provides a clue to the word's meaning.
B. If there are signal words that indicate contrast, circle them.
C. Guess the meaning of the vocabulary word and write it on the line.

1. It is difficult to drop bad habits like smoking and overeating. Although outside rewards such as praise from friends and family can be helpful, it's the **internal** decision to change that is most important and lasting.

   A. What is your "working definition" for **internal**? ______________________

   B. What does **internal** mean? ______________________

2. Your **resolve** to eat less may be hard to keep if your mother is always offering you homemade fudge and brownies, yet indecision makes it even harder.

   A. What is your "working definition" for **resolve**? ______________________

   B. What does **resolve** mean? ______________________

3. Each **obstacle** can cause frustration, but each step forward increases the possibility of success.

   A. What is your "working definition" for **obstacle**? ______________________

   B. What does **obstacle** mean? ______________________

4. **Anticipating** how you will deal with each temptation will help you succeed. In contrast, if you aren't expecting to have to deal with temptations, you are more likely to fail.

   A. What is your "working definition" for **anticipating**? ______________________

   B. What does **anticipating** mean? ______________________

5. You can **sustain** your new, healthy behaviors by giving yourself frequent rewards. On the other hand, you may be tempted to stop your new habit if you spread out the rewards over too long a time period.

   A. What is your "working definition" for **sustain**? ______________________

   B. What does **sustain** mean? ______________________

—Adapted from Hales, *Invitation to Health*, 12th edition

Synonyms

Synonyms are words that have a similar meaning or the same meaning, such as *huge* and *enormous*. Sometimes you can figure out the meaning of a word by finding its synonym in a context that shows the author means to compare (show the similarities between) the two words. Other times the author actually defines the word, so be on the lookout for phrases that mean the same thing as the word.

Review: Signal Words to Understand Context Clues

Watch out for signal words that may lead you to a context clue for words whose meanings you don't know. Signal words can point to:

- Examples: *for example, for instance, such as, to illustrate*
- Contrast (difference): *on the other hand, in contrast, however, but, yet, instead, even though, although, unlike*
- Comparison (similarity): *like, as, also, as well, or, in other words, similar to, that is, in the same way*

Create EASY Note Cards to Study Words.

You need a way to keep your study of vocabulary organized, and it's a smart idea to keep reminding yourself of the meanings of new words so you can commit them to memory. Creating and then studying EASY note cards is a simple way to learn and remember enough about a new word so that you can start to use it comfortably.

Here is an example of an EASY note card.

The word

(the part of speech--
noun, verb, adjective, adverb)

FRONT

Example-- Write a sentence using the word that shows you know its meaning.
Antonym (if there are any)
Synonym (if there are any)
Your Logic-- Use your logic to make up a definition in your own words.

BACK

Here is a sample note card for the word "compose," which was discussed earlier in Part 2 in relation to Bethany Hamilton.

FRONT

Example: Marita composed a picture in the sand using a stick, and then her brother ran through it and ruined it.

Antonyms: fall apart, disturb

Synonyms: put together, make up, arrange, write, create

Your logic: Compose—arrange something to create something new

BACK

As you learn about each word, you may find that other words are related to it. You can add this information to the front of the card as you learn it. You may also choose to draw a picture on the front of the card that reminds you of the meaning, or you can write how to pronounce the word. If you write the pronunciation, you can base it on the pronunciation key on page 156 or you can use your own method, as shown on this card.

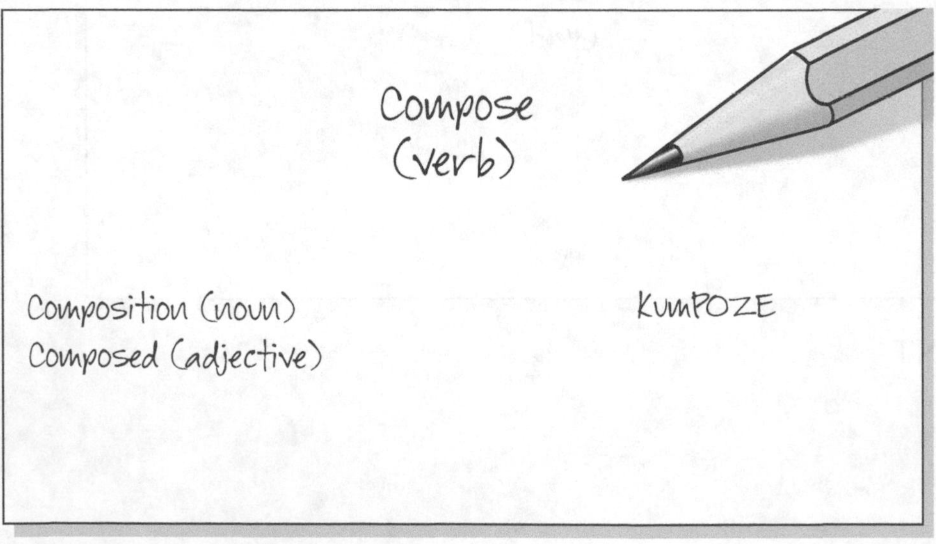

FRONT

Lesson 6

While You Read and After You Read, Use the Dictionary.

When you are reading, first try to use word parts and context clues to understand the meaning of a word. If those clues don't work, and you think the word is important to know so you can understand the reading selection, look up the word in the dictionary.

Understand Different Types of Dictionaries.

Print, online, and cell phone app dictionaries are available today. You should know how to use all three types. Even when you look a word up in a dictionary, you will need to stay aware of the context of the word in the reading selection. Words often have more than one definition, and knowing which one to use depends on the context.

- **Print Dictionaries.** Print dictionaries come in different sizes:
    - **Pocket dictionaries** include brief definitions of words used frequently. For example, *Webster's New Pocket Dictionary* contains 35,000 definitions. One limitation of pocket dictionaries is that they give only one or two definitions for most words, when many words have multiple definitions. A strength of pocket dictionaries is that they are small and easy to carry, so you can carry them in your backpack.

Sample entry from *Webster's New Pocket Dictionary* (2007)

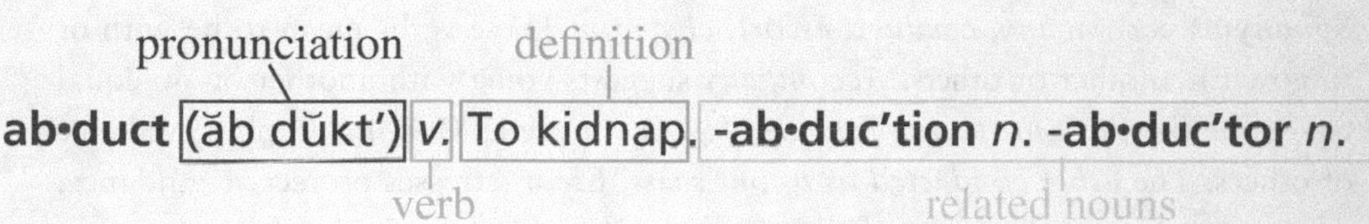

- **Collegiate dictionaries** include more and different kinds of information. *Webster's New College Dictionary,* for instance, gives fuller definitions than the pocket dictionary. It also gives examples of words in use. Other features that collegiate dictionaries typically have are comparisons of synonyms and their precise meanings, word histories, and illustrations of some words.

Sample entry from *Webster's New College Dictionary* (3rd edition, 2008)

verb forms — word history and word parts

ab•duct (ăb dŭkt) *vt* **-duct•ed,-duct•ing, -ducts.** [Lat. *abducere, abduct: ab-,* away + *ducere,* to lead.] 1. To carry off by force. 2. *Physiol.* To draw away from the median line of a bone or muscle or from an adjacent part or limb. **-abduc'tion** *n.* **-abduct'or** *n.*

general definition — definition related to field of physiology

- **Comprehensive dictionaries** are bigger and more valuable still. In addition to the features that collegiate dictionaries include, comprehensive dictionaries define more words; give more examples of words used in context; sometimes provide photographs of people, places, and other subjects; and include sections on word roots from different languages. *The American Heritage Dictionary of the English Language* is an example of a comprehensive dictionary.

Sample feature from *American Heritage Dictionary of the English Language* (4th edition, 2000)

Synonyms accompany, conduct, escort, chaperon These verbs mean to be with or to go with another or others. *Accompany* suggests going with another on an equal basis: *She went to Europe accompanied by her colleague. Conduct* implies guidance of others: *The usher conducted us to our seats. Escort* stresses protective guidance: *The party chairperson escorted the candidate through the crowd. Chaperon* specifies adult supervision of young persons: *My mom helped chaperon the prom.*

You can see from this example that the more specific information you need, the bigger the dictionary you should consult. For quicker or more casual use, go to a smaller dictionary.

- **Online Dictionaries.** Online dictionaries may be based on textual definitions (definitions given in words) or visual definitions. In either case, audio files may be provided that allow you to hear how a word is pronounced.
  - **Online text-based dictionaries** are available at the following Web addresses:
    - Merriam-Webster Online www.merriam-webster.com
    - Your Dictionary www.yourdictionary.com
    - Dictionary http://dictionary.reference.com

  The online format is useful because you can hear the word spoken in an audio file. It's also convenient to simply type in the word you are looking for instead of leafing through the pages of a book. However, you will often see advertisements when you look up or listen to words, which can be distracting.

Sample definition from *Merriam-Webster Online*

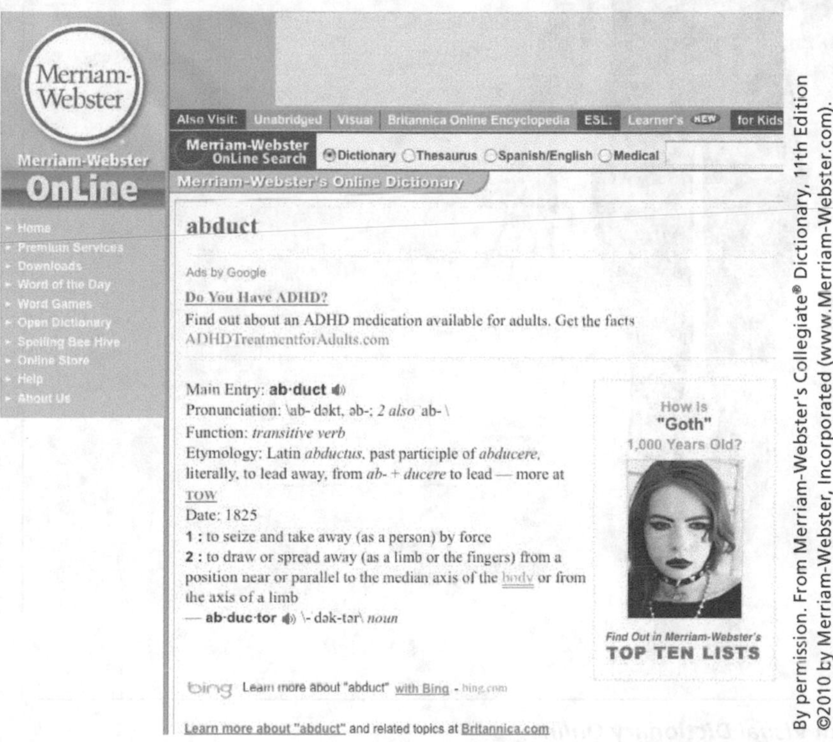

Note that some dictionary sites include other kinds of reference works. Make sure you select the dictionary.

- **Online visual dictionaries** are available in several types. They are limited by the number of words that can be represented in pictures. An example is *Visual Dictionary Online* from Merriam-Webster at http://visual.merriam-webster.com. The dictionary includes about 20,000 words and 6,000 related images. Visual dictionaries may be especially helpful if you need to understand how complex parts fit together, such as in the example that follows. They can also be useful for people who are native speakers of languages other than English.

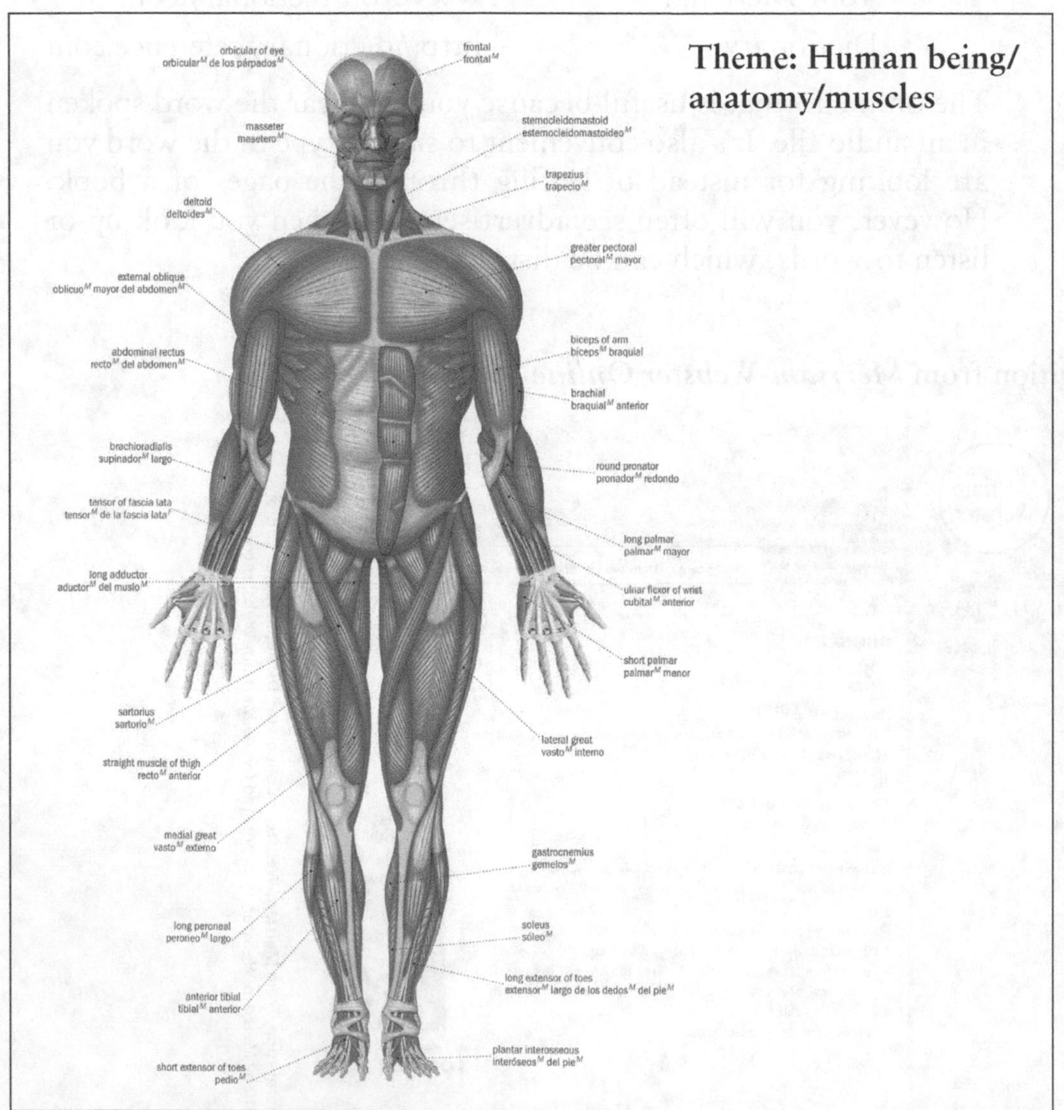

Sample entry from *Visual Dictionary Online*

- **Dictionary Apps for Smart Phones.** Many students now access dictionaries on their smart phones using cell phone apps (applications). If you have a smart phone, such as an iPhone, BlackBerry, Motorola RAZR, or another, you can probably find a dictionary app for it. Some apps are free, some are just a couple of dollars, and others cost much less than a print version of the same dictionary. Some apps require an Internet connection, but others do not. Here are a few choices that were available in 2010.

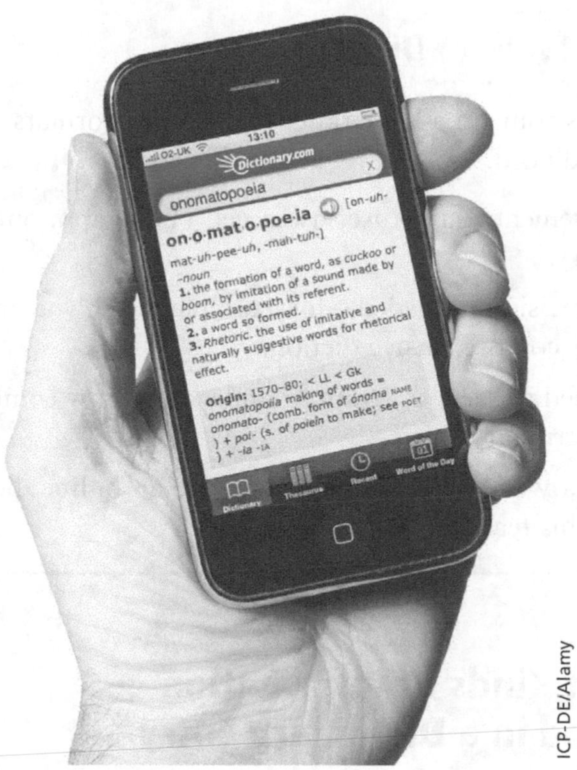

ICP-DE/Alamy

Some dictionary apps:

- Dictionary (for iPhones; free). About 120,000 words.
- Dictionary.com (for BlackBerry, iPhone, and Android; free). About 300,000 words. This dictionary is based on the *Random House Unabridged Dictionary* and includes content from Dictionary.com and Thesaurus.com.
- WordBook English Dictionary and Thesaurus (for iPhones; $1.99). About 150,000 words. Definitions are not as carefully written as in major dictionaries, such as the *American Heritage Dictionary.*

- American Heritage Dictionary, 4th edition (for iPhones and iPod Touches; $29.99). About 300,000 terms—or the entire 2,000-plus page print dictionary.

Just as a pocket-sized print dictionary may not include all the words you need in your college studies, you may not want to rely on free dictionary apps when precise definitions matter. For defining words on the fly, however, they are probably fine.

Review: Types of Dictionaries

Dictionaries come in a wide range of sizes and formats. Use one that is appropriate for your purpose and need.

- For convenient, quick use, use a cell phone app, online text dictionary, or pocket print dictionary.
- When precision is needed—for example, when you are writing a college essay—use a collegiate or comprehensive dictionary.
- If you need to see a diagram to understand how complex parts fit together, use an online visual dictionary.
- To hear a word being pronounced, use an online dictionary. Some cell phone apps also include this feature.

Know What Kinds of Information You Can Find in a Dictionary Entry.

You have seen several examples above of the kinds of information dictionaries provide in a word's definition. Here is a more complete list.

- **Basic form.** The entry word is the basic form of the word, minus any endings that indicate plurals of nouns or tenses of verbs. So if you need to find *harangues,* you look up *harangue.* If you need to find *crippling,* you look up *cripple.*
- **Syllables.** The entry word is divided by little dots or diamonds that show where syllables are: die·sel. If you are writing by hand and want to divide a word at the end of a line, only do so where a syllable break occurs.

- **Pronunciation.** The pronunciation of the word is given in parentheses: (dēzəl, -səl) or between back slashes: \\. To understand the symbols that are used, look for the pronunciation key. This key is usually found at the bottom or side of the dictionary page. It may also be found in the first pages of the dictionary.

Sample List of Abbreviations

Symbol	Example of word with that pronunciation
ă	pat
ā	pay
âr	care
ä	father
ĕ	pet
ē	be
ĭ	pit
ī	pie
îr	pier
ŏ	pot
ō	toe
ô	paw
oi	boy
ou	out
o͝o	took
o͞o	boot
ŭ	cut
ûr	urge
th	thin
th	this
hw	which
zh	vision
ə	about, item
♦	regionalism

Stress marks: ′ (primary); ′ (secondary), as in **dictionary** (dĭk′shə-nĕr′ē)

—Pronunciation key from *The American Heritage Dictionary*, 4th edition

- **Part of speech.** The part of speech is given, usually abbreviated, often in italic type. Here are the main ones:

  n. = noun (person, place, thing, idea)

  v. = verb (action or state of being)

  v.i. or *intr.* = intransitive verb (verb that doesn't need an object, like *die*)

  v.t. or *tr.* = transitive verb (verb that does need an object, like *make*)

  adj. = adjective (describes a noun)

  adv. = adverb (describes a verb, adjective, or another adverb)

  Here is an example of an entry for a noun from *The American Heritage Dictionary* (4th edition):

> **smart bomb** *n.* A bomb that can be guided by radio waves or a laser beam to its target.

- **Definitions and sometimes examples.** Some words have just one or two definitions, but others may have hundreds. The definition you are looking for is the one that fits the context of the sentence you have read.

  Some definitions are in general use. Others are used only in particular fields of study or professions. See the second definition of *handshake* from *The American Heritage Dictionary* (4th edition) for an example.

> **hand·shake** (hănd′shāk′) *n.* 1. The grasping of hands by two people, as in greeting or leave-taking. 2. *Computer Science* An exchange of signals between two devices when communications begin in order to ensure synchronization.

When examples are given, they are often put in italic type or within brackets so you can tell them apart from the definitions.

> **out·growth** (out′grōth′) *n.* 1. The act or process of growing out. 2. A product of growing out; a projecting part or offshoot: *an outgrowth of new shoots on a branch.* 3. A result or consequence: *Inflation is an outgrowth of war.*
>
> —From *The American Heritage Dictionary*, 4th edition

- **Idioms and other common phrases.** Some dictionaries first give all the definitions of the word alone, and then they give all the definitions of that word combined with others in common phrases. *The American Heritage Dictionary* (4th edition), for instance, gives definitions under the word **run** for phrases such as *run against, run along, run away,* and *run down* (and many, many more).

- **Etymology of the word.** The *etymology* is a word's history. To illustrate, here is an etymology for the word *abandon* from *Webster's New College Dictionary* (3rd edition):

  ME *abandounen* < OFr. *Abandoner* < *a bandon*: a, at (< Lat. *ad*) + *bandon* control.

  This word history goes backward in time. It begins with Middle English (ME, spoken from about 1150 to 1500) and then traces the word back to Old French (OFr.) and then back to Latin (Lat.). Etymologies can provide a fascinating glimpse into how a word gradually took on its present meaning and how languages have influenced one another.

INTERACTION 2–21 Using a Dictionary Entry While You Read

Read the following sentence.

> The bank has **stipulated** that the loan amount can't exceed $10,000.

Now read this dictionary entry for the word *stipulate* from *The American Heritage Dictionary* (4th edition).

> **stip·u·late** (stĭp'yə-lāt') *v.* **–lat-ed; -lat-ing, -lates.** *–tr.* **1a.** To lay down as a condition of an agreement; require by contract. **b.** To specify or arrange in an agreement: *stipulate a date of payment and a price.* **2.** To guarantee or promise (something) in an agreement. *–intr.* **1.** To make an express demand or provision in an agreement. **2.** To form an agreement. [Latin *stipulāri, stipulāt-*, to bargain.] *–stip'u·la'tor* n.

Answer the following questions.

_____ 1. What part of speech is *stipulate*?
a. noun
b. verb
c. adjective
d. adverb

_____ 2. Which sentence best describes *stipulate*?
a. It is a transitive verb.
b. It is an intransitive verb.
c. It has both transitive and intransitive uses.
d. It is neither transitive nor intransitive.

_____ 3. Of the intransitive definitions, which one best fits how *stipulate* is used in the sentence above?
a. 1
b. 1a
c. 1b
d. 2

4. What's the meaning of the Latin root that the word *stipulate* comes from?
____

5. Which syllable of *stipulate* is emphasized when it is spoken? __________
____

INTERACTION 2–22 Using a Dictionary While You Read

Read the following paragraph. Look up the four **bold** words in a dictionary—in print, online, or on your phone. Write a brief definition for each word.

> When there is a **devastating** accident, people's explaining away the signs of the **impending** disaster always seems **implausible** to others. Afterward, there is a **tendency** to read about what has taken place and to criticize: "How could those people be so stupid? Fire them. Pass a law against it. Redo the training."
>
> —Norman, *The Design of Everyday Things*

1. **devastating** ____
2. **impending** ____
3. **implausible** ____
4. **tendency** ____

INTERACTION 2–23 Using the Dictionary While You Read

Read the following excerpt from Chapter 2 of *Brian's Return*, a novel by Gary Paulsen.

> It came to a head in of all places the front entryway of Mackey's Pizza Den. Brian had become **aloof,** sometimes unaware of the social life around him, and without knowing it had upset a boy named Carl Lammers. Carl was a football player, a large boy—his nickname was Hulk—and also a bully who **envied** Brian's celebrity. Brian didn't know him. Apparently Carl thought Brian had said something bad about him and he was coming out of Mackey's Pizza Den just as Brian was walking in with a boy and girl from school. The boy was small and thin—he was named Haley—and the girl was named Susan and she thought Brian was great and wanted to know him better and had invited him for a pizza so she could talk to him. Haley had been standing nearby and thought the invitation included him, to Susan's disappointment.
>
> Carl had asked Susan on a date once and she had refused him. Seeing her with Brian made his anger that much worse.
>
> He saw Brian through the glass of the door, saw him walking with Susan, and Carl threw his whole weight into his shoulder and slammed the door open, trying to knock Brian off balance.
>
> It all went wrong. Brian was too far to the side and the door missed him. It caught Haley full on, smashing his nose—blood poured out immediately—and slammed him back into Susan. The two of them went flying backward and Susan fell to the ground beneath Haley and twisted her kneecap.
>
> "Oh . . . ," she moaned.
>
> For a moment everything seemed to hang in place. The door was open, Carl standing there and Brian off to the side, his face **perplexed**—he had been thinking about the woods when it happened—and Susan and Haley on the ground, blood all over Haley's face and Susan moaning, holding her knee.
>
> "What—?" Brian turned back to Carl just as Carl took a swing at his head. Had it connected fully, Brian thought, it would have torn his head off. Dodging before it caught him, he missed the total force of the blow, but even then it struck his shoulder and knocked him **slightly** back and down on one knee.
>
> Then things came very quickly. Haley was blinded by the blood in his eyes but Susan saw it all and still didn't believe it.
>
> "Something happened," she said later. "Something happened to Brian—Carl just disappeared . . ."
>
> In that instant Brian totally **reverted.** He was no longer a boy walking into a pizza parlor. He was Brian back in the woods, Brian with the moose,

Brian being attacked—Brian living because he was quick and focused and intent on staying alive—and Carl was the threat, the thing that had to be stopped, attacked.

Destroyed.

Give the definition for each **bold** word. Then note if you had to use a dictionary to find it.

1. **aloof** ______________________

   Yes No

2. **envied** ______________________

   Yes No

3. **perplexed** ______________________

   Yes No

4. **slightly** ______________________

   Yes No

5. **reverted** ______________________

   Yes No

Review: Kinds of Information in a Dictionary Entry

Dictionary definitions are found under the basic form of a word. Entries typically include the following kinds of information:

- How to break the word into syllables.
- How to pronounce the word.
- What part of speech the word is.
- Definitions, some of which are general definitions and others that are specific to a particular field of study.
- Sometimes, examples of a word in use.

Dictionary entries in larger dictionaries may include other kinds of information, such as the word history (called the *etymology* of the word).

Lesson 7

While You Read and After You Read, Examine the Author's Tone.

How can you tell if people are happy, sad, mad, or experiencing some other emotion? The short answer is that you can use **inference.** Based on what people say and how they say it, you can infer how they are feeling. (Or sometimes, they'll just tell you!) Here's the long answer.

- You can listen closely to a speaker's tone of voice and, using your prior knowledge of hearing many people use different tones of voice under different circumstances, understand what that tone implies (suggests without saying).
- You can listen to the actual words a person says, and, based on your memories of experiences you have had (again, your prior knowledge), you can understand what shade of meaning he or she is using. If someone says "I'm glad to meet you," the phrase means something different than if he or she says, "I'm so delighted to meet you!" The first sentence usually means the person is just being polite. The second suggests that the person has been waiting to meet you for some time or has a special reason for wanting to meet you.
- You can imagine what the person is trying to accomplish with her or his words. The person's emotions probably have something to do with her or his purpose for speaking.

Written language also has a tone—and it, too, can be happy, sad, mad, or a thousand other emotions. The difference is, of course, that you are reading words, not listening to and seeing a person. But the basic idea is the same. The author chooses specific words to get you to understand and even to feel the feelings he or she is trying to evoke in you. One way authors do this is by imagining what associations you will have to certain words. What memories, emotions, or experiences will a word call up for readers?

Spotlight on Inference: Drawing on Memories and Associations to Make Meaning

Read the following sentences from Aldous Huxley's novel *Brave New World,* and think about what the author wants you to think and feel about what he is describing.

> The overalls of the workers were white, their hands gloved with a pale corpse-coloured rubber. The light was frozen, dead, a ghost.

The author could have chosen any color in the world for the workers' overalls. Why did he choose the color white? What other things do you know of that are white?

One is snow. Related to snow is winter. In the next sentence, the author calls the light "frozen," so that confirms the association with winter. What does "corpse-coloured" tell you? The author also calls the light "dead, a ghost."

These kinds of associations are important to consider when you think about tone. The overall effect that Huxley suggests in these two sentences is that of a lifeless, unmoving, cold situation. Even though we don't know what the workers do or where they are, we do know that Huxley wants us to understand that there is nothing there that seems alive or colorful.

Huxley uses words that create certain feelings in his readers. This kind of tone is called **subjective.** Let's see how you can decide if an author's tone is subjective or not.

Understand the Difference Between Denotation and Connotation.

Denotation is the literal meaning of a word. It is straightforward. When you see denotation, think "d"—**d**enotation is the **d**ictionary **d**efinition. When you look up a word in the dictionary, the definition is the denotation of that word.

> **vig·or·ous** (vĭg'ər-əs) *adj.* 1. Strong, energetic, and active in mind or body; robust. 2. Marked by or done with force and energy.
>
> —*American Heritage Dictionary*, 4th edition

TommL/istockphoto.com

Connotation, on the other hand, adds other associations to a word. When you see connotation, think "conn": connotation is the **conn**ection or association of a word to certain emotions or attitudes. Some words have positive connotations, and others have negative connotations. Connotations are related to the context in which a word appears.

Spotlight on Inference: Understanding Connotations

Here are three words and their denotations, or dictionary definitions.

trudge	walk in a heavy-footed way
walk	move by taking steps with the feet at a slower pace than a run
stride	walk with long steps in a vigorous way

Now read each sentence below. Based on the different verbs that are used, what does each sentence connote? What feelings is the student having about taking her final exam?

A. The student **walked** in to take her final exam.

B. The student **trudged** in to take her final exam.

C. The student **strode** in to take her final exam.

No particular emotion is suggested by the verb *walked* in sentence A. The word doesn't have any connotations in this situation. In sentence B, the verb *trudged* suggests that the student may be depressed at the thought of taking her test, which might further suggest that she doesn't feel she will do well on it. In sentence C, the student's energetic act of *striding* may suggest she feels confident and is ready to take the test.

You use **inference** to determine what a word connotes. You base your reading of connotations on your prior experiences. Your memories of taking tests, your experiences of walking in different ways, and how these things are connected to certain emotional states, all come into play. The other important part of understanding connotation is knowing what words mean. Use the strategies you've learned throughout Part 2 when you don't know the meanings of words.

INTERACTION 2–24 Noting the Connotations of Words

Each of the following items starts with the definitions (denotations) of two words. Then the words are used in sentences. For each sentence, decide what feelings or attitudes (connotations) are suggested by the word in **bold.** Some words won't suggest any.

1. house dwelling place

   home dwelling place

   Crying, she said, "I have to go back to my **house** now." ____________________

   ____

   Crying, she said, "I have to go back **home** now." ____________________

   ____

Connotations Suggest a Subjective Tone.

When an author uses words that have connotations, you can assume that the tone is subjective. **Subjective** means that the author is putting himself or herself into the writing as one of the subjects. It's like someone in a conversation giving her opinion. Her opinion becomes part of what you then respond to. Of course, sometimes the author gives opinions directly instead of by using words with connotations—for example, by using phrases such as *I believe, I think, people should,* and *in my opinion*. In either case, the tone is subjective.

Example of subjective tone

Parents [should] [shower] attention on their children.

author's opinion connotation

Lack of Connotations Suggests an Objective Tone.

You may have noticed in Interaction 2–24 that a few bold words did not suggest any connotations. You might call these words the "plain" version of all the choices the author could have made. A lack of connotations suggests that the tone is objective. **Objective** means the author is ignoring his or her own opinions and is focusing on the object of the writing—the facts or ideas he or she is reporting.

Example of objective tone

Many parents [pay attention] to their children.

"plain" words

INTERACTION 2–25 Understanding Tone Based on Connotation

A. In the following excerpts, underline words that have connotations or that suggest the author's opinion.

B. Decide whether the tone is subjective or objective.

1. Something awful has happened—so awful that I can hardly bear to write it. Oh, how could they, how could they?

—Smith, *I Capture the Castle*

subjective objective

2. An estimated twenty million people inhabited the interior [of Southern and Central Africa] when Livingston first arrived. The tribes lived in villages, great and small. Their mud and grass huts with a single low doorway would be clustered within a protective fence of thorn bushes or sharpened sticks.

—Dugard, *Into Africa*

subjective objective

3. According to a recent study in *The Journal of Applied Psychology*, there is another kind of exam that may be more predictive of how successful students will be in medicine: personality testing.

—Chen, "Do You Have the 'Right Stuff' to Be a Doctor?" *New York Times*, January 14, 2010

subjective objective

4. Some snow in a Buffalo neighborhood turned a deep shade of pink after a cloud of powder was released during demolition of a business that used to make food coloring. As surprised parents and pet owners wondered whether to ban outdoor play, state health and environmental officials collected samples.

—Associated Press, *Ft. Worth Star-Telegram*, January 17, 2010

subjective objective

5. She was on her throne, the chair at the head of the mahogany dining table. It's a wonder of the world she has fit her parents' furniture into that room, including a cupboard for dishes. The old carved chairs are so enormous she looks like a child, feet swinging below her ruffled skirts and not quite reaching the floor.

—Kingsolver, *The Lacuna*

subjective objective

Review: Denotation and Connotation

Two kinds of word meanings are denotative and connotative.

- Denotative meaning is the dictionary definition of a word. Connotative meaning is the emotional tone of a word.
- Connotations vary depending on the context in which a word is used.
- When an author uses words with connotations, the tone of a reading selection is subjective. The author has put himself or herself into the writing as a subject.
- When an author does not use words with connotations, the tone of a reading selection is objective. The author focuses on what happened, not on his or her opinion about what happened.

Consider a Word's Degree of Intensity.

Several kinds of words can have connotations. To take examples from Interaction 2–24, one noun that has connotations is the word *home,* and one verb with connotations is the word *scamper.* There is another kind of word, however—the adjective—that has the job of stating outright what the characteristics of a person, place, thing, or idea are. Some examples from Interaction 2–24 are *cute* and *beautiful, contented* and *ecstatic.*

When you are trying to understand an author's tone, look for adjectives that will show you the degree of intensity with which the author describes ideas and events. Many words can have the same basic meaning, but they express different degrees of intensity. Look at these words, which all share the same working definition of "not cold":

cool lukewarm warm hot boiling

LOW INTENSITY HIGH INTENSITY

Review: Degrees of Intensity

Nouns and verbs can both carry connotative meaning, but it is the job of adjectives to state the characteristics of a person, place, thing, or idea.

- Look for adjectives to determine the author's attitude.
- Decide what degree of intensity the adjective reveals.

The larger your vocabulary becomes, the more you will be able to take advantage of degrees of intensity to understand the author's tone.

Tone Supports the Author's Purpose.

As you learned in Lesson 1, the author's general purpose might be to persuade readers, to inform readers, or to entertain readers. The tone of voice an author uses supports the purpose. (See Table 2.1.)

Subjective writing uses words with connotations and different degrees of intensity. The author's emphasis is on creating emotional states—either persuading readers to feel certain emotions or

Table 2.1 Tone Supports Purpose

General Purpose	General Tone
To inform (teach) readers	• **Objective:** The reading selection focuses on facts and ideas. Connotative language is not used much. • **Impersonal:** The author does not describe his or her point of view.
To entertain readers or to express the feelings or thoughts of the writer	• **Subjective:** The reading selection includes emotional connotations. • **Personal:** The author focuses attention on one particular point of view.
To persuade readers to believe or do something	• **Subjective:** The reading selection includes emotional connotations. • **Personal:** The author focuses attention on a particular point of view although much time may also be given to supporting that opinion with fact.

Review: Tone and Purpose

Tone reflects an author's purpose.

- When the purpose is informative, the tone will be objective and factual.
- When the purpose is to entertain or express, the tone will be subjective and emotional.
- When the purpose is to persuade, the tone will be subjective and emotional.

Facts and objective information are included in all writing, so don't automatically think that writing is informative and objective because these are present.

Learn to Use More Specific Tone Words.

The words *subjective* and *objective* are very general. It is helpful to become familiar with a range of more specific words you can use to describe an author's tone, especially a subjective tone. If you want to be able to talk in class about an author's ideas, or write about them for a college assignment, you will probably need to use words like these to describe the author's tone. Here are some possibilities.

Lesson 12

Recognize Patterns of Organization.

In Part 3, you studied MAPP. MAPPing is a system of structuring your reading so that you understand the main idea of a paragraph or longer passage and the details the author provides as support. In this lesson, we are going to study how the major details of a paragraph are organized into patterns. Understanding patterns is a significant help in making sense of what you read.

Major Details Are Often Organized in Patterns.

The major details of a paragraph or longer passage are often organized according to a certain pattern. For example, a recipe is organized by the steps in a process that you have to follow to make the dish. A story is often organized by when things happen, in time order. Identifying the pattern of organization can help you distinguish the major supporting details the author uses to make his or her point from the less important, minor details.

You Can Predict Paragraph Patterns—Sometimes

You have been turning titles, headings, and topic sentences into questions in order to predict what a reading selection is going to be about. For example, you might read the heading "The Causes of the Civil War" in an American history textbook and form the question, "What are the causes of the Civil War?" This prepares you to search for the parts of the answer to the question, which are the main ideas.

In addition to predicting content, you may also be able to predict the **structure** or **pattern** of the information that you will be reading. The question "What are the causes of the Civil War?" will lead you to search for these causes while you read. As another example, suppose you read the following sentence:

Achieving an ethnic identity seems to occur in three phases. (A *phase* is a stage or step.)

First, you can turn the sentence into a question:

What three phases are involved in achieving an ethnic identity?

Second, you can mentally prepare a structure for the answers to this question, which you are about to learn by reading the paragraph. Your mental structure might look like this:

Phase 1: ?

Phase 2: ?

Phase 3: ?

You don't know yet what the phases are, but you have prepared yourself to pick them out from all the other details in the passage. As you read, you will mentally fill in phases 1, 2, and 3.

INTERACTION 4–1 Fill in the Structure with Information

Read the following paragraphs to find out what the three phases of forming an ethnic identity are. After you read, fill in the blanks on page 392 with the three phases.

1 Roughly one third of the adolescents (that, is teenagers) and young adults living in the United States are members of ethnic minority groups, including African Americans, Asian Americans, Latino Americans, and Native Americans. These individuals typically develop an **ethnic identity:** They feel a part of their ethnic group and learn the special customs and traditions of their group's culture and identity.

2 Achieving an ethnic identity seems to occur in three phases. **At first,** adolescents have not examined their ethnic roots. A teenage African American girl in this phase remarked, "Why do I need to learn about who was the first Black woman to do this or that? I'm just not too interested." **In the second phase,** adolescents begin to explore the personal impact of their ethnic heritage. The curiosity and questioning that is characteristic of this stage is captured in the comments of a teenage Mexican American girl who said, "I want to know what we do and how our culture is different from others." **In the third phase,** individuals achieve a distinct ethnic self-concept. One Asian American adolescent explained his ethnic identification like this: "I have been born Filipino and am born to be

Filipino. . . . I'm here in America, and people of many different cultures are here, too. So I don't consider myself only Filipino, but also American."

—Adapted from Kail & Cavanaugh, *Human Development: A Life-Span View*, 4th edition

Phase 1: ______________________________

Phase 2: ______________________________

Phase 3: ______________________________

Remember: Noticing the paragraph pattern will help you grasp which details are more important to the author's main idea. In the second paragraph in Interaction 4–1, each major supporting detail—phase 1, 2, and 3—was supported by a quotation from a teenager. These quotations make the paragraph more lively and interesting, but it's important to keep in mind that they are minor supporting details. Focus mostly on the main idea and the major details in order to comprehend what you read.

You Can Search for Signal Words to Find Paragraph Patterns

Sometimes the main idea of a paragraph will not tell you which pattern of organization a paragraph uses. In these cases, you can search for signal words as you read. (Signal words are also called "transitions.") For example, if you see the words *when, then, tonight,* and *tomorrow,* you might realize the paragraph is organized in time order.

In this lesson and in Lesson 13, you will study seven patterns of organization, and for each one, a list of signal words is given. Also, on page 426, a master list of signal words is provided in alphabetical order. You can search for a word on this list while you are reading to see which pattern of organization it signals.

Each Pattern Answers a Question

Each pattern of organization answers a general question that corresponds to the 5W's and H words you learned in Lesson 1. The question and the signal words naturally go together.

Question	Sample Signal Words	Pattern of Organization
When did that happen?	then, now, a week ago	time order
Where are things located?	above, below, on the left	space order
What does this mean?	means, is, namely	definition
What are examples of this general idea?	for example, to illustrate	examples
What made this happen? What does this lead to?	reasons, because, consequences	cause and effect
How are these the same? How do they differ?	similar, alike, in contrast, however	comparison and contrast
What kinds are there?	types, kinds, forms	classification

Review: Patterns of Details

Pay attention to patterns when you are reading. Patterns can help you decide which details are major and which are minor.

- Sometimes you can predict the pattern of a paragraph by turning the topic sentence into a question and forming a mental structure for the answers. Then as you read you can put the answers into the structure.
- You can search for signal words to help you find patterns.

Time Order: When Did That Happen?

Time order tells readers when things happen, and in what order: first, second, third, and so on. Words that signal time include *before, after, during, meanwhile,* and *later.* Two kinds of writing often use time order: narrative writing and process writing.

Reading Narrative Writing

One kind of time order is called **narration** (also called "story"). In narrative writing, the author uses time order to show what events a person or character experiences. The Harry Potter series happens in time order. Each book takes place during a different school year at Hogwarts School of Witchcraft and Wizardry.

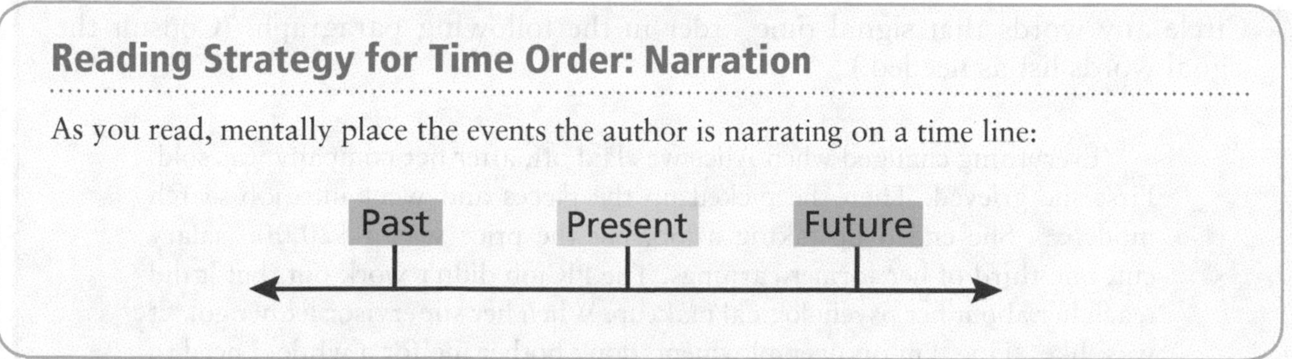

Reading Strategy for Time Order: Narration
As you read, mentally place the events the author is narrating on a time line:
Past
Present
Future

Time Order: Narrative Paragraph — Novel

Use the reading strategy for time order as you read the following paragraph. Then go back and read the highlighted words and the annotations that explain their function in the narration pattern. A list of signal words for narration follows the paragraph.

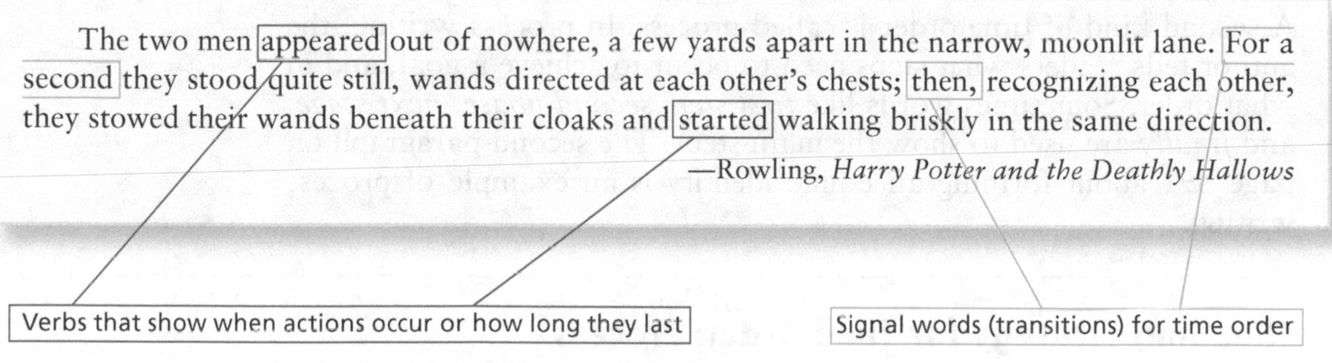

The two men appeared out of nowhere, a few yards apart in the narrow, moonlit lane. For a second they stood quite still, wands directed at each other's chests; then, recognizing each other, they stowed their wands beneath their cloaks and started walking briskly in the same direction.
—Rowling, Harry Potter and the Deathly Hallows
Verbs that show when actions occur or how long they last
Signal words (transitions) for time order

Signal Words (Transitions) for Time Order

When you are reading, look for phrases that will help you figure out when things have occurred. Here are some examples.

- before, during, after
- first, second, third
- next, then, later

- preceding, following, afterward
- as soon as, when, while, until, since
- days, dates, and times, such as Monday through Friday; on March 17, 2010; since 2009; during the week

INTERACTION 4–2 Recognizing the Features of Narration

Circle any words that signal time order in the following paragraph. (Consult the signal words list as needed.)

> Everything changed when Alice was laid off, after her company was sold. First she grieved. Then she picked up the pieces and went into job-search mode. . . . She ended up taking a job, but the price was a $20,000 salary cut, one-third of her former earnings. The PR job didn't work out, but it did teach her about her psychological makeup. When her supervisor let her go, "it was, like, 'Fine, I'm on unemployment, don't bother me for a while. I need to think, about what I want and what I need.'" So she did a little networking, made some contacts, and began freelancing for an advertising company.
>
> —Schor, *The Overspent American*

Reading Process Writing

A second kind of time order is called **process.** In process writing, the author tells readers what steps need to occur to achieve a goal, and in what order. Sometimes words like *first step, second phase, next stage,* and *finally* are used to show the main steps. The second paragraph on page 391 about forming an ethnic identity is an example of process writing.

Reading Strategy for Time Order: Process

To keep the order of events clear as you read, mentally fill in the events on a generalized time line:

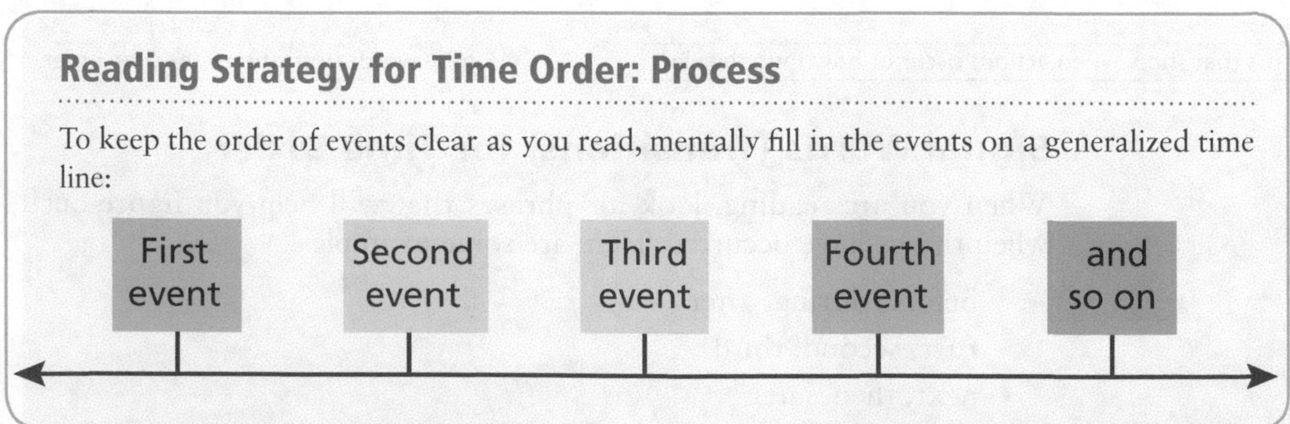

Time Order: Process Paragraph Forensic Science Textbook

Use the reading strategy for process writing as you read the following paragraph. Then go back and read the highlighted words and the annotations that explain their function in the process pattern. A list of signal words for process writing follows the paragraph.

Crime-Scene Investigation of Blood

In an attempt to hide evidence of a violent crime, a perpetrator may try to remove blood evidence by cleaning the area. Although a room may look perfectly clean and totally free of blood after a thorough washing of the walls and floor, blood evidence still remains. Red blood cells contain hemoglobin, the iron-bearing protein that carries oxygen. To detect hemoglobin, an investigator's first step is to mix Luminol powder with hydrogen peroxide in a spray bottle. The mixture is then sprayed on the area to be examined for blood. The iron from the hemoglobin, acting as a catalyst, speeds up the reaction between the peroxide and the Luminol. As the reaction progresses, light is generated for about 30 seconds on the surface of the blood sample.

—Bertino, *Forensic Science: Fundamentals and Investigations*

Words showing steps

The goal or result of the process

Time order words

Signal Words (Transitions) for Process Writing

When you are reading, look for phrases that will help you figure out in what order steps have to occur in order to achieve the desired result.

- first step, second step, third step; first stage, second stage; first phase, second phase
- first, next, then, eventually, last
- start, continue, end
- any of the words from the Signal Words for Time Order list on page 393

INTERACTION 4–3 Recognizing the Features of Process Writing

Circle the words that signal the stages of a process in the following paragraph. (Consult the signal words list as needed.) Underline any other words that indicate time order.

> Once found, there are several steps used in processing a bloodstain, and each can provide a different kind of critical information. The first step is to confirm the stain is blood. Could ketchup, ink, or any other red substance cause the red stain? Before trying to collect the blood, it is necessary to confirm that the evidence is blood, either by using the Kastle-Meyer test or the Leukomalachite green test. If the substance proves to be blood, the second step is to confirm that the blood is human. One test that can be used to determine this is the ELISA test. The third step is to determine the blood type. Depending on the circumstances, blood typing may not be done at all, just DNA analysis.
>
> —Adapted from Bertino, *Forensic Science: Fundamentals and Investigations*

Space Order: Where Are Things Located?

Space order shows readers where things are located in space. Some signal words for space order are *above, below, behind, in front of,* and *near.* Space order is often used in **descriptions.** In a description, the author asks the reader to use sight, hearing, and feeling to imagine experiencing the events or items the author has written about.

Reading Strategy for Space Order

As you read, mentally use your senses, especially your sense of sight, to recreate the scene the author is describing.

Space Order Paragraph — Novel

Use the reading strategy for space order as you read the following paragraph. Then go back and read the highlighted words and the annotations that explain their function in the description pattern. A list of signal words for space order follows the paragraph.

Located on a hill with open views in the middle of the city, the dormitory compound sat on a large quadrangle surrounded by a concrete wall. A huge, towering zelkova tree stood just inside the front gate. People said it was at least a hundred and fifty years old. Standing at its base, you could look up and see nothing of the sky through its dense cover of green leaves.

—Murakami, *Norwegian Wood*

Descriptive details

Signal words (transitions) for space order

Signal Words (Transitions) for Space Order

When you are reading, look for words that signal how the author wants you to picture the scene, and how the elements of the scene are arranged.

- on the left, in the middle, on the right
- in front of, in back of
- above, below, underneath, behind, forward
- off in the distance, beyond, up close, near, far
- at, in, on (as in *at the store, in the wilderness, on the table*)
- inside, outside, inward, outward

INTERACTION 4–4 Recognizing the Features of Space Order

Circle any words that signal space order in the following paragraph. (Consult the signal words list as needed.)

The tide is going out. Near the shore the water is flat, metal-colored, although out past Longway Rock, it's starting to get choppy; there's even a whitecap or two. Lobster buoys down in the cove bob slightly, and seagulls circle the wharf near the marina. The sky is still blue, but off to the northeast, the horizon is lined with a rising cloud bank, and the tops of the pine trees are bending, over there on Diamond Island.

—Strout, *Olive Kitteridge*

Definition: What Does This Mean?

Definition tells what a word or idea means—what it is. Definitions include the term being taught and a description of its meaning. Often, examples are given to illustrate the meaning of the term. Sometimes, illustrations of what the term does *not* include are also provided.

Reading Strategy for Definition

As you read a definition, mentally slot the various parts of the definition into these categories:

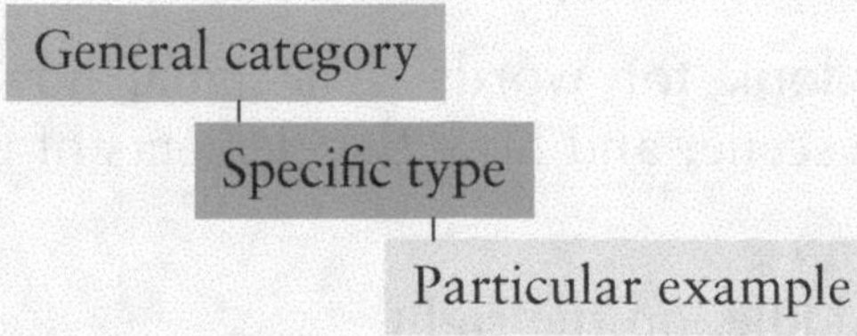

Definition Paragraph — Health Textbook

Use the reading strategy for definition as you read the following paragraph. Then go back and read the highlighted words and the annotations that explain their function in the definition pattern. A list of signal words for definition follows the paragraph.

By simplest definition, **health** means being sound in body, mind, and spirit. The World Health Organization defines health as "not merely the absence of disease or infirmity," but "a state of complete physical, mental, and social well-being." Health is the process of discovering, using, and protecting all the resources within our bodies, minds, spirits, families, communities, and environments.

—Hales, *An Invitation to Health*, 12th edition

Word to be defined — Definition signal word — General term — Specific detail

Signal Words (Transitions) for Definitions

As you read, look for words that suggest definitions are being used.

- is, that is
- is called, can be understood as
- means, has come to mean
- defined as
- consists of
- is not (used to show what a term does not mean)

INTERACTION 4–5 **Recognizing the Features of Definition Writing**

Circle the words that signal definition in the following paragraph. (Consult the signal words list as needed.) Then underline the definitions themselves.

> Wellness can be defined as purposeful, enjoyable living, or, more specifically, a deliberate lifestyle choice characterized by personal responsibility and optimal enhancement of physical, mental, and spiritual health. John Travis, MD, author of *The Wellness Workbook,* notes that "The 'well' person is not necessarily the strong, the brave, the successful, the young, the whole, or even the illness-free being. No matter what your current state of health, you can begin to appreciate yourself as a growing, changing person and allow yourself to move toward a happier life and positive health."
>
> —Adapted from Hales, *An Invitation to Health,* 12th edition

Examples: What Are Examples of This General Idea?

Examples give the specific, down-to-earth details that help readers understand the general statements a writer is making. Examples are often provided for definitions as well. Examples help make general statements come alive.

Reading Strategy for Examples

As you read, create a mental list of examples the author is providing.

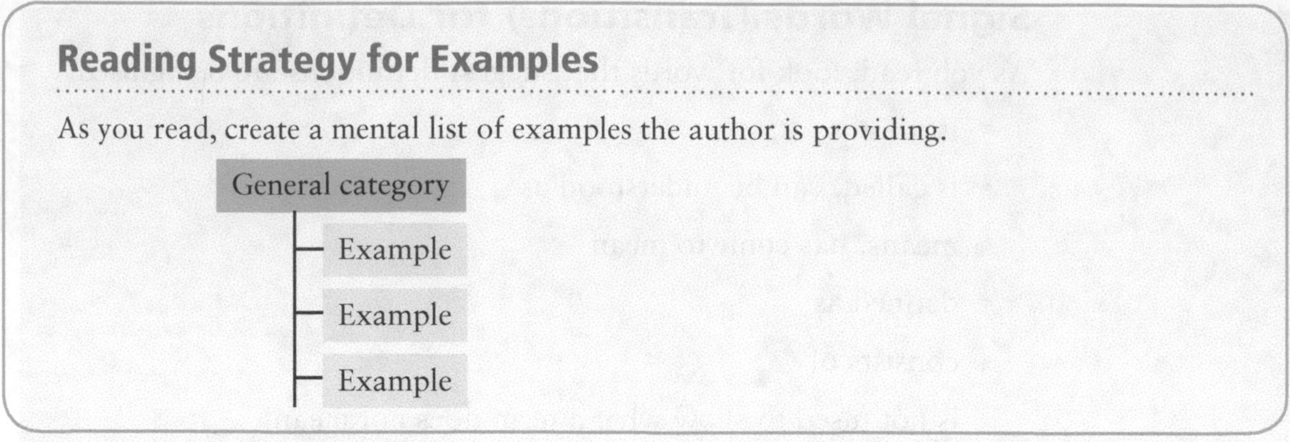

Example Paragraph — Nonfiction Book

Use the reading strategy for examples as you read the following paragraph. Then go back and read the highlighted words and the annotations that explain their function in the example pattern. A list of signal words for examples follows the paragraph.

Body Posture

Body posture is an important influence on one's state. For example, most people would probably find it very difficult to learn effectively with their heads down and their shoulders hunched forward. If you put yourself into that physiology, you will find it's going to be difficult to be inspired. When people are visualizing, for instance, they often tend to be in an erect posture. When people are listening, they tend to lean back a bit with their arms folded or heads tilted. When people are having feelings, they tend to lean forward and breathe more deeply. These cues won't necessarily tell you if the feeling is positive or negative, only that an individual is accessing feelings. So somebody might be feeling very relaxed and have the same general posture as somebody who's feeling depressed.

—Dilts, *Effective Presentation Skills*

General idea | Example signal words | Examples

Signal Words (Transitions) for Examples

- for instance,
- to illustrate,

- namely,
- for example,

Notice that example phrases are often followed by a comma.

INTERACTION 4–6 **Recognizing the Features of Writing That Uses Examples**

Circle the words that signal examples in the following paragraph. (Consult the signal words list as needed.) Then underline all the examples themselves.

> Anger typically emerges between 4 and 6 months. Infants will become angry, for example, if a favorite food or toy is taken away. Reflecting their growing understanding of goal-directed behavior, infants also become angry when their attempts to achieve a goal are frustrated. For example, if a parent restrains an infant trying to pick up a toy, the guaranteed result is a very angry baby.
>
> —Kail & Cavanaugh, *Human Development,* 4th edition

Review: Four Patterns of Organization

Recognize the features of four patterns of organization as you read.

- **Time order:** Time order describes when things occur in relation to one another—*last Friday, this minute, later tonight, first this happens, then that happens.*
- **Space order:** Space order describes where things are in relation to one another—*above, below, beyond.*
- **Definition:** Definition provides the meanings of words by telling what general category a term belongs in and then what makes it different from others of its kind. Words such as *means* and *defined as* are used.
- **Examples:** Examples provide specific instances of a general concept, sometimes introduced by phrases such as *for example* and *to illustrate.*

Lesson 13

Recognize More Patterns of Organization.

In Lesson 12 you learned that the major details of a paragraph (or longer selection) are often arranged in a particular pattern of organization. Sometimes you can predict the pattern from the topic sentence. You can also look for signal words to find paragraph patterns. In that lesson you also studied four patterns: time order, space order, definition, and example. In this lesson you will learn three more: cause and effect, comparison and contrast, and classification.

Cause and Effect: What Made This Happen? What Does This Lead To?

Cause-and-effect paragraphs may focus on the causes of an event, in which case they answer a question such as "What made this happen?" or "What's the reason this occurred?" When they focus on the effects that came about because of something else that happened, a cause-and-effect paragraph answers a question like "What does this lead to?" or "What is the result of this action?"

A cause-and-effect paragraph may describe how a single cause leads to multiple effects, or how multiple causes create a single effect. A piece of writing may even describe how one cause leads to an effect, which then becomes the cause of a second effect, which then becomes the cause of yet another effect, and so on. Think of dominoes falling. The first one knocks over the second one, and when the second one falls, it knocks over the third one, and so on. This last type is called a *causal chain.*

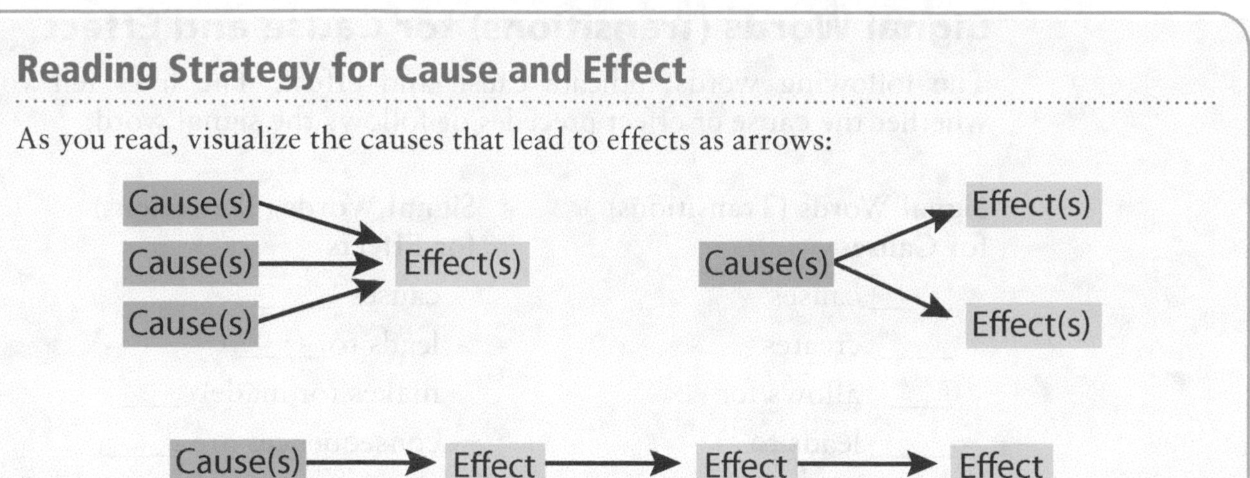

Cause-and-Effect Paragraph **Blog Posting**

Use the reading strategy for cause and effect as you read the following paragraph. Then go back and read the highlighted words and the annotation that explains their function in the cause-and-effect pattern. A list of signal words for cause and effect follows the paragraph.

Medical Bills Cause Most Bankruptcies

Nearly two out of three bankruptcies stem from medical bills, and even people with health insurance face financial disaster if they experience a serious illness, a new study shows. The study data, published online Thursday in *The American Journal of Medicine,* likely understate the full scope of the problem because the data were collected before the current economic crisis. In 2007, medical problems contributed to 62.1 percent of all bankruptcies. Between 2001 and 2007, the proportion of all bankruptcies caused by medical problems rose by about 50 percent.

—Adapted from Parker-Pope, Well Blog, *New York Times,* June 4, 2009

Signal words showing cause or effect

Signal Words (Transitions) for Cause and Effect

The following words indicate cause and effect. The lines tell you whether the cause or effect precedes or follows the signal word.

Signal Words (Transitions) for Causes	Signal Words (Transitions) for Effects
_____ causes	causes _____
_____ creates	leads to _____
_____ allows for	makes (or made) _____
_____ leads to	consequences are _____
_____ makes	produces _____
_____ produces	_____ depends on
are due to _____	_____ were the effects
because _____	_____ is the result
reason is _____	

INTERACTION 4–7 **Recognizing the Features of Cause-and-Effect Writing**

Circle the words that signal causes and effects in the following paragraph. (Consult the signal words list as needed.) Then underline all the causes and effects.

Staying Healthy Longer

The unexercised body—though free of the symptoms of illness—will rust out long before it could ever wear out. Inactivity can make anyone old before his or her time. Just as inactivity accelerates aging, activity slows it down. The effects of ongoing activity are so profound that gerontologists sometimes refer to exercise as "the closest thing to an antiaging pill." Exercise slows many changes associated with advancing age, such as loss of lean mus-

Signal Words and the Patterns They Indicate

The following chart lists signal words that point to the different patterns of organization you have learned about in Lessons 12 and 13. You may want to consult the chart when you are trying to determine how a reading is organized.

Signal Words	Organizational Patterns
above	space order
after, afterward	time order
agree	comparison
alike	comparison
allows for	cause and effect
although	contrast
are called	definition
as	time order
as soon as	time order
at	space order
because	cause and effect
before	time order
behind	space order
below	space order
beyond	space order
both	comparison
brought about by	cause and effect
but	contrast
can be understood as	definition
categories	classification
cause, causes	cause and effect
closer	space order

Signal Words	Organizational Patterns
consequences are	effect
consists of	definition
continue	time order
contrasts with	contrast
creates	cause and effect
defined as	definition
depends on	cause and effect
difference	contrast
different groups	classification
differs by, differs from	contrast
due to	cause and effect
during, during that time	time order
effect	effect
end	time order
eventually	time order
ever since	time order
factors	causes
farther away	space order
first (or second, third, fourth, etc.)	time order, example
first stage, first step	time order (process)
first type	classification
following	time order
for example	example
for instance	example
forms (used as a noun)	classification
forward	space order

Signal Words	Organizational Patterns
here	space order
however	contrast
identical	comparison
if . . . then . . .	cause and effect
immediately	time order
in	space order, time order
in addition	example
in back of, in the background	space order
in contrast	contrast
in front of, in the foreground	space order
in the middle	space order
inside	space order
instead	contrast
is	definition
kinds	classification
last	time order
later	time order
leads to	cause and effect
like, likewise	comparison
makes, made	cause and effect
means, has come to mean	definition
meantime, meanwhile	time order
namely	definition
near, nearby	space order
next	time order
not only . . . but also	comparison

Signal Words	Organizational Patterns
off in the distance	space order
on	space order, time order
on the one hand . . . on the other hand	contrast
outside, outward	space order
phases	process, classification
preceding	time order
rather	contrast
reason is	cause
result is	effect
second; second stage or step; second type	time order, example
share	comparison
similar, similarity, similarly	comparison
since	time order
start	time order
still	time order
subsequently	time order
that is	definition
the same	comparison
then	time order
there	space order
third; third stage or step; third type	time order, example
through	space order, time order
to illustrate	example
to the contrary	contrast
types	classification
under, underneath	space order

Signal Words	Organizational Patterns
until	time order
up close	space order
when	time order, cause
while	time order, contrast

Review: Four More Patterns of Organization

Recognize the features of four patterns of organization as you read.

- **Cause and effect:** Cause and effect describes what made something happen and what it leads to. Signal words such as *because, leads to, due to, causes,* and *consequences* are used.
- **Comparison:** Comparison shows how things are similar to each other. Signal words such as *like, similar,* and *same* are used.
- **Contrast:** Contrast shows how things are different from each other. Signal words such as *different, in contrast,* and *however* are used.
- **Classification:** Classification describes the different kinds or types of a larger idea or event. Signal words include *types, kinds,* and *groups.*

Lesson 16

Analyze Facts, Opinions, and Inferences.

Being able to identify and understand the difference between fact and opinion is an important part of comprehension. If you can clarify what is factual, what is an opinion, and the details that support or refute them, you will be better able to analyze the author's tone and purpose. In addition, you can keep your reactions to a reading separate from the author's tone or from the facts of the reading itself. The basics of fact and opinion as well as the issues that complicate them will be discussed in the first part of this lesson. The second part of the lesson is about inference, which is a process of adding up all the facts and drawing conclusions from them.

Facts Can Be Verified.

Verified means that something can be proven to be accurate, true, and correct. The ability to be verified is at the core of all facts. You can confirm facts by reading different sources on that topic, such as newspapers and magazines that check facts carefully, encyclopedias, nonfiction books, and textbooks. Facts can be verified by science, statistics, or specifics.

The tone word that goes with facts is *objective*. As you learned in Lesson 7, **objective** means "just the facts," not influenced by personal feelings or opinion. You are likely reading facts when the author provides a lot of details such as people's names, place names, events, specific dates and times, numbers, and other items that are observable and provable. Here is an example:

Escada's couture line includes a pair of jeans covered in designs made with Swarovski crystals, which the design house sold for $10,000.

The previous sentence is a fact. It can be verified by checking reliable sources, such as *Forbes* magazine, from which this information was taken, or maybe Escada's Web site. The sources used to verify a particular fact will vary. For instance, if you wanted to verify that the African country of Somalia is east of Ethiopia, you would use a globe, map, or encyclopedia.

INTERACTION 5–9 Finding Factual Sentences

Mark the sentences that are facts with an F. If you think a sentence is a fact, ask yourself, "How can the information be verified?"

____ 1. More than 1,800 people died in Hurricane Katrina.

____ 2. Agriculture arose on plateaus in the Americas and Mexico, unlike in Mesopotamia, Egypt, or China, where it arose in river valleys.

____ 3. The ancient inscription was rather unremarkable.

____ 4. Channing Tatum is one of Hollywood's hottest young stars.

____ 5. People with nightmare disorder typically experience terrible dreams on a nightly basis and are often jarred awake.

____ 6. There are five things that research has shown improves happiness: being grateful, being optimistic, counting your blessings, using your strengths, and being kind to others.

____ 7. Kona coffee is one of the most balanced coffees of the world, with a smooth, medium body and crisp finish.

____ 8. More than 1 million users include "John" in their profile name, making it the most popular name on Facebook.

____ 9. Jim Carrey became a grandfather in 2010 at age 48.

____ 10. Wearing lashes by UR Elegant Eyes brings out your inner Diva.

Opinions Cannot Be Verified.

Unlike facts, opinions cannot be verified. An opinion is a personal view or judgment about something. Opinions change from person to person and from one point in time to another. For example, you may hate onions, but your friend Cedric loves them. However, when Cedric was a kid he did not like onions. As he grew up, his taste buds changed, and as an adult he loves them. Taste is one kind of opinion. Opinions are **subjective.** They are based on personal feelings, tastes, imaginings, predictions, and judgments, and they may change over time.

Remember the crystal-studded Escada jeans that cost $10,000? The price tag was a fact. However, your reaction to paying $10,000 for a pair of jeans would be an opinion. Take a class poll:

- How many of you think that $10,000 is a ridiculous amount to pay for a pair of jeans?
- How many of you think it would be fine to pay $10,000 if you could afford it?

Each answer is an opinion, even if several of you have the same opinion.

INTERACTION 5–11 Finding Opinions in Sentences

Mark the sentences that are opinions with an O. Circle the words you think make the sentence an opinion. If you think a sentence is a fact, ask yourself, "How can the information be verified?"

____ 1. Lil Wayne's song lyrics are degrading to women.

____ 2. The Winter Olympics offered some fierce competition, especially in women's figure skating.

____ 3. The BlackBerry is better than the iPhone for business.

____ 4. In a speech, *volume* means the loudness of a speaker's voice.

____ 5. Never trust a person who does not have at least one bad habit.

____ 6. Daylight saving time allows people to use less energy by taking advantage of the longer daylight hours during spring and summer.

____ 7. Las Vegas casinos do not have clocks in them.

Facts and Opinions Often Appear Together.

Fact seems simple enough to understand; it is something you can prove is true. An opinion is based on someone's feelings or beliefs. What's so complicated about that? One issue that complicates fact and opinion is that they are often mixed together. Here's an example:

> Clint Eastwood, who won best director at the Oscars for the films *Million Dollar Baby* and *Unforgiven,* is also a fantastic actor.

While it is true that Clint Eastwood has directed two Oscar-winning films, to say that he is a fantastic actor is an opinion.

In addition, facts can be misleading. For example:

> In 2006 ExxonMobil had fewer oil spills than in 2005.

This information is factual. What Exxon neglected to say was that even though it had fewer spills, the amount of oil spilled in 2006 was more than three times greater than the amount spilled in 2005 (40,000 barrels vs. 12,200 barrels). This information can be found in the ExxonMobil *2006 Corporate Citizenship Report*, p. 7.

Moreover, opinions can be hidden in unexpected places sometimes. For example, here is a headline from the *New York Times:*

> Sweeping Health Care Plan Passes House

It is a fact that a health care plan passed a House vote, but what does "sweeping" mean? Is this fact or opinion? The word "sweeping" suggests that the plan will cover and fix many issues. This might seem like a fact, but "sweeping" is an opinion. If the health care plan leaves out an issue you find very important, then you would not agree that it is "sweeping."

INTERACTION 5–13 **Is It Fact or Opinion?**

A. In each item, underline the sentence that is fact. Circle the opinion word(s) in the sentence you do not underline.

1. John Fitzgerald Kennedy was assassinated on November 22, 1963. To this day, JFK remains an extremely popular figure in history.
2. The *Mona Lisa* hangs in the Louvre in Paris, France. It is possibly the most beautiful painting in the world.
3. The beauty of sunsets and sunrises is amazing. Although, you know, the sun does not actually "rise" or "set;" rather, the earth rotates.
4. Reading is a required skill in many jobs. In fact, it is the most important skill for success.
5. Salespersons should avoid the use of slang in their speech. Guidelines for proper speech use can be found in the new employee handbook.

B. In each item, underline the part of the sentence that includes a fact. Circle the opinion word(s) that make the other part an opinion.

6. On average, a drunk driver in the United States kills a person every 40 minutes, making this one of the most serious social issues we face.
7. *Avatar* became the second-highest-grossing film worldwide in just four weeks, which is hard to believe.
8. A few cultures do not practice kissing, so kissing must be a learned behavior.
9. Monopoly, which first became available during the Great Depression, was probably popular because people could pretend they were wealthy.
10. Although dating experts hotly debate the precise timeframe, a standard time period in which to return a call after first meeting a person is two to four days.

A Fact Is a Fact, But an Opinion Needs to Be Supported by Proof.

Once proven, a fact remains a fact, except in cases in which scientific advances uncover new information. An opinion, though, needs to be supported by proof to be credible—that is, to be believable by others. The stronger the proof, the more likely others will agree with the opinion.

How do you get support for an opinion? Just because you believe aliens have visited Earth doesn't mean anyone else does. "Where is your proof?" your friends will ask. "Do you have an 'un-Photoshopped' picture of an alien at the mall? Is it possible there is another explanation for what you saw?" While the alien example might be a bit of a stretch, there are ways to lend credibility to opinions.

Credibility comes from strong proof. Strong proof does not make an opinion a fact, but it does make it easier to consider. The strength of proof is usually determined by the source. There are two types of sources that can lend credibility to an opinion:

- An expert
- Direct experience

Expert Opinions

An **expert** is a person who has extensive knowledge, education, or experience about a topic. He or she probably works or has worked in the field, and may have written a book about the topic. For example, a doctor is an expert on medical care. Your doctor has an opinion about what is wrong with you, but his or her experience and education provides support for that opinion and makes it credible. That does not mean doctors do not make mistakes. They do. That is why you get second opinions on more serious health issues.

In addition, a doctor is an expert in the field of medicine, but that doesn't automatically make him or her an expert in other fields. If you want your car repaired, you don't go to a doctor. An expert is an expert in his or her field only, not in all things.

Direct Experience

Direct experience refers to a person's firsthand exposure to something. For example, if a friend has been to Maui for vacation, he has direct experience of the island. His vacation does not make him an expert on Maui unless he has written a travel book, been there twenty times, or produced a TV show for the Travel Channel. However, his personal experience, stories, and tips about vacationing there do have a certain degree of credibility, especially if he is trustworthy.

A word of caution: At times, people try to pass off **secondhand information** such as gossip as credible evidence. An example is when someone starts by saying, "Well, I heard . . ." or "My friend said. . . ." In order for an opinion to be strongly supported, the proof or evidence needs to be reliable, direct, and credible (believable).

INTERACTION 5–14 **Expert Opinion or Direct Experience**

For the following situations, decide if the source is expert opinion or direct experience. Write Expert or Direct. If it is secondhand information, then write NO!

_____ 1. A doctor sharing his opinion about the current state of the U.S. economy.

_____ 2. Your neighbor, who is a mechanic, giving you car advice.

_____ 3. A grandmother giving advice to a new mother.

_____ 4. A movie director critiquing a film.

_____ 5. A soldier talking about his war experience.

_____ 6. An accountant giving tax advice.

_____ 7. Information about Beijing from an Olympic athlete who participated in the 2008 Summer Olympics.

_____ 8. A senior in college giving academic advice to a freshman.

_____ 9. President Obama on the prospects of his favorite football team, the Chicago Bears.

_____ 10. A person you meet on the bus giving you a stock tip.

Review: Supporting Opinions

For an opinion to have credibility, it should be supported in one of the following ways:

- An expert's opinion, gained through education and/or skill.
- Direct experience, gained through personal exposure.

Certain Kinds of Words Indicate Opinions.

One way to identify a fact is to ask yourself, "Is this information verifiable?" Visualizing how you would verify it can help you answer that question. Can you see it, duplicate the results, or check a reliable source? If the information is not verifiable, then it is probably an opinion. Often when you decide something is an opinion, it is because it contains one of the following:

- A value word
- An all-or-nothing word

The first category is "value words." These words mainly consist of adjectives that place a value on something. Here are some examples:

best beautiful awful ugly cool great fantastic good bad
awesome attractive hard easy interesting boring immature

- The book was **great.**
- That movie is **awesome.**
- His sister is **beautiful.**
- This game is **boring.**
- This test was **easy.**

As you can see in each of these sentences, not everyone would agree. The value word makes these statements individual opinions rather than verifiable facts.

The second category is "all-or-nothing words." These words do not automatically express opinions, but you should always be suspicious when you see them and visualize whether they are verifiable facts or just opinions. Here are some examples:

always all any every none never must have to will

- You are **always** late.
- I **never** win.

- **Everybody** is going!
- You **must** listen to me.
- I **will** be there.

As you can see, each of these sentences allows no room for chance. These words are absolute, meaning there is no middle ground. Words like *should, sometimes, usually, often, might,* and *frequently* are more reasonable. However, absolute words do not *always* mean that the sentence will be an opinion. For example, take these sentences:

- Molly is **always** on time.
- The sun **always** rises in the east.

Both sentences use *always,* but in the first one, there is a probability that Molly will be late once, even if she is usually on time. The second sentence is a scientific certainty: the sun does *always* rise in the east and set in the west. So again, determining whether something is a fact or an opinion usually comes down to this one thing: Can the information be verified?

INTERACTION 5–15 Finding Opinion Words

Circle any word that indicates an opinion. If the whole sentence is factual, circle F. If it is an opinion, circle O. Discuss your answers with a classmate and then with your instructor when you are done.

1. Macs are cooler than PCs. F O
2. David Beckham is married to Victoria Adams, a former Spice Girl. F O
3. Classical music is soothing. F O
4. Laughter is the best medicine. F O
5. The number of people in prisons has outgrown current facilities in recent years, causing overcrowding and increased public spending to build new prisons. F O
6. The Black Eyed Peas' song "Boom Boom Pow" was the most frequently downloaded song on iTunes in 2009. F O
7. Everyone needs at least eight hours of sleep per night for the body to function. F O

Review: Words That Indicate Opinions

Certain words suggest opinions. They fall into two categories:

- Words that indicate a value or belief.
- Words that indicate "all or nothing."*

*Remember that "all or nothing" words do not guarantee that the sentence they are in is an opinion, but look closely because they often do indicate an opinion.

Inferences Are Made from the Author's Words and Your Logic.

Facts, as you have learned, are verifiable and observable. Facts are evidence. Sometimes, the author does not "connect all the dots" of the evidence—so you, the reader, have to. When you add up all the available evidence and draw a logical conclusion from it, you are making an inference.

Fact: Last night the temperature dropped below freezing.

Fact: I left my plants outside on the patio.

Fact: The leaves all shriveled and dried up.

Inference: My plants were damaged by the freezing temperatures and may have died.

The writer of the preceding statements inferred (made an inference) that because of the freezing temperature, his or her plants might have died.

When you are inferring from facts, it's important to be logical. You can't ignore any of the evidence, and you can't add any evidence if the author hasn't given it. Think about the inferences that doctors make when you visit them, for example. Doctors write a prescription or give a diagnosis based on the evidence they find when they examine you. A doctor would probably get sued pretty quickly if he or she simply ignored important symptoms you shared or recommended an operation without adequate evidence that you needed it.

The auto mechanic profession is another one that uses inference. The mechanic's job is to check the symptoms to diagnose what is wrong with your car. Mechanics probably wouldn't stay in business long if they ignored what needed to be fixed or started recommending expensive, unnecessary repairs without evidence of a real need.

You make multiple inferences every day. If clouds fill the sky, you infer that it's going to rain and you take along an umbrella. If traffic is backed up, you infer there is an accident and you take an alternative route. If you see a person eating only a salad for lunch every day, you might infer that he or she is on a diet or is a vegetarian. Each of these inferences is logical and based on evidence.

When you read, you make inferences based on what the author says. You may have heard this process referred to as "reading between the lines." You have used inference in every lesson of *Activate: College Reading*. For example, you have been using inference with the following skills:

- Lesson 1: Identifying an author's purpose
- Lesson 2: Predicting what the author will say
- Lesson 3: Thinking, talking, and writing about a reading selection
- Lessons 4 and 5: Defining vocabulary by using word parts and context
- Lesson 6: Using a dictionary effectively for understanding new words and connecting them to prior knowledge
- Lesson 7: Recognizing the connotation of words and how that connects to author's tone
- Lessons 8–11: Understanding the role of topics, stated main ideas and implied main ideas, and supporting details
- Lessons 12 and 13: Analyzing and using patterns of organization
- Lesson 14: Applying the MAPP annotating and reading strategy to textbooks

- Lesson 15: Developing your ability to think critically
- Lesson 16: Understanding the difference between a fact and opinion

Each of these skills involves inference. You are not given the answer directly, but through your logic and using the clues from the text, you are able to *infer* the answer.

INTERACTION 5–18 Using Details to Make Inferences from Situations

Read each situation. Use inference to answer the questions that follow.

Situation A

- Maurice plays soccer.
- Maurice had a soccer game last night.
- Maurice is limping this morning at school.

1. What is the best inference about Maurice?

____ a. He stubbed his toe on his way to school.

____ b. He injured himself playing soccer.

____ c. He is looking for attention.

Situation B

- You go to visit your grandmother.
- You walk in the door and it smells like fresh-baked cookies.

2. What is the best inference about your grandmother?

____ a. She is burning a candle that smells like fresh-baked cookies.

____ b. She is wearing a new perfume that smells of cookies.

____ c. She has baked cookies for you.

Situation C

- You pull up next to a Ferrari at a traffic light.
- The driver is dressed in the latest style.

WRITING

Preface

Our objective with *WRITE 1: Sentences and Paragraphs* and its companion *WRITE 2: Paragraphs and Essays* is to help you function, and even flourish, in college and in the workplace. Now more than ever, you need effective communication skills in order to take your place in our information-driven world. There really is no alternative. Writing, speaking, collaborating, thinking critically—these are the survival skills for the twenty-first century. We have kept this crucial directive clearly in mind during the development of *WRITE 1* and *WRITE 2*.

Overview of *WRITE 1*

WRITE 1 covers all of the essential communication skills needed to succeed in the college classroom:

Part 1 features **writing to learn**, **reading to learn**, and making the **writing-reading** connection.

Inti St. Clair/Digital Vision/Getty Images

Part 2 helps you learn about using the **writing process** and the **traits of effective writing**.

Part 3 covers **the forms of paragraph and essay writing** that you will be expected to develop in the college classroom: description, illustration, definition, narration, classification, process, comparison, cause-effect, and argumentation.

Hervé Hughes/Hemis/Corbis

Part 4 provides in-depth **sentence workshops** to help you master sentence basics and overcome sentence challenges.

Part 5 offers many **word workshops** to help you understand and master using the parts of speech in your writing.

Part 6 includes **punctuation and mechanics workshops** that cover commas, apostrophes, semicolons, colons, hyphens, dashes, quotation marks, italics, and capitalization.

Part 7 is **a reader with short, medium, and long professional essays** for the major forms of paragraph writing covered in part 3.

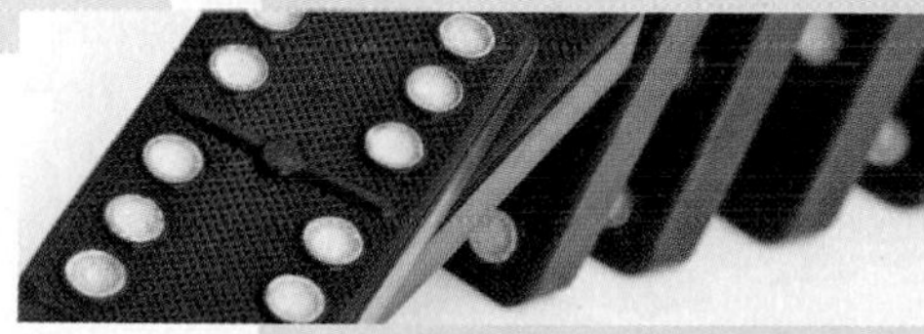

Brian A Jackson, 2010/used under license from www.shutterstock.com

"[Student writers] are frustrated when they are not able to visualize before the first draft what will appear on the page. We must be honest and let them know how much writing is unconscious and accidental."
—Donald Murray

Research-Based Approach

The Writing Process *WRITE 1* presents writing as a process rather than an end product. Too often, writers try to do everything all at once and end up frustrated, thinking that they can't write.

WRITE 1 shows you that writing must go through a series of steps before it is ready to submit. As you work on the various writing tasks, you will internalize strategies that you can employ in all of your future writing, whether analytical essays in college or quarterly reports in the workplace.

The Traits of Writing *WRITE 1* not only explains the steps you should take during a writing project but also tells you what to include—the traits. These traits comprise *ideas, organization, voice, word choice, sentence fluency, conventions,* and *design.*

Working with the traits helps you in two important ways: It (1) identifies the key elements of successful paragraphs and essays and (2) provides a vocabulary for discussing writing with others. This information will give you the background knowledge you need to engage thoughtfully with writing.

Connecting the Process and the Traits *WRITE 1* helps students address the appropriate traits at different points during the writing process. For example, during your prewriting, or planning, you should focus on the ideas, organization, and intended voice in your writing.

The traits are especially useful when revising an initial draft because they help you know what to look for. All of the revising checklists in *WRITE 1* are traits based.

Revise Improve your writing, using your partner's comments on the response sheet and the following checklist. Continue working until you can answer yes to each question.

Ideas:

1. Do I compare two subjects—myself and another person? ____
2. Do I use three points of comparison? ____
3. Do I include details that show instead of tell? ____

Organization:

4. Do I have a topic sentence, middle, and a closing sentence? ____
5. Have I used a point-by-point organizational plan? ____
6. Have I used transitions to connect my sentences? ____

Voice:

7. Do I sound knowledgeable and interested? ____

The Writing-Reading Connection *WRITE 1* provides you with accessible and exemplary models of sentences, paragraphs, and essays. Before you begin to write, you read and respond both verbally and on the page. And as you write, you will read and respond to other students' works. Numerous activities throughout *WRITE 1* support the writing- reading and speaking-listening connections.

■ Grammar in Context *WRITE 1* is designed to provide grammar instruction, as much as possible, within the context of your own writing—to merge skills with craft. Study after study has shown this to be the most effective approach to teaching grammar.

In a typical writing chapter, you are introduced to two or three new grammar skills or concepts. After practicing each skill, you apply what you have learned as you edit your own writing. Additional practice activities are provided in the workshop section of the text.

Developmental Design

WRITE 1 employs the following proven strategies:

■ Helpful Visuals Research shows that visuals help writers learn new concepts and processes. As a result, charts, graphs, and illustrations are used throughout each chapter; and you are encouraged to use graphic organizers as you develop your own writing.

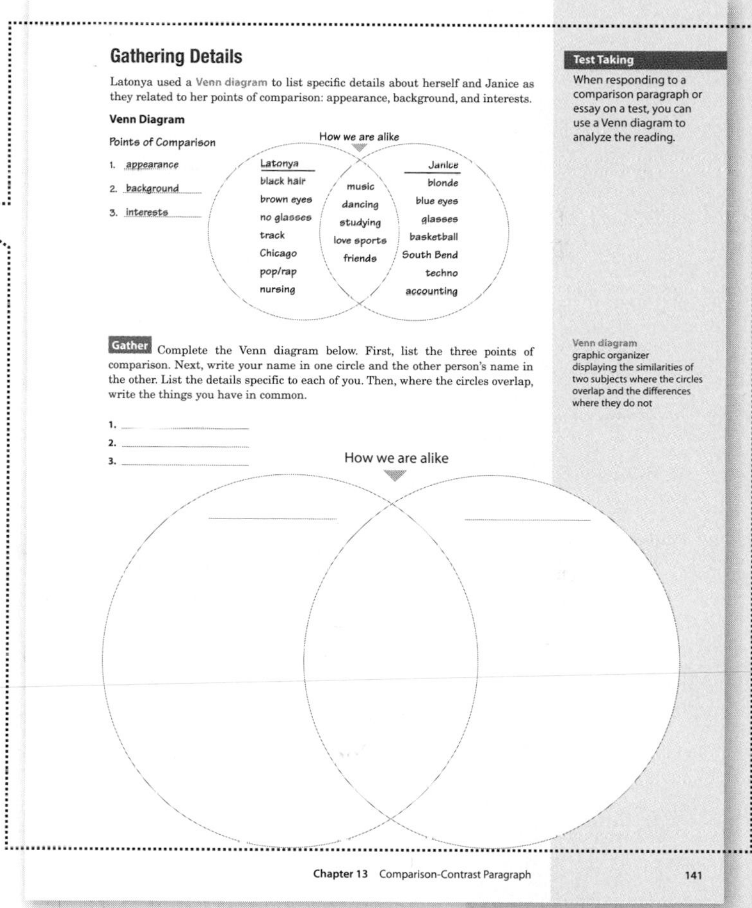

Gathering Details

Latonya used a Venn diagram to list specific details about herself and Janice as they related to her points of comparison: appearance, background, and interests.

Venn Diagram

Gather Complete the Venn diagram below. First, list the three points of comparison. Next, write your name in one circle and the other person's name in the other. List the details specific to each of you. Then, where the circles overlap, write the things you have in common.

1. ________
2. ________
3. ________

Test Taking
When responding to a comparison paragraph or essay on a test, you can use a Venn diagram to analyze the reading.

Venn diagram
graphic organizer displaying the similarities of two subjects where the circles overlap and the differences where they do not

Chapter 13 Comparison-Contrast Paragraph 141

■ Structured Instruction Each chapter in *WRITE 1* is carefully structured and easy to follow, guiding you through the writing process and helping you produce writing that reflects your best efforts. This approach is essential to help you stay with a piece of writing until it is truly ready to submit.

After completing the work in *WRITE 1,* you will have internalized key strategies for producing effective writing.

■ Clear Format Objectives, explanations, and directions in *WRITE 1* are clearly marked so you know what you are expected to do and why. In addition, each two-page spread offers definite starting and ending points for your work, eliminating the necessity to page back and forth within a chapter.

Because *WRITE 1* is so easy to follow, it lends itself to small-group work and independent study.

"Students need opportunities to think for themselves, to build intellectual confidence as well as intellectual competence."
—Dave Kemper

■ Reflection and Reinforcement
WRITE 1 asks you to reflect on your writing after completing the various paragraph and essay assignments. This self-assessment or reflection is a critical activity, helping you to internalize the different forms and strategies.

Learning Outcome
Review description, illustration, and definition.

LO7 Reviewing Description, Illustration, and Definition

Describe Pick out an object within view. Study it with your senses, handling it if possible. Then fill out the following sensory chart with details about the object. Afterward, on your own paper, write a paragraph describing the object.

See	Hear	Smell	Taste	Touch

Illustrate In the following statement, circle the word in parentheses that best describes your current schedule. Then write four examples that illustrate the statement. On your own paper, write an illustration paragraph about your schedule.

Statement: My current schedule is (incredibly/not) busy.
Example A: ______
Example B: ______
Example C: ______
Example D: ______

Define In the top box below, write a word that intrigues you. Then, in the boxes under it, write information about the word. On your own paper, write a definition paragraph about the term.

Word to define:

definition	origin	history	quotation

94

■ Familiar Connections
WRITE 1 compares new, perhaps difficult concepts with old familiar ones, establishing a comfortable context.

Learning Outcome
Read to learn.

LO1 Reading to Learn

Thoughtful, active reading encompasses a number of related tasks: previewing the text, reading it through, taking notes as you go along, and summarizing what you have learned. Active reading gives you control of reading assignments and makes new information part of your own thinking.

"The books that help you the most are those that make you think the most."
—Theodore Parker

Effective Academic Reading

Follow the guidelines listed below for all of your academic reading assignments. A few of these points are discussed in more detail later in the chapter.

1. **Know the assignment:** Identify its purpose, its due date, its level of difficulty, and so on.
2. **Set aside the proper time:** Don't try to read long assignments all at once. Instead, try to read in 30-minute allotments.
3. **Find a quiet place:** The setting should provide space to read and to write.
4. **Gather additional resources:** Keep on hand a notebook, related handouts, Web access, and so on.
5. **Study the "layout" of the reading:** Review the study-guide questions. Then skim the pages, noting titles, headings, graphics, and boldfaced terms.
6. **Use proven reading strategies:** See pages 10–13.
7. **Look up challenging words:** Also use context cues to determine the meaning of unfamiliar terms.
8. **Review difficult parts:** Reread them, write about them, and discuss them with your classmates.
9. **Summarize what you learned:** Note any concepts or explanations that you will need to study further.

Traits
Effective writing has strong ideas, clear organization, appropriate voice, precise words, smooth sentences, correct conventions, and a strong design. Use these traits to understand what you read.

context cues using the words surrounding an unfamiliar term to help unlock its meaning

Reflect Circle the star that best identifies your study-reading skills. Then explain your choice on the lines below. In your explanation, consider which of the above guidelines you do or do not follow. Weak ★ ★ ★ ★ ★ Strong

8

■ Vocabulary Key terms related to instruction are defined.

Additional Special Features

The following features appear as side notes or special call-outs to help you develop your communication skills and to connect your work with other learning situations—both in school and in the workplace.

Traits

The traits are used for writing and reading.

Test Taking

When appropriate, tips for taking exams are provided.

Speaking & Listening

Optional oral activities complement the writing instruction.

WAC

Special notes connect your work to writing in different classes.

Workplace

Special notes connect your work to writing in the workplace.

ESL Support

These features will help those who speak English as a second language to improve their understanding as they complete the activities in *WRITE 1*.

Insight

The insights explain or reinforce concepts for students who are just learning English.

Vocabulary

Challenging words and idioms are defined throughout, helping ESL students—or any student.

Insight

As you've seen, commas are needed to set off extra information in a sentence. Sometimes the extra information comes between the subject and the verb:

Lupe, who is a great singer and dancer, loves theater.

Commas are needed in the sentence above. But when there is no extra information to set off, do not separate the subject and verb with a comma.

Incorrect: Lupe, loves theater.
Correct: Lupe loves theater.

Fuse /Getty Images

Part 1 Writing and Reading for Success

"I hear and I forget; I see and I remember;
I write and I understand."
—Proverb

Inti St. Clair/Digital Vision/Getty Images

1 Writing and Learning

Why should you care about writing? The answer is simple: You'll be doing a lot of it in college and in the world beyond. Today's technology, in fact, has made writing more important than ever before. Just ask anyone in the workplace. In one respect, writing is an invaluable learning tool because it helps you **sort out** your thoughts about new ideas and concepts. In another respect, it is an essential communication tool because you write to pass on what you have learned.

This chapter serves two important functions: (1) It introduces you to "writing to learn"—a way to use writing to succeed in college, and (2) it **initiates** the discussion of writing to share—developing paragraphs, essays, and other forms of writing.

Please know that there are no secrets or shortcuts to becoming an effective writer and learner. But also know that if you sincerely try, you will succeed.

What do you think?

What does the quotation on the previous page say about the learning process? And how does it match up with your own learning process?

Vocabulary

sort out
make clear

initiates
starts, begins

Learning Outcomes

LO1 Write to learn for yourself.

LO2 Write to share learning.

LO3 Consider the range of writing.

LO4 Review writing and learning.

Learning Outcome

Write to learn for yourself.

LO1 Writing to Learn

Gertrude Stein made one of the more famous and unusual statements about writing when she said, "To write is to write is to write is to write . . . ." The lofty place that writing held in her life echoes in the line. As far as she was concerned, nothing else needed to be said on the subject.

What would cause a writer to become so committed to the process of writing? Was it for fame and recognition? Not really. The real fascination that experienced writers have with writing is the frame of mind it puts them in. The act of filling up a page stimulates their thinking and leads to exciting and meaningful learning.

Changing Your Attitude

If you think of writing in just one way—as an assignment to be completed—you will never discover its true value. Writing works best when you think of it as an important learning tool. It doesn't always have to lead to an end product submitted to an instructor.

A series of questions, a list, or a quick note in a notebook can be a meaningful form of writing if it helps you think and understand. If you make writing an important art of your learning routine, two things will happen: (1) You'll change your feelings about the importance of writing, and (2) you'll become a better thinker and learner.

Speaking & Listening

As a class, discuss this writing experience: Did it help you focus your thinking on the topic? Did you surprise yourself in any way? Could you have written more? If so, about what?

Reflect Write nonstop for 5 minutes about one of the topics below. Don't stop or hesitate, and don't worry about making mistakes. You are writing for yourself. Afterward, checkmark two things that you learned about yourself.

My Expectations About College (or) **My Goals in Life**

Keeping a Class Notebook

Keeping a class notebook or journal is essential if you are going to make writing to learn an important part of your learning routine. Certainly, you can take notes in this notebook, but it is also helpful to reflect on what is going on in the class. Try these activities:

- **Write freely about anything from class discussions to challenging assignments to important exams.**
- **Discuss new ideas and concepts.**
- **Argue for and against any points of view that came up in class.**
- **Question what you are learning.**
- **Record your thoughts and feelings during an extended lab or research assignment.**
- **Evaluate your progress in the class.**

WAC

Note taking is a common form of writing to learn in most classes. Always try to explore your thoughts and feelings alongside the basic notes. This makes note taking more meaningful. (See page 12.)

Special Strategies

Writing or listing freely is the most common way to explore your thoughts and feelings about your course work. There are, however, specific writing-to-learn strategies that you may want to try:

Sent or Unsent Messages Draft messages to anyone about something you are studying or reading.

First Thoughts Record your first impressions about something you are studying or reading.

Role-Play Write as if you are someone directly involved in a topic you are studying.

Nutshelling Write down in one sentence the importance of something you are studying or reading.

Pointed Question Keep asking yourself why? in your writing to sort out your thoughts about something.

Debate Split your mind in two. Have one side defend one point of view, and the other side, a differing point of view.

"You never really understand something until you can explain it to your grandmother."
—Albert Einstein

Practice In a notebook, explore your thoughts throughout a unit of study in one of your courses. Use a few of the strategies discussed above, starting with basic free writing. Afterward, assess the value of this writing.

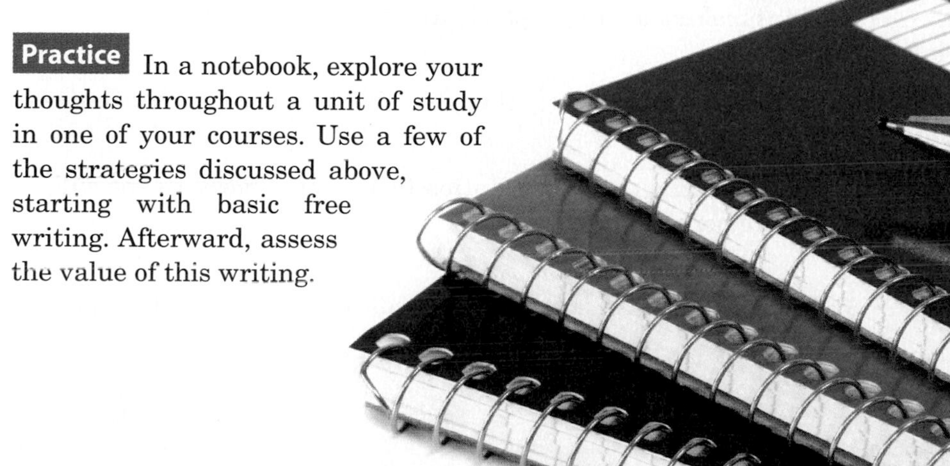

Learning Outcome

Write to share learning.

LO2 Writing to Share Learning

The other important function of writing is to share what you have learned. When you write to learn, you have an audience of one, yourself; but when you write to share learning, you have an audience of many, including your instructors and classmates.

All writing projects (paragraphs, essays, blog entries) actually begin with writing to learn, as you collect your thoughts about a topic. But with a first draft in hand, you turn your attention to making the writing clear, complete, and ready to share with others.

Note:
Writing is called a process because it must go through a series of steps before it is ready to share. (See pages 24–79.)

A Learning Connection

As the graphic below shows, improved thinking is the link between the two functions of writing. Writing to learn involves exploring and forming your thoughts; writing to share learning involves clarifying and fine-tuning them.

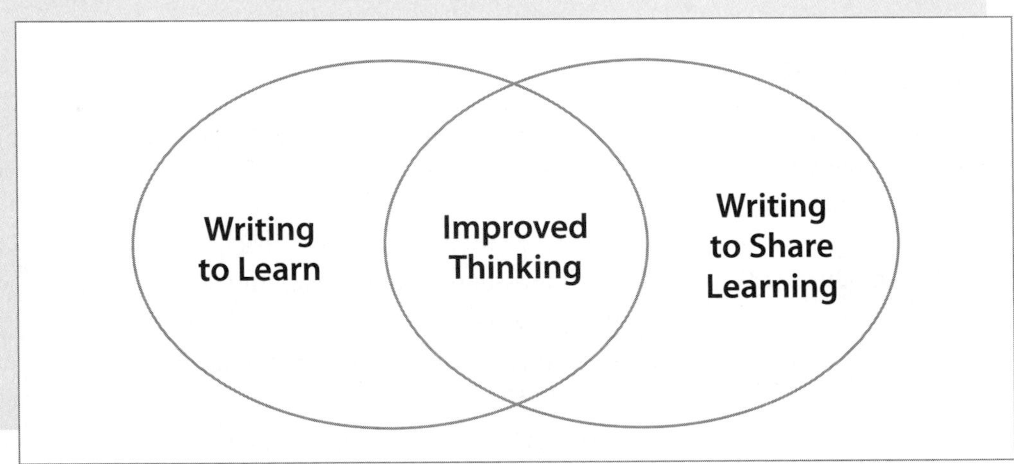

Speaking & Listening

As a class, explore the following question: Why is writing often called "thinking on paper"?

Identify Label each scenario below as an example of writing to learn (WL) or writing to share learning (WSL).

1. Carlos is freely exploring his thoughts about a reading assignment.

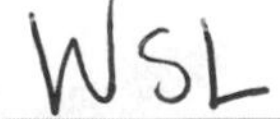

2. Oki is making a paragraph clearer before turning it in.

WL
3. Ferrin is listing his early thoughts about a topic for a blog entry.

WSL
4. Thea is adding more information to an e-mail message she will send to her instructor.

5. Steve is developing a letter to the editor to submit to the college newspaper.

Michaelpuche,2010 / Used under license from Shutterstock.com

LO3 Considering the Range of Writing

The forms of writing to share cover a lot of territory as you can see in the chart below. Some of the forms are quick and casual; others are more thoughtful and formal. As a college student, your writing may cover this entire spectrum, but the instruction you receive will likely focus on the more formal types.

Learning Outcome

Consider the range of writing.

The Writing Spectrum

Formal and Thoughtful ↑

- Multimedia Reports
- Research Papers
- Stories/Plays/Poems
- Responses to Literature
- Persuasive Paragraphs and Essays
- Expository Paragraphs and Essays
- Business Letters
- Personal Narratives
- Blogs
- E-Mails
- Microblogs
- Text Messages

Casual and Quick

Insight

Completeness and correctness are not critical in quick and casual writing, but they are important for all of the other forms on the chart.

React After studying the chart, answer the following questions. Then discuss your responses as a class.

1. How many of these forms of writing have you used?

2. Which ones have you never used?

3. How has technology affected the way you write?

Learning Outcome

Review writing and learning.

LO4 Reviewing Writing and Learning

Writing to Learn Answer the following questions about writing as a learning tool. (See pages 2–3.)

1. What is the difference between writing to learn and the writing that you have traditionally done in school?

 ____

 ____

2. Name two different ways to use a classroom notebook or journal.

 ____

 ____

3. What is meant by nutshelling? By pointed questions?

 ____

 ____

 ____

Writing to Share Learning Answer the following questions about writing to share learning. (See page 4.)

1. What is the difference between writing to learn and writing to share learning?

 ____

 ____

2. How can writing to share learning help you form your thoughts?

 ____

 ____

The Range of Writing Identify the function or reason for using each of the following forms of writing. (See page 5.)

Text Messages ______________________________

____

E-Mails ______________________________

____

Business Letters ______________________________

____

Persuasive Essays ______________________________

____

"To read without reflecting is like eating without digesting."
—Edmund Burke

Fuse/Getty Images

2 Reading and Learning

Reading and learning just naturally go hand in hand. You read to learn about new concepts and ideas; you read to learn how to do something or how something works; you read to better understand the past, the present, and the future. In most of your college classes, of course, reading is an essential learning tool.

Your instructors will expect you to become thoughtfully involved in each of your reading assignments, not only to gain a basic understanding of the material, but also to compare it with what you already know and to reflect on its importance. The guidelines and strategies presented in this chapter will help you become an active, thoughtful reader—someone engaged in the material rather than someone simply "reciting" the words.

Learning Outcomes

- **LO1** Read to learn.
- **LO2** Use reading strategies.
- **LO3** Read graphics.
- **LO4** Review reading and learning.

What do you think?

What does the quotation above have to say about becoming thoughtfully involved in reading?

Learning Outcome

Read to learn.

LO1 Reading to Learn

Thoughtful, active reading encompasses a number of related tasks: previewing the text, reading it through, taking notes as you go along, and summarizing what you have learned. Active reading gives you control of reading assignments and makes new information part of your own thinking.

"The books that help you the most are those that make you think the most."
—Theodore Parker

Effective Academic Reading

Follow the guidelines listed below for all of your academic reading assignments. A few of these points are discussed in more detail later in the chapter.

1. **Know the assignment:** Identify its purpose, its due date, its level of difficulty, and so on.
2. **Set aside the proper time:** Don't try to read long assignments all at once. Instead, try to read in 30-minute allotments.
3. **Find a quiet place:** The setting should provide space to read and to write.
4. **Gather additional resources:** Keep on hand a notebook, related handouts, Web access, and so on.
5. **Study the "layout" of the reading:** Review the study-guide questions. Then skim the pages, noting titles, headings, graphics, and boldfaced terms.
6. **Use proven reading strategies:** See pages 10–13.
7. **Look up challenging words:** Also use **context cues** to determine the meaning of unfamiliar terms.
8. **Review difficult parts:** Reread them, write about them, and discuss them with your classmates.
9. **Summarize what you learned:** Note any concepts or explanations that you will need to study further.

Traits

Effective writing has strong ideas, clear organization, appropriate voice, precise words, smooth sentences, correct conventions, and a strong design. Use these traits to understand what you read.

Vocabulary

context cues
using the words surrounding an unfamiliar term to help unlock its meaning

Reflect Circle the star that best identifies your study-reading skills. Then explain your choice on the lines below. In your explanation, consider which of the above guidelines you do or do not follow. **Weak** ★ ★ ★ ★ ★ **Strong**

Using a Class Notebook

To thoughtfully interact with a text, you need to write about it, so reserve part of your class notebook for responses to your readings. Certainly, you can take straight notes on the material (see page 12), but you should also personally respond to it. Such writing requires you to think about the reading—to agree with it, to question it, to make connections. The following guidelines will help you get started:

- **Write whenever you feel** a need to explore your thoughts and feelings. Discipline yourself to write multiple times, perhaps once before you read, two or three times during the reading, and one time afterward.
- **Write freely and honestly** to make genuine connections with the text.
- **Respond to points of view** that you like or agree with, information that confuses you, connections that you can make with other material, and ideas that seem significant.
- **Clearly label and date your responses.** These entries will help you prepare for exams and other assignments.
- **Share your discoveries.** Think of your entries as conversation starters in discussions with classmates.

Insight

If you are a visual person, you may understand a text best by mapping or clustering its important points. (See page 39 for a sample cluster.)

Special Strategies

Here are some specific ways to respond to a text:

Discuss Carry on a conversation with the author or a character until you come to know him or her and yourself a little better.

Illustrate Use graphics or pictures to help you think about a text.

Imitate Continue the article or story line by trying to write like the author.

Express Share your feelings about a text in a poem.

Practice Follow the guidelines on this page to explore your thoughts about one of your next reading assignments. Afterward, assess the value of responding in this way to the text.

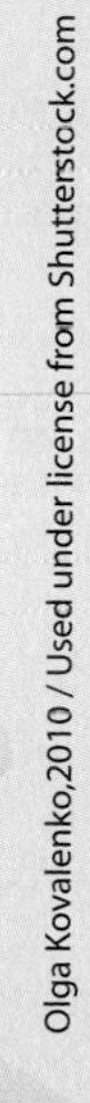

Olga Kovalenko,2010 / Used under license from Shutterstock.com

Learning Outcome

Use reading strategies.

LO2 Using Reading Strategies

To make sure that you gain the most from each reading assignment, employ the additional strategies on the next four pages.

Note: Annotate reading material only if you own the text or if you are reading a photocopy.

Annotating a Text

annotating the process of underlining, highlighting, or making notes in a text

Annotating a text allows you to interact with the writer's thoughts and ideas. Here are some suggestions:

- Write questions in the margins.
- Underline or highlight important points.
- Summarize key passages.
- Define new terms.
- Make connections to other parts.

Annotating in Action

Los Chinos Discover el Barrio
by Luis Torres

He's contrasting the colorful art with the drab surroundings.

There's a colorful mural on the asphalt playground of Hillside Elementary School, in the neighborhood called Lincoln Heights. Painted on the beige handball wall, the mural is of life-sized youngsters holding hands. Depicted are Asian and Latino kids with bright faces and ear-to-ear smiles.

The mural is a mirror (reflection) of the makeup of the neighborhood today: Latinos living side by side with Asians. But it's not all smiles and happy faces in the Northeast Los Angeles community, located just a couple of miles up Broadway from City Hall. On the surface there's harmony between Latinos and Asians. But there are indications of simmering ethnic-based tensions. (contrast)

personal connection

That became clear to me recently when I took a walk through the old neighborhood—the one where I grew up. As I walked along North Broadway, I thought of a joke that comic Paul Rodriguez (Who?) often tells on the stage. He paints a picture of a young Chicano walking down a street on L.A.'s East Side. He comes upon two Asians having an animated conversation in what sounds like babble. "Hey, you guys, knock off that foreign talk. This is America—speak Spanish!"

Ha! This shows how two different immigrant groups struggle to fit in.

Annotate Carefully read the excerpt below from an essay by Stephen King. Then annotate the text, according to the following directions:

- Circle the main point of the passage.
- Underline or highlight one idea in the first paragraph that you either agree with, question, or are confused by. Then make a comment about this idea in the margin.
- Do the same for one idea in the third paragraph and one idea in the final paragraph.
- Circle one or two words that you are unsure of. Then define or explain these words in the margin.

Why We Crave Horror Movies by Stephen King

I think that we're all mentally ill; those of us outside the asylums only hide it a little better—and maybe not all that much better, after all. We've all known people who talk to themselves, people who sometimes squinch their faces into horrible grimaces when they believe no one is watching, people who have some hysterical fear—of snakes, the dark, the tight place, the long drop . . . and, of course, the final worms and grubs that are waiting so patiently underground.

When we pay our four or five bucks and seat ourselves at tenth-row center in a theater showing a horror movie, we are daring the nightmare.

Why? Some of the reasons are simple and obvious. To show that we can, that we are not afraid, that we can ride this roller coaster. Which is not to say that a really good horror movie may not surprise a scream out of us at some point, the way we may scream when the roller coaster twists through a complete 360 or plows through a lake at the bottom of the dip. And horror movies, like roller coasters, have always been the special province of the young; by the time one turns 40 or 50, one's appetite for double twists or 360-degree loops may be considerably depleted.

We also go to re-establish our feelings of essential normality; the horror movie is innately conservative, even reactionary. Freda Jackson as the horrible melting woman in *Die, Monster, Die!* confirms for us that no matter how far we may be removed from the beauty of a Robert Redford or a Diana Ross, we are still light-years from true ugliness.

And we go to have fun.

Ah, but this is where the ground starts to slope away, isn't it? Because this is a very peculiar sort of fun, indeed. The fun comes from seeing others menaced—sometimes killed. One critic suggested that if pro football has become the voyeur's version of combat, then the horror film has become the modern version of the public lynching. . . .

Taking Effective Notes

Taking notes helps you focus on the text and understand it more fully. It changes information you have read about to information that you are working with. Personalizing information in this way makes it much easier to remember and use.

Insight

Note taking should be more than writing down what you read. It should also be connecting with and questioning new information.

Note-Taking Tips

- Use your own words as much as possible.
- Record only key points and details rather than complicated sentences.
- Consider boldfaced or italicized words, graphics, and captions as well as the main text.
- Employ as many abbreviations and symbols as you can (vs., #, &, etc.).
- Decide on a system for organizing or arranging your notes so they are easy to review.

An Active Note-Taking System

To make your note taking more active, use a two-column system, in which one column (two-thirds of the page) is for your main notes and another column (one-third of the page) is for comments, reactions, and questions.

Two-Column Notes

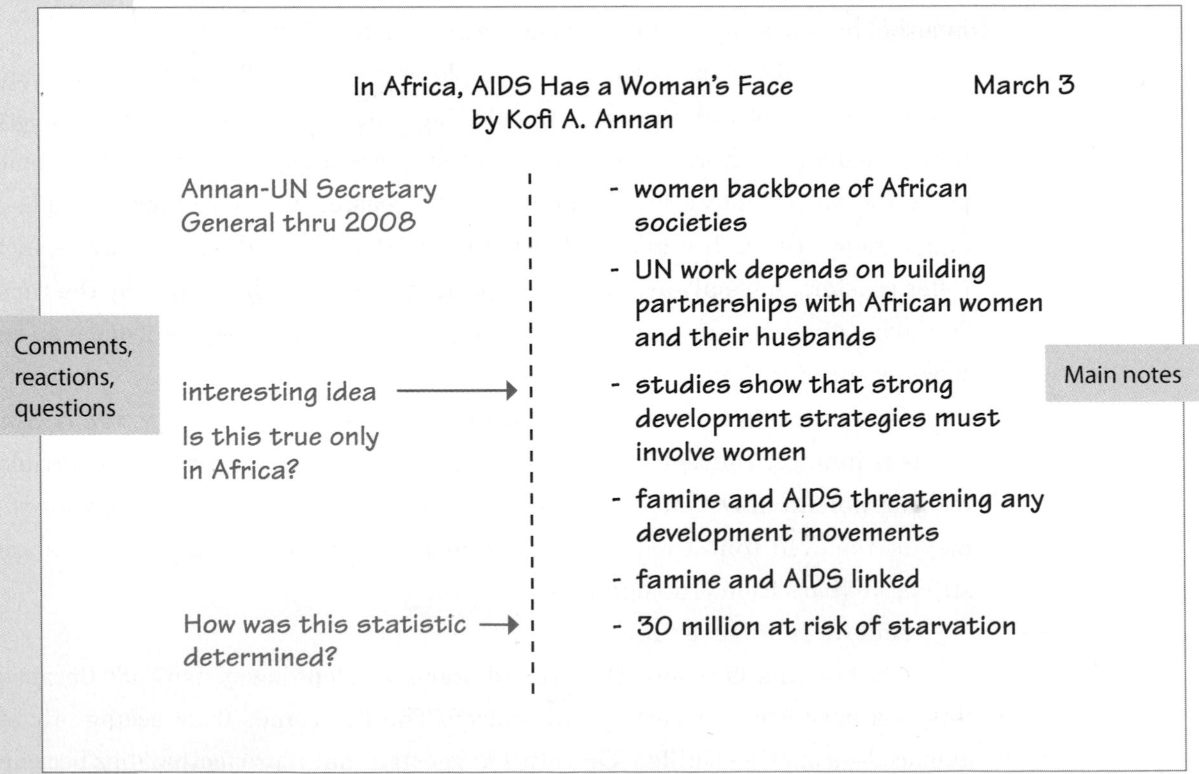

Practice Use the two-column note system for one of your next reading assignments. Use the left-hand column to react with questions, comments, and reflections about the information that you record.

Summarizing a Text

Summarizing a reading assignment is an effective way to test how well you understand the information. **Summarizing** means to present the main points in a clear, concise form using your own words (except for those few words from the original text that can't be changed). Generally speaking, a summary should be no more than one-third as long as the original.

Summarizing Tips

- Start with a clear statement of the main point of the text.
- Share only the essential supporting facts and details (names, dates, times, and places) in the next sentences.
- Present your ideas in a logical order.
- Tie all of your points together in a closing sentence.

Example Summary

The example below summarizes a two-page essay by Kofi A. Annan concerning the suffering caused by AIDS and famine in southern Africa.

Main points (underlined)

Essential supporting facts

Closing sentence (underlined)

Famine and AIDS are threatening the agricultural societies in southern Africa. Tragically, women, the main unifying force in African societies, make up 59% of individuals worldwide infected by the HIV virus. With so many women suffering from AIDS, the family structure and the agricultural infrastructure are suffering severely. These conditions have significantly contributed to the famine conditions and resulting starvation. Any traditional survival techniques used by African women in the past won't work for these twin disasters. International relief is needed, and it must provide immediate food and health aid. A key focus of health aid must be the treatment of women infected with HIV and preventative education to stop the spread of the disease. The future of southern Africa depends on the health and leadership of their women.

Practice Summarize the information in one of the essays on pages 397–463 or in an essay provided by your instructor. Use the tips and sample above as a guide.

iofoto, 2010/used under license from www.shutterstock.com

summarizing
presenting the main points of a text in a clear, concise form using, for the most part, your own words

Learning Outcome

Read graphics.

LO3 Reading Graphics

In many of your college texts, a significant portion of the information will be communicated via charts, graphs, diagrams, and drawings. Knowing how to read these types of graphics will help you become a more effective and informed college student. Follow the guidelines listed below when you read a **graphic**.

- **Scan the graphic.** Consider it as a whole to get an overall idea about its message. Note its type (bar graph, pie graph, diagram, table, and so forth), its topic, its level of complexity, and so on.
- **Study the specific parts.** Start with the main heading or title. Next, note any additional labels or guides (such as the horizontal and vertical guides on a bar graph). Then focus on the actual information displayed in the graphic.
- **Question the graphic.** Does it address an important topic? What is its purpose (to make a comparison, to show a change, and so on)? What is the source of the information? Is the graphic dated or biased in any way?
- **Reflect on its effectiveness.** Explain in your own words the main message communicated by the graphic. Then consider its effectiveness, how it relates to the surrounding text, and how it matches up to your previous knowledge of the topic.

Vocabulary

graphic
a visual representation of information that reveals trends, makes comparisons, shows how something changes over time, and so on

horizontal
parallel to ground level, at right angles to the vertical

vertical
straight up and down, at right angles to the horizontal

Analysis of a Graphic

Review the vertical bar graph below. Then read the discussion to learn how all of the parts work together.

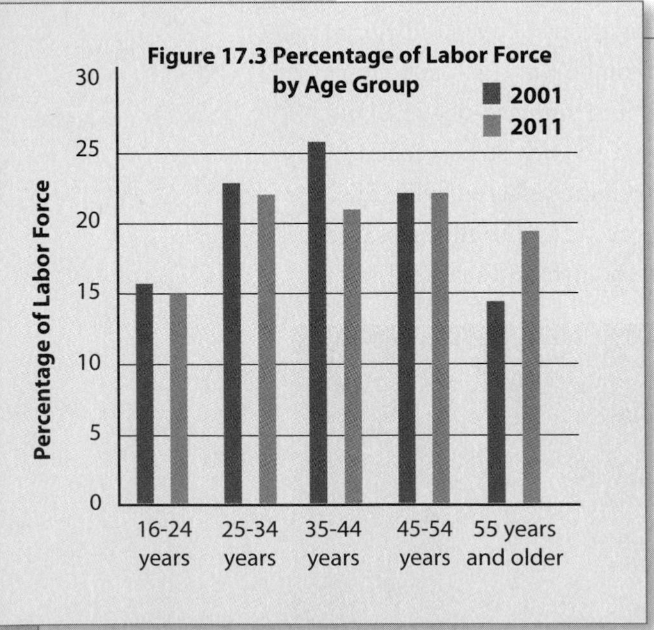

Discussion: This bar graph compares the labor force in 2001 to the labor force in 2011 for five specific age groups. The heading clearly identifies the subject or topic of the graphic. The **horizontal** line identifies the different age groups, and the **vertical** line identifies the percentage of the labor force for each group. The key in the upper right-hand corner of the graphic identifies the purpose of the color coding used in the columns or bars. With all of that information, the graphic reads quite clearly—and many interesting comparisons can be made.

React Read and analyze the following graphics, answering the questions about each one. Use the information on the previous page as a guide.

Graphic 1

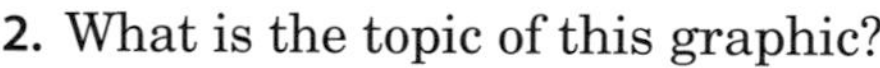

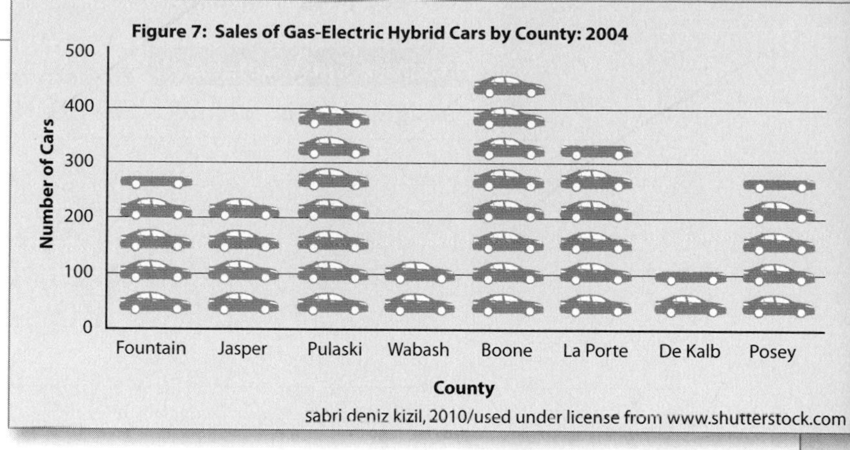

sabri deniz kizil, 2010/used under license from www.shutterstock.com

1. This graphic is called a pictograph rather than a bar graph. What makes it a "pictograph"?

2. What is the topic of this graphic?

3. What information is provided on the horizontal line? On the vertical line?

4. What comparisons can a reader make from this graphic?

Graphic 2

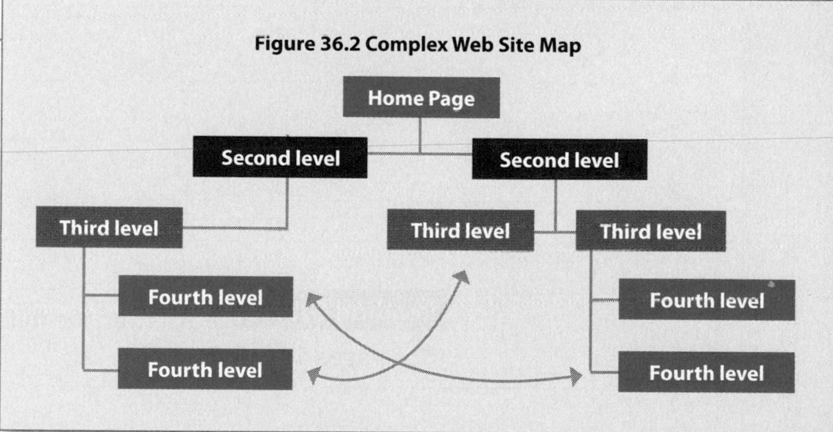

1. This graphic is called a line diagram, mapping a structure. What structure does this diagram map?

2. What two working parts are used in this diagram: *words, lines,* and *symbols?* Circle the appropriate choices.

3. How are the different navigational choices on a complex Web site shown on this graphic?

Learning Outcome

Review reading and learning.

LO4 Reviewing Reading and Learning

Complete these activities as needed to help you better understand the concepts covered in this chapter.

Using a Class Notebook Explain why responding in writing to your reading assignments is valuable. (See page 9.)

Annotating a Text Explain what it means to annotate a text; also identify the main value of this reading strategy. (See pages 10–11.)

Taking Effective Notes Identify three note-taking tips that you find the most helpful. (See page 12.)

1. ______
2. ______
3. ______

Reading Graphics Answer the following questions about a graphic in *WRITE 1*. (See pages 14–15.)

1. The graphic on page 14 is a basic type of graph containing columns of information. What is the topic of this graph?
2. How is the information arranged?
3. Identify one main point represented in this graphic.

"There are some things you learn best in calm, and some in storm."
—Willa Cather

Donovan Reese/Photodisc/Getty Images

3 Making the Writing-Reading Connection

One obvious conclusion can be drawn from the first two chapters in *WRITE 1*: Writing and reading are really **two sides of the same coin**. You write to learn, and you read to learn. You use writing to help you understand your reading. You use reading to help you with your writing. Writing is thinking; reading is thinking. The connections go on and on.

This chapter provides three common strategies that enhance college-level writing and reading: (1) using questions to analyze writing and reading assignments, (2) using the traits of effective writing to analyze your writing and reading, and (3) using graphic organizers to arrange ideas in your writing and reading.

What do you think?

In the quotation above, what distinction is Cather making about learning? How would you apply her point to reading and writing?

Learning Outcomes

- LO1 Analyze the assignment.
- LO2 Use the traits of writing.
- LO3 Use graphic organizers.
- LO4 Review the writing-reading connection.

Vocabulary

two sides of the same coin
an idiom meaning "different but closely related"

Learning Outcome

Analyze the assignment.

LO1 Analyzing the Assignment

At the start of any writing or reading assignment, you should analyze the **dynamics** of the situation to make sure that you fully understand what is expected of you. The dynamics of an assignment are similar to the key ingredients in a recipe. If you forget any one of them, the final product will suffer.

The STRAP Strategy

You can use the **STRAP strategy** to analyze your writing and reading assignments. The strategy consists of answering questions about these five features: *subject, type, role, audience,* and *purpose*. Once you answer the questions, you'll be ready to get to work. This chart shows how the strategy works:

For Writing Assignments		For Reading Assignments
What specific topic should I write about?	**Subject**	What specific topic does the reading address?
What form of writing *(essay, article)* will I use?	**Type**	What form *(essay, text chapter, article)* does the reading take?
What position *(student, citizen, employee)* should I assume?	**Role**	What position *(student, responder, concerned individual)* does the writer assume?
Who is the intended reader?	**Audience**	Who is the intended reader?
What is the goal *(to inform, to persuade)* of the writing?	**Purpose**	What is the goal of the material?

The STRAP Strategy in Action

Suppose you were given the following reading assignment in a sociology class:

> Read the essay "Fatherless America" in your text. Then prepare a summary paragraph, highlighting the author's main claim and key supporting points.

Here are the answers to the STRAP questions for this assignment:

Subject: U.S. society becoming "fatherless"
Type: Persuasive essay
Role: Concerned citizen/advocate
Audience: Americans in general
Purpose: To persuade or take a stand

Test Taking

The STRAP questions help you quickly understand a writing prompt or a reading selection on a test.

Vocabulary

dynamics
main features or elements

STRAP strategy
a strategy for identifying the main features in a writing or reading assignment

Respond Use the STRAP strategy to analyze the two assignments that follow.

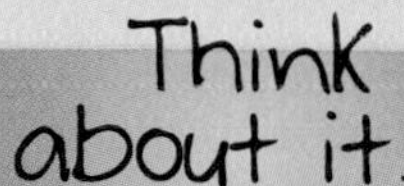

Before you begin any reading assignment, you should also consider these issues:

- The importance of the assignment
- The time you have to complete it
- The way the assignment fits into the course as a whole

Assignment 1: Read "From 'How to Handle Conflict' " starting on page 416 in *WRITE 1*. Then, in your class notebook, respond to the reading, noting its key features and your reactions to them.

Subject: What specific topic does the reading address?

____

____

Type: What form *(essay, text chapter)* does the reading take?

____

____

Role: What position does the writer assume?

____

____

Audience: Who is the intended audience?

____

____

Purpose: What is the goal of the material?

____

____

Assignment 2: Analyze a reading assignment provided by your instructor or given in one of your other classes.

Subject: What specific topic does the reading address?

____

____

Type: What form *(essay, text chapter)* does the reading take?

____

____

Role: What position does the writer assume?

____

____

Audience: Who is the intended audience?

____

____

Purpose: What is the goal of the material?

____

____

Learning Outcome

Use the traits of writing.

LO2 Using the Traits

Chapter 4 in *WRITE 1* goes into great detail about using the **traits** to help you with your writing. (See pages 25–34.) You can use these same traits to help you analyze and discuss your reading assignments.

Previewing the Traits

The traits of writing are highlighted below. Each one addresses an important feature in a reading selection, whether an essay, a chapter, an article, or a piece of fiction. (The questions will help you analyze a reading selection for the traits.)

- **Ideas** The information contained in reading material
  What is the topic of the reading?
  What main point is made?
  What supporting details are provided?
- **Organization** The overall structure of the material
  How does the reading selection begin?
  How is the middle part arranged?
  How does the selection end?
- **Voice** The personality of the writing—how the writer speaks to the reader
  To what degree does the writer seem interested in and knowledgeable about the topic?
  To what degree does the writer engage the reader?
- **Word Choice** The writer's use of words and phrases
  What can be said about the nouns, verbs, and modifiers in the reading? (Are the words too general, or are they specific and effective? Does the writer use **figurative language**?)
- **Sentence Fluency** The flow of the sentences
  What stands out about the sentences? (Are they varied in length, do they flow smoothly, do they seem stylish, and so on?)
- **Conventions** The correctness or accuracy of the language
  To what degree does the writing follow the conventions of the language?
- **Design** The appearance of the writing
  What, if anything, stands out about the design? (Does it enhance or take away from the reading experience?)

Traits

Throughout *WRITE 1*, the traits are used to help you read and write. Watch for this advice in annotations like this one.

Vocabulary

traits
the key elements found in effective writing

figurative language
metaphors, personification, or other creative comparisons used to describe something or to make a point

A Sample Analysis of a Reading Selection

Here is a traits analysis of "Two Views of the Same News Find Opposite Biases," a comparison essay on pages 425–426 in *WRITE 1.*

- **Ideas**

The essay focuses on biased behavior—more specifically, why people reach different conclusions about the same event. The writer refers to an experiment that analyzes and compares pro-Arab and pro-Israeli responses to the reporting of the 1982 war in Lebanon. (The experiment shows that both sides feel that the reporting was biased against them.)

- **Organization**

The first three paragraphs establish the main point (thesis) of the essay.

The middle paragraphs cite and analyze the main findings of the experiment, following a point-by-point pattern of organization.

The closing paragraph provides a quotation by an authority and sums up the essay.

- **Voice**

The writer seems knowledgeable about and interested in his topic. He speaks to the reader in a friendly but professional way. The opening line—"You could be forgiven . . ." —draws the reader into the essay.

- **Word Choice**

The writer uses some technical or unfamiliar terms—*recursive, partisan, raison d'etre,* and so on. However, these terms are defined for the reader. Otherwise, the word choice reflects the vocabulary of an educated and informed writer.

- **Sentence Fluency**

The sentences are, for the most part, on the long side. A few of them require a second or third reading to pick up all of the information they contain. Overall, however, the sentences flow smoothly. Most of the paragraphs are brief (one or two sentences), which adds to the readability of the essay.

- **Conventions**

The writer clearly follows the conventions, presenting error-free writing.

- **Design**

The brief paragraphs give the essay a somewhat unusual appearance. Headings may have made the essay more readable.

Respond Analyze "From 'How to Handle Conflict' " on pages 416–418 for the traits. To develop your analysis, ask and answer each of the trait questions on page 20, or use the questions as an overall response guide, as is done in the analysis above. (Use your own paper.)

Speaking & Listening

Work on this activity with a partner or a small group of classmates if your instructor allows it.

Learning Outcome

Use graphic organizers.

WAC

See page 48 for six common graphic organizers that you can use to organize ideas in any class.

LO3 Using Graphic Organizers

Graphic organizers visually represent ideas or concepts and are commonly used to organize the ideas that you collect for your writing. You can use the same organizers to "chart" the key information in reading assignments.

Charting a Reading Assignment

Provided below is a line diagram that charts the key points in the definition essay on page 180 in *WRITE 1*. (A line diagram shows the logical relationships between the main ideas.)

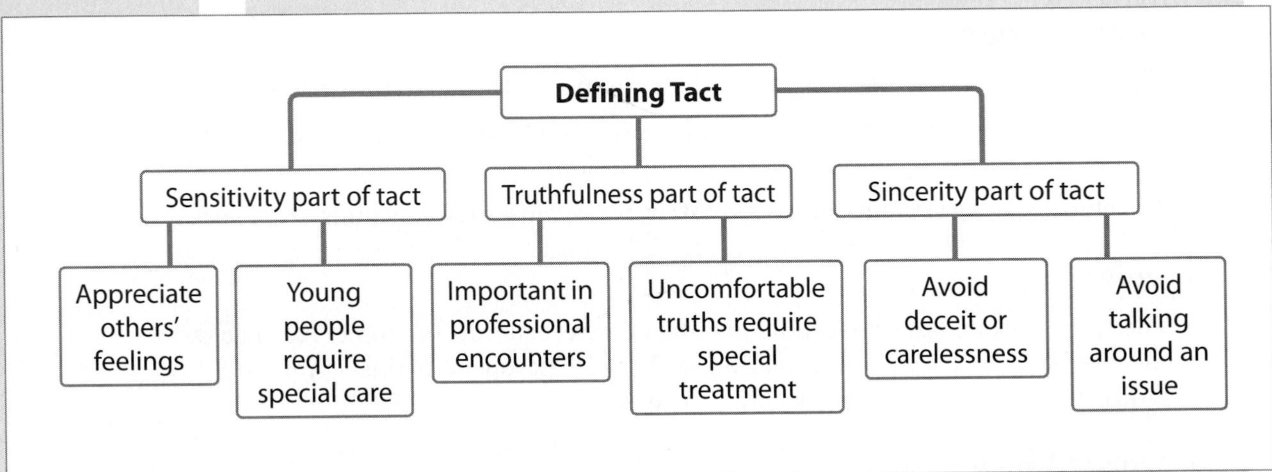

Respond In the space below, create a line diagram to chart the information in the classification paragraph on page 114. (Ignore the errors in the sample.)

LO4 Reviewing the Writing-Reading Connection

Learning Outcome

Review the writing-reading connection.

Complete these activities as needed to help you better understand the writing-reading connection.

Analyze the Assignment Use the STRAP strategy to analyze the following reading assignment: (See pages 18–19.)

Read "What Adolescents Miss When We Let Them Grow Up in Cyberspace" starting on page 441 in your text.

Subject: ______________________

Type: ______________________

Role: ______________________

Audience: ______________________

Purpose: ______________________

Use the Traits Analyze "What Adolescents Miss When We Let Them Grow Up in Cyberspace" for the following traits. (See pages 441–442.)

Ideas: ______________________

Organization: ______________________

Voice: ______________________

Part 2 The Writing Process and the Traits of Writing

"I tell them [writing a novel is] like driving a car at night. You never see farther than your headlights, but you can make the whole trip that way."

—E. L. Doctorow

4 Using the Writing Process and the Traits

Have you ever taken a nighttime trip in a remote area? The headlights of your car carve out a cave of light in an otherwise dark world. That sensation might be a little disconcerting, but, as Doctorow says in the quotation on the previous page, you can make the whole journey that way.

With writing, you have two similar lights—the writing process and the traits of writing. They illuminate the way for you, helping you get where you need to go. This chapter tells how.

What do you think?

How has your writing experience been like driving at night? What has lit your path?

Learning Outcomes

LO1 Think about writing as a process.

LO2 Learn about the steps in the writing process.

LO3 Learn about the traits of effective writing.

LO4 Connect the process and the traits.

Think about writing as a process.

LO1 Understanding the Writing Process

Few things in life can be as unpleasant as having a root canal. All of the drilling, scraping, pulling, pushing, cracking—please! Unfortunately, for some of you, writing can also be unpleasant, not for any physical discomfort, but because you struggle with it.

Part of the problem may be your approach. You may think that you should know everything you want to say before you get started. Well, writing doesn't work that way. Certainly, you should do some planning before you get started, but as the quotation on the part-opening page says, "You never [have to] see farther than your headlights." That is why writing is called a **process:** You often discover what you want to say while writing. Knowing this can make writing a lot easier—and help you do your best work.

The Process in Action

Read/React Read the following quotations by experienced writers who describe different aspects of the writing process. Discuss these quotations with a partner or a small group of classmates. Then explain below what one or two of the statements mean to you.

"The inspiration comes while you write."

—Madeleine L'Engle

"In writing, the more a thing cooks, the better."

—Doris Lessing

"Easy writing makes hard reading, but hard writing makes easy reading."

—Florence King

"The best advice on writing I've ever received was, 'Rewrite it!' A lot of editors said that. They all were right."

—Robert Lipsyte

Reactions: ________________________________

____

____

____

____

____

____

____

Vocabulary

writing process
the process a writer uses to develop a piece of writing, from planning through publishing

Thinking About Your Own Writing

Respond Answer the following questions about your writing experiences. Be sure to explain each of your answers.

1. Rate your experience as a writer by circling the appropriate star:
   negative ★ ★ ★ ★ ★ **positive**

   Explain. ____

   ____

   ____

   ____

2. What is the easiest part of writing for you? ____________________

   ____

   ____

   ____

3. What is the hardest part of writing for you? ____________________

   ____

   ____

   ____

4. What types of writing assignments challenge you the most? __________

   ____

   ____

   ____

5. What is the best thing you have ever written? ____________________

   ____

   ____

   ____

6. What is the most important thing you have learned about writing?

   ____

   ____

   ____

   ____

   ____

Marc Brasz/Corbis

Spotlight on Writing

"If not for writing, I would have been shut behind a wall of silence."

Edwidge Danticat was born in Haiti, a small, impoverished Caribbean country bordering the Dominican Republic. She came to New York City as a shy young lady of 12, having to deal with a new language, new schools, new everything.

As a high school student, Danticat began writing for a citywide newspaper called *New Youth Connections* and soon realized that writing was something she had to do—for the rest of her life. What she has accomplished has been extraordinary.

Danticat has published several books, including *Krik? Krack!* (1996), a National Book Award finalist, and *Brother, I'm Dying* (2007), a National Book Critics Circle Award winner.

Today, she is recognized as the most significant writer of the modern Haitian experience, all because she had the courage to put pen to paper.

Learning Outcome

Learn about the steps in the writing process.

"Writing should be seen from the inside, as a process, rather than from the outside, as a product."
—Donald Murray

LO2 The Steps in the Process

The writing process helps you pace yourself. When you try to do everything all at once, writing becomes a real struggle; but by following the steps that are explained below, you can do one thing at a time.

Process	Activities
Prewriting	Start the process by (1) selecting a topic to write about, (2) collecting details about it, and (3) finding your focus, the main idea or thesis.
Writing	Then write your first draft, using your prewriting plan as a general guide. Writing a first draft allows you to connect your thoughts about your topic.
Revising	Carefully review your first draft and have a classmate review it as well. Change any parts that could be clearer and more complete.
Editing	Edit your revised writing by checking for style, grammar, punctuation, and spelling errors.
Publishing	During the final step, prepare your writing to share with your instructor, your peers, or another audience.

Explain In the space provided, tell how the writing process above compares with how you complete your writing assignments. Consider what you usually do first, second, third, and so on.

Think about it.

Writing leads to making discoveries, forming new understandings, and analyzing information—the types of thinking so essential to doing well in college.

The Process in Action

As the chart indicates, you will likely move back and forth between the steps in the writing process. For example, after writing a first draft, you may decide to collect more details about your topic—a prewriting activity.

Process Chart

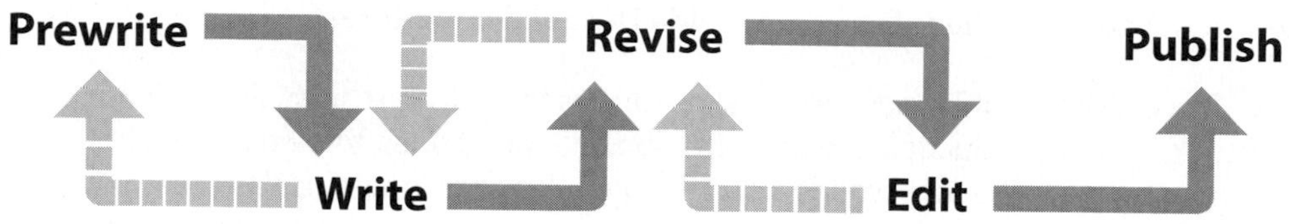

Create In the space provided below, create a chart that shows your own process—the one you described on page 28. Discuss your chart with a partner or small group of classmates.

Reasons to Write

The four main reasons to write are given below. Always use the writing process when **writing to show learning** and when **writing to share**.

Reason	Forms	Purpose
Writing to show learning	Summaries, informational essays	To show your understanding of subjects you are studying
Writing to share	Personal essays, blog postings, short stories, plays	To share your personal thoughts, feelings, and creativity with others
Writing to explore	Personal journals, diaries, unsent letters, dialogues	To learn about yourself and your world
Writing to learn	Learning logs, reading logs, notes	To help you understand what you are learning

Explain Why is using the writing process unnecessary for **writing to explore** and **writing to learn?**

Speaking & Listening

If you are having trouble explaining your process, talk about it with a partner.

Test Taking

When you respond to a prompt on a test, use an abbreviated form of this process. Spend a few minutes gathering and organizing ideas, then write your response. Afterward, read what you have done and quickly revise and edit it.

Learning Outcome

Learn about the traits of effective writing.

LO3 Understanding the Traits of Writing

What makes one particular pizza your favorite? It's all in the ingredients, isn't it? The crust might be crispy and light; the toppings, fresh; the spices, perfect.

It's all in the ingredients with effective writing, too. The ingredients, or **traits**, that you find in the best articles and essays are described below.

■ **Strong Ideas** Good writing contains plenty of good information (ideas and details). And all of the information holds the reader's interest.

> The University of Tennessee's most notorious farm doesn't specialize in grain, livestock, or milk production. It deals with bodies—dead ones, to be exact. Technically speaking, the 2.5-acre wooded plot is called the Anthropological Research Facility, but it's more commonly referred to as the Body Farm. It hosts more than 150 decomposed corpses. Since 1971, research on the Body Farm has led to many critical breakthroughs in forensic science and crime-scene investigation.
>
> — Zackary Dean

1. Rate the passage for ideas by circling the appropriate star:
   weak ★ ★ ★ ★ ★ strong

   Explain. ____________________

   ____

2. What is the main point? ____________________

   ____

3. What is the most interesting detail in the passage? ____________________

   ____

   ____

WAC

The traits help you write and read in any subject area. Each discipline has its own ideas and organizational structures that you should learn, and writing always benefits from strong words, smooth sentences, correctness, and effective design.

■ **Logical Organization** Effective writing has a clear overall structure—with a beginning, a middle, and an ending. Transitions (*first, later on, for a brief time*) link the ideas.

> For five years, I have worked in one of the busiest emergency rooms in southeastern Michigan. For the last two years, I have picked up overtime by working in four other hospitals, including the busiest emergency room in inner-city Detroit. No matter where I am, I experience the same problem—too many patients and not enough staff.
>
> — Paul Duke

1. Rate the passage for organization by circling the appropriate star:
   weak ★ ★ ★ ★ ★ strong

   Explain. ____________________

   ____

2. How is this passage arranged—by time, by location, by logic? ____________________

   ____

3. What transitional phrases does the writer use? ____________________

   ____

Vocabulary

traits
the key elements, or ingredients, found in effective writing

Fitting Voice In the best writing, you can hear the writer's voice— her or his special way of saying things. It shows that the writer cares about the subject.

Snake haters beware: Scientists in Colombia unearthed a prehistoric snake fossil so large it makes a cobra look like an earthworm. How large? Try 42 feet. That's longer than a school bus! Researchers concluded this snake species would have weighed up to one ton. With proportions so colossal, no wonder scientists named it *Titanoboa.*

— Amira Halper

1. Rate the passage for voice by circling the appropriate star:
   weak ★ ★ ★ ★ ★ strong

   Explain. ______________________________

   ____

2. Does the writer seem to care about the topic? Explain. ______________________________

   ____

   ____

3. How would you identify the voice in this passage—sincere, silly, bored?

   ____

   ____

Well-Chosen Words In strong writing, nouns and verbs are specific and clear, and the modifiers add important information.

She strutted to the microphone with the swagger of a rock star. The sparse crowd, busy with their coffee and crosswords, offered her a polite smattering of applause. This was it. For four months, she had poured her private feelings into poetry. For the next four minutes, she would reveal those feelings to twenty-some odd strangers. But before she could begin, a woman interrupted: "Excuse me, miss," she said. "You wouldn't happen to know a four-letter word meaning 'obstruct'?"

— Latisha Jones

1. Rate the passage for word choice by circling the appropriate star:
   weak ★ ★ ★ ★ ★ strong

   Explain. ______________________________

   ____

2. Which, if any, specific verbs stand out for you? ______________________________

   ____

   ____

3. What other words do you find interesting? (Name two.) ______________________________

   ____

   ____

Speaking & Listening

Read this model aloud to a partner. Then have the partner read the model. How do your different voices and expression affect the overall impact of the model?

Traits

The traits help you in two important ways: (1) They name the key ingredients that you must consider when writing. (2) They provide a vocabulary to discuss writing with your peers.

■ **Smooth Sentences** The sentences in good writing flow smoothly from one to the next. They carry the meaning of the essay or article.

> On any given day in Delaware's Wilmington State Park, rock climbers safely glide down treacherous 40-foot cliff faces as if they're riding invisible elevators. The technique is known as *rappelling.* Adventure enthusiasts and rescue teams alike use harnesses, gears, anchors, and ropes to descend slopes that are too dangerous to travel down on foot. Make no mistake; rappelling can be dangerous without proper training and equipment.
>
> — Reid Haywood

1. Rate the sentences in the passage by circling the appropriate star:
   weak ★ ★ ★ ★ ★ strong

   Explain. ______________________________

   ____

2. In what ways does the writer vary the sentences she uses?

   ____

   ____

3. Which sentence do you like best? Why? ______________________________

   ____

   ____

■ **Correct Copy** Strong writing is easy to read because it follows the conventions or rules of the language.

> Have you ever wondered who owns Antarctica? You might ask who would want the earth's coldest, driest, and least hospitable continent? The truth is that seven different countries claim areas of the continent. In accordance with the 1959 Antarctic Treaty, though, the land mass remains a politically neutral space for scientific exploration and environmental conservation.
>
> — Emila Carmen

1. Rate the conventions in the passage by circling the appropriate star:
   weak ★ ★ ★ ★ ★ strong

   Explain. ______________________________

   ____

2. What punctuation marks, other than periods, are used in this passage?

   ____

   ____

3. How is one of these other punctuation marks used? ______________________________

   ____

   ____

■ **Appropriate Design** In the best academic writing, the design follows the guidelines established by the instructor or school.

LaShawna Wilson

Ms. Davis

Forces in Science

February 11, 2011

Physics of Rainbows

"Why are there so many songs about rainbows?" asks the old tune. Perhaps it's because rainbows are beautiful, multicolored, and huge, arching over cities and mountains. But rainbows have captured human imagination as much because of their mystery as their beauty. In his work with prisms, Sir Isaac Newton demonstrated that something as beautiful and mysterious as a rainbow could be created through the simple property of refraction.

Basics of Refraction

The key to understanding rainbows is refraction. When light passes from one medium to another, it bends. Simply look at a straw in a glass, and the apparent break in the straw when it enters the water demonstrates refraction. Light is bending as it passes through the water, showing the straw in a different place.

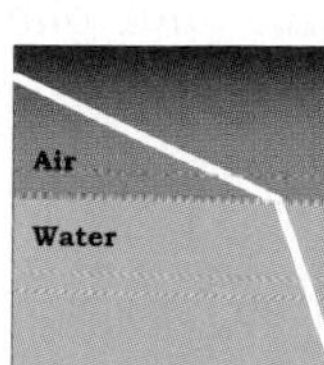

Figure 1: Basic refraction. Light moving from one medium to another slows down. When entering at an angle, the light is more sharply refracted.

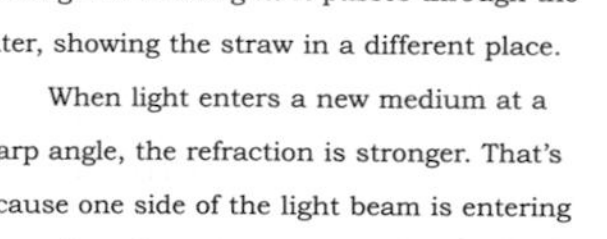

When light enters a new medium at a sharp angle, the refraction is stronger. That's because one side of the light beam is entering the medium first, thereby slowing down, as the other side of the light beam continues longer at its previous speed. The result is a turn in the angle of the light ("Prism" 13). This effect is demonstrated in Figure 1.

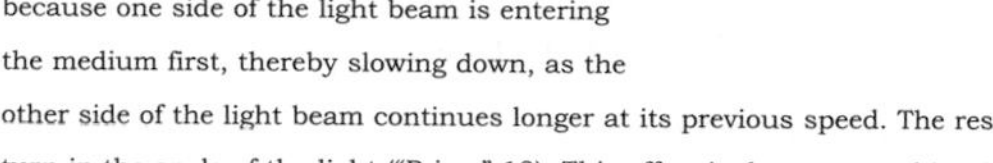

Frequencies and Refraction

Different frequencies of light bend at different angles. The relatively long wavelengths of red light do not bend as much as the relatively short wavelengths of purple light, which is why a prism splits white light into its colors.

A raindrop can do the same thing. Figure 2, derived from the Web site "How Stuff Works," shows how white light is bent when passing through a raindrop.

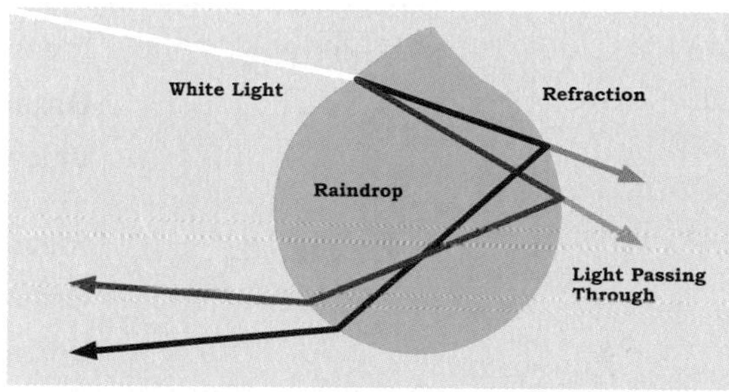

Figure 2: Refraction of light through a raindrop. Note that the purple light exits at a higher angle than the red. Drops lower in the air will reflect violet light to viewers' eyes, while higher drops reflect red light. (Source http://science.howstuffworks.com/rainbow2.htm.)

Bands of Color

The reason that a rainbow looks like bands of color is that the observer sees only one color coming from each droplet. As Figure 2 shows, a droplet that is higher in the sky will refract red into the eyes of the viewer. A droplet that is lower in the sky will refract violet into the viewer's eyes. This same pattern holds for all of the colors in between—orange, yellow, green, blue, and indigo. This effect creates the bands of color that the person sees when looking at the rainbow.

1. Circle the appropriate star to rate the headings, margins, and graphics on these pages: weak ★ ★ ★ ★ ★ strong

   Explain. ______________________________

   ____

   ____

2. What one design feature stands out for you? ______________________________

   ____

   ____

3. Why is format and design important for a finished piece of writing? __________

   ____

   ____

Workplace

Design becomes especially important when you create a workplace document. Using correct format for letters, memos, and reports helps readers understand the content and projects a professional image.

Learning Outcome

Connect the process and the traits.

LO4 Connecting the Process and the Traits

The writing process guides you as you form a piece of writing. The writing traits identify the key elements to consider in the writing. This chart connects the two. For example, it shows that during prewriting, you should focus on ideas, organization, and voice.

Process	Traits
Prewriting	**Ideas:** selecting a topic, collecting details about it, forming a thesis **Organization:** arranging the details **Voice:** establishing your stance (objective, personal)
Writing	**Ideas:** connecting your thoughts and information **Organization:** following your planning **Voice:** sounding serious, sincere, interested, . . .
Revising	**Ideas:** reviewing for clarity and completeness **Organization:** reviewing for structure/arrangement of ideas **Voice:** reviewing for appropriate tone
Editing	**Word choice:** checking for specific nouns, verbs, and modifiers **Sentences:** checking for smoothness and variety **Conventions:** checking for correctness
Publishing	**Design:** evaluating the format

Traits

The first three traits—ideas, organization, and voice—deal with big issues, so they dominate the beginning of the writing process. Words, sentences, conventions, and design become important later.

Think Critically Team up with a classmate to discuss the following questions. Record your answers in the spaces provided below.

1. Which writing trait interests you the most? Why?

____

____

____

2. Which step in the writing process should probably take the most time? Explain. ____

____

____

____

3. How could you use this chart during a writing project? _______________

____

____

____

Monkey Business Images, 2010/used under license from www.shutterstock.com

"Success is 10 percent inspiration and 90 percent perspiration."

—Thomas Edison

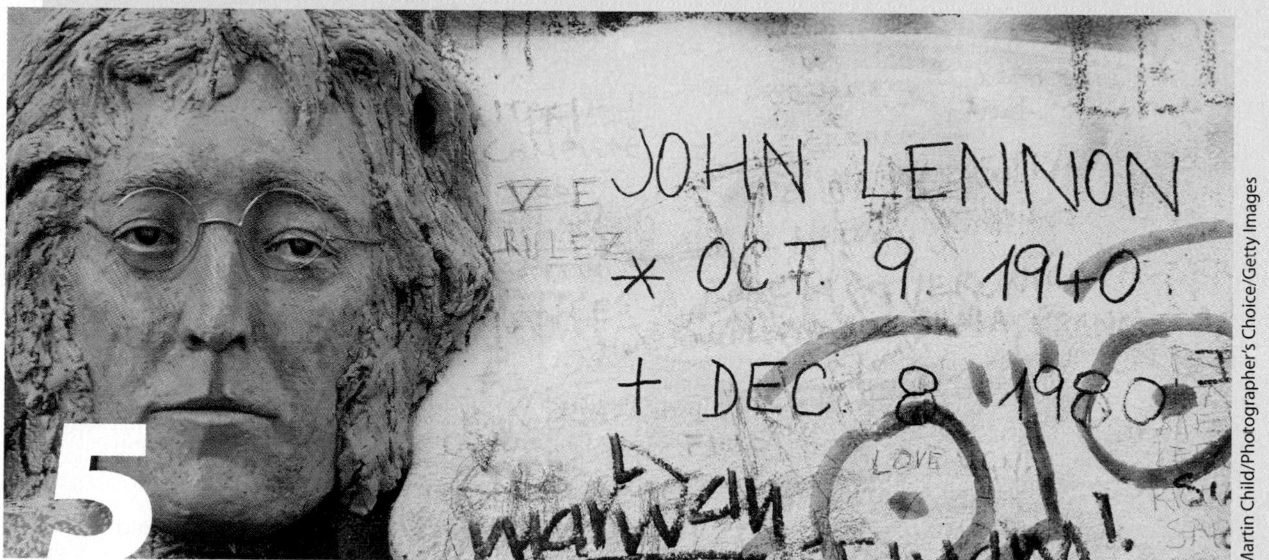

Martin Child/Photographer's Choice/Getty Images

Prewriting

Who doesn't enjoy a spellbinding movie, an awesome concert, a nail-biting championship game? Witnessing great performances is one of life's great pleasures, and we remember each one for a long, long time.

What most of us don't think about is all the **behind-the-scenes** work that makes such a performance possible. Consider moviemaking. Among other things, there's a script to craft, a cast to pick, a filming location to select, a budget to establish, and on and on.

There is a lot of behind-the-scenes work that goes into effective writing, too. This work is called **prewriting**, and it consists of, among other things, selecting a writing idea, gathering details, and establishing a focus. In this chapter, you will learn about and practice important prewriting strategies.

What do you think?

Do you agree with the Edison quotation above? Why or why not? What percentages would you give to inspiration and perspiration?

Learning Outcomes

- LO1 Analyze the assignment.
- LO2 Select a topic.
- LO3 Gather details about a topic.
- LO4 Establish a writing focus.
- LO5 Identify a pattern of organization.
- LO6 Organize your information.
- LO7 Review prewriting.

Vocabulary

behind-the-scenes
an idiom meaning "out of public view"

prewriting
the first step in the writing process, the preparation leading to the actual writing

Learning Outcome

Analyze the assignment.

LO1 Analyzing the Assignment

The writing process starts as soon as one of your instructors makes a writing assignment. And, of course, each assignment will call to mind many questions—the first one being *What will I write about?* You can use the **STRAP strategy** to help first answer your questions about the assignment and begin your preparation.

How the Strategy Works

The **STRAP** strategy consists of key questions that you answer about a writing assignment.

Subject: What specific topic should I write about?

Type: What form of writing *(essay, article, report)* will I use?

Role: What position *(student, citizen, employee, family member)* should I assume?

Audience: Who *(classmates, instructor, government official, parent)* is the intended reader?

Purpose: What is the goal *(to inform, to analyze, to persuade, to share)* of the writing?

The STRAP Strategy in Action

Suppose you were given the following assignment in a sociology class:

> Write a personal essay or blog post in which you analyze a common expression that you find bothersome.

Here are the answers to the STRAP questions for this assignment:

Subject: a common, bothersome expression

Type: a personal essay or blog post

Role: student

Audience: classmates

Purpose: to analyze

Test Taking

For some assignments, you may not find a direct answer to every STRAP question. Use your best judgment when this happens.

Vocabulary

STRAP strategy
a strategy helping a writer identify the key features of an assignment—the subject, type of writing, writer's role, audience, and purpose

Respond Analyze the two writing assignments below using the STRAP strategy. Refer to the previous page to help you complete your work.

Assignment 1: In a letter to the editor suitable for a community publication, take a stand on a relevant environmental issue. Be sure to select an issue that deserves immediate attention.

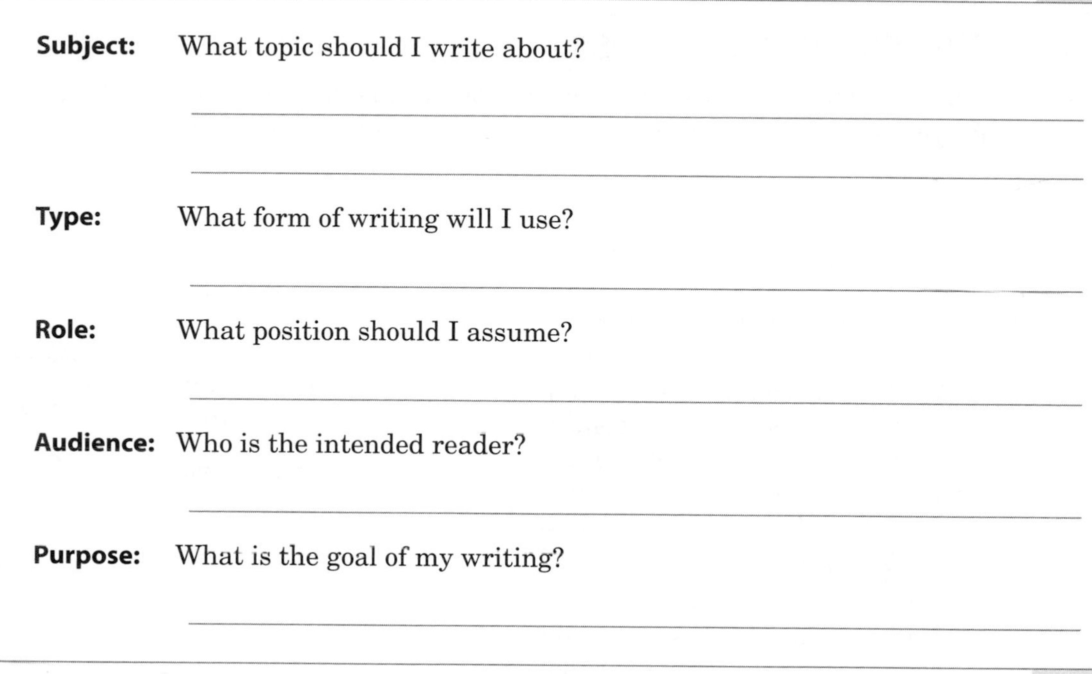

Subject: What topic should I write about?

____

____

Type: What form of writing will I use?

____

Role: What position should I assume?

____

Audience: Who is the intended reader?

____

Purpose: What is the goal of my writing?

____

Assignment 2: As part of your take-home exam, write an informational essay explaining the main characteristics of a stress-related condition.

Subject: What topic should I write about?

____

____

Type: What form of writing will I use?

____

Role: What position should I assume?

____

Audience: Who is the intended reader?

____

Purpose: What is the goal of my writing?

____

Think about it...

Before you begin any writing assignment, you should also consider these issues:

- How the writing will be assessed
- How much time you have to complete your work
- How much importance the assignment carries

Tip

Look for key words in an assignment—*explain, compare, analyze*—so you know exactly what you should do.

Learning Outcome

Select a topic.

LO2 Selecting a Topic

Novelist Kurt Vonnegut gave good advice for selecting a writing idea. He said, "Find a subject you care about and which you in your heart feel others should care about." Having strong feelings about a writing idea makes it that much easier to produce a finished piece that you feel good about and that your reader will enjoy.

The Narrowing Process

Typically, when your instructors make assignments, they provide a starting point for your topic search. Suppose you were given this assignment from page 37:

As part of your take-home exam, write an informational essay explaining the main characteristics of a stress-related condition.

The general subject area, "a stress-related condition," serves as the starting point for a topic search. However, to identify a topic limited enough for an informational essay, a writer would first have to narrow the subject, perhaps to stress-related *physical* conditions. With this focus in mind, a writer could then identify a specific topic like *dehydration*.

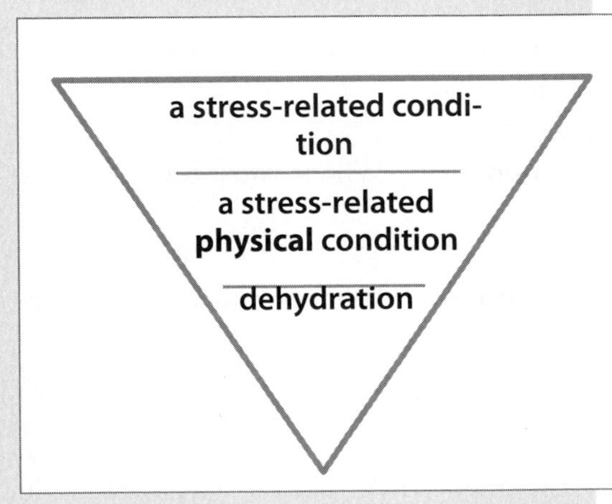

Tip

When evaluating a possible topic, always ask yourself if it is too general or too specific for the assignment.

Choose Identify a specific writing idea by filling in the inverted pyramid for the following assignment. (Use the example above as a guide.)

Writing assignment: In a letter to the editor suitable for your community newspaper, take a stand on a relevant environmental issue.

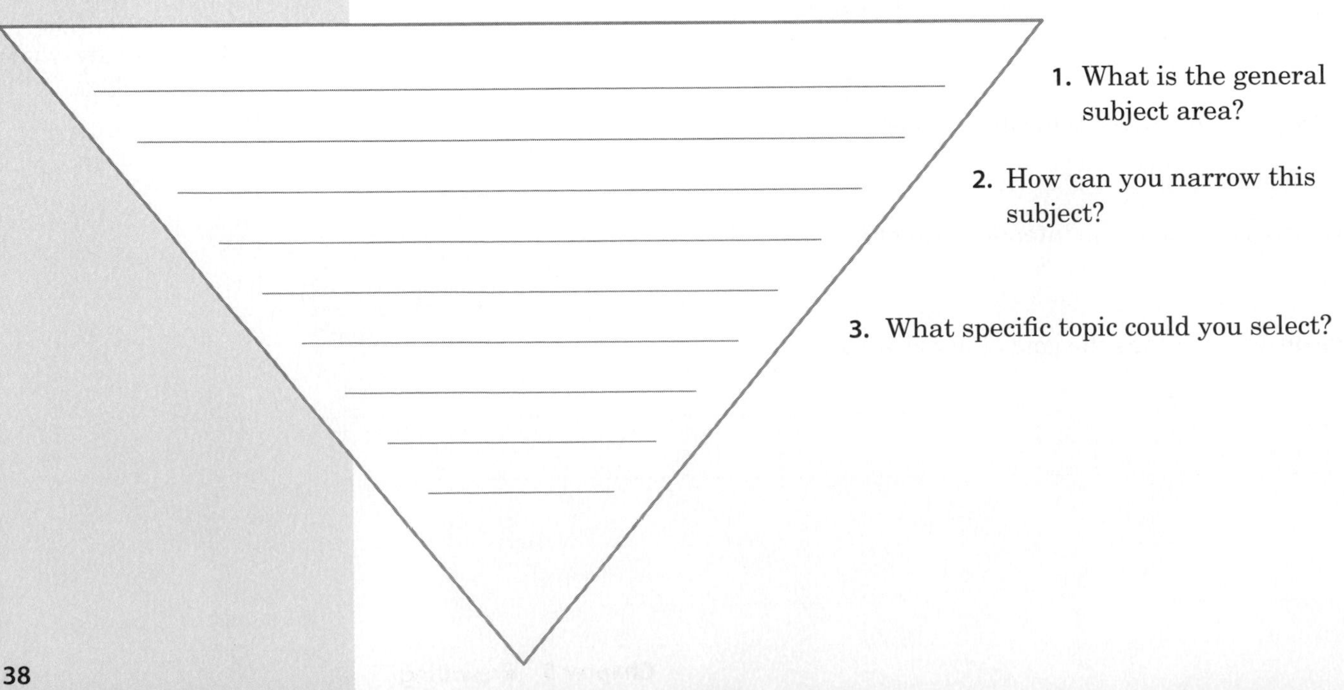

1. What is the general subject area?
2. How can you narrow this subject?
3. What specific topic could you select?

Selecting Strategies

If you have trouble identifying a specific topic for an assignment, first review your notes, text, and appropriate Web sites for ideas. Also consider using one of these selecting strategies:

- **Clustering** Begin a cluster (or web) with a nucleus word or phrase related to the assignment. (The general subject area or narrowed subject would work.) Circle it and then cluster related words around it. As you continue, you will identify possible writing ideas.

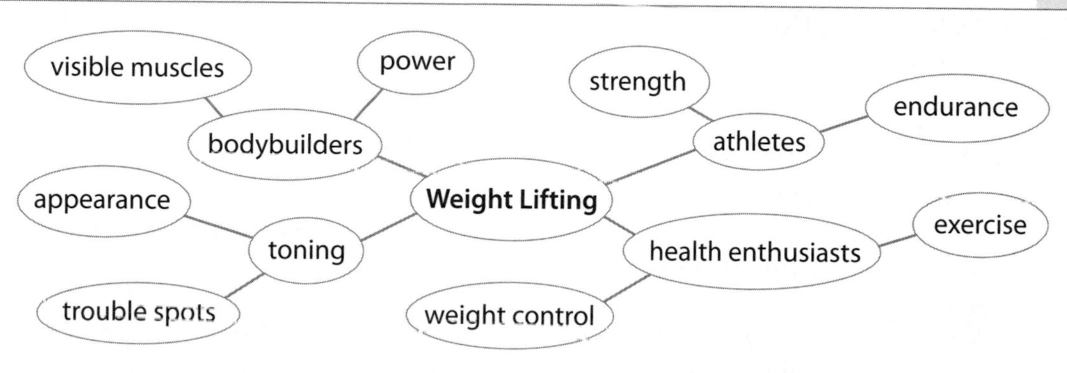

Extend

If one of the clustering ideas truly interests you, write freely about it for 5 minutes to see what you can discover.

- **Listing** Freely list ideas as you think about your writing assignment. Keep going as long as you can. Then review your list for possible topics.

- **Freewriting** Write nonstop for 5–10 minutes about your assignment to discover possible topics. Begin by writing down a particular thought about the assignment.

Practice Use one of the strategies explained above to identify possible topics related to one of the following general subject areas:

exercise	popular music	careers	freedom/rights	technology

Learning Outcome

Gather details about a topic.

"Knowledge is of two kinds. We know subjects ourselves, or we know where we can find information [about] it."
—Samuel Johnson

LO3 Gathering Details

Once you identify a specific writing topic, you need to gather information about it. Obviously, if you already know a lot about a topic, you may not need to do much collecting. For other topics, however, try the following strategies.

Gathering Your First Thoughts

Use one of these strategies to find out what you already know about the topic.

- **Clustering** Create a cluster with your specific topic as the nucleus word. (See page 39.)
- **Listing** List thoughts and ideas about your topic as well as questions about it that come to mind. Record as many ideas as you can.
- **Focused Freewriting** Write nonstop for at least 5–8 minutes to see what ideas you unlock about your topic. Do not stop to think what to say next; simply go where your writing takes you.

Collect Use one of the strategies above to gather your first thoughts about a topic you identified on page 39. (Select an activity different from the one you used on the previous page.)

Traits

At this stage, the most important trait is ideas. Hunt them down, gather them up. More is better.

Learning More About a Topic

For most college writing assignments, you will need more than your own thoughts to develop an effective piece of writing. To gather additional information about a topic, try these activities.

■ **Analyzing** Explore your topic from a number of different angles by answering the following questions:

- What parts does my topic have? *(Break it down.)*
- What do I see, hear, or feel when I think about my topic? *(Describe it.)*
- What is it similar to and different from? *(Compare it.)*
- What value does it have? *(Evaluate it.)*
- How useful is it? *(Apply it.)*

■ **Imagining** Think creatively about a topic by writing and answering **unconventional** questions. Note these examples:

Writing About an Important Issue

- What game would this issue enjoy?
- What type of clothing does it resemble?

Writing About a Person

- What type of food is this person like?
- What type of book do you associate with the person?

Collect In the space provided below, use the analyzing or imagining strategy to discover more about the topic you worked with on page 40. (If you choose the imagining strategy, ask and answer at least three questions about the topic.)

WAC

Conducting **primary** and **secondary** research is another important way to learn more about a topic. Common methods of research include reading, exploring Web sites, consulting experts, and so on.

Vocabulary

unconventional
out of the ordinary, unusual, or offbeat

primary sources
original sources of information such as participating or interviewing

secondary sources
secondhand sources of information such as reading an article about a topic

Learning Outcome

Establish a writing focus.

LO4 Finding a Focus

Selecting a topic and collecting information about it are important first steps. But you still have some important decisions to make, the first of which involves finding a focus for your writing.

Choosing a Focus

An effective **focus** establishes boundaries for your writing and helps you decide what information to include about your topic. Let's say you are writing an editorial about the food in your school cafeteria and want to make the point that a huge amount of food is wasted during each meal. This particular feeling could serve as a focus for an editorial because it is reasonable, clear, and worthy of discussion.

Insight

Academic writing in the United States tends to be direct and focused. If you come from a cultural tradition with a less direct approach, practice writing in both ways.

Topic: food in your school cafeteria

Focus: amount of food that is wasted

Review Rate the effectiveness of each focus below by circling the appropriate star. Consider whether the focus is clear, reasonable, and worth developing. Then explain your rating.

1. **Topic:** sports drinks
   Focus: the best choice during long workouts

   weak ★ ★ ★ ★ ★ strong

   ____

   ____

2. **Topic:** society's view of beauty
   Focus: seems good

   weak ★ ★ ★ ★ ★ strong

   ____

   ____

3. **Topic:** cultural comparisons between Korea and the United States
   Focus: contrasting views on cleanliness

   weak ★ ★ ★ ★ ★ strong

   ____

   ____

4. **Topic:** lacrosse
   Focus: a fast-growing sport

   weak ★ ★ ★ ★ ★ strong

   ____

   ____

Vocabulary

focus
a particular feeling about or a specific part of a topic that determines what information is included in a piece of writing

Forming a Thesis Statement

For most of your college writing, you will state your focus in a **thesis statement** (or in a **topic sentence** if you are writing a paragraph). A strong thesis statement highlights a special part or feature of a topic or expresses a particular feeling about it. You can use the following formula to write a thesis statement or topic sentence.

A specific topic	+	A particular feeling, feature, or part	=	An effective thesis statement or topic sentence
arrival of Hernán Cortés in Mexico		marked the beginning of the end of the Aztec empire		The arrival of Hernán Cortés in Mexico marked the beginning of the end of the Aztec empire.

Tip

Keep working with a thesis statement or topic sentence until it accurately expresses the main point of your writing.

Create Identify a focus and then write a topic sentence or thesis statement for each of the following assignments. The first one is done for you.

1. **Writing assignment:** Paragraph describing a specific style of clothing

   Specific topic: Zoot suit

   Focus: Popular during the swing era

   Topic sentence: The zoot suit *(specific topic)* became a popular fashion symbol in the swing era *(a particular feature)*.

2. **Writing assignment:** Paragraph explaining how to do something

   Specific topic: Using chopsticks

   Focus: ______________________________

   Topic sentence: ______________________________

   ____

3. **Writing assignment:** Essay analyzing a popular type of cooking

   Specific topic: Cajun cooking

   Focus: ______________________________

   Thesis statement: ______________________________

   ____

4. **Writing assignment:** Essay exploring technology and education

   Specific topic: Electronic textbooks

   Focus: ______________________________

   Thesis statement: ______________________________

   ____

Vocabulary

thesis statement
the controlling idea in an essay, highlighting a special part or feature of a topic or expressing a particular feeling about it

topic sentence
the controlling idea in a paragraph

Learning Outcome

Identify a pattern of organization.

LO5 Choosing a Pattern of Organization

Once you've established a focus or thesis, you must identify an appropriate pattern of organization for the information you plan to include in your writing. Here's how to proceed:

1. **Study your thesis statement or topic sentence.** It will usually indicate how to organize your ideas. For example, consider the following thesis statement:

   > Eating locally grown produce will improve the local economy.

   This thesis suggests arranging the information by order of importance, because you are trying to prove a point.

2. Then **review the information you have gathered**. Decide which ideas support your thesis and arrange them according to the appropriate method of organization. For the thesis statement above, you would either arrange your reasons from most important to least important or vice versa.

Patterns of Organization

Listed below are some common patterns of organization that you will use in your writing.

- Use **chronological order** (time) when you are sharing a personal experience, telling how something happened, or explaining how to do something.
- Use **spatial order** (location) for descriptions, arranging information from left to right, top to bottom, from the edge to the center, and so on.
- Use **order of importance** when you are taking a stand, arguing for or against something, and so on. Either work from most important to least important or the other way around.
- Use **deductive** organization if you want to follow your topic sentence or thesis statement with supporting reasons, examples, and facts.
- Use **inductive** organization when you want to present specific details first and conclude with your topic sentence or thesis statement.
- Use **compare-contrast** organization when you want to show how one topic is different from and similar to another one.

Traits

Think about your purpose as you choose a pattern of organization. Often, your working thesis statement will suggest how you should organize details.

Choose Study each of the following thesis statements. Then choose the method of organization that the thesis suggests. Explain each of your choices. The first one is done for you.

1. **Thesis statement:** The bottom of the hill in my childhood neighborhood offered everything young boys wanted.

   Appropriate method of organization: spatial order

   Explain: The thesis statement suggests that the writer will describe the area at the bottom of the hill, so using spatial order seems appropriate.

2. **Thesis statement:** In most cases, people involved in recreational fishing should use barbless hooks.

   Appropriate method of organization: __________

   Explain: __________

3. **Thesis statement:** To become an effective leader, a person must develop three main traits.

   Appropriate method of organization: __________

   Explain: __________

4. **Thesis statement:** Meeting my grandmother for the first time rates as one of my most important personal encounters.

   Appropriate method of organization: __________

   Explain: __________

5. **Thesis statement:** (Choose one that you wrote on page 43.)

   Appropriate method of organization: __________

   Explain: __________

Speaking & Listening

Work on this activity with a partner if your instructor allows it.

"An effective piece of writing has focus. There is a controlling vision which orders what is being said."
—Donald Murray

Learning Outcome

Organize your information.

LO6 Organizing Your Information

After selecting an appropriate method of organization, you're ready to arrange the supporting information for your writing. Here are three basic strategies for doing that:

- **Make a quick list** of main points.
- **Create an outline** or organized arrangement of main points and subpoints.
- **Fill in a graphic organizer**, arranging main points and details in a chart or diagram.

Using a Quick List

A quick list works well when you are writing a short piece or when your planning time is limited. Here is a quick list for a descriptive paragraph about zoot suits. (The list organizes details in spatial order, from top to bottom.)

Sample Quick List

Topic sentence: The zoot suit became a popular fashion symbol in the swing era.
- begins with a stylish wide-brimmed hat turned down
- follows with an oversized, tapered long jacket
- under jacket, a dress shirt with a tie
- pleated pants taper to narrow bottoms
- ends with two-tone, thin-soled shoes

Create Write a topic sentence and a quick list for a narrative paragraph about a funny, scary, or otherwise significant personal experience. Include four to six details in your list, organized chronologically.

Topic sentence: ______________________

____

____

Quick list:

____

____

____

____

____

____

____

Using an Outline

An effective outline shows how ideas fit together and serves as an effective blueprint for your writing. You may be familiar with topic and sentence outlines, which follow specific guidelines: If you have a "I," you must have at least a "II." If you have an "A," you must have at least a "B," and so on. You can also make up your own kind of outline to put your ideas in order.

Sample Customized Outline

What follows is the first part of a **customized** outline that includes main points stated in complete sentences and supporting details stated as phrases.

Thesis statement: Humpback whales are by far the most playful and amazing whale species.

1. Most observers note that humpbacks appear to enjoy attention.
   - lift bodies almost completely out of water (breaching)
   - slap huge flippers against the water
   - thrust their flukes (tail portion) straight out of water
2. Humpback whales "sing" better than other whales.
   - song lasts up to 30 minutes
   - head pointed toward ocean floor when singing
   - seem to engage in group singing

WAC

For research papers and other formal pieces of writing, you may be expected to complete a traditional topic or sentence outline.

Create Using the sample above as a guide, develop a customized outline for an essay about becoming a leader. A thesis statement and three main points are identified for you. Put the main points in the most logical order and make up two or three details to support each main point. (Work on this activity with a partner if your teacher allows it.)

Vocabulary

customized
changed or altered to meet individual or personal needs

Thesis statement: To become an effective leader, a person must develop three main traits.

Main points: Leaders must earn the respect of others. Leaders must display good work habits. Leaders must be confident.

1. ____________________
   - ____________________
   - ____________________
   - ____________________
2. ____________________
   - ____________________
   - ____________________
   - ____________________
3. ____________________
   - ____________________
   - ____________________
   - ____________________

Using Graphic Organizers

Note: A cluster is another type of graphic organizer. (See page 39.)

Graphic organizers are charts or diagrams for arranging information. You can use them either to collect information or to organize the supporting facts and details you have already gathered.

Sample Graphic Organizers

Time Line Use for personal narratives to list actions or events in the order they occurred.

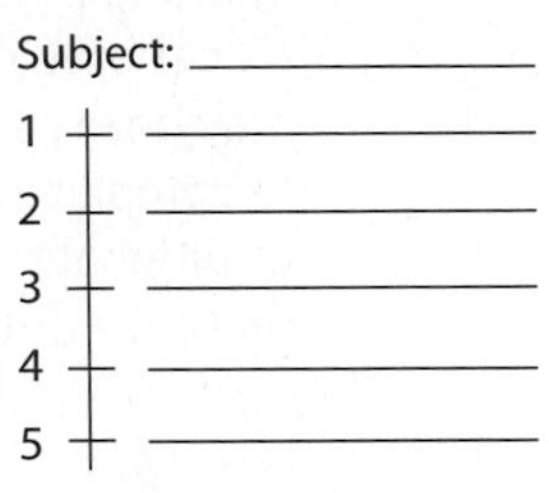

Process Diagram Use to collect details for science-related writing, such as the steps in a process.

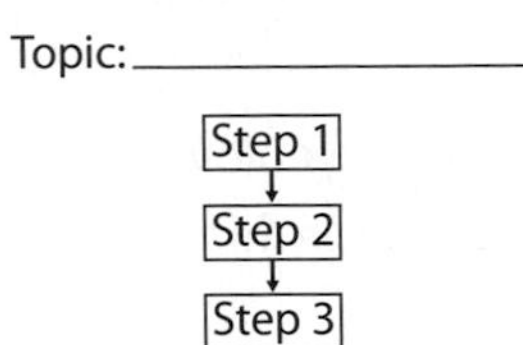

Line Diagram Use to collect and organize details for academic essays.

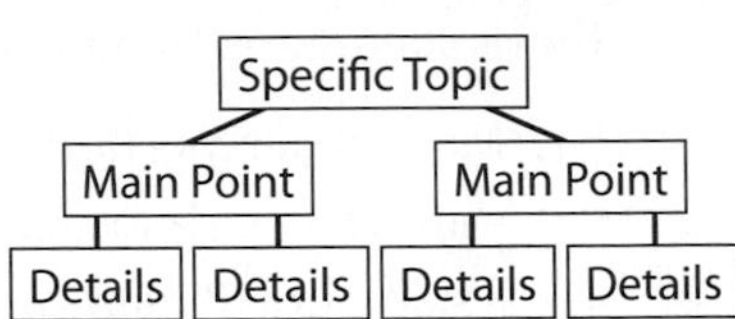

Venn Diagram Use to collect details to compare and contrast two topics.

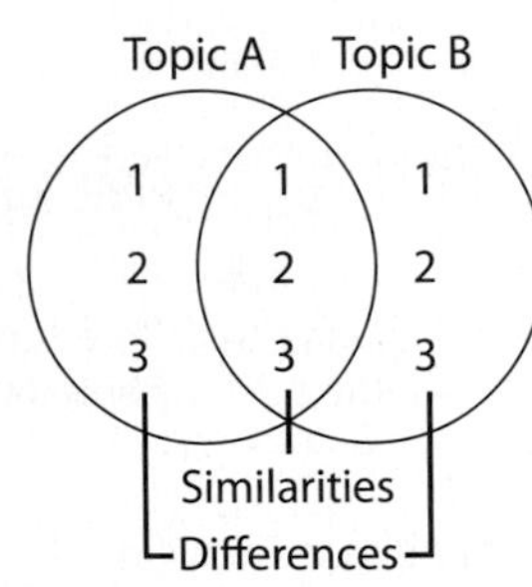

Cause-Effect Organizer Use to collect and organize details for cause-effect essays.

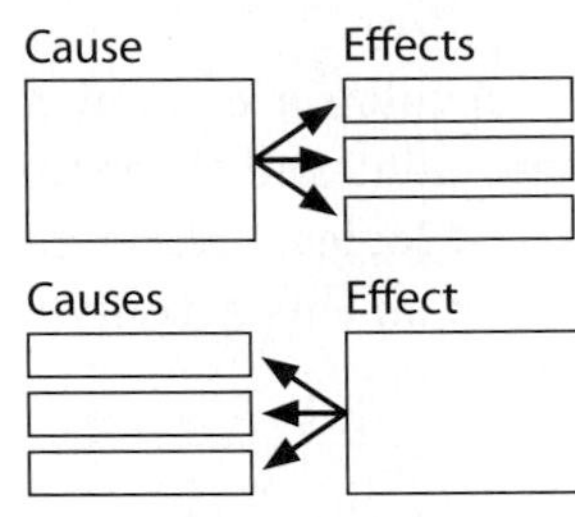

Problem-Solution Web Use to map out problem-solution essays.

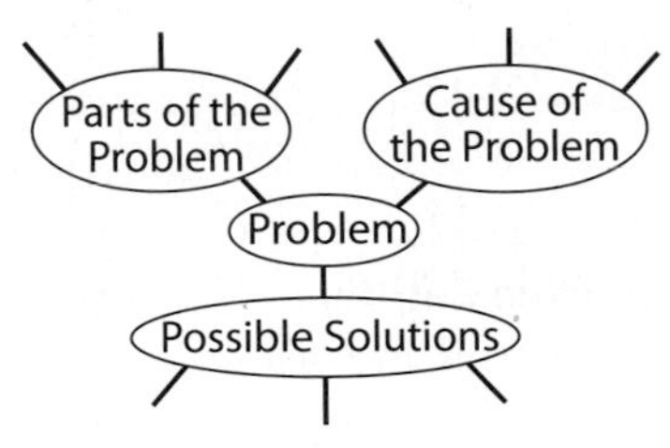

Create Use the appropriate graphic organizer to organize the information for an essay about becoming an effective leader.

LO7 Reviewing Prewriting

Learning Outcome

Review prewriting.

Prewriting is the planning step in the writing process. Here is a quick overview of key prewriting strategies covered in this chapter.

■ Using the STRAP Strategy

This strategy helps you to analyze the following parts of an assignment:

Subject:	What specific topic should I write about?
Type:	What form of writing will I use?
Role:	What position should I assume?
Audience:	Who is the intended reader?
Purpose:	What is the goal of the writing?

■ Selecting a Topic

Choosing a topic for a paragraph or an essay involves selecting a specific topic related to the general subject area identified in the assignment.

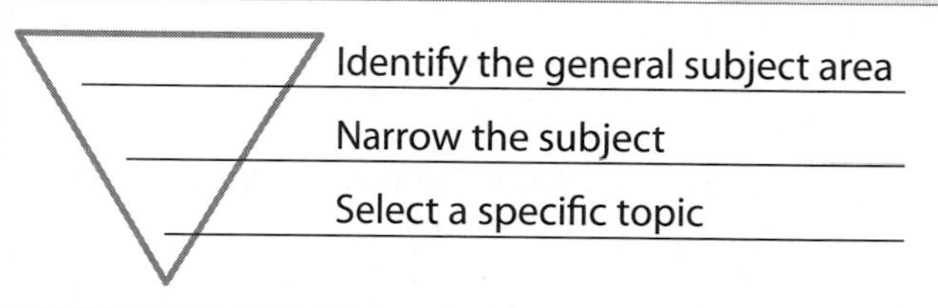

■ Gathering Details

Gathering involves discovering what you already know about a topic and what you need to find out. Here are some of the strategies that you can use to collect information.

- Listing
- Clustering
- Freewriting
- Analyzing
- Researching

■ Forming a Topic Sentence or Thesis Statement

A topic sentence (for a paragraph) or a thesis statement (for an essay) provides a focus for writing. The following formula can be used to create either one.

A specific topic + A particular feeling, feature, or part = An effective topic sentence or thesis statement

■ Organizing Information

A writer can use a quick list, an outline, or a graphic organizer to arrange supporting information for writing. Here is a list of common graphic organizers.

- Time Line
- Process Diagram
- Line Diagram
- Venn Diagram
- Cause-Effect Organizer
- Problem-Solution Web

Reflect Think of two of the most important things you learned about prewriting in this chapter. Explain your choices below.

Reinforcement

Complete these activities as needed to help you better understand key strategies covered in this chapter.

Analyze an Assignment Use the STRAP questions (see pages 36–37) to analyze the following writing assignment:

Write an informational blog essay suitable for a school publication in which you introduce the reader to an important new form of physical training.

Subject: What topic should I write about?

____

Type: What form of writing will I use?

____

Role: What position should I assume?

____

Audience: Who is the intended reader?

____

Purpose: What is the goal of my writing?

____

Selecting a Topic Select a specific topic for the following general subject area (or a subject of your own choosing): *green energy sources*. (See page 38.)

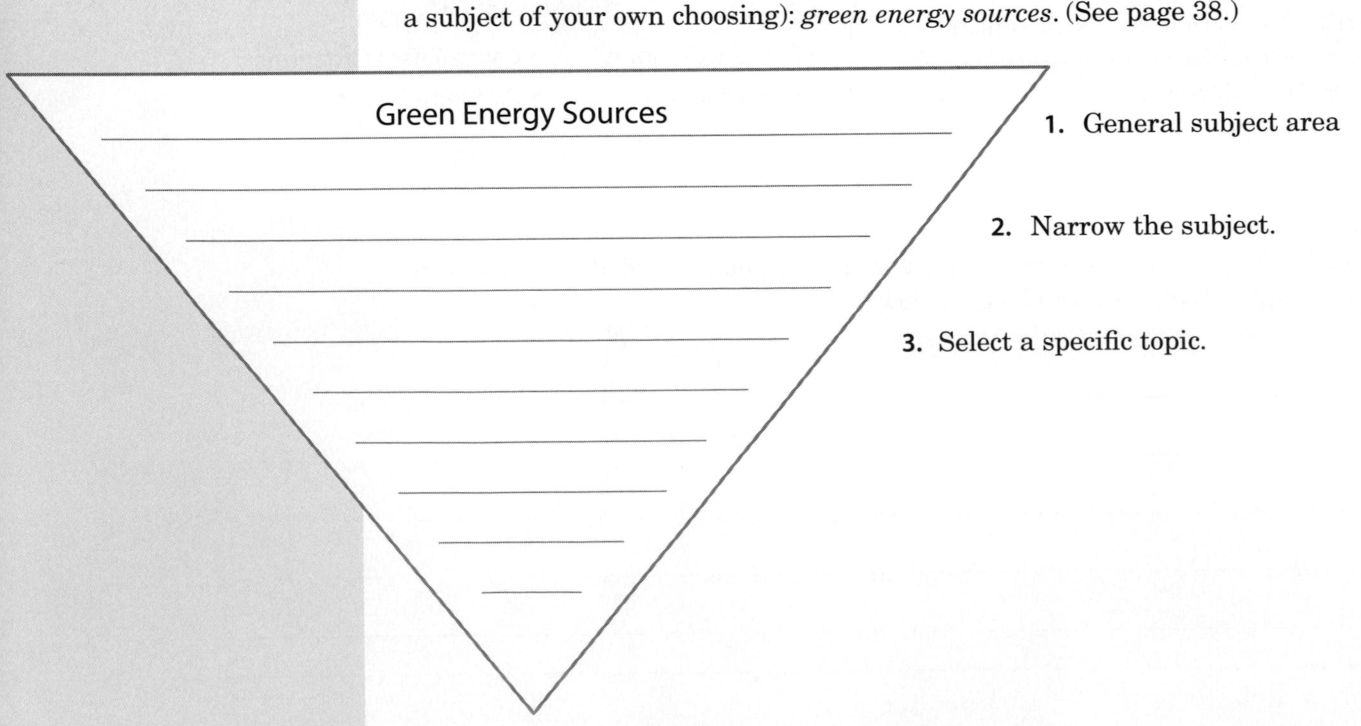

"Writing and rewriting is a constant search for what one is trying to say."
—John Updike

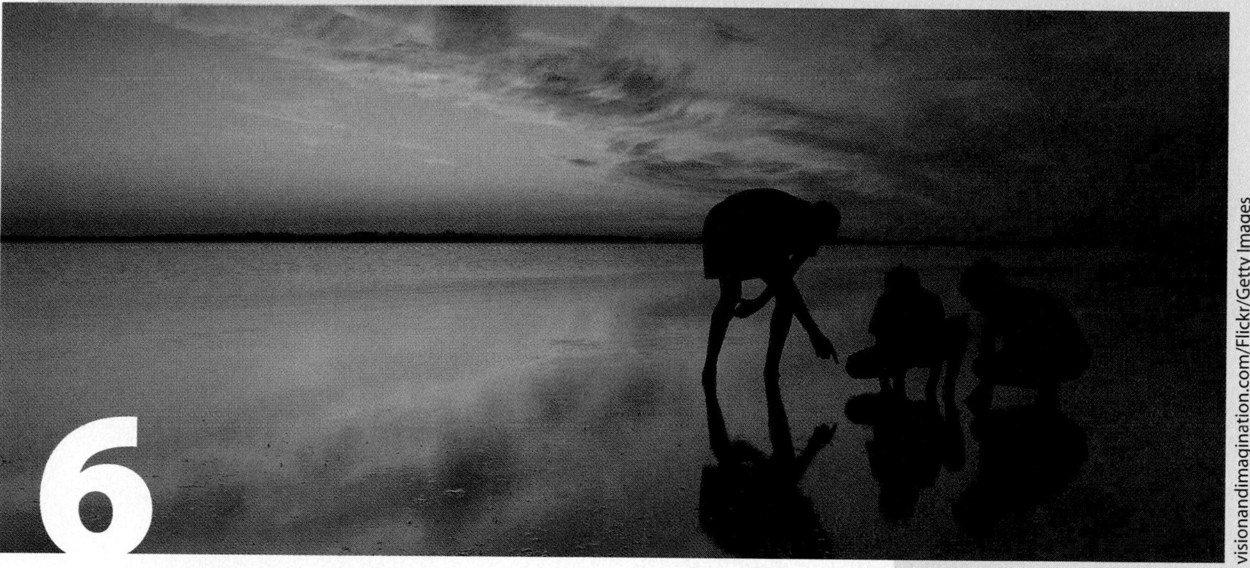

visionandimagination.com/Flickr/Getty Images

6 Drafting

The word "draft" as related to writing means "a preliminary or early version." So developing a draft is your first (or early) attempt to connect your thoughts about a writing idea. This writing should go smoothly if you have completed the necessary prewriting.

Writing a first draft becomes difficult only if you try to get everything just right. By all means, follow your plan and refer to your notes, but don't get bogged down with the wording of every single sentence. The purpose of drafting is simply to get your ideas on paper, to see what you have to work with. Think of a first draft as an **emerging** piece of writing.

The advice and strategies provided in this chapter will help you develop effective first drafts. Among other things, you'll learn how to avoid writer's block and how to include different levels of detail in your writing.

Learning Outcomes

LO1 Follow a drafting plan.

LO2 Form a meaningful whole.

LO3 Develop your ideas in different ways.

LO4 Use different levels of detail.

LO5 Review drafting.

Vocabulary

emerging
coming into being, still forming

What do you think?

How is writing, as John Updike says, "a constant search for what one is trying to say"?

Learning Outcome

Follow a drafting plan.

LO1 Following a Drafting Plan

You're ready to develop a first draft once you have completed the necessary prewriting: gathering enough information about your topic, establishing a focus or thesis, and organizing your supporting ideas. (See pages 35–50.)

How you approach this writing is up to you. You may want to spend a little extra time with your opening paragraph. Then, with the beginning set, you may find it easier to complete the draft. Or you may want to get all your thoughts on paper right away—beginning, middle, and ending.

A Writing Plan

Use the following points as a guide when developing a first draft:

- Focus on developing your ideas, not on trying to produce a final copy.
- Follow your prewriting and planning notes, but also feel free to include new ideas as they come to mind during your writing.
- Continue writing until you cover all of your main points or until you come to a logical stopping point.
- Express yourself honestly and sincerely, using other sources of information to support what you have to say.
- If you get stuck, employ one of the strategies covered on the next page.

Traits

Focus first on your ideas, pouring them out into the paragraph or essay structure. As you work, let your voice develop.

React Explain the meaning of the following idea: *When writing a first draft, focus on producing possibilities rather than perfection.*

Avoiding Writer's Block

Writer's block is the condition of not knowing what to say in a piece of writing. You've got pen in hand or fingers on the keyboard, but the words just won't come. It's quite natural to experience writer's block every once in a while. But your chances of facing this condition are greatly reduced if you know a lot about your topic and have strong feelings about it. That is why prewriting is so important.

"The inspiration comes while you write."
—Madeleine L'Engle

Strategies to Try

When writer's block strikes, try one of these strategies to get the words flowing.

1. **Write as if you are in a conversation with the reader.** Don't worry about sounding academic or correct. Instead, talk to the reader.

   Liz, I want to tell you about . . .

2. **Write nonstop in short, fluid bursts of 3–5 minutes.** Don't worry about making mistakes, or you'll stop the flow of ideas.

   Dehydration occurs when the body loses more fluids than it takes in. When the body doesn't have these fluids . . .

3. **Start in the middle.** The traditional Latin term for such a beginning is *in media res* (literally, "in the middle of things"). Don't waste time with building an elaborate opening. Just identify your topic or focus, if necessary, and go from there.

   I was an eyewitness to a drug deal at work. I was at work about 20 feet from the alley when I heard . . .

Speaking & Listening

Exchange your writing with a classmate and discuss the effectiveness of the strategy that you used.

Write Develop the first part of a draft in which you discuss something in everyday life that bugs you *(noisy eaters, sniffers and coughers, braggarts, barking dogs, and so on).* Use one of the strategies above to get started.

Learning Outcome

Form a meaningful whole.

"If you want to write, you must begin by beginning, continue by continuing, finish by finishing. This is the great secret. . . . Tell no one."
—Jack Heffron

LO2 Forming a Meaningful Whole

Novelist John Steinbeck said, "throw the whole thing on paper" when it comes to drafting. By "the whole thing," he meant connecting all of your thoughts and feelings about your topic. You should also think in terms of forming a meaningful whole, a complete draft with a beginning, a middle, and an ending. Until you do that, you won't know how to proceed.

Forming a meaningful whole for a paragraph means including a topic sentence, body sentences, and a closing sentence. For an essay, it means including an opening part (including a thesis statement), a number of supporting paragraphs, and a closing paragraph. (See pages 179–193.)

Graphically Speaking

The graphics below show the structure of both basic forms of writing.

Paragraph Structure

Topic Sentence
A **topic sentence** names the topic.

Detail Sentences
Detail sentences support the topic.

Closing Sentence
A **closing sentence** wraps up the paragraph.

Essay Structure

Opening Paragraph
The **opening paragraph** draws the reader into the essay and provides information that leads to a thesis statement. The thesis statement tells what the essay is about.

Middle Paragraphs
The **middle paragraphs** support the thesis statement. Each middle paragraph needs a topic sentence, a variety of detail sentences, and a closing sentence.

Closing Paragraph
The **closing paragraph** finishes the essay by revisiting the thesis statement, emphasizing an important detail, providing the reader with an interesting final thought, and/or looking toward the future.

Review Study each of these writing samples. Put a plus (+) next to the sample if it forms a meaningful whole; put a minus (–) next to the sample if it doesn't. Explain what is missing if you label a sample with a minus.

☐ In first grade, I found out that circuses don't necessarily live up to all of the hype. We were going to the circus for our class trip, and I was really excited about it. Our class had worked for weeks on a circus train made of shoe boxes, and Carrie Kaske told me her mom had fainted when she saw the lion tamer perform. When the day finally came, the wonderful circus turned out to be one disappointment after another. We were so high up in the arena, I had a hard time making out the performers scurrying around in the three rings, and the lion tamer was so far away that I didn't even try to watch him. After the first half hour, all I wanted to do was buy a soda and a monkey-on-a-stick and get out of there. Of course, nothing in life is that easy. We weren't allowed to buy anything, so I couldn't have my souvenir. And instead of a cold soda, I had a carton of warm milk the room mothers had so thoughtfully brought along. I returned to school tired and a little wiser. I looked at our little circus train and thought I'd rather play with it than go to another circus.

Explanation: ____

____

____

____

____

____

☐ Uncle John is normally a likeable man, except at family reunions when he appoints himself official photographer. He spends the whole time with one eye looking through a lens and the other scoping out potential victims for his photographs. Uncle John doesn't believe in candids, so he insists upon interrupting all activity to persuade his prey to pose for his pictures. In return he gets photographs of people arranged in neat rows smiling through clenched teeth. We've told him time and time again to chill out with the staged photos, but he continues to insist that we, "Come over here, so I can take your picture."

Explanation: ____

____

____

____

____

____

Learning Outcome

Develop your ideas in different ways.

LO3 Developing Your Ideas

As you develop your ideas in a first draft, you are consciously or unconsciously describing, explaining, analyzing, comparing, defining, classifying, reflecting, and so on. Think of these as your basic writing moves.

In most pieces of writing, you will employ a variety of these moves. For example, when writing a descriptive paragraph or essay, you might *describe* a favorite place in your childhood, *reflect* on its importance, and then *compare* it to other places. In an essay of definition, you might *define* the subject, *compare* it to something similar, and *share* a brief story about it.

Basic Writing Moves

If for some reason you get stuck during a draft, try one or more of these moves to unlock some new ideas.

Narrating — sharing an experience or a story
Describing — telling how someone or something appears, acts, or operates
Explaining — providing important facts, details, and examples
Analyzing — carefully examining a subject or breaking it down
Comparing — showing how two subjects are similar and different
Defining — identifying or clarifying the meaning of a term
Reflecting — connecting with or wondering about
Evaluating — rating the value of something
Arguing — using logic and evidence to prove something is true

Workplace

Workplace documents require each of these moves in different situations. That's because each of these basic writing moves reflects a different purpose.

Respond Review the list of writing moves and then answer the following questions. Work on this activity with a classmate if your instructor allows it.

1. Which writing move would be very easy to employ and why?

____

____

2. Which one would be very challenging to employ and why?

____

____

3. Which of these writing moves have you used most often in the past?

____

____

4. Which ones do you have little experience with and why?

____

____

Identify Name the main writing move exhibited in each of these writing samples and briefly explain your choice.

1. My grandmother's rose garden was a symphony of color, and she was the conductor. Shears in hand, she would step confidently toward the rose trellis and spread her hands before the bushes. With a quick downbeat her sheers sliced through the sharp thorns. . . .

   Main writing move: ______________________________

   ____

   ____

2. Most people think of smokestacks and car fumes when they think of air pollution. However, individuals are exposed to more air pollution when they are inside their own homes than when they are outside. The biggest reason for in-home air pollution is the lack of air circulation. As people make their houses airtight, they trap dirty air inside. . . .

   Main writing move: ______________________________

   ____

   ____

3. In *Native Son* by Richard Wright and *Equus* by Peter Schaffer, the two main characters, Bigger and Alan, struggle to take control of their lives. Both boys are entering adulthood and realize that what they do and say is severely restricted by the workplace, the media, and religion. Because of his family's desperate financial situation, Bigger is forced to . . . Alan experiences the pressure of working . . .

   Main writing move: ______________________________

   ____

   ____

4. *Webster's* defines *eclectic* as selecting or choosing elements from different sources or systems. *Eclectic* implies variety. But what a great way of saying variety. Variety sounds so generic, so Brand X. But *eclectic* is rich with imaginative sound. . . .

   Main writing move: ______________________________

   ____

   ____

5. Throughout life, we meet individuals that move us, shape us, affect the way in which we go about life. Many people have influenced my life, but none more than Mr. Schneider, one of my high school English teachers. You always had a way of making me feel good about myself. The little talks you had with all of us brought up important things that I needed to hear. For example, . . .

   Main writing move: ______________________________

   ____

   ____

LO4 Using Levels of Detail

Learning Outcome

Use different levels of detail.

Your college instructors will require a certain level of **depth** in your writing. When you make a point, they will expect you to fully explain it with specific examples and details before you make another. The process of making important points and supporting them with details is at the core of most writing.

To write with depth, you should include different levels of detail. Here are three basic levels.

Level 1: A **controlling sentence** names a topic (usually a topic sentence) or makes a main point.

Level 2: A **clarifying sentence** explains a level 1 sentence.

Level 3: A **completing sentence** adds details to complete the point.

Test Taking

Graders of writing tests watch for an elaboration of ideas—including different levels of details.

Details in Action

The passage that follows uses three different levels of detail. Notice how each new level adds depth to the writing.

(Level 1) Louis Braille, a blind French student, developed a system of communication for people with this handicap. **(Level 2)** The system consists of an alphabet using combinations of small raised dots. **(Level 3)** The dots are imprinted on paper and can be felt, and thus read, by running the fingers across the page.

Here's another passage containing a combination of the three levels of detail.

(Level 1) Cartoons helped to shape the way I think. **(Level 2)** Most of them taught me never to take life too seriously. **(Level 3)** Many of the characters made their way through life with smirks on their faces. **(Level 3)** And all but a few of them seized the day, living for the moment. **(Level 2)** In an offhanded way, cartoons also provided me with a guide on how to act. **(Level 3)** Good versus evil was usually clearly defined. **(Level 3)** Other cartoons stressed the importance of loyalty.

Note: To "complete" this passage, the writer could add another level of detail (level 4) by including references to specific cartoon characters.

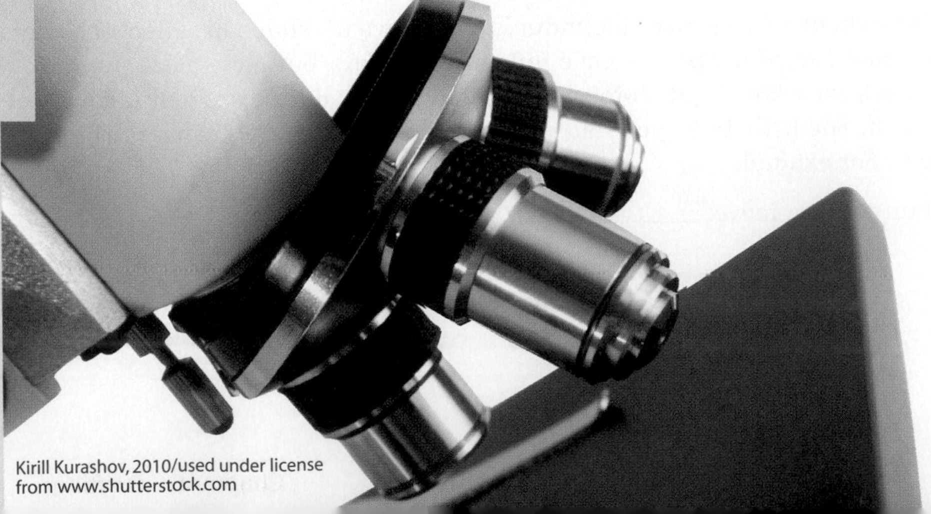

Kirill Kurashov, 2010/used under license from www.shutterstock.com

Vocabulary

depth
carefully worked out, detailed, thorough

Identify Carefully read the following passage; then label its levels of details. (Work on this activity with a partner if your instructor allows it.)

(__________) Jim Thorpe was one of the star athletes representing the United States in the 1912 Summer Olympics in Sweden. (__________) Thorpe, a Native American, was an extremely versatile athlete, but he was especially skilled in track and field. (__________) He won a gold medal in the pentathlon, a track-and-field event of five parts. (__________) He also won a gold medal in the decathlon, a ten-part track-and-field event.

"The writer writes with information, and if there is no information there will be no effective writing."
—Donald Murray

Create Write a brief paragraph about one of the following topics (or a topic of your own choosing): *types of friends, the causes of good (or poor) grades, your definition of courage, a favorite Web site, an interesting career*. Be sure that your paragraph includes at least five or six sentences.

Identify Label the sentences in your paragraph with the numbers 1, 2, or 3, depending on the level of detail they include. Then in the space below, explain where you could add even more detail in your paragraph.

Note: Your paragraph will surely contain level 1 (the topic sentence) and level 2 details. It may also contain level 3 details to support or illustrate the nearest level 2 sentence, and so on.

Learning Outcome

Review drafting.

LO5 Reviewing Drafting

Here is a quick review of drafting, the second step in the writing process.

Follow a drafting plan.

Focus on developing your ideas, not on producing a final copy, and use your prewriting and planning notes as a general writing guide.

Form a meaningful whole.

A complete first draft includes a beginning, a middle, and an ending. Until you complete all three parts, you won't know how to proceed.

A complete paragraph:	A complete essay:
Topic Sentence	Thesis Statement
Body	Supporting Paragraphs
Closing Sentence	Closing Paragraph

Develop your ideas in different ways.

In most pieces of writing, you will make a variety of writing moves. You may start with some **description**, add some **reflection**, then make a **comparison**, and so on.

Use different levels of detail.

In your college writing, you will be expected to include at least three different levels of detail.

Level 1: Controlling sentences name a topic or make a main point.
Level 2: Clarifying sentences explain level 1 sentences.
Level 3: Completing sentences add details to complete the point.

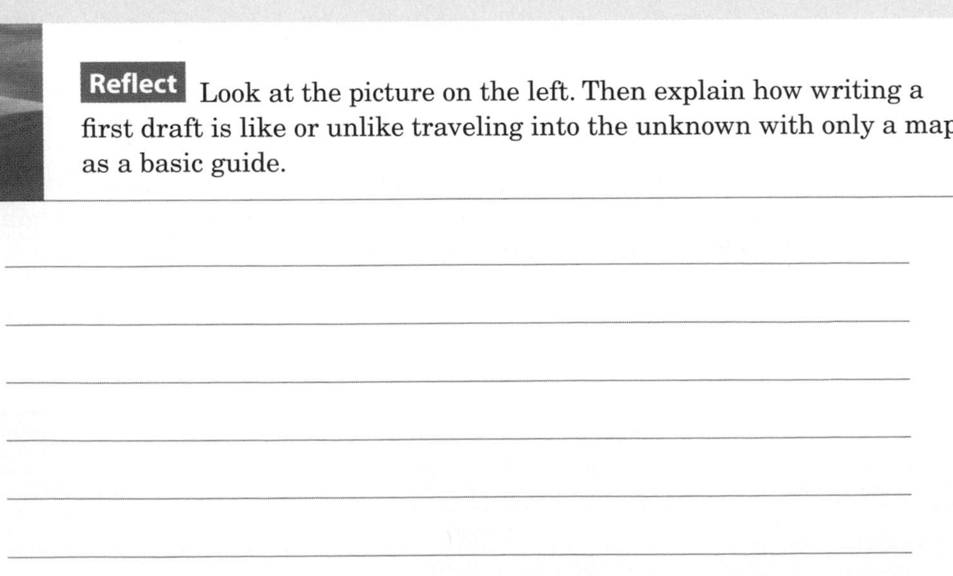

Dave & Les Jacobs/Blend Images/Getty Images

Reflect Look at the picture on the left. Then explain how writing a first draft is like or unlike traveling into the unknown with only a map as a basic guide.

"The first draft is the down draft—you just get it down. The second draft is the up draft—you fix it up."
—Anne Lamont

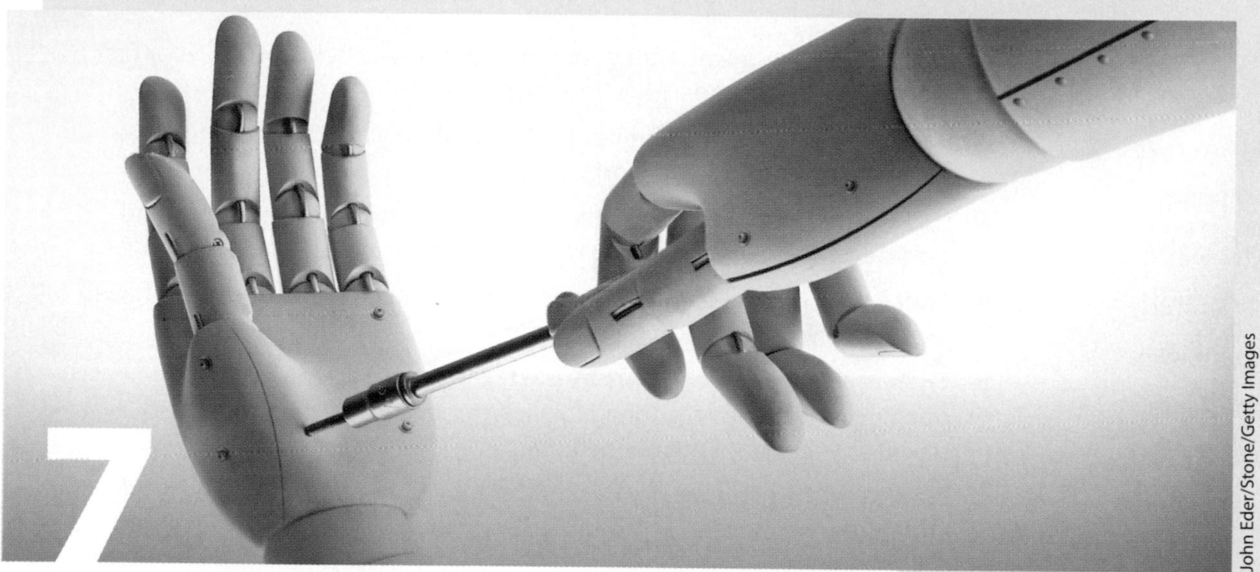

John Eder/Stone/Getty Images

7 Revising

Someone once said, "Hard writing makes easy reading." In this context, "hard writing" refers to writing that is strong from start to finish because of the effort put into it. And "easy reading" refers to the pleasurable (informative, stimulating) reading experience such writing provides.

Revising is really **synonymous** with hard writing because when you revise, you improve a first draft until it says what you want it to say. The amount of time spent revising is directly related to the quality of the finished piece. If you put in the necessary time, the results will please both you and your instructors.

This chapter provides guidelines and strategies for revising your first drafts. You will learn, among other things, the traits of strong writing and how they can direct the changes you make.

Learning Outcomes

LO1 Understand the revising process.

LO2 Recognize the traits of strong writing.

LO3 Understand the basic revising moves.

LO4 Learn the basics of peer reviewing.

LO5 Review the revising process.

Vocabulary

synonymous
alike in meaning or significance

What do you think?

In the quotation above, what does Lamont mean by the second draft being the "up draft"?

____

____

____

____

Learning Outcome

Understand the revising process.

"It would be crazy to begin revising immediately after finishing the first draft, and counter to the way the mind likes to create."
—Kenneth Atchity

Traits

Don't pay undue attention to surface issues—usage, spelling, punctuation—at this point in the process. Instead, focus on the ideas, organization, and voice of your writing.

Vocabulary

ties everything together an idiom meaning "to make important connections"

LO1 Understanding Revising

Revising is the process of improving your message—the ideas, organization, and voice in your writing. To make the best revising decisions, follow these guidelines:

- **Take some time away from your writing.** This will help you see your first draft more clearly, and with a fresh outlook.
- **Read your first draft a number of times,** silently and out loud, to get an overall impression of your work.
- **Have a trusted peer or two react to your writing.** Their questions and comments will help you decide what changes to make.
- **Check your overall focus or thesis.** Decide if it still works and if you have provided enough support for it.
- **Then review your work, part by part.** Pay special attention to the opening, since it sets the tone of your writing, and the closing, since it serves as your final word on the topic.
- **Plan a revising strategy** by deciding what you need to do first, second, and third.

Select Checkmark the statements below that clearly refer to revising. Work on this activity with a classmate if your instructor allows it.

_____ 1. Reviewing the opening part to make sure it effectively introduces your thesis

_____ 2. Looking up a specific comma rule

_____ 3. Adding supporting details in one of your paragraphs

_____ 4. Changing the order of two parts to strengthen your message

_____ 5. Replacing one word with a synonym

_____ 6. Deleting a part that is not really related to your thesis

_____ 7. Moving a prepositional phrase from the beginning to the end of a sentence

_____ 8. Rewriting the closing part so it more effectively **ties everything together**

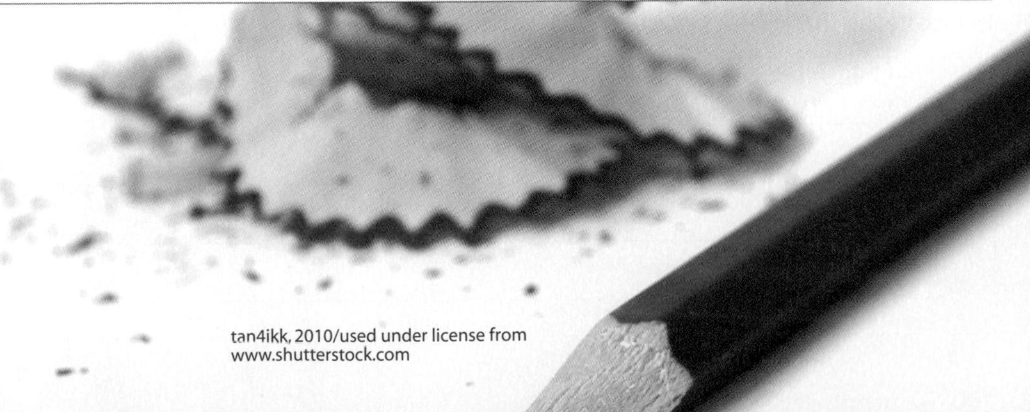

Review Carefully read the following first draft at least two times. As you read, notice parts that you like and parts that need work.

When I was a kid, there was this guy who used to hang around all the time. My father built houses and fixed up people's kitchens and stuff. Ted worked for my father for about five years. He would work until he had enough money for awhile, then he'd come back for more work. Beats me what he did when he wasn't working for us. He scraped and painted and hauled equipment and other stuff. He was about 60 and lived in a Crown Victoria car with maroon leather upholstery. He had a funny patchwork quilt and lace pillows in the backseat. It looked just like a living room for little people. He even had a little TV that hooked up to his car's lighter. He parked the car on his brother's farm. On sunny days, he'd open up the trunk where he kept a cooler, take out a lawn chair, and sit there sipping root beer. I don't know what else he did. It was funny to see him pull up in his house every morning, his Cubs hat pushed back on his balding head. After a cup of coffee, he'd say, "Well I guess I need a few more chores, Tony."

Respond React to this writing by answering the following questions. Try to make specific references to the text in your explanations.

Speaking & Listening

Discuss your responses with a classmate. Did each of you react in the same way to the writing?

1. Are the contents interesting and worth sharing? Explain.

2. Does the paragraph begin with a clearly expressed topic sentence? If not, what is wrong with it?

3. How effective is the middle part? Explain.

4. Does the paragraph have a strong ending? Explain.

5. If you were revising this paragraph, what change would you be sure to make?

Learning Outcome

Recognize the traits of strong writing.

LO2 Recognizing Strong Writing

What traits or elements make writing strong? Most writing experts would agree on the list that follows. You will find this list helpful when you review and revise your first drafts. If your writing doesn't "pass" certain descriptors, then you should make the necessary improvements.

Tip

Here's another important point to consider: Does your writing meet the requirements of the assignment? To check for this, revisit your answers to the STRAP questions. (See pages 18–19.)

Revising Checklist

Ideas

- ☐ **1.** Does an interesting and relevant topic serve as a starting point for the writing?
- ☐ **2.** Is the writing focused, addressing a specific feeling about or a specific part of the topic? (The focus is usually expressed in the thesis statement.)
- ☐ **3.** Are there enough specific ideas, details, and examples to support the thesis?
- ☐ **4.** Overall, is the writing engaging and informative?

Organization

- ☐ **5.** Does the writing form a meaningful whole—with beginning, middle, and ending parts?
- ☐ **6.** Does the writing follow a logical pattern of organization?
- ☐ **7.** Do transitions connect ideas and help the writing flow?

Voice

- ☐ **8.** Does the writer sound informed about and interested in the topic?
- ☐ **9.** In addition, does the writer sound sincere and genuine?

Word Choice

- ☐ **10.** Does the word choice clearly fit the purpose and the audience?
- ☐ **11.** Does the writing include specific words as much as possible?

Sentence Fluency

- ☐ **12.** Are the sentences clear and do they flow smoothly?
- ☐ **13.** Are the sentences varied in terms of their beginnings and length?

Traits

Word choice and sentence fluency are not as important as the other traits at this point. But they become very important during the editing step.

React Carefully read the passages below. Then answer the questions dealing with ideas in the first passage, organization in the second, and voice in the third.

Ideas As a wrestling cheerleader in high school, I witnessed many meets and many matches. But one meet, in particular, really stands out. Just as the meet against Parkview was to start, the 98-pounder from the other school came out on the mat. He was small and narrow in every way, except for his oversized shoulder muscles. But it wasn't the boy's build that shocked me as much as the way he moved. He could barely walk, even with the help of crutches. And once on the mat, he had to drag himself into position. We all were in awe; we couldn't believe that this boy was going to wrestle. The next year, he wrestled again. He lost both matches that I saw, but he didn't quit. . . .

1. Is the topic relevant and interesting? Explain.

____

2. Is the writing focused? Explain.

____

3. Does the writing contain plenty of detail? Explain.

____

Organization Being vice president of the United States is not necessarily the road to the presidency. In fact, fewer than half of our country's vice presidents have gone on to the Oval Office. To be exact, 14 vice presidents have become president, while 30 have not. At certain times in our history, a number of consecutive terms have expired before a vice president followed a president into office. Between 1805 and 1837, seven consecutive terms passed before a vice president—Martin Van Buren—was elected president. . . .

1. What transitions are used in this passage? Underline two or three of them.
2. What do the transitions add to or do for the writing?

____

____

Voice The appearance of comets in the night skies has puzzled people for thousands of years. The first stargazers thought they were distant planets. Aristotle and the astronomers of his time theorized that they were the result of air escaping from the earth's atmosphere and catching fire. It wasn't until the fifteenth and sixteenth centuries that scientists realized comets were unique heavenly bodies. But that didn't change the long-standing myth that the sighting of a comet meant impending disaster. . . .

Does the writer sound informed about and interested in the topic? Explain.

____

____

Learning Outcome

Understand the basic revising moves.

"By the time I reach a fifth version, [my writing] begins to have its own voice."
—Ashley Bryan

LO3 Understanding the Basic Moves

You have four basic moves that you can make when you are ready to improve your writing. Depending on the situation, you can add, cut, rewrite, or reorder your ideas.

Add information if . . .

- your beginning or ending lacks **impact**.
- additional main points are needed.
- you need to clarify or complete a main point.

> , and to a homesick girl they held no holiday promise.
> The cinder-block walls of the living room were cold and unfriendly. The forlorn evergreen stood in the corner like a misbehaving child . . .

Cut information if . . .

- it doesn't support or explain your main points (including your thesis).
- it simply repeats what has already been said.

> Quietly I tiptoed into the room, my eyes darting like water bugs, searching for lizards. ~~I looked left and right for the bugs.~~ What a strange, silent Christmas it was going to be. . . .

Rewrite information if . . .

- it isn't clear and easy to follow.
- the level of language (voice) doesn't fit with the rest of the writing.

> Slowly I crept toward the electrical outlet and inserted the plug. ~~To my utter amazement the lights illuminated the room quite impressively.~~ A thousand brilliant lights danced upon the tree. And in the darkness beyond the window . . .

Reorder information if . . .

- it is out of logical order.
- it would make a clearer impact in another spot.

> The villagers stood hand in hand by the living room window. I found out that I wasn't alone. I could see the wonder and delight in each of their eyes.

Test Taking

For some prompted writing tasks, you may be expected to revise your work. For others, you may not. Make sure you understand the way the test will be graded.

Vocabulary

impact
effect or value

Write Develop the first draft of a paragraph in which you describe a favorite class or instructor or a favorite job or employer. Include at least six or seven sentences.

React Evaluate your writing using pages 64 and 65 as a guide. Then, in the space provided below, identify two or three changes that you would make to improve the paragraph.

1.

2.

3.

Learning Outcome

Learn the basics of peer reviewing.

"What you say must be honest, but you don't have to say everything you feel."
—Ken Macrorie

Insight

Working with your writing peers may be one of the most important strategies that you can use to improve your writing. So get into the habit of sharing your work.

Andresr, 2010/used under license from www.shutterstock.com

Vocabulary

constructively
in a helpful manner

LO4 Reviewing with Peers

It always helps to have your peers review your work during the revising process. Their reactions can help you find ways to strengthen your writing. The following guidelines tell you how to conduct peer-review sessions, whether you are working with one partner or in a small group.

The Role of the Writer

1. **Have a complete piece of writing to share.** Make a copy for each group member.
2. **Set the scene** by making a few introductory comments about your work. But don't say too much.
3. **Read your work out loud.** Don't stop for explanations; just read the text as clearly as you can.
4. **Afterward, listen carefully to the reactions,** and answer any questions. Don't try to defend yourself or your writing. Just listen and take notes on important points.
5. **Ask for help** if you have concerns about certain parts.

The Role of the Listeners/Responders

1. **Pay careful attention during the reading.** Take brief notes if you think it would help. Then read the text silently.
2. **React positively and constructively.** Instead of saying "Nice start," for example, say something more exact, such as "Sharing that dramatic story in the beginning really made me take notice."
3. **Comment on specific things you noticed.** Saying, "It would be good to add more style to your writing" isn't very helpful. But saying, "Many of the sentences start in the same way" gives the writer a specific idea for improving the writing.
4. **Question the writer** if you are unsure of something. "What is the purpose of . . . ?" or "Why did you start the . . . ?"
5. **Show that you are really interested in helping.** Have at least one positive comment and one suggestion to offer. Also listen to others' comments and add to them.

Share Following the guidelines on the previous page, conduct a peer-responding session for the first draft you wrote on page 67. (Work with one partner or a small group of your peers.) List one or two helpful suggestions that were made about your work.

1. __________

2. __________

Revise In the space below, write another draft of your paragraph based on your own review and the response of your peers.

Learning Outcome

Review the revising process.

LO5 Reviewing Revision

Complete these activities as needed to help you better understand the revising process.

Understanding Reviewing and Revising Number these revising steps so they are in the correct order. (See page 62.)

_____ Read your first draft a number of times.
_____ Take some time away from your writing.
_____ Lastly, plan your revising strategy.
_____ Have a trusted peer or two react to your writing.
_____ Check your overall focus or thesis.
_____ Then review your work, part by part.

Recognizing Strong Writing Donald Murray said that without good information there can be no good writing. So how can you tell if a piece of writing contains good ideas or information? Name two things that you will find. (See pages 64–65.)

1. ____

2. ____

Understanding the Basic Moves Fill in the blank with the appropriate revising move—adding, cutting, rewriting, or reordering information—for each of the following situations. (See page 66.)

____________________ 1. A main point needs more support.
____________________ 2. The language doesn't fit the rest of the draft.
____________________ 3. An idea is unrelated to your focus or thesis.

Reviewing with Peers The first responsibility of a peer reviewer is to carefully listen to or read a writer's draft. What are two additional responsibilities for a reviewer? (See page 68.)

____
____
____
____
____

"Grammar is the piano I play by ear."

—Joan Didion

masahiro Makino/Flickr/Getty Images

8 Editing

Editing is the process of checking the style and accuracy of your writing. You're ready to focus on this step once you have completed all of your major revisions. Think of editing as the process of **fine-tuning** your writing before sharing it.

The first part of this chapter covers style, with special attention given to word choice and sentence **fluency**. The second part covers correctness, offering strategies for finding and fixing errors, an explanation of the common editing symbols, and information about editing academic writing. When you are ready to edit for correctness, be sure to refer to pages 194–394 in *WRITE 1* for explanations and examples of the rules or conventions of the language.

Learning Outcomes

LO1 Understand the basics of word choice.

LO2 Learn about sentence fluency.

LO3 Learn how to check for correctness.

LO4 Edit academic writing.

LO5 Review editing.

Vocabulary

fine-tuning
making small changes or adjustments

fluency
smooth expression or flow of ideas

What do you think?

How can grammar be "played by ear"?

Learning Outcome

Understand the basics of word choice.

LO1 Understanding Word Choice

When it comes to word choice, the first **rule of thumb** is to use words that fit the audience and purpose of your writing. For example, the words used in a personal essay would not necessarily be appropriate for a report or research paper.

Pay special attention to the nouns and verbs you use since they carry and influence much of the meaning and style of your writing. The information that follows serves as a guide to using nouns and verbs.

Using Specific Nouns

Nouns name people, places, ideas, and objects, and they range from the very general (*man* or *drink*) to the very specific (*Barack Obama* or *mango juice*). Notice how the nouns become more specific in the chart below. When it comes to your writing, specific nouns almost always work better than general ones.

Insight

To build a strong working vocabulary for your writing, do these three things: (1) become a regular reader; (2) keep a vocabulary notebook, recording new and interesting words as you come across them; and (3) learn how to use a thesaurus and a dictionary.

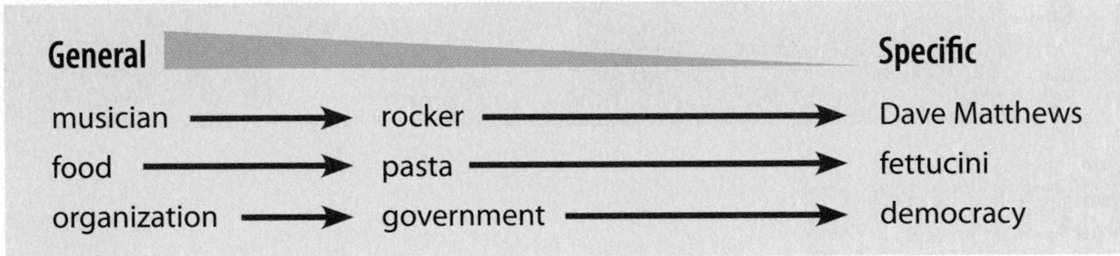

Complete Fill in the blanks below with nouns that become more specific.

General → Specific

People:

_______________ _______________ _______________

_______________ _______________ _______________

Objects:

_______________ _______________ _______________

_______________ _______________ _______________

Ideas:

_______________ _______________ _______________

_______________ _______________ _______________

Extend

On your own paper, write five or six sentences about one of your favorite classes or one of your best jobs. Afterward, underline the nouns that you have used; then replace at least two of these nouns with more specific ones.

Vocabulary

rule of thumb
a practical or useful approach based on experience

Using Specific Verbs

Action verbs tell what is happening in a sentence. A specific action verb like *examine* will usually work better than a general one like *look* because it is more exact. Listed below are a few additional **synonyms** for *look*; each one is more exact and interesting.

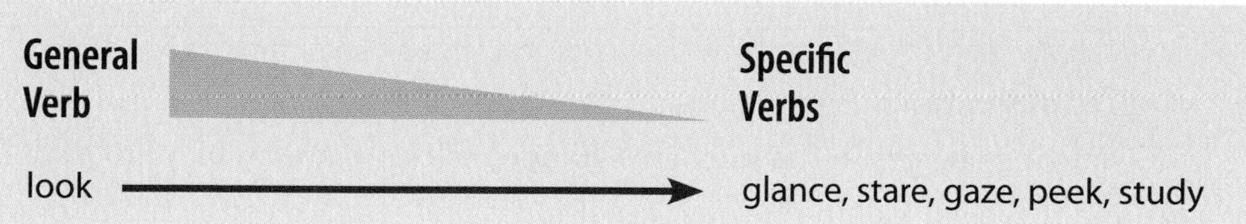

"It is with words as with sunbeams—the more they are condensed, the deeper they burn."
—Robert Southey

Complete List three or four specific verbs for two of the following general verbs: *give, laugh, think,* or *make*. Use the example above as a guide.

General verb: ______________ Specific verbs: ______________

General verb: ______________ Specific verbs: ______________

______________ ______________

______________ ______________

Watch for "Be" Verbs

Overusing "be" verbs (*is, are, was,* and *were*) can weaken your writing, so always look for ways to use action verbs.

Sentence with a "be" verb:

Maria Posada **is** the supervisor of the nursing trainees.

Sentence with an action verb:

Maria Posada **supervises** the nursing trainees.

Extend

Circle the main verbs that you used in the sentences that you wrote for the Extend feature on the previous page. Replace at least two or three of these verbs (including linking verbs) with more specific action verbs.

Revise Rewrite each of the following sentences so that it contains a specific action verb rather than a linking verb. (You can often form an action verb from another word in the sentence.)

Sentence with a "be" verb: Ben Franklin was a promoter of free access to books.

Sentence with an action verb: ______________

____

Sentence with a "be" verb: Scooters are a dominant feature of modern European traffic.

Sentence with an action verb: ______________

____

Vocabulary

synonyms
words having similar meaning

Learning Outcome

Learn about sentence fluency.

Traits

Sentences that all sound the same become too predictable and are actually hard to read.

LO2 Writing Fluent Sentences

Your writing will be stylistic if the sentences are fluent, or flow smoothly from one idea to the next. To achieve sentence fluency, vary your sentences in terms of their length and beginnings. Note how the sentences in the following passage flow smoothly:

> Fred's Sandwich Shop opens in the back onto an alley. Last night, while cutting veggies in the kitchen, I happened to see a man in a tailored suit and a typical looking townie in a T-shirt and jeans meet in the alley behind our dumpster. They were not more than 20 feet away from me. Without any real caution, the townie handed the man a roll of bills, and in return, received a package wrapped in brown paper. A quick examination of the goods and a simple nod signaled the end of the transaction, and they both went their separate ways. This whole drug deal took less than 45 seconds.
>
> **Discussion:** The passage reads smoothly because, among other things, no two sentences start in the same way, and the sentences vary in length from 9 to 35 words.

Create In the space provided below, describe an exciting or surprising event that you witnessed. Try to write at least five or six sentences.

____

____

____

____

____

____

____

____

____

____

Review Circle the first two or three words in each of your sentences. Also count the number of words in each sentence. Then decide if you need to vary some of the beginnings or lengths of your sentences to make them more fluent. If so, rewrite the passage on your own paper.

A Closer Look at Fluency

One way to achieve sentence fluency is to combine series of shorter sentences into longer ones that read more smoothly. Combining sentences is one of the keys to becoming a better writer, helping you to present your ideas in a more **sophisticated** way.

Vocabulary

sophisticated
improved and polished

Read Study the three short sentences that follow. Then notice how the ideas flow more smoothly when they are combined.

Shorter Sentences

Last weekend, Moira prepared lunches at Brighton Hall.
Brighton Hall is a local community center.
The lunches consisted of soup and sandwiches.

Combined Sentence

Last weekend, Moira prepared lunches of soup and sandwiches at Brighton Hall, a local community center.

"Putting style in almost always clutters up writing; removing clutter gives writing style."
—William Zinsser

Create Follow the directions below to combine the following sentences in various ways. (Add, delete, or change words as necessary.)

1. There was a power failure.
2. The power failure hit the school.
3. The power failure hit without warning.
4. The failure left the lower-level classes completely in the dark.
5. The failure left the tech-ed classes without operable equipment.
6. The failure left the cafeteria with half-cooked food.

1. Combine the first three sentences.

____

____

2. Combine the last three sentences.

____

____

3. Combine sentences three and four using the word *which* to introduce one of the ideas.

____

____

4. Complete this sentence:

When the power failure hit, ____

____

Learning Outcome

Learn how to check for correctness.

LO3 Checking for Correctness

You're ready to focus on correctness once you have edited your writing for style. When editing for correctness, you check your writing for punctuation, capitalization, spelling, and grammar errors.

Traits

If you pay too much attention to correctness too soon, you may ignore the most important part of your writing—your ideas. Think ideas before conventions, always.

Strategies for Editing

There are many different types of errors to look for. This means you must examine your writing word for word and sentence by sentence. The following strategies will help you edit thoroughly and effectively.

- If possible, first set your writing aside for a day or two.
- Work with a clean copy of your writing, one that incorporates your revisions and stylistic changes.
- Check one element at a time—spelling, punctuation, subject-verb agreement, and so on.
- For spelling, start at the bottom of the page to force yourself to look at each word. (Remember that your spell-checker will not catch all types of spelling errors.)
- For punctuation, circle all the marks to force yourself to look at each one.
- Read your work aloud at least once, noting any errors as you go along.
- Refer to a list of common errors or a personal list of errors you often make.
- Have an editing guide (see pages 194–394 in this text) and a dictionary handy.
- Also ask a trusted classmate to edit your work.

Respond In the space provided below, identify three of these strategies that you think would be most helpful. Explain your choices. Afterward, share responses with your classmates.

Using Editing Symbols

You, as well as an instructor or a writing tutor, can use editing symbols to mark errors in your writing. Listed below are some of the most common symbols.

Symbol	Meaning	Symbol	Meaning
chicago (C above, triple underline)	Capitalize a letter.	my ∧ speech (first)	Insert here.
Fall (slash through F)	Make lowercase.	∧ ∧ ∧ (, : ;)	Insert a comma, a colon, or a semicolon.
Mr. Ford (circled period)	Insert (add) a period.	∨ ∨ ∨ (' " ")	Insert an apostrophe or quotation marks.
Sp. or (recieve)	Correct spelling.	? ! ∧ ∧	Insert a question mark or an exclamation point.
Mr. Lott ~~he~~	Delete (take out) or replace.	possible worst (switch)	Switch words or letters.

"No iron can pierce the heart with such force as a period put just at the right place."
—Isaac Babel

tan4ikk, 2010/used under license from www.shutterstock.com

Edit Use the editing symbols above to mark the errors in the following piece and show how they should be corrected. The first error has been marked for you.

When we lived on Maple street (S), we had a neighbor who seemed to have two personalities his name was Mr. Bunde. I worked for him one Summer while I was in grade school, cutting his lawn and doing other yard work. After a few months of working for him I'd had more than enough. In general, he was a nice enough guy and he likes to joke around some of the time. Unfortunately, it was hard to tell if he was really kidding or if his mood was suddenly changing. When he was in one of his moods I couldn't do anything rite. Sometimes he would complain about other neighbors and he would expect me to agree with him, even though he new they were my friends. I not only have to concentrate on my work but I also had to be on my guard, trying to predict Mr. Bundes mood. Why did I have to work for him

Traits

The second part of *WRITE 1* provides grammar, punctuation, capitalization, and spelling practice to help you improve your editing skills.

Learning Outcome

Edit academic writing.

Insight

The level of language used by your friends may be much different from the level of language expected in academic writing. Develop the ability to shift into semiformal language as needed.

Extend

On your own paper, write the same brief message twice, using a different writing style for each version. You can choose between these three styles: very personal, informal, or semiformal.

LO4 Editing Academic Writing

Everyday writing may have an informal style, but academic writing should have a semiformal writing style. The following information identifies the basics of these two styles.

Informal

This is a somewhat relaxed style of writing often used when communicating via e-mail, letters, blogs, narratives, personal essays, and so on. This style is often signaled by . . .

- **contractions** *(I'll, she's, can't)*,
- **popular expressions** *(Can you believe that!)*,
- **cliches** *(blew his top)*,
- **first-person references** *(It took me a long time . . .)*, **and**
- **occasional fragments** *(Not if I can help it)*.

Semiformal

This is a careful, all-purpose style of writing that you will use in most of your academic essays, articles, reports, and papers. This style is signaled by . . .

- **few contractions** *(A strict vegetarian will not . . .)*,
- **carefully chosen words** *(The recycled lumber can withstand . . .)*,
- **few, if any, cliches,**
- **few, if any, first-person references** *(The election proved . . .)* **and**
- **carefully constructed sentences.**

Respond Decide if each of the following passages demonstrates an informal or a formal style of writing. Explain each of your choices.

1. Science fiction is not always, as some people believe, a second-rate, comic-book literary **genre**.

   ____ Informal ____ Semiformal

   ____

   ____

2. We were really scared when the cops pulled us over on I-65. Who wouldn't be?

   ____ Informal ____ Semiformal

   ____

   ____

3. Elderly people in Milwaukee often struggle to pay their utility bills during the coldest months of the year. One utility advocacy group reports that . . .

   ____ Informal ____ Semiformal

   ____

   ____

cliches
overused expressions or ideas, such as *sharp as a tack*

genre
category, type, or class

LO5 Reviewing Editing

Learning Outcome

Review editing.

Complete these activities as needed to help you better understand the editing process.

Word Choice In the space provided below, write two or three sentences about your favorite restaurant. Afterward, underline the nouns and circle the verbs in your writing. Replace any general words with more specific ones. (See pages 72–73 for help.)

Sentence Fluency Explain, in the space below, two ways that you can vary your sentences and make them read more smoothly. (See pages 74–75 for help.)

Editing for Correctness Edit the following sentences using the symbols on page 77 to mark the errors and show how they should be corrected.

have you ever traveled to another Country I no from personal experience that it can be an exciting experience. I spent six moths in london England.

Academic Writing Style There are two basic writing styles—informal and semiformal. Explain the differences between the two styles. (See page 78 for help.)

Informal style

Semiformal style

Part 3 Developing Paragraphs and Essays

"Art is the imposing of a pattern on experience, and our aesthetic enjoyment is recognition of the pattern."

—Alfred North Whitehead

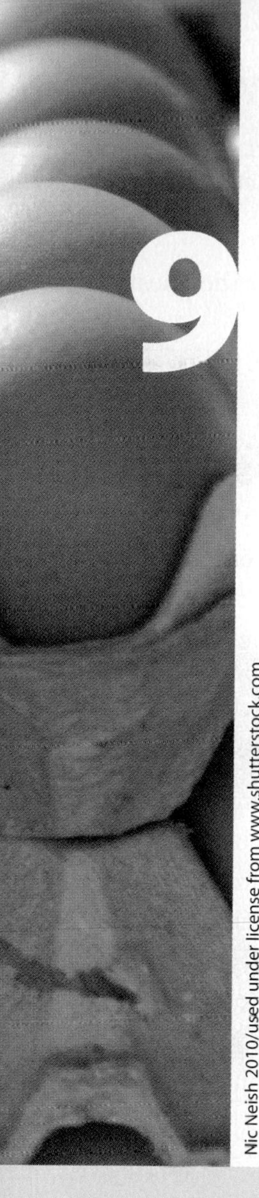

Nic Neish 2010/used under license from www.shutterstock.com

9 Description, Illustration, and Definition

Consider the lowly egg carton. It has a very simple pattern—a series of hollows designed to preserve eggs in their dozens. A milk carton has a different pattern—rectangular, with a cardboard spout for pouring. And a Chinese-food carton has another pattern, a single piece of waxed cardboard folded into a trapezoid and clasped at the top.

Paragraphs have different patterns, too, based on what they hold. Some paragraphs hold descriptions, others illustrations, and others definitions. This chapter provides models and prompts to help you develop these basic patterns of paragraphs. Later chapters guide you through developing even more advanced patterns. Each is designed to hold a certain kind of thinking.

What do you think?

What would happen to eggs in a milk carton, or Chinese food in an egg carton, or milk in a cigarette carton?

Learning Outcomes

LO1 Analyze a descriptive paragraph.

LO2 Write a descriptive paragraph.

LO3 Analyze an illustration paragraph.

LO4 Write an illustration paragraph.

LO5 Analyze a definition paragraph.

LO6 Write a definition paragraph.

LO7 Review description, illustration, and definition.

Learning Outcome

Analyze a descriptive paragraph.

LO1 Analyzing a Descriptive Paragraph

A descriptive paragraph paints a word picture. It uses strong sensory details—sights, sounds, smells, tastes, and textures—to describe its subject. Descriptive writing is often used in narratives.

Read/React Read the following descriptive paragraph and answer the questions at the bottom of the page.

A Quixotic Statue

The **topic sentence** identifies the subject and expresses the writer's thought about it.

Body sentences provide an overall impression and specific sensory details.

The **closing sentence** describes the importance of the object.

The Don Quixote statuette my dad gave me isn't worth much. It stands about a foot high and depicts a gaunt old man in battered armor sitting astride a swayback horse. The helmet on Quixote's head is dented, its visor bent above bushy eyebrows, squinting eyes, a wide wedge of a nose, and a rampant mustache and beard. His breastplate and shield are so worn that whatever emblems they once held have been pummeled into obscurity. The statue looks like rough-cast pewter, but when I accidentally knocked it over, it smashed on the floor, revealing itself to be painted plaster. I scooped up the jaggy chunks and did my best to stick them back together. Now seams of seeping glue and off-color paint crisscross the figure, and electrician's tape clings to the bent lance. Despite these flaws, despite dust and cobwebs, Quixote still manages to stare out with a look of inexhaustible hope. The statuette wasn't worth much when Dad gave it to me, and it's worth even less now. But somehow, after all this time and all this glue and tape, the statue means even more to me.

dubassy 2010/used under license from www.shutterstock.com

1. What does the paragraph describe?

____

____

2. Write down key details from the model:

Sights	Sounds	Textures

3. How does the writer organize the details of this description?

____

____

____

Vocabulary

quixotic
idealistic; unrealistic

Don Quixote
(Don Kee-HOE-tee) an idealistic man who thinks he is a knight of old and battles windmills, thinking they are dragons; from Cervantes' book of the same name

LO2 Writing a Descriptive Paragraph

To write your own descriptive paragraph, follow these guidelines for prewriting, writing, revising, and editing.

Learning Outcome

Write a descriptive paragraph.

Prewriting

List/Select Under each category, list favorite objects. Then choose one object you know well and could describe in a paragraph.

Clothes	Foods	Decorations

Gather Write down key sensory details about the object you have chosen.

See	Hear	Smell	Taste	Touch

Create Answer the following questions to create a topic sentence for your essay.

1. What is your topic? ______

2. What interesting thought or feeling do you have about it? ______

3. Write a sentence that names the topic and expresses the thought or feeling.

______

Write Create a first draft of your description paragraph, following the paragraph outline below:

Paragraph Outline

Topic Sentence: Begin with the topic sentence you wrote on the previous page.

Body Sentences: Write a sentence that provides an overview of the favorite object. Follow with sentences that provide sensory details in a reasonable order (top to bottom, left to right, outside to inside).

Closing Sentence: Write a sentence that sums up the object's meaning to you.

WAC

Description is crucial in all branches of study, whether you are describing a natural system, a computer component, a form of government, or a famous sculpture.

Revising

Revise Read your paragraph and, if possible, have someone else read it as well. Then use the following checklist to guide your revision. Keep revising until you can check off each item in the list.

Ideas

☐ **1.** Does my paragraph describe an interesting object?
☐ **2.** Do I provide an overview of the object?
☐ **3.** Do I include a variety of sensory details—sights, sounds, smells, and so on?

Organization

☐ **4.** Does my topic sentence name the object and provide an interesting thought or feeling about it?
☐ **5.** Do the body sentences provide sensory details in a logical order (top to bottom, left to right, outside to inside)?
☐ **6.** Does my closing sentence tell what the object means to me?

Voice

☐ **7.** Does my writing voice reflect the object's meaning to me?
☐ **8.** Does my voice engage the reader?

Editing

Edit Create a clean copy of your paragraph and use the following checklist to check it for words, sentences, and conventions.

Words

☐ **1.** Have I used specific nouns and verbs? (See page 103.)
☐ **2.** Have I used more action verbs than "be" verbs? (See page 73.)

Sentences

☐ **3.** Have I varied the beginnings and lengths of sentences? (See pages 226–231.)
☐ **4.** Have I combined short choppy sentences? (See page 232.)
☐ **5.** Have I avoided shifts in sentences? (See page 278.)
☐ **6.** Have I avoided fragments and run-ons? (See pages 261–266, 270–271.)

Conventions

☐ **7.** Do I use correct verb forms (*he saw,* not *he seen*)? (See pages 320, 324.)
☐ **8.** Do my subjects and verbs agree (*she speaks,* not *she speak*)? (See pages 245–260.)
☐ **9.** Have I used the right words (*their, there, they're*)?
☐ **10.** Have I capitalized first words and proper nouns and adjectives? (See page 386.)
☐ **11.** Have I used commas after long introductory word groups? (See page 358.)
☐ **12.** Have I carefully checked my spelling?

Learning Outcome

Analyze an illustration paragraph.

LO3 Analyzing an Illustration Paragraph

An illustration paragraph provides examples to support a main point. Many types of college writing require the use of illustrations and examples.

Read/React Read the following illustration paragraph and answer the questions at the bottom of the page.

The Elsewhere Generation

The **topic sentence** provides the main point.

Body sentences give examples that illustrate the main point.

The **closing sentence** recasts the main point in an interesting way.

With their immersion in social media, **millennials** are being called the "Elsewhere Generation." Quite often, a millennial will ignore people in the same room while virtually interacting with people elsewhere. A teenage boy plays a massively multiplayer online role-playing game with people in a different country while his brothers beg him to play basketball outside. A group of friends sits in a cafe, but instead of talking to each other, they are texting people who are miles away. A student is listening to a lecture while typing a status update on Facebook. Two joggers run side by side, but each is talking on a headset to someone elsewhere. This constant **multitasking** means that millennials can interact with many people in many places at once. Sometimes, though, millennials seem to be everywhere and nowhere at the same time.

1. What is the main point of the paragraph?

____

____

____

2. List examples that illustrate the main point:

Example A: ______________________________

Example B: ______________________________

Example C: ______________________________

Example D: ______________________________

3. How does the writer sum up the main point of this paragraph?

____

____

____

Bakaleev Aleksey/iStockphoto.com

Vocabulary

millennial
a person born between the mid 1970s and the early 2000s

multitasking
doing many things simultaneously

LO4 Writing an Illustration Paragraph

To write your own illustration paragraph, follow these guidelines for prewriting, writing, revising, and editing.

Learning Outcome

Write an illustration paragraph.

Prewriting

Answer Respond to the following questions to select a topic and gather details about it.

1. What is the best thing about your generation? ____________________

____

2. What is the worst thing about your generation? ____________________

____

3. How is your generation unique? ____________________

____

____

4. Which observation above could you write about in an illustration paragraph?

____

____

5. Considering your chosen observation, write a topic sentence that states this idea and expresses a thought or feeling about it.

____

____

____

6. Write four examples that illustrate the main point you have made in your topic sentence.

Example A: ____________________

____

Example B: ____________________

____

Example C: ____________________

____

Example D: ____________________

____

Write Create a first draft of your illustration paragraph, following the paragraph outline below:

Paragraph Outline

Topic Sentence: Begin with the topic sentence you wrote on the previous page.

Body Sentences: Write sentences that provide examples that illustrate the main point you made about your generation. Use transitions as needed to connect your ideas.

Closing Sentence: Write a sentence that sums up your main point or recasts it in an interesting way.

Traits

As you write, focus on ideas—supporting your topic sentence with a variety of interesting, engaging details.

Revising

Revise Read your paragraph and, if possible, have someone else read it as well. Then use the following checklist to guide your revision. Keep revising until you can check off each item in the list.

Ideas

- ☐ **1.** Do I make an interesting observation about my generation?
- ☐ **2.** Do I provide a number of examples that illustrate the observation?

Organization

- ☐ **3.** Does my topic sentence state the observation and a thought or feeling about it?
- ☐ **4.** Do the body sentences give examples that illustrate my main point?
- ☐ **5.** Does my closing sentence reflect on my main point?

Voice

- ☐ **6.** Does my writing voice sound knowledgeable and interested?
- ☐ **7.** Do I share ideas in a way that engages the reader?

Editing

Edit Create a clean copy of your paragraph and use the following checklist to check it for words, sentences, and conventions.

Words

- ☐ **1.** Have I used specific nouns and verbs? (See page 103.)
- ☐ **2.** Have I used more action verbs than "be" verbs? (See page 73.)

Sentences

- ☐ **3.** Have I varied the beginnings and lengths of sentences? (See pages 226–231.)
- ☐ **4.** Have I combined short choppy sentences? (See page 232.)
- ☐ **5.** Have I avoided shifts in sentences? (See page 278.)
- ☐ **6.** Have I avoided fragments and run-ons? (See pages 261–266, 270–271.)

Conventions

- ☐ **7.** Do I use correct verb forms (*he saw,* not *he seen*)? (See pages 320, 324.)
- ☐ **8.** Do my subjects and verbs agree (*she speaks,* not *she speak*)? (See pages 245–260.)
- ☐ **9.** Have I used the right words (*their, there, they're*)?
- ☐ **10.** Have I capitalized first words and proper nouns and adjectives? (See page 386.)
- ☐ **11.** Have I used commas after long introductory word groups? (See page 358.)
- ☐ **12.** Have I carefully checked my spelling?

Learning Outcome

Analyze a definition paragraph.

Insight

If you speak a language other than English, you could write a definition paragraph based on an English word that comes from your home language.

LO5 Analyzing a Definition Paragraph

A definition paragraph explores the meaning of a word, using the dictionary definition, origin, history, and other details. Definition writing is important in many forms of academic writing.

Read/React Read the following definition paragraph and then fill in the graphic organizer with details from the paragraph.

Looking for Utopia

The **topic sentence** identifies the term and gives a basic definition.

Body sentences explore the term in a number of ways.

The **closing sentence** leaves the reader with a final thought.

Everyone wishes to find a perfect place—a utopia that has no crime and no disease, where everyone is happy, healthy, wealthy, and wise. In fact, the word "utopia" would seem to mean "good place," coming from the Greek "eu" (good) and "topos" (place). However, the prefix in Greek is not "eu" but "ou," which means "not" or "no." That's right; "utopia" means "no place." Sir Thomas More coined the term in 1516, writing a book about a perfect place that didn't exist. His book was a satire, trying to show that a utopia wasn't possible. That didn't stop a number of utopian movements from springing up. In fact, one utopian community established in New Harmony, Indiana, proudly announced that it was based on ideas commended by Sir Thomas More. This 2,000-person communal city banned money but quickly dissolved due to quarrelling. Nathaniel Hawthorne tells in *The Scarlet Letter* why such utopias are bound to fail: "The founders of any new colony, whatever Utopia of human virtues and happiness they originally project, have invariably recognized it among their earliest practical necessities to allot a portion of the virgin soil as a cemetery, and another portion as the site of a prison." In other words, no utopia can exist as long as any humans are in it.

Utopia

definition	origin	history	quotation

LO6 Writing a Definition Paragraph

To write your own definition paragraph, follow these guidelines for prewriting, writing, revising, and editing.

Learning Outcome

Write a definition paragraph.

Prewriting

Associate Read each word below and write down the first word that occurs to you. Then choose one of the words you thought of as the subject of a definition essay.

Eat ______	Paint ______	Crab ______
Hand ______	Man ______	Goof ______
Heal ______	Light ______	Water ______
Leaf ______	Hook ______	Heap ______
Lie ______	Mistake ______	Lucky ______

Gather In the top box below, write the word you will define in your paragraph. Then research the term and write notes about its definition, origin, and history. Also find and record a quotation that uses the term.

Word to define:

definition	origin	history	quotation

Write Create a first draft of your definition paragraph, following the paragraph outline below:

Paragraph Outline

Topic Sentence: Write a topic sentence that names the term and gives a basic definition.

Body Sentences: Write sentences that explore the meaning and history of the term. Provide a quotation that uses the term.

Closing Sentence: Write a sentence that leaves the reader with an interesting final thought about the term.

WAC

Every discipline has a different vocabulary. Defining terms is an important starting point for any discussion.

Revising

Revise Read your paragraph and, if possible, have someone else read it as well. Then use the following checklist to guide your revision. Keep revising until you can check off each item in the list.

Ideas

☐ **1.** Does my paragraph focus on an interesting term?

☐ **2.** Do I explore the definition, origin, and history of the term?

☐ **3.** Do I include a quotation that uses the term?

Organization

☐ **4.** Does my topic sentence name the term and give a basic definition?

☐ **5.** Do the body sentences provide a variety of details about the term?

☐ **6.** Does my closing sentence leave the reader with a final interesting thought?

Voice

☐ **7.** Does my writing voice show my interest in the term?

☐ **8.** Does my voice engage the reader?

Editing

Edit Create a clean copy of your paragraph and use the following checklist to check it for words, sentences, and conventions.

Words

☐ **1.** Have I used specific nouns and verbs? (See page 103.)

☐ **2.** Have I used more action verbs than "be" verbs? (See page 73.)

Sentences

☐ **3.** Have I varied the beginnings and lengths of sentences? (See pages 226–231.)

☐ **4.** Have I combined short choppy sentences? (See page 232.)

☐ **5.** Have I avoided shifts in sentences? (See page 278.)

☐ **6.** Have I avoided fragments and run-ons? (See pages 261–266, 270–271.)

Conventions

☐ **7.** Do I use correct verb forms *(he saw,* not *he seen)*? (See pages 320, 324.)

☐ **8.** Do my subjects and verbs agree (*she speaks,* not *she speak*)? (See pages 245–260.)

☐ **9.** Have I used the right words (*their, there, they're*)?

☐ **10.** Have I capitalized first words and proper nouns and adjectives? (See page 386.)

☐ **11.** Have I used commas after long introductory word groups? (See page 358.)

☐ **12.** Have I carefully checked my spelling?

Learning Outcome

Review description, illustration, and definition.

LO7 Reviewing Description, Illustration, and Definition

Describe Pick out an object within view. Study it with your senses, handling it if possible. Then fill out the following sensory chart with details about the object. Afterward, on your own paper, write a paragraph describing the object.

See	Hear	Smell	Taste	Touch

Illustrate In the following statement, circle the word in parentheses that best describes your current schedule. Then write four examples that illustrate the statement. On your own paper, write an illustration paragraph about your schedule.

Statement: My current schedule is (incredibly/not) busy.

Example A: ______________________

Example B: ______________________

Example C: ______________________

Example D: ______________________

Define In the top box below, write a word that intrigues you. Then, in the boxes under it, write information about the word. On your own paper, write a definition paragraph about the term.

Word to define:

definition	origin	history	quotation

"I've never tried to block out the memories of the past, even though some are painful. I don't understand people who hide from their past. Everything you live through helps to make you the person you are now." —Sophia Loren

Photo by Jason Rogers

10 Narrative Paragraph

People are often inspired to *live in the now.* On this topic, American philosopher Ralph Waldo Emerson said, "With the past, I have nothing to do; nor with the future. I live now." In other words, what's done is done and your future is dependent on the opportunities you have today. Certainly this is worthy inspiration, but living in the moment doesn't mean you should let your past slip away.

Reflecting on a memorable past experience can give your life meaning as you discover how the experience shaped you to be the person you are today. A paragraph that shares such a memory is called a narrative paragraph.

This chapter will guide you through the process of writing a narrative paragraph about an unforgettable memory from your life. As well as sharing your story with others, be ready to relive it yourself.

Learning Outcomes

LO1 Understand personal paragraphs.

LO2 Plan a personal paragraph.

LO3 Write the first draft.

LO4 Revise the writing.

LO5 Edit the writing.

LO6 Reflect on the experience.

What do you think?

What does living in the now mean to you? Do you subscribe to this lifestyle? Why or why not?

Learning Outcome

Understand personal paragraphs.

LO1 Reviewing a Narrative Paragraph

Read/React Read the following paragraph. Then answer the questions below to identify your first impressions about it.

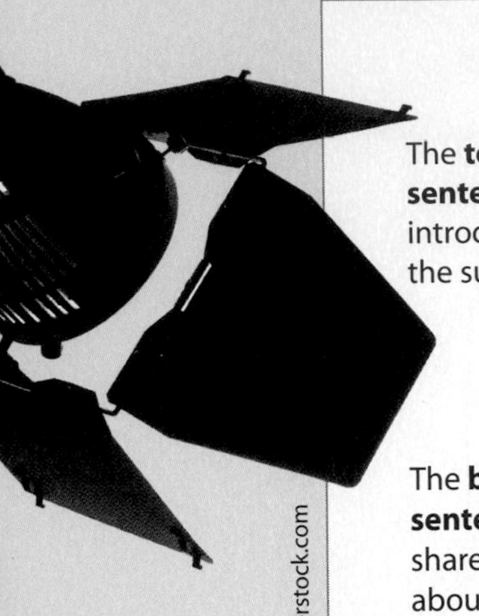

Taking a Bow

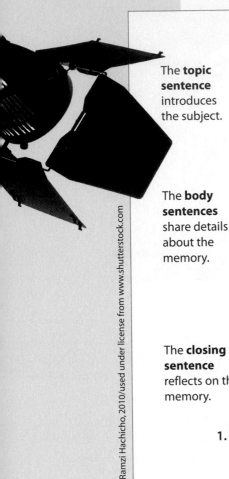

The **topic sentence** introduces the subject.

The **body sentences** share details about the memory.

The **closing sentence** reflects on the memory.

My final moments on stage during the musical *Grease* are ones I'll never forget. It was a Saturday night, and my high school's matchbox-sized theater was filled to capacity, only no one was sitting. We had finished singing our closing number and the cast, crew, and I stood hand in hand, soaking in a standing ovation. I couldn't help but feel a supreme sense of satisfaction. This was the culmination of three months of hard work. Heck, *tonight* was hard work. My voice was shot. My hair was frizzy. And sweat beads trickled down my brow, streaking globs of black mascara under my eyes. I looked like a mess, but I didn't care. Four rows into the audience my family was going bonkers. Dad pumped his fist as if the Steelers won the Super Bowl, while mom waved her hands in the air wildly. Under normal conditions, this type of behavior would make me run for cover, but not tonight. Eventually the curtain closed and my special night was over. I never did pursue a career in theater, but on that night, in that moment, Broadway didn't seem so faraway.

1. Name two things that you like about the paragraph. (Consider specific details, main ideas, particular sentences, and so on.)

   a. ______________________________

   ____

   b. ______________________________

   ____

2. List two questions that you have about the paragraph. (Is there something that you would like to know more about? Are there any words or phrases that you don't understand completely?)

   a. ______________________________

   ____

   b. ______________________________

   ____

A Closer Look

Rochelle used **thought details** to reveal her personal insights and feelings about her theater experience. Such details add meaning and authenticity to a personal paragraph.

Identify This chart includes three different kinds of thought details—sensations, emotions, and reflections. Review Rochelle's personal paragraph to find the thought details. Then write them in the appropriate column of the chart.

Thought Details

Sensations Think about sights, sounds, smells, tastes, feelings (touch).	**Emotions** Think of feelings—happiness, loneliness, indifference.	**Reflections** Think of opinions and conclusions.

Explain What type of thought detail are you most interested in hearing about from a writer? Why?

Traits

This graphic organizer helps you analyze the ideas in the reading. A similar organizer will help you gather ideas for your own writing.

Vocabulary

thought details
details that explore a writer's impressions, emotions, and reflections

Learning Outcome

Plan a personal paragraph.

LO2 Prewriting: Planning

In your own personal paragraph, you will write about an unforgettable memory. Think of a past time, place, or experience that holds significant meaning for you.

Selecting a Topic

Dan listed four experiences that he vividly remembers: the first day on his first job, his grandfather's funeral, his high school track championship, and his backpacking trip. He chose to write about his backpacking trip with his brother.

Select In the space below, list four unforgettable memories from your life. Then circle the one memory you would like to write about in a personal paragraph.

1. ________________
2. ________________
3. ________________
4. ________________

Traits

Transition words connect one sentence to another, strengthening organization. Narrative writing requires transitions that show time (see page 101).

Using Chronological Order

Once you have selected a topic, you should think closely about the order of events in your memory. In most cases, personal paragraphs are arranged according to time, or **chronological order**, placing events in the order in which they happened.

Vocabulary

chronological order
time order; relating details in the order that they occurred

Identify Use the time line below to list the main events of your memory chronologically.

1. ________________
2. ________________
3. ________________
4. ________________

Gathering Details

The most vivid personal paragraphs use plenty of sensory details. Such details allow the reader to picture, hear, and touch what you describe. Dan used a sensory chart to list specific sensory details about his backpacking trip.

Sensory Chart

Sights	Sounds	Smells	Tastes	Feelings (touch)
-forests of evergreens -dirt path -mountain ranges -thick fog	-talk with brother -birds chirping -crunching leaves	-fresh air -smell of rain	-peanut butter granola bar	-achy thighs -burning lungs

Gather Complete the sensory chart below. Collect any sights, sounds, smells, tastes, or feelings about your subject in the appropriate column.

Sights	Sounds	Smells	Tastes	Feelings (touch)

Learning Outcome

Write the first draft.

LO3 Writing: Creating a First Draft

Provided below is Dan's personal paragraph about a special moment in his life. He uses sensory and other thought details to clearly describe the moment.

Read/React Carefully read Dan's paragraph, paying attention to the way he organizes his story into a beginning, a middle, and an ending. Afterward, answer the questions about the paragraph.

A Rugged Ride

Topic Sentence | **Body Sentences** | **Closing Sentence**

Riding up the mountain trail, my thighs ached and my lungs burned, but I couldn't be happier. Fifty feet in front of me pedaled my brother, Keith, fresh off his tour with the Marines. This mountain biking adventure was his idea. The green, forest-lined trail was rugged, with sharp turns and steep descents. At one point we hit a patch of fog and I lost sight of Keith. It felt as if we were riding through clouds. The ghostly air was damp and smelled like rain. I slowed down and called for my brother, "Are you still up there?" "Would I be anywhere else?" he yelled back. When the fog disappeared, we stopped for a **breather** on a ridge that overlooked a vast valley. A sea of pointy **evergreens** stretched for miles, ending near the peak of a distant mountain. While I snacked on a peanut butter granola bar, Keith glanced over at me. "This is fun, isn't it," he commented. "It's good having you back, man," I responded. With that, we hopped on our bikes and continued our adventure.

1. What main feeling does Dan share in the topic sentence?

____

____

2. Identify at least three sensory or other thought details in the paragraph. Write them down.

____

____

3. What two things do you especially like in the paragraph? (Consider words, sentences, or ideas.)

____

____

Vocabulary

breather
a rest used to relax and slow your heartbeat

evergreens
trees with needle-like leaves that stay green throughout the year

Write Create a first draft of your paragraph using the ideas and details from your sensory chart (page 99). Use the paragraph outline below and transition words as you need them.

Paragraph Outline

Topic Sentence: Write a topic sentence that sets the stage for the paragraph. To set the right course, you should identify your topic and put it in perspective in an interesting way.

Body Sentences: Write body sentences that share details (sensations as well as emotions and reflections) about the subject and each main point.

Closing Sentence: Write a closing sentence (or two) that captures the significance of your experience.

Traits

Transition words that show time: after / at / before / during / finally / first / later / next / next week / now / second / soon / suddenly / third / then / today / until / when / while / yesterday

Learning Outcome

Revise the writing.

Speaking & Listening

Have your partner read your paragraph aloud. Then complete the response sheet together.

LO4 Revising: Improving the Writing

Revising involves sharing your work with a peer and improving your writing by adding, cutting, reworking, or rearranging material.

Peer Review

Sharing your writing is especially important when you are revising a first draft. The feedback that you receive will help you improve your paragraph. Use a peer-response sheet to respond to a classmate's writing, or to have a classmate respond to yours.

Respond Complete this response sheet after reading the first draft of a classmate's paragraph. Then share the sheet with the writer. (Keep your comments helpful and positive.)

Paragraph title: ______________________________

Writer: ____________________ Reviewer: ____________________

1. Which part seems to work best: topic sentence, middle, or closing sentence?

   Why? ______________________________

   ____

   ____

2. Which part needs some work? Why? ______________________________

   ____

   ____

   ____

3. Does the piece include any sensations, emotions, or reflections? Name them.

   ____

   ____

   ____

4. Identify a portion of the paragraph that illustrates the writer's passion for the subject.

   ____

   ____

   ____

Specific Nouns and Verbs

You can strengthen your paragraph by substituting specific nouns and verbs for those that are too general. Thoughtful, vivid words will make your writing more interesting.

General Noun vs.	Specific Noun
The **place** was beautiful.	The **valley** was beautiful.

General Verb vs.	Specific Verb
My thighs **hurt**.	My thighs **ached**.
My brother **rode** in front of me.	My brother **pedaled** in front of me.
There **were** evergreens everywhere.	The evergreens **stretched** for miles.
I **ate** a granola bar.	I **snacked** on a granola bar.

Revising in Action:

Read aloud the unrevised and then the revised version of the following excerpt. Note how the specific words energize the writing.

. . . we stopped for a ~~rest~~ breather on a ridge that overlooked ~~a large opening~~ a vast valley. ~~There were evergreens everywhere~~ A sea of pointy evergreens stretched for miles, ending near the peak of a distant mountain. While I ~~ate~~ snacked on a peanut butter granola bar…

Revise Improve your writing, using the checklist below and your partner's comments on the response sheet. Continue working until you can check off each item in the list.

Ideas

- ☐ **1.** Do I focus on one specific memory?
- ☐ **2.** Is the memory meaningful to me?
- ☐ **3.** Do I include sufficient sensory and other thought details?

Organization

- ☐ **4.** Do I have a topic sentence, body sentences, and a closing sentence?
- ☐ **5.** Is the paragraph organized chronologically?
- ☐ **6.** Have I used transitions to connect my sentences?

Voice

- ☐ **7.** Do I sound interested and sincere?

Insight

To learn new, more precise nouns and verbs, use a thesaurus to find new words, but then use a dictionary to understand the exact meaning of different words.

Learning Outcome

Edit the writing.

Speaking & Listening

Direct quotations should sound natural, as if the person is speaking. Read direct quotations out loud to check the way they sound.

LO5 Editing: Punctuating Dialogue

Dialogue refers to the words spoken by people and set apart with quotation marks.

Quotation Marks and Dialogue

In some personal paragraphs, **dialogue** may be used to capture the unique voices of the people involved in the story. When you recall or create conversations between people, you must use quotation marks before and after the speaker's exact words, also called a **direct quotation**. However, when you use an **indirect quotation**—one that does *not* use the speaker's exact words—quotation marks are not needed. See the examples that follow.

Direct quotation:

Sitting in my one-room apartment, I remember Mom saying, **"Don't go to the party with him."**

Indirect quotation:

I remember Mom saying **that I should not go to the party with him.**

Note: The words *if* and *that* often indicate dialogue that is being reported rather than quoted.

Punctuation Practice Read the sentences below. Place quotation marks (" ") before and after the words in direct quotations. If the sentence contains no direct quotations, write *correct* next to the sentence.

1. Christina, could you give me a ride to the airport? I asked. ________
2. You are one lucky guy, said Reid. ________
3. The tour guide said that we should get our cameras out. ________
4. There's little chance I'll ever eat octopus, joked Hailey. ________
5. Before we left I said, Don't forget your wallet and cell phone! ________
6. Kyle said if he goes to the movie tonight, he will miss the party. ________
7. Where did you get that dress? asked Brianna. ________
8. Derrick says that he thinks your sweater shrunk in the dryer. ________

Vocabulary

dialogue
a conversation between two people

direct quotation
a person's exact words

indirect quotation
a statement that reports a speaker's words

Apply Read your narrative paragraph. If you included any direct quotations, make sure they are properly marked with quotation marks. If you did not use any direct quotations, consider adding one or two to enliven and improve the voice of your writing.

Punctuation Used with Quotation Marks

As you edit your narrative paragraph, pay special attention to the punctuation marks used with quotation marks. In general, there are three special rules to follow:

- When periods or commas follow the quotation, place them before the closing quotation mark.

  "Never be afraid to ask for help**,**" advised Mr. Lee.

  "With the evidence we now have**,**" Professor Howard said**,** "many scientists believe there could be life on Mars**.**"

- When question marks or exclamation points follow the quotation, place them before the closing quotation mark if they belong with the quoted words. Otherwise, place them after the quotation mark.

  "Bill, do you want to go to the gym with me**?**" I asked.

  Were you telling the truth when you said, "Let's go home"**?**

- When semicolons or colons follow the quotation, place them after the quotation mark.

  He said, "Absolutely not"**;** however, he relented and left work early.

Insight

These rules for punctuating quotations reflect the U.S. standards. British English follows different rules.

Punctuation Practice In each sentence, correct the misplaced punctuation marks. (Use the transpose sign ∿.) Refer to the rules above for help.

1. "Please hand your papers in by the end of the week", advised Professor Hopkins.
2. Mark said, "See you soon;" however, he missed his flight.
3. "With everything that happened", my boss said ", it might be best to take Friday off."
4. "Don't be late"! exclaimed Lisa.
5. "Should we meet tomorrow"? asked Renee.
6. Did you really mean it when you said, "We are just looking?"
7. "Remember, you have a doctor appointment on Thursday", my mom reminded me.
8. "Can you pass me the ketchup"? I asked.

Apply Read your narrative paragraph. Check the punctuation of dialogue closely.

Marking a Paragraph

The model that follows has a number of errors.

Punctuation Practice Correct the following paragraph, using the correction marks to the left. One correction has been done for you.

Correction Marks

- 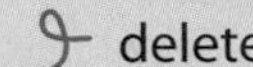 delete
- capitalize
- lowercase
- insert
- add comma
- add question mark
- add word
- add period
- spelling
- switch

Habits

People say I'm a creature of habit, but that's not entirely true. For instance I like try new foods. When I was in New hampshire, I ate raw oysters. People say they taste like the ocean Indeed they are very salty. I do enjoy the thrill of a new food however, oysters will not become a staple of my diet. Besides eating bizarre foods, I also enjoy going on weeknd adventures. Last saturday, my friends and I went camping outside of the city. We didn't even set up tents, opting to sleep under the stars. Unfortunately the rising sun woke us up at about 6:00 a.m. I only got about for hours of sleep, so I tired and crabby for the rest of the day. I guess that's won way I am a creature of habit. I like my sleep. Another unusual activity I enjoy is Pilates. For some reason my friends think this makes me a wimp but I bet they couldn't make it threw one class. I would love to see them try

Insight

You have seen how quotation marks are used before and after direct quotations. Quotation marks are also used around special words: (1) to show that a word is being discussed as a word, (2) to indicate that a word is slang, or (3) to point out that a word is being used in a humorous or ironic way.

(1) In our society, the word **"honesty"** is often preceded by the modifier **"old-fashioned."**

(2) You are wearing an **"old-school"** style of jeans.

(3) In an attempt to be popular, he works very hard at being **"cute."**

Correcting Your Paragraph

Now it's time to correct your own paragraph.

Apply Create a clean copy of your writing and use the following checklist to check for errors. When you can answer yes to a question, check it off. Continue working until all items are checked.

Editing Checklist

Words

- ☐ **1.** Have I used specific nouns and verbs? (See page 103.)
- ☐ **2.** Have I used more action verbs than "be" verbs? (See page 73.)

Sentences

- ☐ **3.** Have I varied the beginnings and lengths of sentences? (See pages 226–231.)
- ☐ **4.** Have I combined short choppy sentences? (See page 232.)
- ☐ **5.** Have I avoided shifts in sentences? (See page 278.)
- ☐ **6.** Have I avoided fragments and run-ons? (See pages 261–266, 270–271.)

Conventions

- ☐ **7.** Do I use correct verb forms *(he saw,* not *he seen)*? (See pages 320, 324.)
- ☐ **8.** Do my subjects and verbs agree (*she speaks,* not *she speak*)? (See pages 245–260.)
- ☐ **9.** Have I used the right words (*their, there, they're*)?
- ☐ **10.** Have I capitalized first words and proper nouns and adjectives? (See page 386.)
- ☐ **11.** Have I used commas after long introductory word groups? (See page 358.)
- ☐ **12.** Have I punctuated dialogue correctly? (See pages 104–105.)
- ☐ **13.** Have I carefully checked my spelling?

WAC

Use this checklist for editing writing assignments in all of your classes.

Adding a Title

Make sure to add an attention-getting title. Here are three simple strategies for creating one.

- **Use a phrase or a word from the paragraph:** Habits
- **Use a main idea from the paragraph:** Taking a Bow
- **Use strong, colorful words from the paragraph:** A Rugged Ride

Insight

Have a classmate, friend, or family member read your work to catch any missed errors.

Create Prepare a clean final copy of your paragraph and proofread it.

Learning Outcome

Reflect on the experience.

Photo by Jason Rogers

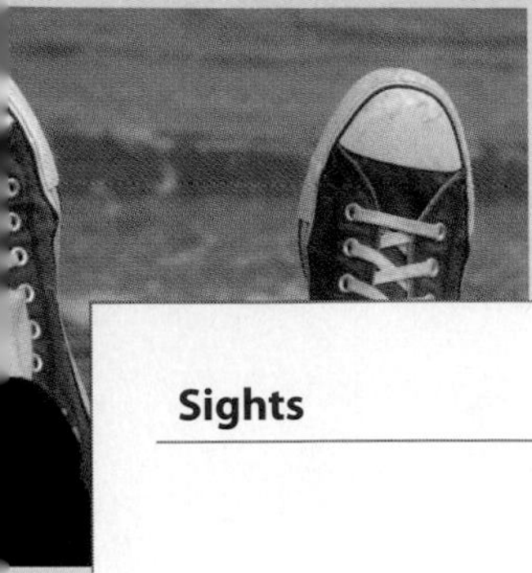

LO6 Reviewing Narrative Writing

Complete these activities as needed to help you better understand writing narrative paragraphs.

Fill In Look closely at the photograph. Imagine you are the person on the beach with the red shoes. What sensory details—sights, smells, sounds, and so on—do you experience? Write as many as you can in the sensory chart. (See page 99.)

Sights	Sounds	Smells	Tastes	Feelings (touch)

Define In your own words, define **chronological order**. (See page 98.)

Sort Circle the transitions that *show time:* (See page 101.)

first above before near next then

"I want all my senses engaged. Let me absorb the world's variety and uniqueness."

—Maya Angelou

11 Classification Paragraph

The word *fruit* describes thousands of varieties, from cherries to blueberries to plums. But each of those varieties has subcategories. For example, there are two main types of cherries—sweet and sour—and within those categories are many, many varieties, including the two shown above. Believe it or not, those yellow cherries are maraschinos *before* being dyed and processed into that sweet thing in a Shirley Temple.

A classification essay explores the varieties of something. It breaks down a topic into categories and subcategories. In this chapter, you will be writing a classification paragraph about a topic of your own selection.

Learning Outcomes

- **LO1** Understand classification paragraphs.
- **LO2** Plan a classification paragraph.
- **LO3** Write the first draft.
- **LO4** Revise the writing.
- **LO5** Edit the writing.
- **LO6** Review classification writing.

What do you think?

What is you favorite type of apple? Is it tart or sweet, red or green, soft or crisp? Why is it your favorite?

Learning Outcome

Understand classification paragraphs.

LO1 Reviewing a Paragraph

A classification paragraph analyzes a subject by breaking it into different categories or types.

Read/React Read the following classification paragraph and answer the questions below.

A Question of Taste

The **topic sentence** introduces the categories.

The **body sentences** describe each category.

The **closing sentence** leaves the reader with a final thought.

All the flavors that a person can taste are made up of a few basic taste sensations. In the Western world, people are used to thinking about four tastes: salty, sweet, sour, and bitter. The salty taste comes from substances that include sodium, such as snacks like potato chips or pretzels. The sweet sensation comes from sugars, whether in processed foods like sweetened cereals or naturally occurring in fruit or honey. Sour tastes come from acidic foods (pH below 7) such as lemons and grapefruit, and bitter tastes come from alkaline foods (pH above 7) such as coffee or dark chocolate. But in the Eastern world, two other taste sensations are recognized. A savory taste (**umami**) comes from amino acids, which are a basic part of meats and proteins. And a spicy taste (**piquancy**) comes from substances like the capsaicin in hot peppers. Given the savory and spicy nature of Indian, Thai, Chinese, and other Eastern foods, it's no wonder that these tastes are recognized. But other nontaste sensations also add to the enjoyment of food—aroma, color, shape, temperature, texture, dryness, and sound, just to name a few. With all the senses to appeal to, chefs can make every dish a unique work of art.

1. Name two things that you like about the paragraph. (Consider specific details, main ideas, particular sentences, and so on.)

   a. ____

   ____

   b. ____

   ____

2. Name two questions you have about the paragraph. (Is there something that you would like to know more about? Are there any words or phrases that you don't understand completely?)

   a. ____

   ____

   b. ____

   ____

Vocabulary

umami
the quality of being savory, or rich and meaty

piquancy
the quality of being spicy

A Closer Look

List Complete the chart below by writing the name of each taste sensation, a definition of that sensation, and examples of foods that create the taste. The first one has been done for you.

Type/Category	Definition	Examples
salty	a taste that contains sodium	potato chips or pretzels

Traits This organizer helps you analyze the reading, and will help you write your own classification paragraph.

Consider What nontaste sensations does the writer list? Why are these sensations not included in the main classification?

Learning Outcome

Plan a classification paragraph.

LO2 Prewriting: Planning

In your own classification paragraph, you will explore the categories or types of something. These two pages will help you select a topic and gather details about it.

Explore Read through the "Essentials of Life" list below. Select four general subject areas that you would like to explore. Then, for each subject area, write a possible topic. An example has been done for you.

Essentials of Life

food	intelligence	resources
clothing	personality	energy
shelter	senses	money
education	emotions	government
work	goals	laws
entertainment	health	rights
recreation	environment	science
religion	plants	measurement
family	animals	machines
friends	land	tools
community	literature	agriculture
communication	arts	business

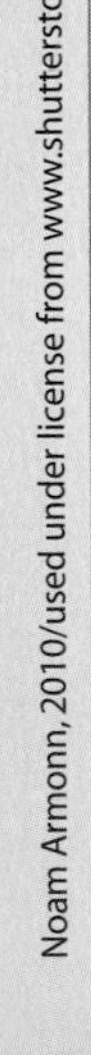

Example Subject Area:	**Example Topic:**
energy	Types of solar energy
1. Subject Area:	**Topic:**
____________	Types of ____________
2. Subject Area:	**Topic:**
____________	Types of ____________
3. Subject Area:	**Topic:**
____________	Types of ____________
4. Subject Area:	**Topic:**
____________	Types of ____________

Select Review the topics listed above and select one that could be broken down into 3 to 6 types (a number you could cover in a single paragraph).

Researching Your Topic

Once you have selected a topic, you'll want to find out more about it. Search Internet sites, encyclopedias, school texts, and other sources as necessary. As you break your topic into types or categories, consider the following:

Types or categories should be . . .

- **exclusive**, which means that one example doesn't fit into more than one category
- **consistent**, which means that examples of this category have the same traits

Organize In the chart below, list each type or category in the first column. In the second column, define the type or category. In the third column, write examples of the type or category.

Type/Category	Definition	Examples

WAC

Classification writing is key to the sciences, which classify everything from rocks and species to governments and people.

Vocabulary

exclusive category
a type that does not overlap with other types

consistent category
a type that contains examples that share the same traits

Learning Outcome

Write the first draft.

LO3 Writing: Creating a First Draft

As you prepare to write your own first draft, read the sample classification paragraph below, which focuses on different uses of solar power.

Read/React Carefully read the paragraph below, paying attention to the ways that the categories are named and defined as well as the examples that are provided. Afterward, answer the questions about the paragraph.

Plugging into Sunlight

Topic Sentence

With fossil fuels running out, people are learning more and more ways to use the free energy of the sun.

Body Sentences

The simplest form of solar energy is solar lighting, which means designing buildings to take advantage of natural light. A more advanced form is solar heating, or gathering the sun's warmth and using it to heat a building. The sun heats up a "thermal mass"—whether stone, cement, or water—which then radiates the heat. A third use of solar energy is solar cooking. Box cookers are insulated boxes with clear tops, and parabolic cookers use solar rays to boil water or cook food. A fourth use of solar energy provides drinkable water to millions of people. Solar water treatment devices can turn salt water into fresh water and can disinfect water using the sun's rays. Photovoltaic cells produce a fifth type of solar energy, converting sunlight into electrical energy. The energy can power household devices and even electrical vehicles. Finally, solar chemical systems use the sun to power chemical reactions, from producing hydrogen to purifying natural gas.

Closing Sentence

Of course, the oldest type of solar power was not invented by people but by plants. Photosynthesis turns sunlight, water, and minerals into food for plants and the whole world!

1. What six uses of solar power does the writer define?

a. ____________________ d. ____________________

b. ____________________ e. ____________________

c. ____________________ f. ____________________

2. What transition words does the writer use to connect the sentences?

____

____

____

____

Markus Gann 2010/used under license from www.shutterstock.com

Write Create a first draft of your paragraph using the ideas and details from your prewriting (pages 112–113). Consider the paragraph outline below:

Paragraph Outline

Topic Sentence: Write a topic sentence that introduces the subject and refers to the types or categories.

Body Sentences: Write body sentences that name each category, define it, and provide examples.

Closing Sentence: Write a closing sentence that leaves the reader with an interesting final thought.

Learning Outcome

Revise the writing.

Speaking & Listening

Have your partner read your paragraph aloud. Then complete the response sheet together.

LO4 Revising: Improving the Writing

Revising involves sharing your work with a peer and improving your writing by adding, cutting, reworking, or rearranging material.

Peer Review

Having a peer read and review your writing will help you revise. The following peer response sheet will guide the peer review process.

Respond Read a classmate's paragraph and complete the following response sheet. (Keep comments helpful and positive.) Share the sheet with the writer.

Paragraph title: ______________________________

Writer: ____________________ Reviewer: ____________________

1. Which part seems to work best: topic sentence, middle, or closing sentence? Why?

____

____

____

2. Which part needs some work? Why?

____

____

____

3. What types or categories did the paragraph explain?

a. ____________________ d. ____________________

b. ____________________ e. ____________________

c. ____________________ f. ____________________

4. What two details did you like most?

____

____

5. Identify a phrase or two that shows the writer's level of interest in the topic.

____

____

____

Using Transitions

Transition words and phrases can help you identify each type or category and rank them, perhaps by complexity, rareness, age, or some other factor:

One type	The simplest	The most common	The earliest
A second	A more complex	A less common	A later
A third	An advanced	A rare	A recent
The last	The most complex	A very rare	The newest

Traits

Transitions help you organize your writing and improve sentence fluency.

Revising in Action

Read aloud the unrevised and then revised version of the following excerpt. Note how the transition words identify and rank the categories.

> The simplest form of solar energy is
> . . . people are learning more and more ways to use the free energy of the sun. ^Solar
> , which   A more advanced form is
> lighting^ means designing buildings to take advantage of natural light. ^Solar heating
> , or
> ~~is~~^ gathering the sun's warmth and using it to heat a building. The sun heats up a "thermal mass"—whether stone, cement, or water—which then radiates the heat.
> A third use of solar energy is solar cooking.
> ^Box cookers are insulated boxes with clear tops, and parabolic cookers use solar rays to boil water or cook food. . . .

Revising

Revise Improve your writing, using the following checklist and your partner's comments on the response sheet. Continue working until you can check off each item in the list.

Ideas

☐ **1.** Do I identify my subject?

☐ **2.** Do I name and define the types or categories?

☐ **3.** Do I provide examples of each type?

Organization

☐ **4.** Do I have an effective topic sentence, body sentences, and a closing sentence?

☐ **5.** Do I use transition words and phrases to identify and rank the types?

Voice

☐ **6.** Does my voice sound knowledgeable and interested?

Learning Outcome

Edit the writing.

LO5 Editing: Subject-Verb Agreement

Subjects and verbs must agree in number. These two pages cover basic subject-verb agreement and agreement with compound subjects.

Basic Subject-Verb Agreement

A singular subject takes a singular verb, and a plural subject takes a plural verb:

One type of instrument is percussion.
singular subject (type) — singular verb (is)

Two percussion instruments are drums and cymbals
plural subject (instruments) — plural verb (are)

In order to identify the correct subject, disregard any words that come between the subject and verb.

One of the types of instruments is percussion.
singular subject (One) — singular verb (is)

(*Types* and *instruments* are not subjects, but objects of the prepositions.)

Test Taking

Some tests require you to correct subject-verb agreement errors. For more practice, see pages 246–260.

Agreement Practice In each sentence, create subject-verb agreement by circling the correct verb in parentheses.

1. The percussion category (include/includes) instruments that make noise by striking something.
2. Pianos, by that definition, (is/are) percussion instruments.
3. The hammers inside a piano (strike/strikes) the strings to make the sound.
4. Of course, drums (is/are) also types of percussion.
5. The drumsticks, made of hardwood, (hit/hits) the skin of the drumhead.
6. Another of the instrument types (is/are) winds.
7. This family of instruments (include/includes) flutes, clarinets, and even brass.
8. When wind (produce/produces) the sound, the instruments (is/are) winds.
9. Some winds like the clarinet or oboe (make/makes) sound with a reed.
10. Other winds like the trumpet or trombone (make/makes) sound with the player's lips.

Apply Read your classification paragraph, making sure that your subjects and verbs agree.

Agreement with Compound Subjects

A compound subject is made of two or more subjects joined by *and* or *or*. When the subjects are joined by *and*, they are plural and require a plural verb:

A baritone and a trombone play the same range.
(A baritone and a trombone = plural compound subject; play = plural verb)

When the subjects are joined by *or*, the verb must match the number of the last subject.

Either the woodwinds or the brass plays the main theme.
(brass = singular subject; plays = singular verb)

Either the brass or the woodwinds play the main theme.
(woodwinds = plural subject; play = plural verb)

Agreement Practice In each sentence, create subject-verb agreement by circling the correct verb in parentheses.

1. Stringed instruments and their players (fill out/fills out) the orchestra.
2. Violins and violas (play/plays) the higher notes.
3. A cello or bass (handle/handles) the lower notes.
4. The horsehair bow and the string (make/makes) the sound.
5. Either music or screeches (emerge/emerges) depending on the player's talent.
6. A soloist or all the violins (carry/carries) the melody.
7. The conductor or the concertmaster (indicate/indicates) when to bow.
8. The concertmaster and the strings (sit/sits) closest to the audience.
9. The orchestra and any soloist (perform/performs) to packed audiences.
10. Either the musicians or their director (thank/thanks) the crowd.

Write Write the end of each sentence, matching the verb to the compound subject.

1. The director and the orchestra ______________________________

____

2. The orchestra or the director ______________________________

____

Apply Read your classification paragraph, making sure that your compound subjects and verbs agree.

Marking a Paragraph

The model classification paragraph that follows has a number of errors.

Editing Practice Correct the following paragraph, using the marks on the left. The first error has been corrected for you.

Correction Marks

- 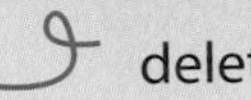 delete
- d (triple underline) capitalize
- Ɗ lowercase
- ∧ insert
- ∧, add comma
- ?∧ add question mark
- word∧ add word
- ⊙ add period
-  spelling
-  switch

My Condiments to the Chef

When most Americans talk about mustard they mean a type of bright-yellow goo that the rest of the world hardly recognizes as mustard. Actually four basic types of mustard. Yellow mustard are the most common in America, made from finely ground mustard seed, vinegar, and a bright yellow coloring called turmeric. Yellow mustard is mild, a constant companion of hot dogs. For a spicier mustard, people in the united states and outside as well enjoy brown mustard. it is made from coarse-ground mustard seeds, and so it looks yellow and brown. For an even stronger flavor, mustard lovers turn to the famous mustard called Dijon, named after the French city where it begun Dijon mustard is fine ground and most often contains wine instead of viniger. In addition to these basic types of mustard, their are all kinds of specialty mustards, mixed with everything from honey to jalapenos, when it comes to taste, there's a mustard for just about anybody.

Insight

In academic writing, the pronouns *I* and *you* have special rules for subject-verb agreement:

- *I* takes the verb *am* instead of *is*: I *am* (**not** I *is*).
- *I* also takes plural action verbs: I *sit* (**not** I *sits*).
- *You* always takes a plural verb: You *are;* you *sit* (**not** You *is;* you *sits*).

For more information, see pages 250–251.

Correcting Your Paragraph

Now it's time to correct your own paragraph.

Apply Create a clean copy of your paragraph and use the following checklist to check for errors. When you can answer yes to a question, check it off. Continue working until all items are checked.

WAC

Use this checklist for editing writing assignments in all of your classes.

Editing Checklist

Words

☐ **1.** Have I used specific nouns and verbs? (See page 103.)

☐ **2.** Have I used more action verbs than "be" verbs? (See page 73.)

Sentences

☐ **3.** Have I varied the beginnings and lengths of sentences? (See pages 226–231.)

☐ **4.** Have I combined short choppy sentences? (See page 232.)

☐ **5.** Have I avoided shifts in sentences? (See page 278.)

☐ **6.** Have I avoided fragments and run-ons? (See pages 261–266, 270–271.)

Conventions

☐ **7.** Do I use correct verb forms (*he saw,* not *he seen*)? (See pages 320, 324.)

☐ **8.** Do my subjects and verbs agree (*she speaks,* not *she speak*)? (See pages 245–260.)

☐ **9.** Have I used the right words (*their, there, they're*)?

☐ **10.** Have I capitalized first words and proper nouns and adjectives? (See page 386.)

☐ **11.** Have I used commas after long introductory word groups? (See page 358.)

☐ **12.** Have I punctuated dialogue correctly? (See pages 104–105.)

☐ **13.** Have I carefully checked my spelling?

Adding a Title

Make sure to add a title that calls attention to your paragraph. Here are some simple strategies for coming up with a catchy title.

- **Use a number:** Four Types of Mustard
- **Use an expression:** A Matter of Taste
- **Think outside the box:** Plugging into Sunlight
- **Be clever:** My Condiments to the Chef

Insight

Have a classmate, friend, or family member read your work to catch any missed errors.

Create Prepare a clean final copy of your paragraph and proofread it.

Learning Outcome

Review classification writing.

LO6 Reviewing Classification Writing

Complete these activities as needed to help you better understand writing classification paragraphs.

Gather Think about the types of friends you have. Do you have different friends for different locations or experiences? List the types of friends and a definition for each type. Then list examples of each type. (See pages 111 and 113.)

Type/Category	Definition	Examples

Correct For each sentence below, create subject-verb agreement by circling the correct verb in parentheses. (See pages 118–119.)

1. My friends Carl and Leon (is/are) what I call "football buddies."
2. Either Carl or Leon or both (attend/attends) every game at my house.
3. They or I (provide/provides) the food for the big game.
4. The Bears (is/are) my favorite, but the Packers (is/are) Carl and Leon's.
5. Either I or my friends (get/gets) humiliated when those two teams meet.

"Shall I compare thee to a summer's day?"

—William Shakespeare

Hervé Hughes/Hemis/Corbis

13 Comparison-Contrast Paragraph

Take a look at this photo. It is full of contrasts: a tree is contrasted with a power station, nature with technology, green with blue, horizontal with vertical. But the photo also contains some interesting comparisons. The water vapor from the power plant looks much like the clouds overhead. The green tree matches the green grass. And, moving beyond appearances, the plants and the power station are both involved with energy use and production.

By looking at the similarities and differences between two things, you can come to understand both things better. A paragraph that examines similarities and differences is called a comparison-contrast paragraph.

This chapter will guide you through the process of writing a paragraph that compares and contrasts two people—you and someone you know well.

Learning Outcomes

LO1 Understand comparison paragraphs.

LO2 Plan a comparison paragraph.

LO3 Write the first draft.

LO4 Revise the writing.

LO5 Edit the writing.

LO6 Reflect on the experience.

What do you think?

How are you similar to a summer's day? How are you different?

Learning Outcome

Understand comparison paragraphs.

LO1 Reviewing a Comparison Paragraph

When you show how two things are similar, you are **comparing** them, and when you show how they are different, you are **contrasting** them. This chapter focuses on writing comparison-contrast paragraphs. The paragraph that follows demonstrates this form.

Read/React Read the following paragraph. Then answer the questions below to identify your first impressions about it.

Old Versus New

The **topic sentence** summarizes the comparison-contrast theme.

The **body sentences** share details about the subjects.

The **closing sentence** finishes the comparison.

People often say I look like a younger version of my father, but in most ways, we are very different. Our appearance is similar in that I have Dad's brown eyes and black hair. We even have similar smiles, according to my mom. But no one would say we look the same in the clothes we wear. Dad dresses **old school** in work pants and button-down shirts, always tucked in. For me, it's jeans and a Padres jersey, never tucked in. Our different dress shows our different personalities. Dad is quiet, shy, and hardworking, while I am very friendly and sometimes a little crazy. Neither of us, however, is interested in causing trouble. Most of our differences come from our different backgrounds. Dad was born in Mexico in a small town south of Monterrey. He moved to San Diego as a young man and has worked very long hours as a cook ever since. It has taken him a long time to feel comfortable in this country, while the United States is all I have ever known. Dad's tough life has made him more careful and serious than I am, but if he had lived my life, he would be much more like me.

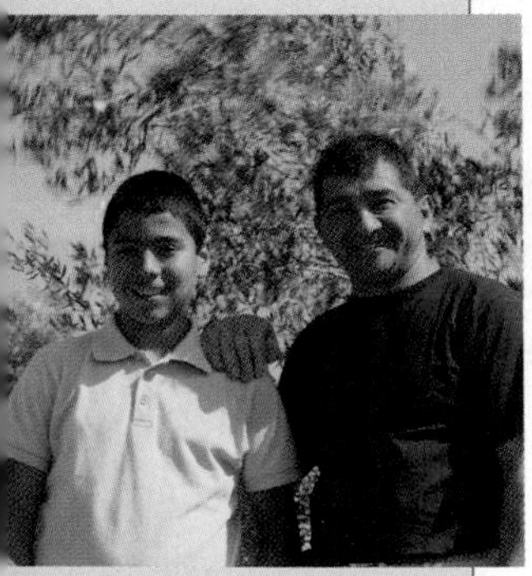

Monty Rakusen/Getty Images

1. Name two things that you like about the paragraph. (Consider specific details, main ideas, particular sentences, and so on.)

   a. ______________________________

   b. ______________________________

2. List two questions that you have about the paragraph. (Is there something that you would like to know more about? Are there any words or phrases that you don't understand completely?)

   a. ______________________________

   b. ______________________________

Vocabulary

comparing
pointing out the similarities between two things

contrasting
pointing out the differences between two things

old school
an idiom meaning "traditional or following past practices"

A Closer Look

Miguel used a **point-by-point pattern of organization** to arrange the details in his paragraph. He discussed each point of comparison for both himself and his father before moving on to the next one.

Traits

Points of comparison help you gather and organize your thoughts.

Identify This chart shows the three points of comparison in Miguel's paragraph: *appearance, personality,* and *background.* Fill in the chart with specific details about Miguel and his father for each point of comparison.

Point of Comparison	Father	Miguel
Appearance Think of size, shape, hair color, eye color, skin color, gender, clothing, and so on.		
Personality Think of attitude, outlook, feelings, actions, and so on.		
Background Think of place of birth, schooling, family, home town, and so on.		

Explain In your opinion, which point of comparison is the most interesting, and which is the least interesting? Why?

____

____

____

____

Vocabulary

point-by-point pattern of organization
a pattern in which one point of comparison is discussed for both subjects before moving on to the next point

Learning Outcome

Plan a comparison paragraph.

Speaking & Listening

Complete the "Identify" activity with a partner. Ask your partner about the person he or she is writing about. Discuss physical appearance, personality, background, and interests. Then switch roles and have your partner ask you the same questions.

LO2 Prewriting: Planning

In your own paragraph, you, too, will compare and contrast yourself with a friend or relative. Think of someone that you know very well so that you have plenty of details to use in your writing.

Selecting a Topic

Latonya began by listing four people that she knew well: her sister, aunt, roommate, and father. She chose her roommate, Janice.

Select In the space below, list four people you know well. Then circle the one person you would like to compare and contrast in a paragraph.

______________________	______________________
______________________	______________________

Selecting Points of Comparison

Once you have selected a topic, you need to decide on points of comparison.

Identify Complete the chart below. In the first column, list your characteristics for each point of comparison to the left. In the second column, list the characteristics of the person you have chosen. Finally, choose three points of comparison to use in your paragraph.

Point of Comparison	You	Other Person
Appearance Think of size, shape, hair color, eye color, skin color, gender, clothing, and so on.		
Personality Think of attitude, outlook, feelings, actions, and so on.		
Background Think of place of birth, schooling, family, hometown, and so on.		
Interests Think of favorite activities, friends, restaurants, and so on.		
(Other)		

Gathering Details

Latonya used a **Venn diagram** to list specific details about herself and Janice as they related to her points of comparison: appearance, background, and interests.

Venn Diagram

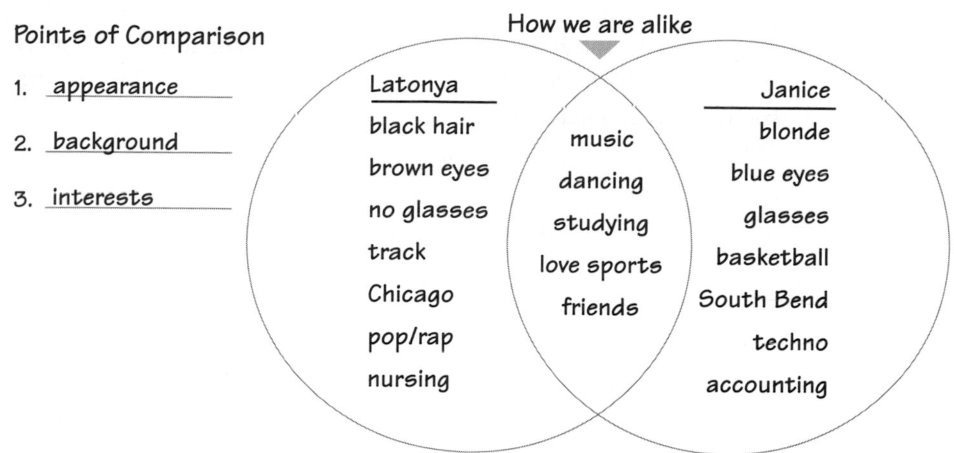

Gather Complete the Venn diagram below. First, list the three points of comparison. Next, write your name in one circle and the other person's name in the other. List the details specific to each of you. Then, where the circles overlap, write the things you have in common.

1. ________________
2. ________________
3. ________________

How we are alike

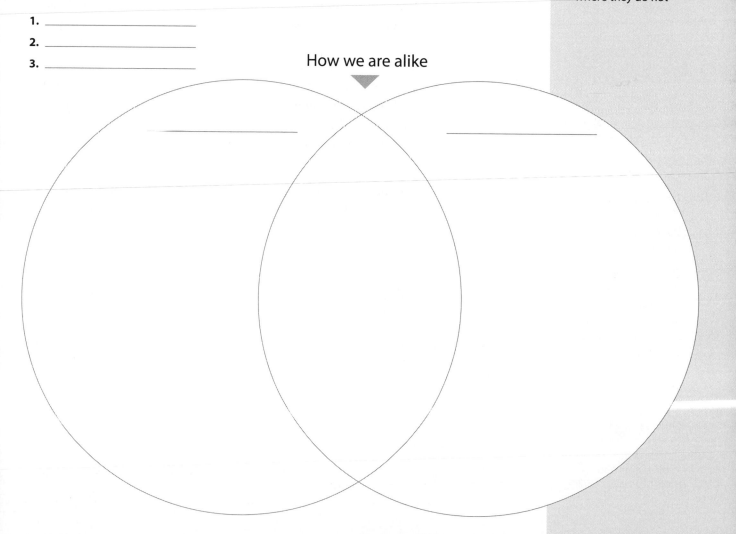

Test Taking

When responding to a comparison paragraph or essay on a test, you can use a Venn diagram to analyze the reading.

Vocabulary

Venn diagram
graphic organizer displaying the similarities of two subjects where the circles overlap and the differences where they do not

Learning Outcome

Write the first draft.

Workplace

In the workplace, you may need to compare two products, services, or bids. You'll need to choose points of comparison then, too.

LO3 Writing: Creating a First Draft

Provided below is Latonya's paragraph, comparing herself with her friend Janice. Latonya has used the point-by-point pattern of organization and her three points of comparison are *appearance, background,* and *interests.*

Read/React Carefully read Latonya's paragraph, paying attention to the way she organizes her ideas. The three points of comparison are labeled. Afterward, answer the questions about the paragraph.

We Can Dance

Appearance

Background

Interests

To look at my roommate and me, you'd think we have nothing in common. First of all, we look like complete opposites. Janice is tall, with long blonde hair and blue eyes, while I'm short, with black curly hair and brown eyes. Janice loves wearing her basketball jersey from her Indiana State Championship team. I prefer dressing in my cross-country gear and taking off down the road. We're also from completely different places. I'm a city girl, born and raised on the south side of Chicago, right in the heart of Barack Obama country. Janice grew up on a farm in a sea of corn, near South Bend, Indiana. So why do Janice and I get along so well? Some might think it is our interest in sports, but that's only a small part of it. When we first moved in together, I turned on some hip-hop, and Janice started **popping and locking**. She was good! So I showed her some of my moves, and even tried the techno music she likes. Before you know it, we came to be the best of friends, going to parties and dances together and having a blast.

1. What is the topic sentence in the paragraph? (Underline it.) What main feeling does Latonya state in that sentence?

____

____

2. Why do you think she talks about their mutual interests last in the paragraph?

____

____

3. What two things do you especially like in the paragraph? (Consider words, sentences, or ideas.)

____

____

Vocabulary

popping and locking
the jerky movements and rigid postures of a classic funk dance

Write Create the first draft of your paragraph using the ideas and details from your chart and Venn diagram (pages 140–141). Follow the steps in the paragraph outline below, and use the transitional words to the right to make your writing flow.

Paragraph Outline

Topic Sentence: Write a topic sentence that tells who you are comparing yourself to.

Body Sentences: Write body sentences that share details about each subject for each point of comparison.

Closing Sentence: Write a closing sentence that sums up your comparison.

Traits

Transitions to compare:
as / as well / also / both / in the same way / much as / much like / one way / like / likewise / similarly

Transitions to contrast:
although / even though / by contrast / but / however / on the one hand / otherwise / though / still / while / yet

Learning Outcome

Revise the writing.

Speaking & Listening

Have your partner read your paragraph aloud. Then complete the response sheet together.

LO4 Revising: Improving the Writing

Revising involves sharing your work with a peer and improving your writing by adding, cutting, reworking, or rearranging material.

Peer Review

Sharing your writing is especially important when you are revising a first draft. The feedback that you receive will help you improve your paragraph. To help you respond to a classmate's writing or receive help with your own writing, use a peer-response sheet.

Respond Complete this response sheet after reading the first draft of a classmate's paragraph. Then share the sheet with the writer. (Keep your comments helpful and positive.)

Paragraph title: ______________________________

Writer: ______________________ Reviewer: ______________________

1. Which part seems to work best: topic sentence, middle, or closing sentence?

   Why? ______________________________

   ____

   ____

2. Which part needs some work? Why? ______________________________

   ____

   ____

3. What are the three points of comparison in the paragraph?

   a. ______________________________

   b. ______________________________

   c. ______________________________

4. Name two favorite details.

   a. ______________________________

   b. ______________________________

5. Identify a phrase or two that shows the writer's level of interest.

   ____

   ____

   ____

Show, Don't Tell

Your paragraph will be stronger if you **show** similarities and differences, not just **tell** about them. Consider the examples that follow. The improvement can be dramatic when you revise to "show."

Showing vs.	**Telling**
She's popping and locking.	She likes to dance.
She lives on a farm in a sea of corn.	She is a country girl.
She lives in her championship jersey.	She is an athlete.
She has blonde hair and blue eyes.	She is white.

Revising in Action:

Read aloud the unrevised and then the revised version of the following excerpt. Note how much the first draft is improved by showing instead of telling. The writer provides more information, creates more interest, and gives the reader something to "see."

with long blonde hair and blue eyes,
. . . First of all, we look like complete opposites. Janice is ~~white and~~ tall,
with black curly hair and brown eyes. wearing her basketball jersey from her Indiana State Championship team.
while I'm ~~black and~~ short. ~~We like different sports.~~ Janice loves ~~basketball,~~
I prefer dressing in my cross-country gear and taking off down the road.
~~and I like track~~. We're also from completely different places. . . .

R. Gino Santa Maria, 2010/used under license from www.shutterstock.com

Revise Improve your writing, using the following checklist and your partner's comments on the response sheet. Continue working until you can check off each item in the list.

Ideas

- ☐ **1.** Do I compare two subjects—myself and another person?
- ☐ **2.** Do I use three points of comparison?
- ☐ **3.** Do I include details that show instead of tell?

Organization

- ☐ **4.** Do I have a topic sentence, middle, and a closing sentence?
- ☐ **5.** Have I used a point-by-point organizational plan?
- ☐ **6.** Have I used transitions to connect my sentences?

Voice

- ☐ **7.** Do I sound knowledgeable and interested?

Vocabulary

show
provide details that let the reader experience an idea or get a clear picture

tell
offer a general fact or circumstance without letting the reader experience it

Learning Outcome

Edit the writing.

LO5 Editing: Comma Use

Commas tell the reader when to pause, making the writing easy to follow.

Commas After Introductory Words

Many sentences naturally start with the subject. Some sentences, however, start with an introductory phrase or clause. A comma is used to separate a long introductory word group from the rest of the sentence. When you read sentences like these out loud, you will naturally pause after the introductory words. That tells you that a comma is needed to separate these words from the rest of the sentence. See the examples that follow.

Phiseksit 2010/used under license from www.shutterstock.com

Introductory Word Groups:

After my third birthday**,** my brother was born. (prepositional phrase)

When he arrived on the scene**,** life changed for me. (dependent clause)

Punctuation Practice Read the sentences below, out loud. Listen for the natural pause after an introductory phrase or clause. Place a comma to set off the introductory words.

1. When my younger brother was born I was jealous.
2. Before he showed up I had Mom all to myself.
3. At the beginning of our relationship we didn't get along very well.
4. As the years passed my brother stopped being a pest and became a friend.
5. As a matter of fact we both came to love basketball.
6. Without my younger brother I wouldn't have anyone to push my basketball skills.
7. Taking that into account our long rivalry has helped us both.
8. Since our teenage years we've become best friends.
9. Although we still tease each other we're not being vicious.
10. When we bump fists I sometimes remember when we bumped heads.

Apply Read your comparison paragraph and look for sentences that begin with introductory phrases or clauses. If you do not find any, add an introductory phrase or clause to a few sentences to vary their beginnings. Does this help your writing read more smoothly? Remember to use a comma to separate a long introductory word group from the rest of the sentence. (For more information, see page 358.)

Commas with Extra Information

Some sentences include phrases or clauses that add information in the middle or at the end of sentences. This information should be set off with commas. You can recognize this extra information because it can be removed without changing the basic meaning of the sentence. When you read the sentence out loud, there's a natural pause before and after the phrase or clause. This indicates where you are to place the commas.

Insight

Commas are very important in written English. For more practice with comma use, see pages 357–366.

Extra Information:

I have a tough time waking up, not surprisingly.

My mother, who works two jobs, makes me breakfast every morning.

Punctuation Practice In each sentence, use a comma or commas to separate extra information. Listen for the natural pause. Some sentences may not have extra information.

1. My mother works as a waitress which is a tough job.
2. She also works as a licensed practical nurse which is an even tougher job.
3. The nursing home the one on Main and 7th is strict.
4. A time card punched one second late is docked fifteen minutes an unfair policy.
5. A time card punched ten minutes early does not earn overtime.
6. The restaurant job pays minimum wage which is not much.
7. Tips from a good lunch not the busiest time can double Mom's pay.
8. What I've learned about determination real grit I learned from Mom.
9. She wants to help me qualify for a better job a selfless goal.
10. I want exactly the same thing no surprise there.

Apply Read your comparison paragraph and look for sentences that have extra information. If you haven't included any, add some extra information in a sentence or two. Do these additions make your writing more interesting? Remember to use commas to set off extra information in your sentences. (For more information, see page 364.)

Marking a Paragraph

The model that follows has a number of errors.

Editing Practice Correct the following paragraph, using the marks to the left. One correction has been done for you.

Correction Marks

- delete
- capitalize
- lowercase
- insert
- add comma
- add question mark
- add word
- add period
- spelling
- switch

Into the Spotlight

My wife and I love each other, but it's hard to imagine how we could be more different. Lupe's a social butterfly. She been always meeting people for coffee or talking to people on the phone. By contrast, I'm private. I work at U.S. steel and come home. The only person I really want to be with is Lupe, but she's always dragging me out to partys. Their is another big difference. Lupe who is a great singer and dancer loves theater. She's been in a dozen plays. When it come to me the idea of being on stage is terrifying. She convinced me once to be in a play I forgot my one line. so, is there anything Lupe and I have in common? We love each other. Lupe needs me to keep her grounded, and I need her to pry me out of the house. We've even figured out a way to work around the theater thing. Next play she is in. I'll work set crew. That's how we get along so well. I work backstage, set up props for her, and getting what she needs. Then she walks into the spotlight and performs.

Insight

As you've seen, commas are needed to set off extra information in a sentence. Sometimes the extra information comes between the subject and the verb:

> Lupe, who is a great singer and dancer, loves theater.

But when there is no extra information to set off, do not separate the subject and verb with a comma.

Incorrect: Lupe, loves theater. **Correct:** Lupe loves theater.

Correcting Your Paragraph

Now it's time to correct your own paragraph.

Apply Create a clean copy of your paragraph and use the following checklist to check for errors. When you can answer yes to a question, check it off. Continue working until all items are checked.

WAC

Use this checklist for editing writing assignments in all of your classes.

Editing Checklist

Words

- ☐ **1.** Have I used specific nouns and verbs? (See page 103.)
- ☐ **2.** Have I used more action verbs than "be" verbs? (See page 73.)

Sentences

- ☐ **3.** Have I varied the beginnings and lengths of sentences? (See pages 226–231.)
- ☐ **4.** Have I combined short choppy sentences? (See page 232.)
- ☐ **5.** Have I avoided shifts in sentences? (See page 278.)
- ☐ **6.** Have I avoided fragments and run-ons? (See pages 261–266, 270–271.)

Conventions

- ☐ **7.** Do I use correct verb forms (*he saw*, not *he seen*)? (See pages 320, 324.)
- ☐ **8.** Do my subjects and verbs agree (*she speaks*, not *she speak*)? (See pages 245–260.)
- ☐ **9.** Have I used the right words (*their, there, they're*)?
- ☐ **10.** Have I capitalized first words and proper nouns and adjectives? (See page 386.)
- ☐ **11.** Have I used commas after long introductory word groups? (See page 358.)
- ☐ **12.** Have I punctuated dialogue correctly? (See pages 104–105.)
- ☐ **13.** Have I carefully checked my spelling?

Adding a Title

Make sure to add an attention-getting title. Here are three simple strategies for creating one.

- **Use a phrase from the paragraph:** Into the Spotlight
- **Point to a similarity or difference:** We Can Dance
- **Use the word "versus":** Old Versus New

Insight

Have a classmate, friend, or family member read your work to catch any missed errors.

Create Prepare a clean final copy of your paragraph and proofread it.

Reflect on the experience.

© Ocean/Corbis

LO6 Reviewing Comparison Writing

Complete these activities as needed to help you better understand how to write comparison-contrast paragraphs.

Compare/Contrast Consider this photograph. How are the two creatures represented in it alike? How are they different? Fill in the following Venn diagram, listing similarities and differences.

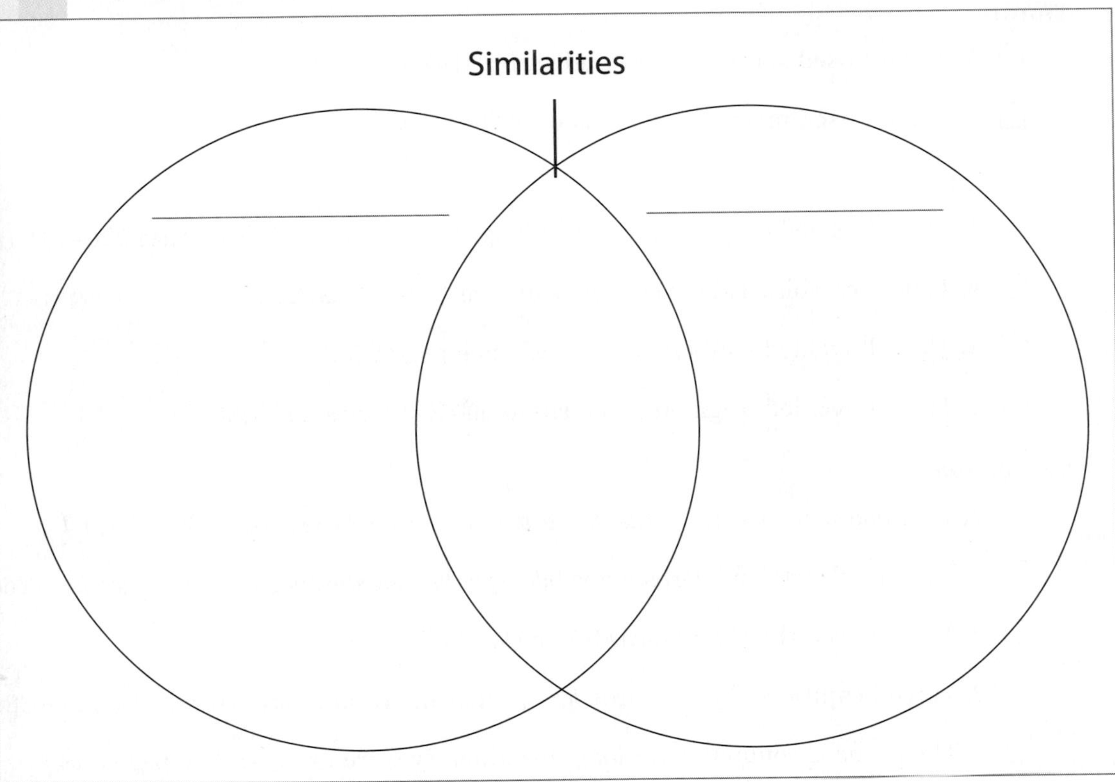

Match Draw a line to connect each organizational pattern below to its description.

1. Point-by-point	■ an organizational pattern focusing first on one subject and then on the other
2. Similarities-differences	■ a pattern in which one point of comparison is discussed for both subjects before moving on to the next point
3. Subject-by-subject	■ an organizational pattern sharing how subjects are alike and how they are different

Sort Circle transitions that *contrast*:

also	both	but	however	like	otherwise	though

"There is only one constant, one universal. It is the only real truth. Causality. Action, reaction. Cause and effect."
—from *The Matrix Reloaded*

Mike Norton, 2010/used under license from www.shutterstock.com

Cause-Effect Paragraph

Studying the causes and effects of a phenomenon can help you better understand why and how things happen around you. Your work in a meteorology class may explain the causes and effects of forest fires, a discussion with a friend may reveal the impact of instant-replay technology on the NFL, and so on.

In this chapter, you will write a paragraph to explain the causes and effects of a past or present incident, event, or circumstance. And during the process, as you learn how one event leads to another, you will grasp the topic in a new way.

Learning Outcomes

LO1 Understand cause-effect paragraphs.
LO2 Plan a cause-effect paragraph.
LO3 Write the first draft.
LO4 Revise the writing.
LO5 Edit the writing
LO6 Reflect on the experience.

What do you think?

Read the quotation above from the movie *The Matrix Reloaded*. Briefly explain an action you have taken that had a cause and an effect.

Learning Outcome

Understand cause-effect paragraphs.

LO1 Reviewing a Paragraph

When you think about the relationship between the causes and effects of an event, an incident, or a circumstance, you are practicing cause-effect reasoning. This chapter focuses on writing a paragraph that clearly explains a cause-effect relationship. The paragraph that follows demonstrates this form.

Read/React Read the following cause-effect paragraph. Then answer the questions below to identify your first impressions about it.

Cutting Down the Atmosphere

The **topic sentence** introduces the cause-effect relationship.

The **body sentences** explain the causes and effects.

The **closing sentence** restates the main point.

Trees make up an essential part of the earth's ecosystem, but rapid deforestation is having harmful effects on the planet. Deforestation refers to the clearance of forests through logging and burning. The main cause of deforestation is the use of trees for lumber and fuel. Forests are also cut down to make room for farming. But while deforestation can boost struggling economies, it is also causing harm to the environment. Adverse effects of deforestation include erosion of soil, disruption of the water cycle, loss of biodiversity, and flooding and drought. The most harmful effect, though, may be on the climate. Deforestation leads to a greater accumulation of carbon dioxide in the atmosphere, which in turn may warm the planet. Those who practice deforestation must determine if the economic benefits outweigh the negative impact on our earth.

1. Name two things that you like about the paragraph. (Consider specific details, main ideas, particular sentences, and so on.)

   a. ______________________________

   ____

   b. ______________________________

   ____

2. List two questions that you have about the paragraph. (Is there something that you would like to know more about? Are there any words or phrases that you don't understand completely?)

   a. ______________________________

   ____

   b. ______________________________

   ____

ArtmannWitte, 2010/used under license from www.shutterstock.com

A Closer Look

Grant used an **effect-focused pattern of organization** to arrange the details in his paragraph. He briefly explains the main causes of deforestation before focusing on specific effects of the practice.

Identify Grant used a cause-effect T-chart to organize his research about deforestation. Fill in the chart with the specific causes and effects of deforestation that are covered in Grant's paragraph.

Subject: The Causes and Effects of Deforestation

Causes	Effects
■	■
■	■
■	■
■	■
■	■

Explain In your opinion, should the writer have paid more attention to the causes of deforestation? Why or why not?

Vocabulary

effect-focused pattern of organization
a pattern of organization that focuses on the "effects" of a cause-effect relationship

Learning Outcome

Plan a cause-effect paragraph.

WAC

Cause-effect relationships are crucial to all areas of study, but especially the sciences and history.

LO2 Prewriting: Planning

In your own paragraph, you will explain the causes and effects of a phenomenon of your choice. Think of an event, a circumstance, or an incident—from the past or present—that has made a lasting impact on the world around you.

Selecting a Topic

If you are having trouble thinking of topics, consider the categories listed below.

Cause-Effect Categories

- Family Life
- Politics
- Society
- Environment
- Entertainment
- Workplace

Select List three or four possible topics on the blanks below. Then circle the topic you would like to write about in a paragraph.

____________________	____________________
____________________	____________________

Researching the Causes and Effects

Once you have selected a topic, you will need to research the causes and effects related to it.

Identify Complete the chart below to show the relationship between the causes and effects of your topic.

Topic: ____________________

1. Cause: ____________________	**1. Effect:** ____________________
2. Cause: ____________________	**2. Effect:** ____________________
3. Cause: ____________________	**3. Effect:** ____________________

Gathering Details

As you research your topic, you should look for clear, factual evidence that links specific causes to specific effects. Using trustworthy sources will lead you to the best information.

While doing her research, Christina avoided sources that took a distorted or overly biased stance on her topic. Here are some examples of information that distorts cause-effect logic:

- **Broad Generalization:** An assertion that is based on too little evidence or allows no exceptions

  Video games are the reason that today's youth have a shorter attention span. *(The claim disregards the possibility of other reasons.)*

- **Straw Man:** A claim that exaggerates or misrepresents an opponent's position

  If you cause deforestation, you hate the planet.

- **False Cause:** A claim that confuses sequence with causation (If A comes before B, A must have caused B.)

  Since that new skate park opened, vandalism among young people has increased. The skate park should never have been built. *(The two factors may have no real connection.)*

Speaking & Listening

Listen to a political debate or watch a political attack ad. See if you can detect any of these distortions in cause-effect logic. What does the distortion do to the speaker's credibility?

Forming a Cause-Effect Topic Sentence

Christina used the following formula to write the topic sentence for her cause-effect paragraph. Using your topic and research from page 154, write your own topic sentence below.

Topic		Cause-Effect Relationship		Topic Sentence
U.S. Airways Flight 1549	+	struck a flock of geese, causing the plane to lose power in both its engines	=	In January 2009, U.S. Airways Flight 1549 struck a flock of geese, causing the plane to lose power in both its engines.

Topic

Cause-Effect Relationship: ______

Topic Sentence: ______

Learning Outcome

Write the first draft.

LO3 Writing: Creating a First Draft

In the paragraph below, Christina wrote about a remarkable airplane landing. The paragraph uses an effect-based approach, beginning with the main cause of the event and then focusing on three specific effects.

Read/React Read Christina's paragraph, paying attention to the way she organizes the causes and effects. Afterward, answer the questions about the paragraph.

Emergency Landing

Topic Sentence | **Body Sentences** | **Closing Sentence**

In January 2009, U.S. Airways Flight 1549 struck a flock of geese, causing the plane to lose power in both its engines. The situation forced pilot Chesley "Sully" Sullenberger to perform an emergency landing on the Hudson River outside of New York City. Not only did he land safely, but all 150 passengers survived without a single serious injury. The event had many meaningful effects. Massive media coverage of the landing made "Sully" a household name. Many hailed him as an American hero. Meanwhile, the passengers on the flight, though safe, suffered emotional trauma from the landing. Many refuse to step back onto a plane. Maybe the greatest effect, however, was the impact on the airline industry. The result of the landing led to a greater awareness of the dangers of bird populations near airways. Government agencies have gone so far as to **eradicate** geese populations in the proximity of airports. For this reason, Sully's remarkable landing may make air travel safer for generations to come.

1. What is the topic sentence in the paragraph? (Underline it.) What does the sentence tell us about the paragraph?

____

____

2. What three specific effects does the author focus on?

____

____

3. What two things do you especially like in the paragraph? (Consider words, sentences, or ideas.)

____

____

Vocabulary

eradicate
to remove completely

ArchMan, 2010/used under license from www.shutterstock.com

Write Create a first draft of your paragraph using the ideas and details from your cause-effect chart on page 154. Follow the paragraph outline below and use the cause-effect transition words to the right as you write your paragraph.

Paragraph Outline

Topic Sentence: Begin with the topic sentence you wrote on page 155.

Body Sentences: Write body sentences that describe specific causes and effects related to your topic.

Closing Sentence: Write a closing sentence that sums up the main point.

Traits

Transitions that show cause-effect relationships: accordingly / as a result / because / consequently / for this purpose / for this reason / hence / just as / since / so / such as / therefore / thus / to illustrate / whereas

Learning Outcome

Revise the writing.

Speaking & Listening

Have your partner read your paragraph aloud. Then complete the response sheet together.

LO4 Revising: Improving the Writing

Revising involves sharing your work with a peer and improving your writing by adding, cutting, reworking, or rearranging material.

Peer Review

Sharing your writing is especially important when you are revising a first draft. The feedback that you receive will help you improve your paragraph. To help you respond to a classmate's writing or receive help with your own writing, use a peer-response sheet.

Respond Complete this response sheet after reading a classmate's paragraph. Then share the sheet with the writer. (Keep your comments helpful and positive.)

Paragraph title: ______________________________

Writer: ____________________ Reviewer: ____________________

1. Which part seems to work best: topic sentence, middle, or closing sentence?

   Why? ______________________________

   ____

   ____

2. Which part needs some work? Why? ______________________________

   ____

   ____

3. What are the causes and effects discussed in the paragraph?

   ____

   ____

   ____

4. Name two favorite details.

   a. ______________________________

   b. ______________________________

5. Identify a phrase or two that shows the writer's level of interest.

   ____

   ____

   ____

Using an Academic Style

Cause-effect paragraphs require an academic style, which sounds knowledgeable and confident without being stuffy. Consider the quick tips below as you revise your paragraph.

Quick Tips for Academic Style

- **Avoid personal pronouns.** Unless your instructor tells you differently, avoid using personal pronouns such as *I, we,* and *you* in your cause-effect paragraph.
- **Define technical terms and jargon.** If your readers are not experts on your topic, make sure to define the specialized vocabulary or technical words you use.
- **Beware of unnecessary intensifiers.** Words such as *really, totally,* and *completely* "overqualify" your writing and create an informal style.

Revising in Action:

Read aloud the unrevised and then the revised version of the following excerpt. Note how the changes improved the excerpt's academic style.

> Maybe the greatest effect, however, was the impact on the airline industry.
> ~~I think the greatest effect was the impact on aviation.~~ The result of the landing led to a ~~completely and totally~~ greater awareness of the dangers of bird populations
> airways.
> near ~~air hubs.~~ ~~You see~~ government agencies have . . .

Insight

Think of writing style in the same way that you think of clothing style. For a formal occasion, you would dress more formally than for an everyday event. In the same way, when you write an academic essay, you use more formal language.

Revise Use the following checklist and your partner's comments on the response sheet to improve your writing. Continue working until you can check off each item in the list.

Ideas

- ☐ **1.** Does the topic sentence clearly introduce the cause-effect relationship?
- ☐ **2.** Are all major causes and effects addressed?
- ☐ **3.** Are all the links between the causes and effects clear and logical?

Organization

- ☐ **4.** Do I have a topic sentence, body sentences, and a closing sentence?
- ☐ **5.** Have I used transitions to show cause-effect relationships and connect my ideas?

Voice

- ☐ **6.** Have I used an academic voice?

Learning Outcome

Edit the writing.

LO5 Editing: Pronoun-Antecedent Agreement

A **pronoun** is a word that is used in place of noun.

Pronoun-Antecedent Agreement

A pronoun usually has an **antecedent**, which is a word that the pronoun refers to or replaces. Each pronoun must agree with its antecedent in three ways: in number, in person, and in gender. When a pronoun and an antecedent fail to agree in number, person, or gender, the sentence can be confusing for the reader.

Number

Somebody needs to bring **his or her** laptop to the meeting.

(The singular pronouns *his* or *her* agree with the antecedent *somebody*.)

Person

If **students** want to do better research, **they** should talk to a librarian.

(The third person pronoun *they* agrees with the antecedent *students*.)

Gender

Chris picked up **his** lawn mower from **his** parents' garage.

(The masculine pronoun *his* agrees with the antecedent *Chris*.)

Insight

Different languages handle pronouns differently. If your heritage language treats pronoun number, person, or gender differently, carefully study the rules in English. For more information, see pages 297–310.

Practice Read the sentences below. Correct the pronouns so that they agree with their antecedents in number, person, and gender.

1. The musicians strummed his guitars.
2. After Shauna finished washing the dishes, it sparkled.
3. If the waitress wants a better tip, he should be more polite.
4. As the basketball players walked onto the court, he waved to the crowd.
5. Mrs. Jackson started their car.
6. Everyone can attend the extra study session if they need help.
7. Eric poured root beer in their favorite mug.

Vocabulary

pronoun
a word that takes the place of a noun or other pronoun

antecedent
the word that a pronoun refers to or replaces

Apply Read your cause-effect paragraph, watching for agreement issues between pronouns and their antecedents. Correct any pronouns that fail to agree with their antecedents in person, number, or gender.

Case of Pronouns

The case of a pronoun tells what role it can play in a sentence. There are three cases: *nominative, possessive,* and *objective*. Examine the information below, which explains how pronouns of each case are correctly used.

The nominative case is used for subjects and predicate nouns.

I, you, he, she, it, we, they

> **She** walked to the bank.

The possessive case shows possession or ownership.

my, mine, our, ours, his, her, hers, their, theirs, its, your, yours

> The jacket is **his.** This jacket is **mine. Your** jacket is gone.

The objective case is used for direct or indirect objects and for objects of prepositions or infinitives.

me, us, you, him, her, it, them

> Reid told **her** that going to the movie was okay with **him.**

Insight

When it comes to understanding the case of pronouns, you may have an advantage over native English speakers, who may never have thought about case. Think about how case works in your heritage language and compare English use of case.

Practice In the sentences below, replace each incorrect pronoun with a pronoun of the correct case.

1. Frank said that him needed someone to pick his up.
2. I looked over theirs expense report, and them went way over budget.
3. Her worked on she new project.
4. The judge commended the competitor on him speed and agility.
5. Theirs lawn service is better than our.
6. It was him who spotted the bird.
7. The CEO increased she pay.
8. My brother and me attended the film festival.

Apply Read your cause-effect paragraph, checking the pronouns you've used. Make sure each pronoun is in the correct case.

Marking a Paragraph

The model that follows has a number of errors.

Editing Practice Correct the following paragraph, using the marks to the left. One correction has been done for you.

Correction Marks

- delete
- capitalize
- lowercase
- insert
- add comma
- add question mark
- add word
- add period
- spelling
- switch

Divided Parallel

Though the fighting ceased in 1953 the effects of the Korean War resonate today. The war began in 1950 when communist-occupied North Korea. Waged war with south Korea. In a larger context, the war was caused by the United States' desire to stop communism and the Soviet Union's desire to spread communism. The effects of the conflict were considerable. Both sides suffered massive casualties, while the battle sparked the start of the cold war between the United States and the Soviet Union. Today, Korea remain divided along the 38th parallel. North Korea maintains a heavy military presence and has suffered much poverty meanwhile, South Korea has thrived economically. Though the countries have taken smalls steps toward political piece, the war has not ended.

Insight

All English clauses (excluding imperatives in which the subject *you* is understood) must include subjects. In sentences with more than one clause, every clause needs a subject, even if a subject has already been established in one of the other clauses.

Incorrect: Though Jerry loves baseball, prefers to play soccer.

Correct: Though Jerry loves baseball, **he** prefers to play soccer.

Correcting Your Paragraph

Now it's time to correct your own paragraph.

Apply Create a clean copy of your paragraph and use the following checklist to check for errors. When you can answer yes to a question, check it off. Continue working until all items are checked.

Editing Checklist

Words

- ☐ **1.** Have I used specific nouns and verbs? (See page 103.)
- ☐ **2.** Have I used more action verbs than "be" verbs? (See page 73.)

Sentences

- ☐ **3.** Have I varied the beginnings and lengths of sentences? (See pages 226–231.)
- ☐ **4.** Have I combined short choppy sentences? (See page 232.)
- ☐ **5.** Have I avoided shifts in sentences? (See page 278.)
- ☐ **6.** Have I avoided fragments and run-ons? (See pages 261–266, 270–271.)

Conventions

- ☐ **7.** Do I use correct verb forms (*he saw,* not *he seen*)? (See pages 320, 324.)
- ☐ **8.** Do my subjects and verbs agree (*she speaks,* not *she speak*)? (See pages 245–260.)
- ☐ **9.** Have I used the right words (*their, there, they're*)?
- ☐ **10.** Have I capitalized first words and proper nouns and adjectives? (See page 386.)
- ☐ **11.** Have I used commas after long introductory word groups? (See page 358.)
- ☐ **12.** Have I carefully checked my spelling?

WAC

Use this checklist for editing writing assignments in all of your classes.

Adding a Title

Make sure to add an effective title. Here are two strategies for creating one.

- **Grab the reader's attention:** Cutting Down the Atmosphere
- **Use an idea from the paragraph:** Emergency Landing

Insight

Have a classmate, friend, or family member read your work to catch any missed errors.

Learning Outcome

Reflect on the experience.

LO6 Reviewing Cause-Effect Writing

Complete these activities as needed to help you better understand writing cause-effect paragraphs.

Cause/Effect Consider the photograph to the right. Think about potential causes and effects of forest fires. Fill in the following cause-effect chart with your ideas.

Topic: Forest Fire

1. Cause:	**1. Effect:**
2. Cause:	**2. Effect:**
3. Cause:	**3. Effect:**

Match In your own words, explain how to write in an academic style. (See page 159.)

Sort Circle transitions that show a *cause-effect relationship*: (See page 157.)

as a result   behind   soon   therefore   because   since

"Prose is architecture, not interior decoration."
—Ernest Hemingway

Ilja Mašík, 2010/used under license from www.shutterstock.com

16 Writing Essays

Architecture is the art or science of building. Using steel, glass, stone, concrete, and other composites, the architect creates unified forms or structures that can stand up to the elements

Writing, too, is the art or science of building. Using sentences and paragraphs, not steel and concrete, the writer creates strong writing forms that can stand up to repeated readings.

This chapter addresses the essay, the academic form most commonly assigned in the college classroom. As you learn about the essay-writing process, you yourself will develop an essay of definition.

Learning Outcomes

LO1 Review an academic essay.
LO2 Plan an essay.
LO3 Draft an essay.
LO4 Revise an essay.
LO5 Edit an essay.
LO6 Prepare the final copy for publishing.

What do you think?

Why does Hemingway connect writing with architecture but not with interior decoration?

Learning Outcome

Review an academic essay.

essay
a multiparagraph paper in which ideas on a topic are explained, argued for, or explored in an interesting way

LO1 Reviewing an Academic Essay

An **essay** is a piece of academic writing containing multiple paragraphs. Because it is a longer piece of writing, you can go into more depth in an essay than you can in a single paragraph. The following essay of definition by student writer Martina Lincoln explores the concept of tact from a number of different angles.

Read Carefully read the following essay and side notes.

Break It to Them Gently

Beginning
The first paragraph gains the reader's attention and states the thesis.

A few years ago, there was a new student in one of my high school classes. (I'll call him Bill.) Bill suffered from unbearably yellow teeth that grossed everyone out. One loudmouthed boor suggested that Bill "Ajax" his teeth. Of course, Bill turned every shade of red and just wanted to disappear. Had the boor any sense of empathy, he would have realized that there were far more tactful ways to address the new student. Tact is the sensitive handling of situations, even those that are potentially hurtful.

Middle
Each middle paragraph addresses an important element of tact.

Sensitivity is a major component of tact. If a person isn't sensitive to another person's feelings, there is no way that he or she can be tactful. Young people are especially vulnerable and must be handled sensitively. My five-year-old nephew proudly announced that he had cleaned the screen on the family television. Unfortunately, he used a furniture polish that left an oily film on the screen. My sister thanked him for his efforts—and then showed him how to clean the screen properly. Her sensitivity enabled my nephew to keep his self-respect. But sensitivity by itself is not enough.

Truthfulness is another important component of tact. A tactful person expresses herself sensitively and truthfully. Doctors, for example, must be truthful when conversing with patients. If a patient is seriously ill, a tactful doctor will truthfully explain the situation but do so with as much sensitivity as possible. Part of the discussion will certainly focus on the best ways to deal with the illness. An understanding doctor will use tact with the patient's relatives as well. Instead of bluntly stating the patient's condition, she might say, "I'm sorry to report that . . ." and/or "The good news is that . . . ." These are tactful ways of dealing with uncomfortable truths.

Tact should not be confused with deceit or cleverness. Deceit occurs when a credit card company fails to clearly explain the penalties for missed or late payments. It occurs in the courtroom when a lawyer phrases his questions in such a way that a witness says something he or she never meant to say. An admiring listener might say, "How tactful he is, this lawyer!" Crafty he may be, but tactful he is not. Being tactful requires speaking sincerely, not talking around or avoiding an issue.

Closing
The last paragraph summarizes the essay's main points and stresses the importance of tact.

Sensitivity, truthfulness, and sincerity are all connected to tactfulness. They all must be utilized, especially in touchy situations when people's feelings are an issue. Tactful people are individuals that we should admire and respect. They should be our role models, showing by example how to deal with our peers, our family members, and our fellow citizens. Thinking of the opposite, living in a society that condones insensitivity and deceit, reveals the importance of tact in our lives.

React Answer the following questions about the essay on page 180.

1. What sentence in the first paragraph states the focus of the essay? Write it here.

2. What is the topic sentence of the second paragraph?

3. How does the writer support or develop this topic sentence?

4. What is the topic sentence of the third paragraph?

5. How does the writer support or develop this topic sentence?

6. What is the topic sentence of the fourth paragraph?

7. How does this paragraph differ from the other middle paragraphs?

8. What is the topic sentence of the closing paragraph?

9. What is the writer attempting to accomplish in this paragraph?

"When I wear high heels, I have a great vocabulary and I speak in paragraphs. I'm most **eloquent**. I plan to wear them more often."
—Meg Ryan

Vocabulary

eloquent
effective or powerful in speech

Learning Outcome

Plan an essay.

WAC

Often, instructors will assign essays to help you deepen your thinking about a topic and share what you know about it.

LO2 Prewriting: Planning

On the following pages, you will learn about the essay-writing process, and at the same time, you will develop an essay of definition, much like the one you read and reacted to on pages 180–181. Refer to that essay as needed while you write your own essay.

Selecting a Topic

In the sample essay, Martina defined the **abstract** term *tact*. A list of other abstract ideas follows. Consider these terms as possible topics for your own essay. (Use a dictionary to look up any words that are unfamiliar.)

courage **empathy** **honesty** **humility** **joy** **envy** **competitiveness**

Create List four or five more abstract terms of your own choosing. Then circle the one idea (above or below) that you want to write about in a definition essay.

_______ _______ _______ _______ _______

Gathering Your Own Thoughts

Once you select an essay topic, explore your thoughts and feelings about it. This will help you discover what you already know about the topic and what you still need to find out about it.

Vocabulary

abstract
something without shape, structure, or any other dimension

Explore In the space provided below, write freely about your topic. Consider why you selected it, what you already know about it, when and where you have seen it in action, and so on. (Use your own paper if you need more space.)

Collecting Additional Information

For most types of academic essays, you will need to find out more information than you already know about a topic. Martina, for example, found a definition of her term and used it in the first paragraph of her essay. Then, in her middle paragraphs, she identified the idea's essential parts and also determined what her topic isn't.

Collect Complete the gathering grid below to collect information about your topic.

Gathering Grid

Dictionary definition	
One component or part of the topic	
Another component or part of the topic	
A third component (optional)	
What your topic is not (consider a key antonym or two)	

Focusing Your Efforts

Once you understand your topic well, you are ready to write a thesis statement that explains the focus of your essay.

Create Write a thesis statement for your essay of definition following this formula:

Topic		Thought or Feeling		Thesis Statement
Tact	+	the sensitive handling of situations, even those that are potentially hurtful	=	Tact is the sensitive handling of situations, even those that are potentially hurtful.

Thesis Statement:

____

____

____

Organizing Your Ideas for Writing

To complete your planning, decide which main points to include (*ideas that support your thesis*) and how to arrange them.

Arrange Number the main points in your gathering grid above to put them in the best order for your essay.

Learning Outcome

Draft an essay.

LO3 Writing: Creating a First Draft

An essay consists of the opening, the middle, and the closing parts, just as a paragraph has a topic sentence, body sentences, and a closing sentence.

- The topic sentence becomes the opening paragraph.
- The body sentences become the middle paragraphs.
- The closing sentence becomes the closing paragraph.

Paragraph Structure

Topic Sentence

A **topic sentence** names the topic.

Body Sentences

Body sentences support the topic.

Closing Sentence

A **closing sentence** wraps up the paragraph.

Essay Structure

Opening Paragraph

The **opening paragraph** draws the reader into the essay and provides information that leads to a thesis statement. The thesis statement tells what the essay is about.

Middle Paragraphs

The **middle paragraphs** support the thesis statement. Each middle paragraph needs a topic sentence, a variety of body sentences, and a closing sentence.

Closing Paragraph

The **closing paragraph** finishes the essay by revisiting the thesis statement, emphasizing an important detail, providing the reader with an interesting final thought, and/or looking toward the future.

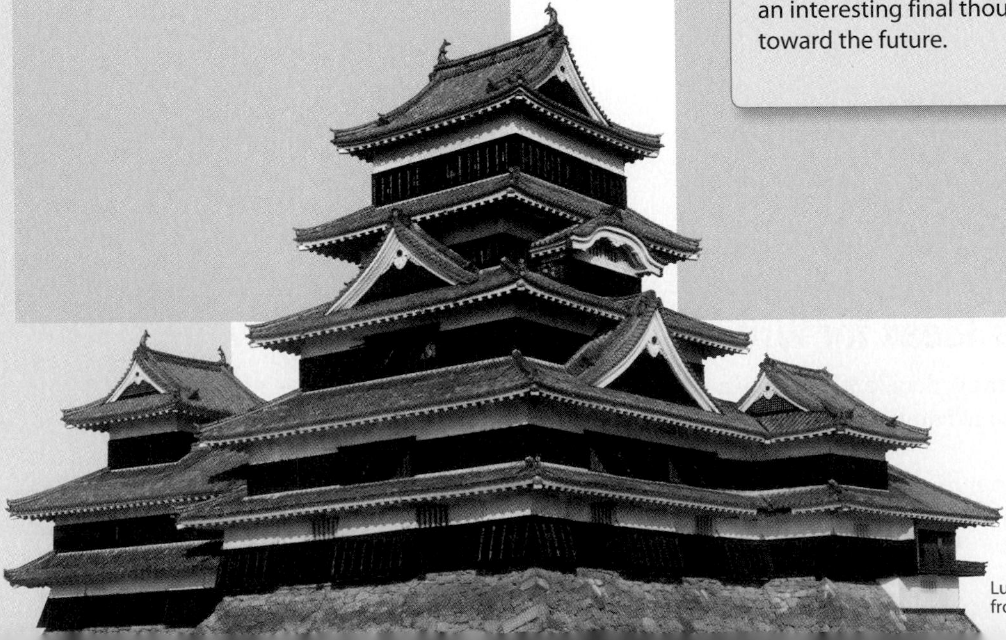

Luftikus, 2010/used under license from www.shutterstock.com

Writing the Opening Paragraph

The thesis statement is the most important part of the opening paragraph. But of course, there is more to an opening than this one statement. The writer must get the reader's attention with (1) a surprising statement, (2) an appropriate quotation, (3) a thought-provoking question, or (4) an anecdote (interesting story). Martina opens her essay with an anecdote and then states her thesis.

Create On your own paper, develop the opening paragraph for your definition essay. Begin by getting your reader's attention using one of the strategies above, then provide any necessary background information, and, finally, state your thesis.

Developing the Middle Part

The middle paragraphs in an essay support or explain the thesis. In most cases, each middle paragraph develops one main supporting point. Here is the thesis statement and the topic sentences for each of the middle paragraphs in Martina's essay.

Thesis Statement

Tact is the sensitive handling of situations, even those that are potentially hurtful.

Topic Sentences:

- *Sensitivity is a major component of tact.*
- *Truthfulness is another important component of tact.*
- *Tact should not be confused with deceit or cleverness.*

Traits

To support each topic sentence in your middle paragraphs, provide examples as Martina does in her paragraphs.

Write Continue your essay by writing the middle paragraphs. Be sure that each middle paragraph focuses on one main supporting point. Refer to your list of main points on page 183.

Ending the Essay

The closing paragraph brings an essay to a logical stopping point. An effective closing will often do one or more of these things: (1) restate the thesis, (2) review the main supporting points, (3) stress a key point, and/or (4) provide a final thought for the reader to consider.

In the sample essay, Martina reviews her main points and provides the reader with a few final key thoughts.

Create Complete your essay with a closing paragraph. Use at least two of the strategies listed above. Be sure to share important thoughts and ideas since they will create the final image of your topic for the reader.

Learning Outcome

Revise an essay.

Traits

Revising deals with improving the ideas and organization in your writing; it does not deal with correcting a few surface errors. That comes later.

LO4 Revising: Improving the Essay

During revising, you review your first draft to determine what parts work and what parts need to be improved. *Remember:* All first drafts require changes before they read clearly and logically. Your basic revising moves include adding, deleting, rewriting, and/or rearranging information.

Having a Peer Review Your Work

Always ask at least one of your writing peers to review your first draft. The feedback you receive will help you identify changes that you need to make. Use a peer-response sheet like the one below.

Respond Exchange first drafts with a classmate and complete this response sheet for each other's writing. (Keep your comments helpful and positive.)

Essay title: ____________________

Writer: ____________________ Reviewer: ____________________

1. What is the thesis of the essay? ____________________

2. List the main points that support the thesis. (There should be three or more.) ____________________

3. Does the closing paragraph bring the essay to an effective stopping point? If so, how?

4. What do you like most about the essay? ____________________

5. What could the writer do to improve the essay? ____________________

Building Coherence

To make sure that your essay is **coherent**, connect your ideas by repeating key words and adding transitions. Martina repeated key words and used a transition in the first and last sentences of her paragraphs to build coherence into her essay.

> "I tell them to use transitions, to start and finish each paragraph with an interlocking nut, a thread, so that the story is seamless."
> —Steve Lovelady

Coherence in Martina's Essay

- **Thesis statement:** Tact is the sensitive handling of situations, even those that are potentially hurtful.
- **First middle paragraph:** Sensitivity is a major component of tact. . . . But sensitivity by itself is not enough.
- **Second middle paragraph:** Truthfulness is another important component of tact. . . . These are tactful ways of dealing with uncomfortable truths.
- **Third middle paragraph:** Tact should not be confused with deceit and cleverness. . . . Being tactful requires speaking sincerely, not talking around or avoiding an issue.
- **Closing paragraph:** Sensitivity, truthfulness, and sincerity are all connected to tactfulness.

Revise Use your classmate's comments and the following checklist to improve the first draft of your essay. Add, cut, rewrite, and rearrange information as needed. Continue revising until you can check off each item in the list.

Ideas

- ☐ **1.** Does my essay draw the reader in and include a clear thesis statement?
- ☐ **2.** Do I support my thesis with at least three main ideas developed in separate paragraphs?
- ☐ **3.** Do I include enough details and examples in each paragraph?
- ☐ **4.** Does my closing paragraph bring the essay to an effective end?

Organization

- ☐ **5.** Does my essay include opening, middle, and closing paragraphs?
- ☐ **6.** Are my middle paragraphs in the best order?
- ☐ **7.** Are all of my details organized in the best way?
- ☐ **8.** Is my essay coherent, with key words or transitions linking paragraphs?

Voice

- ☐ **9.** Do I sound knowledgeable about and interested in my topic?

Vocabulary

coherent
logically ordered and connected

Learning Outcome

Edit an essay.

Test Taking

Some tests require you to correct errors with modifiers. For more practice, see pages 276–277.

LO5 Editing: Modifiers

When you edit your essay, you check it for style and correctness. Editing for style means making sure that you have used the best words and that your sentences read smoothly. Editing for correctness means making sure that you have followed the rules for punctuation, capitalization, usage, grammar, and spelling.

Dangling Modifiers

Dangling modifiers are a type of sentence error that can confuse the reader. They are modifiers that describe a word that isn't in the sentence.

Dangling modifier:

After finishing her routine, the judge rated the performance.
(It sounds as if the judge finished the routine.)

Corrected:

After Juanita finished her routine, the judge rated the performance.

Editing Practice Correct any dangling modifiers below by rewriting the sentences. If a sentence contains no modifying error, write a C on the line. (The first one has been done for you.)

1. Using a computer to diagnose the engine problem, my car was repaired. ________
   Using a computer to diagnose the engine problem, the mechanic repaired my car.
2. While playing the piano, our dog began to howl. ________
   ____
3. Scanning the horizon, a faint plume of smoke appeared. ________
   ____
4. After standing in line all morning, the ticket seller said all tickets were sold out.
   ____
   ____
5. After finishing the main course, the server wheeled out the dessert tray. ________
   ____

Vocabulary

dangling modifiers
phrases that appear to modify the wrong word or a word that isn't in the sentence

Apply Read through your essay, looking for dangling modifiers. Correct any that you find by rewriting the sentence so that the modifier clearly modifies the correct word.

Misplaced Modifiers

Misplaced modifiers are similar to dangling modifiers in that they create a confusing or illogical idea. They occur when a modifier seems to modify the wrong word in a sentence.

> **Misplaced modifier:**
>
> Ms. Jones fixed several snacks for the kids with healthful ingredients. *(It sounds as if the kids contain the healthful ingredients.)*
>
> **Corrected:**
>
> Ms. Jones fixed several snacks with healthful ingredients for the kids.

Editing Practice Underline the misplaced modifier in each of the following sentences. Then correct the error by rewriting the sentence. (The first one has been done for you.)

1. That painting is my favorite piece in the entire gallery <u>with the brilliant colors.</u>

   That painting with the brilliant colors is my favorite piece in the entire gallery.

2. Athletes must train rigorously to prepare for the Olympics without any letup.

3. When women rode bicycles, they were told it was not feminine in the 1890s.

4. I am visiting two apartments that I will consider renting over the weekend.

5. Please review the reśumé describing my qualifications and experience enclosed.

Apply Read through your essay, checking for misplaced modifiers. Correct any that you find by rewriting the sentence so that the modifier is placed next to the appropriate word.

"Essays are how we speak to one another in print."
—Edward Hoagland

Vocabulary

misplaced modifiers
modifying words or phrases that have been placed incorrectly, creating an unclear or confusing idea

Speaking & Listening

When editing, always read the writing out loud, at least once. Hearing the words will help you catch some errors that are easily missed during silent readings.

Correction Marks

- delete
- d ≡ capitalize
- Ɖ lowercase
- ∧ insert
- add comma
- ? ∧ add question mark
- word ∧ add a word
- ⊙ add period
- spelling
- switch

Vocabulary

chivalry
acting like a gentleman, with honesty, courtesy, and bravery

skeptics
people who doubt or question accepted beliefs

Using the Editing Symbols

When editing for correctness, use the correction marks on the left side of this page to mark errors and show how you would correct them.

Editing Practice Correct the following paragraphs from a student's definition essay, using the editing symbols.

Different Shades of Equality

Webster's collegiate Dictionary defines feminism as "the theory of political, economic, and social equality of the sexes." However, feminism is a movement that has significantly affected all women with varied interpretations. Ultimately, it defines itself according to the situation and the people involved.

Some feminists expect to be treated like men, while others want freedoms more closely associated with there own sex. Some feminists find nudity degrading, while others see it as an expression of art. Some feminists still appreciate **chivalry**, while others find it offensive

Some critics of the movement believe that some feminists have gone to far. Individuals that question the movement believe that some feminists equate equality with the freedom to do whatever they want. **skeptics** also say that radical feminists begrudge men their sexual difference. That true equality should negate the facts of life.

A more moderate approach to feminism focuses on issues such as sharing with men the right to justice, the right to be treated with respect and the right to make important lifestyle choices. A moderate feminist wants the freedom to decide whether to focus on a career, on motherhood, or on a combination of the two. What a moderate feminist doesn't want is to be accused of surrendering to male dominance. If she, for example, chooses to be a stay-at-home mom, at least for part of her life.

Some women don't want to be associated with feminism. They don't want to get a job because they are the token woman, they are not interested in recieving any other special favors. They is quite satisfied with being a woman, but in a world where the capabilities and interests of the individual are what really matters.

Correcting Your Essay

When editing your paragraphs and essays, it helps to use a basic checklist as a guide. You may also want to keep a personal list of errors as a handy reference.

Apply Create a clean copy of your essay; then use the following checklist to edit it for errors. When you can answer yes to a question, check it off. Continue editing until all of the items are checked.

Editing Checklist

Words

- ☐ **1.** Have I used specific nouns and verbs? (See page 103.)
- ☐ **2.** Have I used more action verbs than "be" verbs? (See page 73.)

Sentences

- ☐ **3.** Have I varied the beginnings and lengths of sentences? (See pages 226–231.)
- ☐ **4.** Have I combined short choppy sentences? (See page 232.)
- ☐ **5.** Have I avoided shifts in sentences? (See page 278.)
- ☐ **6.** Have I avoided fragments and run-ons? (See pages 261–266, 270–271.)

Conventions

- ☐ **7.** Do I use correct verb forms (*he saw,* not *he seen*)? (See pages 320, 324.)
- ☐ **8.** Do my subjects and verbs agree (*she speaks,* not *she speak*)? (See pages 245–260.)
- ☐ **9.** Have I used the right words (*their, there, they're*)?
- ☐ **10.** Have I capitalized first words and proper nouns and adjectives? (See page 386.)
- ☐ **11.** Have I used commas after long introductory word groups? (See page 358.)
- ☐ **12.** Have I punctuated dialogue correctly? (See pages 104–105.)
- ☐ **13.** Have I carefully checked my spelling?

Adding a Title

Be sure to add an appropriate title to your essay. Here are three simple strategies for creating one.

- **Pick up on a key phrase:** A Movement Gone Too Far?
- **Focus on an important element:** Different Shades of Equality
- **Use strong, colorful words from the paragraph:** A Defining Movement

Create Prepare a clean final copy of your essay and proofread it.

Insight

Remember to have a classmate or writing tutor check your writing for errors. You are too close to your writing to catch everything.

Learning Outcome

Prepare the final copy for publishing.

WAC

The most immediate form of publishing is submitting your writing to your instructor. Other forms of publishing include sharing your work with your writing peers or posting it on a class wiki or your own blog for comments.

LO6 Preparing Your Final Copy

After revising and editing your essay, you're ready to prepare the final copy for publishing. The guide that follows will help you complete this important final step in the writing process.

Preparation Guide

Be sure that you have . . .

- made all of the necessary revising and editing changes.
- responded to peer reviews of your work.
- saved all of your drafts for handy reference.
- developed a neat final copy of your work.
- **proofread** this copy for errors.
- adhered to the design guidelines provided by your instructor.

Effective Design in Action

Maintain a uniform margin.

Double-space throughout.

Use an easy-to-read typeface.

Indent first words of paragraphs.

Martina Lincoln

Dr. Meyer

Composition 101

October 15, 2011

Break It to Them Gently

A few years ago, there was a new student in one of my high school classes. (I'll call him Bill.) Bill suffered from unbearably yellow teeth that grossed everyone out. One loudmouthed boor suggested that Bill "Ajax" his teeth. Of course, Bill turned every shade of red and just wanted to disappear. Had the boor any sense of empathy, he would have realized that there were far more tactful ways to address the new student. Tact is the sensitive handling of situations, even those that are potentially hurtful.

Sensitivity is a major component of tact. If a person isn't sensitive to another person's feelings, there is no way that he or she can be tactful. Young people are especially vulnerable and must be handled sensitively. . . .

Prepare Complete the final copy of your definition essay, using the information on this page as a guide. Be sure to proofread this copy before you submit it.

Vocabulary

proofread
the process of checking a final copy for errors

Reinforcement

Complete these activities as needed to help you better understand the essay-writing process.

Paragraph vs. Essay Explain below the basic differences between a paragraph and an essay. (See pages 54–55.)

____

____

____

Collecting Information Once you select a specific topic for an essay, what first step should you take to gather information, and why is the step important? (See page 182.)

____

____

____

Thesis Statement What formula can you use to write a thesis statement? (See page 183.)

____

Drafting an Essay An essay must have opening, middle, and closing parts. What type of information should you include in each part? (See page 184.)

Opening: ______________________________

____

____

Middle: ______________________________

____

____

Closing: ______________________________

____

____

Part 4 Sentence Workshops

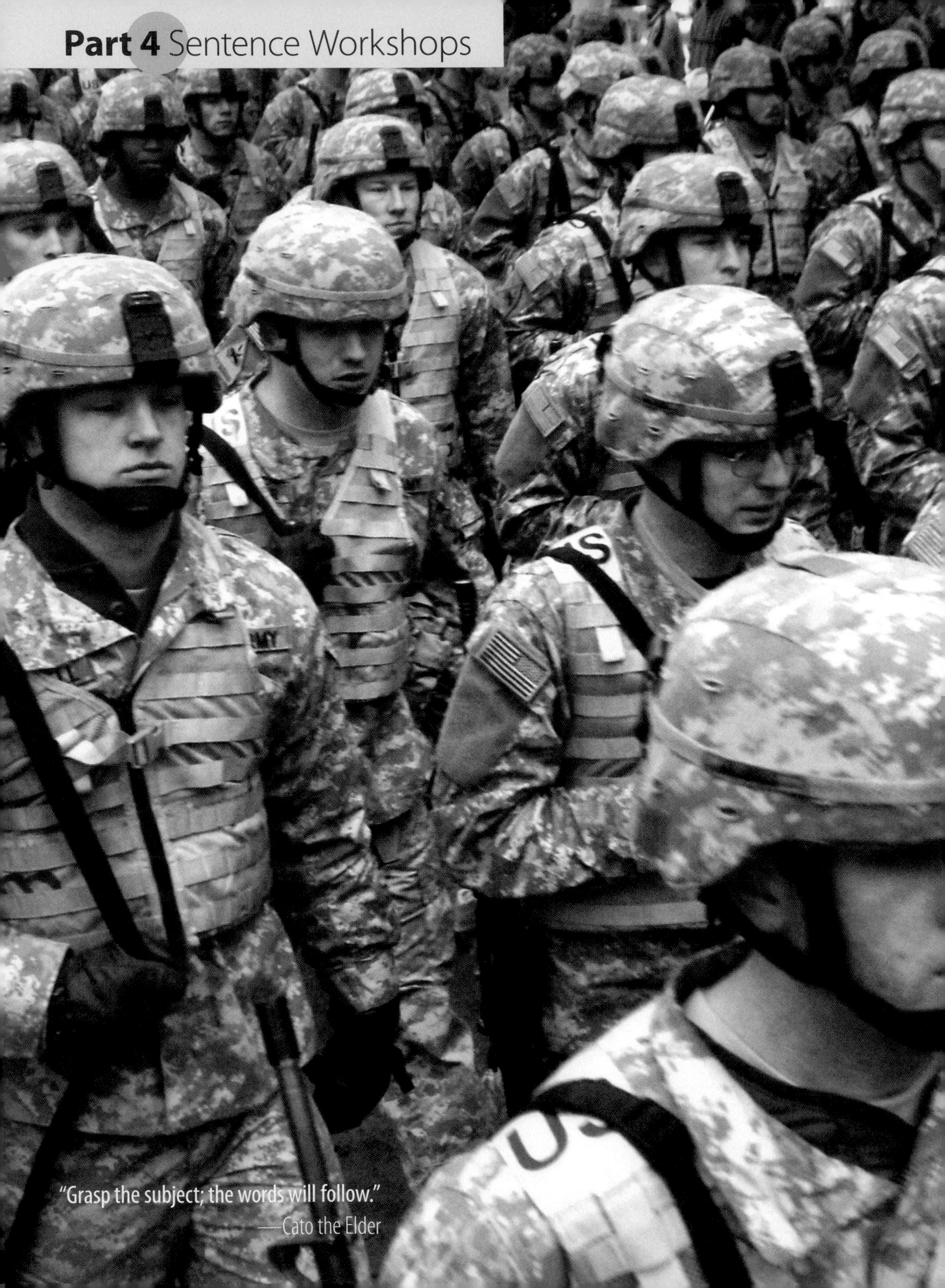

"Grasp the subject; the words will follow."
—Cato the Elder

Courtesy of the U.S. Army/www.army.mil.

Sentence Basics

All right, soldiers, fall in for basic training. Of course, you've studied all of this before, so the following pages will be a review. And the basics of sentences really *are* basic. A sentence is the connection between a noun and a verb (or a subject and a predicate), with all of the other words modifying those two parts.

In the pages that follow, you will explore the ins and outs of subjects and predicates, as well as the words, phrases, and clauses that describe them. Fear not. These are sentence basics, and we'll make sure they are easy to understand.

What do you think?

Read the quotation from Cato the Elder on the facing page. How does grasping the subject of a sentence (or of a longer piece of writing) help you write the rest of the words?

Learning Outcomes

- **LO1** Understand subjects and predicates.
- **LO2** Work with special subjects.
- **LO3** Work with special predicates.
- **LO4** Understand adjectives.
- **LO5** Understand adverbs.
- **LO6** Use prepositional phrases.
- **LO7** Use clauses.
- **LO8** Apply sentence basics in a real-world context.

Learning Outcome

Understand subjects and predicates.

LO1 Subjects and Verbs (Predicates)

The subject of a sentence tells what the sentence is about. The verb (predicate) of a sentence tells what the subject does or is.

Parrots talk.

Subject: what the sentence is about

Predicate: what the subject does

Simple Subject and Simple Predicate

The **simple subject** is the subject without any modifiers, and the **simple predicate** is the predicate without modifiers or objects.

The red and black parrot sang the song all day.
(parrot = simple subject; sang = simple predicate)

Complete Subject and Complete Predicate

The **complete subject** is the subject with modifiers, and the **complete predicate** is the predicate with modifiers and objects.

The red and black parrot sang the song all day.
(The red and black parrot = complete subject; sang the song all day = complete predicate)

Implied Subject

In commands, the subject *you* is implied. Commands are the only type of sentence in English that can have an **implied subject**.

(You) = implied subject   Stop singing! = complete predicate

Inverted Order

Most often in English, the subject comes before the predicate. However, in questions and sentences that begin with *here* or *there*, the subject comes after the predicate.

Why are you so loud? (are = predicate; you = subject)   Here is a cracker. (is = predicate; cracker = subject)

Vocabulary

simple subject
the subject without any modifiers

simple predicate
the predicate without modifiers or objects

complete subject
the subject with modifiers

complete predicate
the predicate with modifiers and objects

implied subject
the word *you* implied in command sentences

Creating Subjects and Verbs (Predicates)

Identify/Write For each sentence below, underline and label the simple subject (SS) and simple predicate (SP). Then write a similar sentence of your own and identify the simple subject and simple predicate in the same way.

1. In the wild, parrots gather in large groups.
2. In a person's home, a parrot needs constant companionship.
3. Without enough attention, some parrots pluck their feathers.
4. A caring pet owner understands the parrot's need for attention.

Identify/Write For each sentence below, underline and label the complete subject (CS) and complete predicate (CP). Then write a similar sentence of your own and identify the complete subject and complete predicate in the same way.

1. A typical pet parrot can live to be eighty years old.
2. A baby parrot bought by a forty-year-old could outlive the person.
3. Parrot owners often place their parrots in their wills.
4. Why do parrots live so long?
5. There must be an explanation.

Learning Outcome

Work with special subjects.

LO2 Special Types of Subjects

As you work with subjects, watch for these special types.

Compound Subjects

A **compound subject** is two or more subjects connected by *and* or *or*.

My brother and sister swim well. Dajohn, Larinda, and I love to dive.
(brother and sister: compound subject; Dajohn, Larinda, and I: compound subject)

"To" Words (Infinitives) as Subjects

An **infinitive** can function as a subject. An infinitive is a verbal form that begins with *to* and may be followed by objects or modifiers.

To complete a one-and-a-half flip is my goal.
(To complete a one-and-a-half flip: infinitive subject)

"Ing" Words (Gerunds) as Subjects

A **gerund** can function as a subject. A gerund is a verb form that ends in *ing* and may be followed by objects or modifiers.

Swimming is his favorite sport. Handing him the goggles would be nice.
(Swimming: gerund subject; Handing him the goggles: gerund subject)

Noun Clause as Subject

A **noun clause** can function as a subject. The clause itself has a subject and a verb but cannot stand alone as a sentence. Noun clauses are introduced by words like *what, that, when, why, how, whatever,* or *whichever*.

Whoever wants to go swimming must remember to bring a swimsuit.
(Whoever wants to go swimming: noun clause subject)

Whatever remains of the afternoon will be spent at the pool.
(Whatever remains of the afternoon: noun clause subject)

Traits

Note that each of these special subjects still functions as a noun or a group of nouns. A sentence is still, at root, the connection between a noun and a verb.

Vocabulary

compound subject
two or more subjects connected by *and* or *or*

infinitive
a verb form that begins with *to* and can be used as a noun (or as an adjective or adverb)

gerund
a verb form that ends in *ing* and is used as a noun

noun clause
a group of words beginning with words like *that, what, whoever,* and so on; containing a subject and a verb but unable to function as a sentence

Say It

Pair up with a partner and read each sentence aloud. Take turns identifying the type of subject—compound subject, infinitive subject, gerund subject, or noun-clause subject. Discuss your answers.

1. Swimming across the pool underwater is challenging.
2. To get a lifesaving certificate is hard work.
3. Whoever gets a certificate can be a lifeguard.
4. You and I should go swimming sometime.

Creating Special Subjects

Identify/Write For each sentence below, underline and label the complete subject: compound subject (CS), infinitive (I), gerund (G), or noun clause (NC). Then write a similar sentence of your own and identify the complete subject in the same way.

1. To clean the car thoroughly requires a vacuum.

2. Wishing for better weather won't stop the rain.

3. The river and the lake are flooding into the streets.

4. Whoever needs to set the table should get started now.

5. Shoes, shirts, and pants are required in this restaurant.

6. Reading us the riot act is not the best way to win us over.

7. To reassure your boss about the expenditures is your first priority.

8. Whatever you plan needs to be simple and affordable.

9. Are Jason, Micah, and Eli in the play?

10. Helping us change the tire will speed everything along.

Learning Outcome

Work with special predicates.

LO3 Special Verbs (Predicates)

As you work with predicates, watch for these special types.

Compound Predicates

A **compound predicate** consists of two or more predicates joined by *and* or *or*.

I sang and danced. The audience laughed, clapped, and sang along.
(sang and danced = compound predicate; laughed, clapped, and sang along = compound predicate)

Predicates with Direct Objects

A **direct object** follows a transitive verb and tells what or who receives the action of the verb.

I sang a song. I danced a few dances. I told a joke or two.
(song = direct object; dances = direct object; joke, two = direct objects)

Aaron Amat, 2010/used under license from www.shutterstock.com

Predicates with Indirect Objects

An **indirect object** comes between a transitive verb and a direct object and tells to whom or for whom an action was done.

I sang Jim his favorite song. I told Ellen her favorite joke.
(Jim = indirect object; Ellen = indirect object)

Passive Predicates

When a predicate is **passive**, the subject of the sentence is being acted upon rather than acting. Often, the actor is the object of the preposition in a phrase that starts with *by*. Using that object as the subject, the sentence can be rewritten to be **active**.

Passive	Active
Teri was serenaded by Josh.	Josh serenaded Teri.
Teri = subject; was serenaded = passive verb; Josh = object of the preposition	Josh = subject; serenaded = active verb; Teri = direct object

Vocabulary

compound predicate
two or more predicates joined by *and* or *or*

direct object
a word that follows a transitive verb and tells what or who receives the action of the verb

indirect object
a word that comes between a transitive verb and a direct object and tells to whom or for whom an action was done

passive
the voice created when a subject is being acted upon

active
the voice created when a subject is acting

Say It

Pair up with a partner and read each sentence aloud. Take turns identifying the sentence as active or passive. If the sentence is passive, speak the active version out loud.

1. I threw out my back.
2. My friends were warned by the bouncer.
3. A camera crew was escorted to the exit by the guard.
4. I plan to go.

Creating Special Predicates

Identify/Write For each sentence below, underline and label any compound predicate (CP), direct object (DO), and indirect object (IO). Then write a similar sentence of your own and identify the compound predicate and direct or indirect object in the same way.

1. Everyone at the party danced and sang.

2. The DJ played dance music.

3. I gave him a request.

4. The crowd twisted and shouted.

5. I gave my date a kiss.

6. The music rattled and boomed.

7. The DJ provided everyone some awesome entertainment.

Identify/Write For each passive sentence below, underline and label the simple subject (SS), the simple predicate (SP), and the object of the preposition *by* (O). Then rewrite each sentence, making it active. (See "Passive Predicates" on the previous page.)

1. Many songs were played by the DJ.

2. A good time was had by the partygoers.

3. My friend was asked by Sarah to the next party.

Learning Outcome

Understand adjectives.

Baloncici 2010/used under license from www.shutterstock.com

Insight

It's less important to know the name of a phrase or clause than to know how it functions. If a group of words answers one of the adjective questions, the words are probably functioning as an adjective.

LO4 Adjectives

To modify a noun, use an adjective or a phrase or clause acting as an adjective.

Adjectives

Adjectives answer these basic questions: *which, what kind of, how many, how much*.

To modify the noun **books,** ask . . .

Which books? → hardbound books

What kind of books? → old books

How many books? → five books

five old hardbound books

Adjective Phrases and Clauses

Phrases and clauses can also act as adjectives to modify nouns.

To modify the noun **books,** ask . . .

What kind of books? → books about women's issues

→ books showing their age

Which books? → books that my mother gave me

Showing their age, the books that my mother gave me about women's issues rest on the top shelf.

Say It

Pair up with a classmate to find adjectives—words, phrases, or clauses—that modify the nouns below. Take turns asking the questions while the other person answers.

1. **Cars**
   Which cars?
   What kind of cars?
   How many cars?
2. **Trees**
   Which trees?
   What kind of trees?
   How many trees?

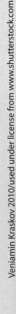

Veniamin Kraskov 2010/used under license from www.shutterstock.com

Use Adjectives

Answer/Write For each noun, answer the questions using adjectives—words, phrases, or clauses. (See page 202 for help.) Then write a sentence using two or more of your answers.

1. **Dogs**

Which dogs? ______

What kind of dogs? ______

How many dogs? ______

Sentence: ______

2. **Classes**

Which classes? ______

What kind of classes? ______

How many classes? ______

Sentence: ______

3. **Ideas**

Which ideas? ______

What kind of ideas? ______

How many ideas? ______

Sentence: ______

Learning Outcome

Understand adverbs.

LO5 Adverbs

To modify a verb, use an adverb or a phrase or clause acting as an adverb.

Adverbs

Adverbs answer these basic questions: *how, when, where, why, how long,* and *how often*.

To modify the verb **jumped,** ask . . .

How did they jump? ⟶ jumped exuberantly

When did they jump? ⟶ jumped today

Where did they jump? ⟶ jumped there

How often did they jump? ⟶ jumped often

The children jumped exuberantly and often today, there on the pile of old mattresses.

Adverb Phrases and Clauses

Phrases and clauses can also act as adverbs to modify verbs.

To modify the verb **jumped,** ask . . .

How did they jump? ⟶ jumped with great enthusiasm

When did they jump? ⟶ jumped before lunchtime

Where did they jump? ⟶ jumped on the trampoline

Why did they jump? ⟶ jumped to get some exercise

⟶ jumped because it's fun

How long did they jump? ⟶ jumped for an hour

To get some exercise before lunchtime, the children jumped on the trampoline with great enthusiasm. I think, though, that they jumped for an hour just because it's fun!

Speaking & Listening

Read the last two sentences aloud. Though they may look imposing on the page, they sound completely natural, probably because adverbs and adjectives are a common part of our speech. Experiment with these modifiers in your writing as well.

Jacek Chabraszewski 2010/used under license from www.shutterstock.com

Using Adverbs

Answer/Write For each verb, answer the questions using adverbs—words, phrases, or clauses. (See page 204 for help.) Then write a sentence using three or more of your answers.

1. Sang

How did they sing? ____________________

When did they sing? ____________________

Where did they sing? ____________________

Why did they sing? ____________________

How long did they sing? ____________________

How often did they sing? ____________________

Sentence: ____________________

____

____

____

____

2. Ate

How did they eat? ____________________

When did they eat? ____________________

Where did they eat? ____________________

Why did they eat? ____________________

How long did they eat? ____________________

How often did they eat? ____________________

Sentence: ____________________

____

____

____

____

Learning Outcome

Use prepositional phrases.

LO6 Prepositional Phrases

One of the simplest and most versatile types of phrases in English is the **prepositional phrase**. A prepositional phrase can function as an adjective or an adverb.

Building Prepositional Phrases

A prepositional phrase is a preposition followed by an object (a noun or pronoun) and any modifiers.

Preposition	+	Object	=	Prepositional Phrase
at		noon		at noon
in		an hour		in an hour
beside		the green clock		beside the green clock
in front of		my aunt's vinyl purse		in front of my aunt's vinyl purse

As you can see, a propositional phrase can be just two words long, or many words long. As you can also see, some prepositions are themselves made up of more than one word. Here is a list of common prepositions.

Insight

A preposition is pre-positioned before the other words it introduces to form a phrase. Other languages have post-positional words that follow the words they modify.

Prepositions

aboard	back of	except for	near to	round
about	because of	excepting	notwithstanding	save
above	before	for	of	since
according to	behind	from	off	subsequent to
across	below	from among	on	through
across from	beneath	from between	on account of	throughout
after	beside	from under	on behalf of	'til
against	besides	in	onto	to
along	between	in addition to	on top of	together with
alongside	beyond	in behalf of	opposite	toward
alongside of	but	in front of	out	under
along with	by	in place of	out of	underneath
amid	by means of	in regard to	outside	until
among	concerning	inside	outside of	unto
apart from	considering	inside of	over	up
around	despite	in spite of	over to	upon
as far as	down	instead of	owing to	up to
aside from	down from	into	past	with
at	during	like	prior to	within
away from	except	near	regarding	without

Vocabulary

prepositional phrase
a group of words beginning with a preposition and including an object (noun or pronoun) and any modifiers

Using Phrases

Create For each item below, create a prepositional phrase by writing a preposition in the first box and an object (and any modifiers) in the second box. Then write a sentence using the prepositional phrase.

1. Preposition + Object (and any modifiers)

Sentence: ______________________________

2. Preposition + Object (and any modifiers)

Sentence: ______________________________

3. Preposition + Object (and any modifiers)

Sentence: ______________________________

4. Preposition + Object (and any modifiers)

Sentence: ______________________________

5. Preposition + Object (and any modifiers)

Sentence: ______________________________

Learning Outcome

Use clauses.

Speaking & Listening

In each example, read the dependent clause out loud. (The dependent clause is in red.) Can you hear how each dependent clause sounds incomplete? Read it to another person, and the listener will probably say, "What about it?" These clauses depend on a complete thought to make sense.

Vocabulary

independent clause
a group of words with a subject and predicate that expresses a complete thought

dependent clause
a group of words with a subject and predicate that does not express a complete thought

adverb clause
a dependent clause beginning with a subordinating conjunction and functioning as an adverb

adjective clause
a dependent clause beginning with a relative pronoun and functioning as an adjective

noun clause
a dependent clause beginning with a subordinating word and functioning as a noun

LO7 Clauses

A clause is a group of words with a subject and a predicate. If a clause can stand on its own as a sentence, it is an **independent clause**, but if it cannot, it is a **dependent clause**.

Independent Clause

An independent clause has a subject and a predicate and expresses a complete thought. It is the same as a simple sentence.

I have nineteen pets.

Dependent Clause

A dependent clause has a subject and a predicate but does not express a complete thought. Instead, it is used as an **adverb clause**, an **adjective clause**, or a **noun clause**.

An adverb clause begins with a subordinating conjunction (see below) and functions as an adverb, so it must be connected to an independent clause to be complete.

after	before	since	when
although	even though	so that	whenever
as	given that	that	where
as if	if	though	whereas
as long as	in order that	unless	while
because	provided that	until	

Because I have nineteen pets, I have a big pet-food bill.

An adjective clause begins with a relative pronoun *(which, that, who)* and functions as an adjective, so it must be connected to an independent clause to be complete.

My oldest pet is a cat that thinks he is a person.

A noun clause begins with words like those below and functions as a noun. It is used as a subject or an object in a sentence.

how	what	whoever	whomever
that	whatever	whom	why

My cat doesn't care about what I think.

Using Clauses

Identify/Write For each sentence below, underline and label any adverb clauses (ADVC), adjective clauses (ADJC), or noun clauses (NC). Then write a similar sentence of your own and identify the clauses.

1. I know a woman who has fifteen cats.

2. The number is so high because she takes care of shelter kittens.

3. When a pregnant cat is dropped at the shelter, this woman takes her home.

4. She provides what the mother and the kittens need.

5. Whatever cat comes to her receives good care.

6. People who are cruel to animals should not have pets.

7. When I visit my friend, I see plenty of kittens.

8. All are safe provided that they don't escape.

9. My friend has a shirt that has the words "Cat Lady" printed on it.

10. Though others might scoff, my friend is proud of what she does.

Learning Outcome

Apply sentence basics in a real-world context.

LO8 Real-World Application

Identify In the e-mail below, underline simple subjects once and simple predicates twice. Circle dependent clauses.

Send | Attach | Fonts | Colors | Save As Draft

To: Robert Pastorelli

Subject: Meeting to Discuss Benefits and Policies

Dear Robert:

I am pleased to hear that you have accepted the Production Manager position at Rankin Technologies. I believe that you'll find many opportunities for professional growth with us.

Our Human Resources Department is here to help you grow. To that end, I would like to discuss Rankin's benefit package, policies, and procedures. Specifically, I'd like to share the following information:

- Profit-sharing plan
- Medical-plan benefits for you and your family
- Procedures for submitting dental and optometry receipts
- Counseling services
- Continuing-education programs
- Advancement policies and procedures
- Workplace policies

On Friday, I'll call to set up a convenient time for your orientation meeting. I look forward to spending time with you reviewing this useful information. In the meantime, if you have questions, please contact me at extension 3925 or simply reply to this message.

Sincerely,
Julia

Expand Answer the adjective and adverb questions below. Then expand the sentence using some of the words, phrases, and clauses you have created.

The manager spoke.

Which **manager?** ______________________________

What kind of **manager?** ______________________________

Spoke ***how?*** ______________________________

Spoke ***when?*** ______________________________

Sentence: ______________________________

"A complex system that works is invariably found to have evolved from a simple system that works."

—John Gaule

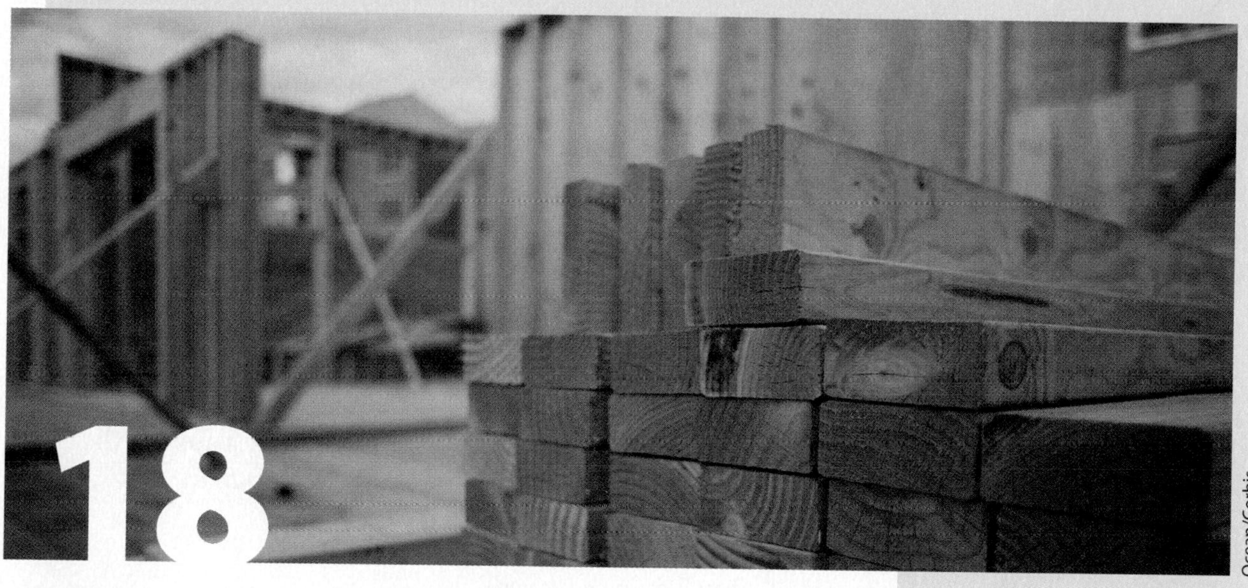

Ocean/Corbis

Simple, Compound, and Complex Sentences

A two-by-four is a simple thing—a board with standard dimensions. But two-by-fours can be used to create everything from a shed to a mansion. It's the way that the boards are connected and combined that determines the proportions of the final structure.

A sentence can be a simple thing as well, just a subject and a verb. But sentences can also be connected to become compound or complex sentences. The way in which writers use simple, compound, and complex sentences determines the maturity of their writing.

What do you think?

If you could build anything out of two-by-fours, what would you build? If you could build anything out of sentences, what would you build? Why?

Learning Outcomes

- LO1 Create simple sentences.
- LO2 Create simple sentences with compound subjects.
- LO3 Create simple sentences with compound verbs (predicates).
- LO4 Create compound sentences.
- LO5 Create complex sentences.
- LO6 Create complex sentences with relative clauses.
- LO7 Apply simple, compound, and complex sentences in a real-world context.

Learning Outcome

Create simple sentences.

LO1 Simple Sentences

A **simple sentence** consists of a subject and a verb. The subject is a noun or pronoun that names what the sentence is about. The verb tells what the subject does or is.

Terrance played.
subject verb

Modifiers

Other words can modify the subject. Words and phrases that modify the subject answer the adjective questions: *which, what kind of, how many, how much.*

My longtime friend Terrance played.
(The phrase tells *which Terrance.*)

Other words can also modify the verb. These words and phrases answer the adverb questions: *how, when, where, why, how long,* and *how often.*

Terrance played **all afternoon and into the evening.**
(The phrases tell *when Terrance played.*)

Direct and Indirect Objects

The verb may also be followed by a **direct object**, a noun or pronoun that receives the action of the verb. The direct object answers the question *what* or *whom.*

Terrance played **basketball.**
(*Basketball* tells *what Terrance played.*)

A noun or pronoun that comes between the verb and its direct object is called an **indirect object**. The indirect object answers the question *to whom* or *for whom* an action is done.

Terrance passed **me** the basketball.
(*Me* tells *to whom Terrance passed the basketball.*)

Vocabulary

simple sentence
a subject and a verb that together form a complete thought

direct object
a noun or pronoun that follows a verb and receives its action

indirect object
a noun or pronoun that comes between a verb and a direct object, telling *to whom* or *for whom* an action is done

Say It

Team up with a partner and follow these steps: One of you speaks the sentence aloud, and the other asks the question in italics. Then the first person says the sentence again, inserting an answer.

1. We played basketball. *(Where did you play basketball?)*
2. The team won. *(Which team won?)*
3. Terrance passed. *(What did Terrance pass?)*
4. We gave a trophy. *(We gave a trophy to whom?)*

Insight

In item 1, you are adding modifiers to the verb, and in item 2, you are adding modifiers to the subject. In item 3, you are adding a direct object, and in item 4, you are adding an indirect object.

Create Simple Sentences

Create For each item below, create a simple sentence by writing a subject in the first box and a verb in the second. Then write the sentence, including modifiers that answer the question in parentheses.

1. **Subject** | **Verb**

(Which?)

Simple sentence: ______________________________

____

2. **Subject** | **Verb**

(What kind of?)

Simple sentence: ______________________________

____

3. **Subject** | **Verb**

(When?)

Simple sentence: ______________________________

____

4. **Subject** | **Verb**

(Where?)

Simple sentence: ______________________________

____

5. **Subject** | **Verb**

(How?)

Simple sentence: ______________________________

____

Learning Outcome

Create simple sentences with compound subjects.

LO2 Simple Sentences with Compound Subjects

A simple sentence can have a **compound subject** (two or more subjects).

A Simple Sentence with Two Subjects

To write a simple sentence with two subjects, join them using *and* or *or*.

One Subject: **Chan** collected donations for the animal shelter.
Two Subjects: **Chan and Lynn** collected donations for the animal shelter.
Chan or Lynn collected the most donations.

One Subject: The **president** of the shelter gave Lynn an award.
Two Subjects: The **president and vice president** of the shelter gave Lynn an award.
The **president or** the **vice president** of the shelter thanked her for her hard work.

Traits

Using a compound subject in a simple sentence does not make the sentence compound. As long as the subjects connect to the same verb, the sentence is still considered simple.

A Simple Sentence with Three or More Subjects

To write a simple sentence with three or more subjects, create a series, using *and* or *or* before the last one.

Three Subjects: **Chan, Lynn, and I** went out to celebrate.
Five Subjects: **Chan, Lynn,** the **president,** the **vice president**, **and I** were interviewed by a reporter.

Note: When a compound subject is joined by *and*, the subject is plural and requires a plural verb. When a compound subject is joined by *or*, the verb should match the last subject.

Chan and Lynn plan to help out again next year.
Chan or Lynn plans to help out again next year.

Say It

Speak each of the following sentences out loud.

1. Chan *volunteers* regularly.
2. Chan *and* Lynn *volunteer* regularly.
3. Chan *or* Lynn *volunteers* once a month.
4. Chan, Lynn, *and* Dave *help* at the shelter each week.
5. Chan, Lynn, *or* Dave *helps* at the shelter each week.

Vocabulary

compound subject
two or more subjects joined by the conjunction *or* or *and*

Using Compound Subjects

Create For each item below, write subjects in the boxes provided. Then connect the subjects using *and* or *or* and use the compound subject in a simple sentence.

1. Subject | Subject

Simple sentence: ______________________________

2. Subject | Subject

Simple sentence: ______________________________

3. Subject | Subject | Subject

Simple sentence: ______________________________

4. Subject | Subject | Subject

Simple sentence: ______________________________

5. Subject | Subject | Subject | Subject

Simple sentence: ______________________________

6. Subject | Subject | Subject | Subject

Simple sentence: ______________________________

Learning Outcome

Create simple sentences with compound verbs (predicates).

Traits

Using a compound verb in a simple sentence does not make the sentence compound. As long as the verbs connect to the same subject, the sentence is still considered simple.

LO3 Simple Sentences with Compound Verbs

A simple sentence can have a **compound verb** (two or more verbs).

A Simple Sentence with Two Verbs

To write a simple sentence with two verbs, join them using *and* or *or*.

One Verb: The tornado **roared**.
Two Verbs: The tornado **roared and twisted**.

Remember that the predicate often includes words that modify or complete the verbs.

One Verb: A tornado **tore** through our town.
Two Verbs: A tornado **tore** through our town **and damaged** buildings.

A Simple Sentence with Three or More Verbs

To write a simple sentence with three or more verbs, create a series, using *and* or *or* before the last one.

Three Verbs: The tornado **roared**, **twisted**, **and shuddered**.
Five Verbs: People **shouted**, **ran**, **gathered**, **hid**, **and waited**.

Each verb in a series can also include modifiers or completing words (direct and indirect objects).

The tornado **tore** apart a warehouse, **ripped** the roofs from homes, **and flattened** trailers in a local park.

Jacek Don Hammond/Design Pics/Corbis

Vocabulary

compound verb
two or more verbs joined by the conjunction *or* or *and*

Using Compound Verbs

Create For each subject below, write verbs, along with modifiers or completing words, in the boxes provided. (See page 216.) Then create a compound verb using *and* or *or* and write the complete simple sentence on the lines.

1. The hailstorm

Verb

Verb

Simple sentence: ______________________________

____

2. Driving rain

Verb

Verb

Simple sentence: ______________________________

____

3. A news crew

Verb

Verb

Simple sentence: ______________________________

____

4. Many homes

Verb

Verb

Verb

Simple sentence: ______________________________

____

____

Learning Outcome

Create compound sentences.

Insight

The word *and* indicates that the second clause provides additional information. The words *but, or, nor,* and *yet* create a contrast. The words *for* and *so* indicate that the idea shared in one clause is the cause of the other.

LO4 Compound Sentences

A **compound sentence** is made out of simple sentences joined by a coordinating conjunction: *and, but, or, nor, for, so,* or *yet*.

Compound of Two Sentences

Most compound sentences connect two simple sentences, or independent clauses. Connect the sentences by placing a comma and a coordinating conjunction between them.

Two Sentences: We drove all night. The sun rose behind us.
Compound Sentence: We drove all night**, and** the sun rose behind us.

You can also join two sentences with a semicolon.

Compound Sentence: We drove all night**;** the sun rose behind us.

Compound of Three or More Sentences

Sometimes, you may want to join three or more short sentences to form a compound sentence.

Three Sentences: I drove. Janice navigated. Paulo slept.
Compound Sentence: I drove**,** Janice navigated**, and** Paulo slept.

You can also join the sentences with semicolons. This approach works well for sharing a long, involved process or a flurry of activity.

I took the shift from Williamsburg to Monticello; Janice drove from Monticello to Louisville; Paulo brought us from Louisville to Indianapolis.

Note: Remember that a compound sentence is made of two or more simple sentences, each containing its own subject and verb.

Image Source/Corbis

Vocabulary

compound sentence
two or more simple sentences joined with a coordinating conjunction

Create Compound Sentences

Write Write a simple sentence for each prompt; then combine them into a compound sentence.

1. What did you do on a road trip? ______

   What did a different person do? ______

   Compound sentence: ______

   ______

2. What do you like to eat? ______

   What does a friend like to eat? ______

   Compound sentence: ______

   ______

3. What did you do last weekend? ______

   What did a friend do? ______

   What did a relative do? ______

   Compound sentence: ______

   ______

4. Where do you want to go? ______

   Where does a friend want to go? ______

   Where does a relative want to go? ______

   Compound sentence: ______

   ______

   ______

5. What is your favorite place? ______

   What is a friend's favorite place? ______

   What is a relative's favorite place? ______

   Compound sentence: ______

   ______

   ______

Learning Outcome

Create complex sentences.

LO5 Complex Sentences

A **complex sentence** shows a special relationship between two ideas. Instead of connecting two sentences as equal ideas (as in a compound sentence), a complex sentence shows that one idea depends on the other.

Using a Subordinating Conjunction

You can create a complex sentence by placing a subordinating conjunction before the sentence that is less important. Here are common subordinating conjunctions:

after	before	so that	when
although	even though	that	where
as	if	though	whereas
as if	in order that	till	while
as long as	provided that	'til	
because	since	until	

The subordinating conjunction shows that the one sentence depends on the other and cannot stand on its own.

Two Sentences: We searched the package. We found no instructions.
Complex Sentence: **Though** we searched the package, we found no instructions.
We found no instructions **though** we searched the package.

Note: The subordinating conjunction begins the dependent clause, but the two clauses can be in either order. When the dependent clause comes second, it is usually not separated by a comma.

Speaking & Listening

Read the example complex and compound-complex sentences aloud. Despite their daunting names, these sentences aren't that complicated and are used often in speech. Experiment with them in your writing.

Compound-Complex

You can also create a **compound-complex sentence** by placing a subordinating conjunction before a simple sentence and connecting it to a compound sentence.

Simple Sentence: I wouldn't give up.
Compound Sentence: Jan went to watch TV, and Bill joined her.
Compound-Complex: **Although I wouldn't give up,** Jan went to watch TV, and Bill joined her.

Vocabulary

complex sentence
a sentence with one independent clause and one or more dependent clauses

compound-complex sentence
a sentence with two or more independent clauses and one or more dependent clauses

Create Complex Sentences

Write Write a simple sentence for each prompt. Then select a subordinating conjunction from the facing page, place it at the beginning of one sentence, and combine the two sentences into a single complex sentence.

1. What did you look for? ______

   What did you find? ______

   Complex sentence: ______

2. Who helped you? ______

   Who did not help? ______

   Complex sentence: ______

3. What do you need? ______

   What did you get? ______

   Complex sentence: ______

4. What did you see? ______

   What did a friend see? ______

   Complex sentence: ______

5. Whom did you meet? ______

   Whom did you avoid? ______

   Complex sentence: ______

6. What did you win? ______

   What did you lose? ______

   Complex sentence: ______

Learning Outcome

Create complex sentences with relative clauses.

Insight

In some languages, if the relative pronoun is the object of the clause it introduces, another pronoun is inserted in the clause:

I liked the gift that my boss gave it to me.

In English, no additional pronoun is inserted:

I liked the gift that my boss gave to me.

Vocabulary

relative clause
a group of words that begins with a relative pronoun and includes a verb but cannot stand alone as a sentence

relative pronoun
a word *(that, which, who, whom)* that relates a dependent clause to another word in the sentence

LO6 Complex Sentences with Relative Clauses

In a complex sentence, one idea depends on the other. You've seen how a dependent clause can start with a subordinating conjunction. Another type of dependent clause starts with a relative pronoun.

Relative Clauses

A **relative clause** is a group of words that begins with a **relative pronoun** *(that, which, who, whom)* and includes a verb and any words that modify or complete it.

Relative Clauses: that celebrates my promotion
which is very generous
who comes to the party
whom I contacted yesterday

Each relative clause above has a subject and a verb, but none of the clauses is a complete sentence. All need to be connected to independent clauses to complete their meaning.

Complex Sentences: I hope you come to the party that celebrates my promotion.
My boss gave me an office, which is very generous.
I'll have a gift for everyone who comes to the party.
I hope to see Lavonne, whom I contacted yesterday.

That and *Which*

The pronoun *that* signals information that is necessary to the meaning of the sentence. The pronoun *which* signals information that is not necessary, so the clause is set off with a comma.

That: Please reserve the room **that** we will use. (The clause beginning with *that* defines the room.)

Which: We'll have cheesecake, **which** I love. (The clause beginning with *which* just adds information about the cake.)

Who and *Whom*

The pronoun *who* is the subject of the relative clause that it introduces. The pronoun *whom* is a direct object in the clause it introduces.

Who: I spoke to the woman **who** baked the cake. (*Who* is the subject.)

Whom: I greeted the Joneses, **whom** I invited. (*Whom* is the direct object.)

Create Complex Sentences with Relative Clauses

Write For each item, write a relative clause beginning with the pronoun provided. Then write a complex sentence that includes the relative clause. (If you need a topic idea, consider writing about a party, concert, or family gathering you attended.)

1. Relative clause: that ________________________

   Complex sentence: ________________________

2. Relative clause: who ________________________

   Complex sentence: ________________________

3. Relative clause: which ________________________

   Complex sentence: ________________________

4. Relative clause: whom ________________________

   Complex sentence: ________________________

5. Relative clause: that ________________________

   Complex sentence: ________________________

6. Relative clause: which ________________________

   Complex sentence: ________________________

Learning Outcome

Apply simple, compound, and complex sentences in a real-world context.

LO7 Real-World Application

Rewrite Read the following invitation to a party. Note how every sentence is a simple sentence. Rewrite the invitation, combining some sentences into compound or complex sentences to improve the flow.

Dear Ms. Jamison:

You are invited to a party. The party celebrates my promotion to store manager. I've been working toward this promotion all year. The store owner notified me yesterday. This is a big step for me. I want to share my day with you.

The party takes place Tuesday, July 13, at 8:00 p.m. at the Lucky Star restaurant. I've invited my colleagues and friends. Don't bring a gift. Just bring an appetite and a party spirit. I will provide beverages and cake. You've been a great support. I hope to see you there.

Workplace

Using a variety of sentences in workplace writing will improve the flow of ideas and give the organization a polished, capable image.

Dear Ms. Jamison:

"Fashion is general. Style is individual."

—Edna Woolman Chase

Jacek Ewan Burns/Fancy/Corbis

19 Sentence Style

Your style of clothing speaks volumes about how you want to be perceived. The young men above have selected every article of clothing very carefully. These guys are dressed to exude "cool skater dude." But the same people in suits and ties would look like congressional pages.

Your sentence style also speaks volumes about who you are and how you want to be perceived. Different sentences have different effects. Short sentences punctuate important thoughts. Long sentences create elaborate relationships.

This chapter focuses on ways to improve and perfect your sentence style. Through varying, combining, expanding, and modeling sentences, you'll hone the look and feel of your writing.

What do you think?

What style of clothing fits you best? How could your writing style reflect your clothing style?

Learning Outcomes

LO1 Vary sentence lengths.

LO2 Vary sentence beginnings.

LO3 Combine with coordination.

LO4 Combine with subordination.

LO5 Combine by moving parts.

LO6 Combine by deleting.

LO7 Expand sentences.

LO8 Model professional sentences.

LO9 Revise a real-world document for sentence style.

Learning Outcome

Vary sentence lengths.

LO1 Varying Sentence Lengths

To create a smooth flow of thought, use a variety of sentence lengths.

Short Sentences

Short sentences are powerful. They make a point. In dramatic circumstances, a series of short sentences can create a staccato effect:

> I came. I saw. I conquered. —Julius Caesar

For less dramatic situations, a series of short sentences may start to sound choppy. So remember to use short sentences in combination with longer sentences.

Medium Sentences

Medium-length sentences do most of the work in everyday writing. They are not overly punchy or overly complicated, and so they communicate well.

> If you want to know what God thinks of money, just look at the people he gave it to. —Dorothy Parker

WAC

Read an article or a speech in your major, noting the lengths of the sentences. Count the words in each. What effect does the variety of sentences (or lack of variety) have on readability?

Long Sentences

Long sentences express complex ideas and create an expansive feeling. The long sentence may be the hardest type to pull off because it needs to have a clear sense of direction. Otherwise, it may begin to ramble.

> The history of our race and each individual's experience are sown thick with evidence that a truth is not hard to kill and that a lie told well is immortal.
>
> —Mark Twain

Varying Lengths

The most effective paragraphs include sentences of different lengths. Read the following famous paragraph from the Gettysburg Address and note the different sentence lengths and their effect.

> Now we are engaged in a great civil war, testing whether that nation, or any nation so conceived and so dedicated, can long endure. We are met on a great battlefield of that war. We have come to dedicate a portion of that field, as a final resting place for those who here gave their lives that that nation might live. It is altogether fitting and proper that we should do this.
>
> —Abraham Lincoln

Varying Sentence Lengths

Create Write the types of sentences requested below.

1. Write a short sentence naming your favorite type of music.

2. Write a medium sentence describing that kind of music.

3. Write a long sentence indicating why you like that kind of music.

4. Write a medium sentence providing a final thought about the kind of music.

Create Write the types of sentences requested below.

1. Write a short sentence naming your favorite actor or writer.

2. Write a medium sentence describing the actor or writer.

3. Write a long sentence indicating why you like this actor or writer.

4. Write a medium sentence providing a final thought about the actor or writer.

Learning Outcome

Vary sentence beginnings.

Test Taking

It is more important to be able to use prepositional phrases and infinitive phrases than to be able to identify them. However, some tests require the ability to identify phrases. For more practice, see pages 206–207 and 326.

Vocabulary

prepositional phrase
a phrase formed from a preposition followed by an object and any modifiers; functioning as an adjective or adverb

infinitive phrase
a verbal phrase that begins with *to* followed by a verb and any objects; functioning as a noun, an adjective, or an adverb

LO2 New Beginnings I

If every sentence begins with the subject, writing can become monotonous. Vary sentence beginnings by starting in these different ways.

Prepositional Phrase

A **prepositional phrase** is formed from a preposition (*in, at, through*) followed by an object (a noun and any modifiers). (For more prepositions, see page 350.)

PR = Preposition
O = Object

After the game . . .	For that matter . . .	With a renewed interest . . .
After = PR, game = O	For = PR, matter = O	With = PR, interest = O

A prepositional phrase functions as an adjective or an adverb. That means that a prepositional phrase can answer any of the adjective or adverb questions:

Adjective Questions	Adverb Questions
Which?	How?
What kind of?	When?
How many?	Where?
How much?	Why?
	How often?
	How long?

Infinitive Phrase

An **infinitive phrase** is formed from the word *to* followed by a verb and any objects and modifiers.

V = Verb
O = Object

To prove my point . . .	To complete the comparison . . .	To do this . . .
prove = V, point = O	complete = V, comparison = O	do = V, this = O

An infinitive phrase functions as a noun, an adjective, or an adverb. It can answer any of the adjective and adverb questions above, but it can also serve as the subject of the sentence:

To complete my degree is my goal.
(*To complete my degree* functions as the subject of the sentence.)

Varying with Prepositional and Infinitive Phrases

Vary For each sentence below, add the requested type of beginning.

1. (Prepositional phrase):

   ____

   a high-calorie diet can lead to weight gain.

2. (Infinitive phrase):

   ____

   you should exercise and reduce calorie intake.

3. (Prepositional phrase):

   ____

   lifestyle changes require time to become habits.

4. (Infinitive phrase):

   ____

   a balanced diet is the most healthful choice.

Create Write the types of sentences requested below.

1. Write a short sentence about exercise. (Begin with a prepositional phrase.)

   ____

2. Write a medium sentence about exercise. (Begin with an infinitive phrase.)

   ____

   ____

3. Write a long sentence about exercise. (Begin with a prepositional phrase.)

   ____

   ____

   ____

4. Write a medium sentence about exercise. (Begin with an infinitive phrase.)

   ____

   ____

Learning Outcome

Vary sentence beginnings.

Insight

Participial phrases and gerund phrases both can start with the *ing* form of a verb, but participial phrases function as adjectives, and gerund phrases function as nouns. For a closer look at these phrases, see page 326.

Vocabulary

participial phrase
a phrase beginning with a participle (*ing* or *ed* form of verb) plus objects and modifiers; used as an adjective

adverb clause
a clause beginning with a subordinating conjunction and functioning as an adverb

LO2 New Beginnings 2

If sentences still sound repetitive, you can start with two other constructions—participial phrases and adverb clauses.

Participial Phrase

A **participial phrase** is formed from a participle (verb ending in *ing* or *ed*) and any objects and modifiers.

PA = Participle
O = Object

Expecting the best . . .	Considering the source . . .	Concerning the plan . . .
PA (Expecting), O (best)	PA (Considering), O (source)	PA (Concerning), O (plan)

A participial phrase functions as an adjective. That means that the phrase answers one of the adjective questions.

Adjective Questions	
Which?	How many?
What kind of?	How much?

Adverb Clause

An **adverb clause** is formed from a subordinating conjunction (see page 208) followed by a noun (or pronoun) and verb (and any objects and modifiers).

SC = Subordinating Conjunction **N** = Noun **V** = Verb

When Bill arrived . . .	Because Jan climbed so high . . .	While Ted watched . . .
SC (When), N (Bill), V (arrived)	SC (Because), N (Jan), V (climbed)	SC (While), N (Ted), V (watched)

Subordinating Conjunctions			
after	before	since	when
although	even though	so that	whenever
as	given that	that	where
as if	if	though	whereas
as long as	in order that	unless	while
because	provided that	until	

An adverb clause functions as an adverb, answering one of the adverb questions.

Adverb Questions	
How?	Why?
When?	How often?
Where?	How long?

Varying with Participial Phrases and Adverb Clauses

Vary For each sentence below, add the requested type of beginning.

1. (Participial phrase):

   ____

   we hiked up the trail toward Bear Lake.

2. (Adverb clause):

   ____

   we spotted a couple of porcupines waddling across the road.

3. (Participial phrase):

   ____

   the porcupines preceded us across a footbridge.

4. (Adverb clause):

   ____

   I realized it was better to encounter porcupines than bears.

Create Write the types of sentences requested below.

1. Write a short sentence about hiking. (Begin with a participial phrase.)

   ____

2. Write a medium sentence about hiking. (Begin with an adverb clause.)

   ____

   ____

3. Write a long sentence about hiking. (Begin with an adverb clause.)

   ____

   ____

   ____

4. Write a medium sentence about hiking. (Begin with a participial phrase.)

   ____

   ____

Learning Outcome

Combine with coordination.

LO3 Using Coordination

When you have too many short sentences, writing begins to sound choppy. Look for sentences that have related ideas and combine them.

Coordination

If two sentences express ideas of equal importance, you can combine the sentences by connecting them with a **coordinating conjunction**. (See the following list.)

Coordinating Conjunctions						
and	but	or	nor	for	so	yet

Choppy: Arthur Marx played the harp. He got the nickname Harpo.

Combined: Arthur Marx played the harp**, so** he got the nickname Harpo.

Note: Remember to place a comma before the conjunction.

The different coordinating conjunctions make different connections between ideas:

Comparison → and
Contrast → but, yet
Options → or, nor
Cause → so, for

Julius Marx was a grump**, so** he got the nickname Groucho.
Another brother was nicknamed Chico**, for** he was a lady's man.
Zeppo was in the Marxes' first films**, but** he left show business.

Traits

The word *coordinate* means "to place together." A *coordinating conjunction,* then, is a word that places ideas of equal importance together.

Vocabulary

coordinating conjunction
a word that connects equal sentence parts

Combining Using Coordination

Coordinate Mark the sentences below to show which coordinating conjunction you would insert to combine them. Use the correction marks as needed to add words and change punctuation and capitalization.

Correction Marks

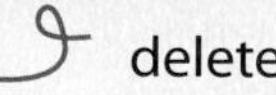
delete

d capitalize

lowercase

insert

add comma

add question mark

word add word

add period

spelling

switch

1. The Marx Brothers began in vaudeville. Their mother managed them.
2. Their father was a bad tailor. He was a great cook.
3. The Marxes grew up in New York. They moved to Chicago.
4. The boys had a singing act. Once Groucho ad-libbed a couple of jokes.
5. Increasingly, they added jokes. The act soon was a comedy routine.
6. The boys had a script. An ad-lib from one would get all off topic.
7. Minnie feared they would be fired. She yelled their mortgage holder's name.
8. Each of the boys had a persona. Their characters suited them.
9. Groucho was a wisecracker. Chico was an Italian huckster.
10. Harpo was a mute tramp. His top hat and shock wig became iconic.
11. The Marx brothers signed with Paramount. *The Cocoanuts* was their first film.
12. *Horse Feathers* made fun of college. A crazy football game ended the show.
13. In *Duck Soup,* they satirized war. This was seven years before WWII.
14. The film featured the fake country Freedonia. The real village Fredonia was unhappy.
15. They said the film hurt their image. Groucho said the town hurt their film.
16. The Marxes moved to MGM. They made *A Night at the Opera.*
17. *The Big Store* was supposed to be their last film. They made two more.
18. The Marx Brothers retired from movies. Groucho had a TV show.

Learning Outcome

Combine with subordination.

LO4 Using Subordination

If sentences sound choppy, you can combine them using subordination.

Subordination

If one sentence is more important than the other, you can combine the sentences by connecting them with a **subordinating conjunction**. (See the list below.) Place the conjunction before the less important sentence.

Subordinating Conjunctions			
after	before	since	when
although	even though	so that	whenever
as	given that	that	where
as if	if	though	whereas
as long as	in order that	unless	while
because	provided that	until	

Choppy: Facebook and Twitter both connect people. They do so in different ways.

Combined: **Though** Facebook and Twitter both connect people**,** they do so in different ways.

Choppy: Facebook connects friends. Twitter connects strangers.

Combined: Facebook connects friends **while** Twitter connects strangers.

Note: If the subordinate clause comes first, put a comma between the clauses.

Different subordinating conjunctions show different kinds of connections:

Time → after, as, as long as, before, since, until, when, whenever, while

Cause → because, given that, if, in order that, provided that, since, so that

Contrast → although, as if, even though, though, unless, whereas, while

Insight

The word *subordinate* means "to place below." A *subordinating conjunction,* then, is a word that makes one idea less important than (or dependent on) another idea.

Alex Mit,2010 / Used under license from Shutterstock.com

Vocabulary

subordinating conjunction
a word or phrase that begins a subordinate (adverb) clause, showing that the ideas in the clause are dependent on those in the main clause

Combining Using Subordination

Subordinate Mark the sentences below to show which subordinating conjunction you would use to combine them. Use the correction marks as needed to add words and change punctuation and capitalization.

Correction Marks

ℓ	delete
d (triple underline)	capitalize
Đ	lowercase
∧	insert
∧ with comma	add comma
? ∧	add question mark
word ∧	add word
⊙	add period
(oval)	spelling
(switch mark)	switch

1. Facebook began in 2004. Twitter got started in 2006.
2. Both applications are social media. They connect people.
3. Facebook helps friends communicate. People share pictures, videos, and thoughts.
4. Twitter is called microblogging. Users send messages of 140 characters.
5. The two platforms connect to each other. They take feeds from each other.
6. Some people are Facebook based. Others use Twitter primarily.
7. Each application thrives on links. They connect to anything on the Internet.
8. Social media are changing ideas of privacy. They encourage sharing.
9. Older Americans want privacy. Younger Americans fear obscurity.
10. Everyone gets 15 minutes of fame. Some get it 140 characters at a time.

Write For each prompt, write a simple sentence with a subject and predicate. Then combine the sentences using subordination.

1. What social media do you use? ______________________________

   What do your friends use? ______________________________

   Combine: ______________________________

   ____

2. What do you share online? ______________________________

   What do your friends share? ______________________________

   Combine: ______________________________

   ____

Learning Outcome

Combine by moving parts.

Speaking & Listening

On the facing page, read each of the sentence pairs out loud. Then ask yourself how you could say the same thing in one sentence. Say it aloud before writing it down. In this way, your conversational skills can help you improve your writing skills.

LO5 Combining by Moving Parts

Sometimes sentences need to be combined because they cover the same material. The way to combine such sentences is to move one part of one sentence into the other sentence.

Moving a Word

Before: Every Fourth of July has fireworks. ~~They are~~ beautiful.

After: Every Fourth of July has beautiful fireworks.

Moving a Phrase

Before: Fireworks were invented in the seventh century. ~~They were invented~~ in China.

After: Fireworks were invented in the seventh century in China.

Before: A peony, which is the most common type of firework. ~~A peony~~ looks like a flower.

After: A peony, which looks like a flower, is the most common type of firework.

Reworking Sentences

Before: ~~Some~~ fireworks that propel themselves. ~~They~~ are called skyrockets.

After: Fireworks that propel themselves are called skyrockets.

Before: ~~Some~~ fireworks ~~are~~ launched from mortars. ~~They~~ are called aerial shells.

After: Fireworks launched from mortars are called aerial shells.

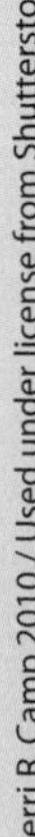

Combining by Moving Parts

Combine Combine each pair of sentences below by moving a word or phrase or by reworking the sentences.

1. Many fireworks are named after plants. They look like the named plants.

2. A willow firework trails long streamers. It looks like a fiery willow tree.

3. A palm firework has a short lateral burst. The burst looks like fronds.

4. Other fireworks have object names. Other fireworks have animal names.

5. The ring firework creates a bright circle. It resembles a ring of stars.

6. A diadem is a type of peony. The diadem has a crown in the center.

7. Some little bursts "swim" away. Those little bursts are called "fish."

8. A spider shell sends out long lines. They look like a spider's legs.

9. One type is called a kamuro. Kamuro is Japanese for "boy's haircut."

10. Another type leaves a long streamer. It is called a horsetail or waterfall.

Learning Outcome

Combine by deleting.

LO6 Combining by Deleting

When writing is wordy or repetitious, the best way to combine sentences is by finding the key pieces of information, deleting the rest, and writing new sentences from what is left.

Finding the Key Pieces

Read the following paragraph, noting how wordy and repetitious it is. Afterward, consider the important ideas that the writer underlined.

> When people go to a city that they haven't ever been to before or a foreign place that is new to them, they often decide that what they have to do is to figure out how to use the mass-transit system. They will try to use a subway or the buses or trains in order to get all around a major city like Paris or London. Another way to tour the capital of another country is to take a walking tour through all of its tourist spots and also many other spots along the way. A walking tour allows the person to get a feel for where everything is in a city and also provides opportunities for the person to meet and greet the people who live and work in the city and go about their daily lives there. Often on a walking tour of a city, a person discovers that all of the many tourist attractions that she or he wants to see are not as interesting or memorable as the unexpected experiences that happen along the way.

Workplace

Workplace writing needs to be concise, clear, and compelling. By finding the important points and deleting the unimportant ones, you can create a message that reaches colleagues and clients.

Rewriting and Combining

Now read the much shorter and more effective paragraph that the writer wrote using the main ideas.

> When people go to a city, they often use mass-transit systems, but another option is to take a walking tour. A walking tour lets the person get a feel for the city's layout and meet the people who live there. Often, tourist attractions turn out to be less memorable than the unexpected experiences along the way.

Aurelie and Morgan David de Lossy/cultura/Corbis

Combining by Deleting

Underline Read the following wordy, repetitive paragraph. Afterward, reread the paragraph, looking for important details. Underline them.

What people seem to forget is that most major cities in the world such as New York, London, Paris, Rome, Athens, and other major cities were originally designed not for traveling through in motorized vehicles like cars, buses, and trains, but for going around on foot. In fact, one of the biggest problems for all of these cities has been having to deal with the headaches of motorized transportation, including the inconvenience and expense of such things as finding and affording a parking place or paying tolls for different bridges or tunnels, not to mention the frustration of fighting through traffic. These problems are solved by taking to the sidewalks for a walking tour rather than by always needing to pay money for taxis or subway rides or having to figure out bus schedules and so forth. With a simple map, whether one printed on paper or one available on a cell phone or through some kind of other digital device like a GPS, the walker can find wherever he or she is currently. If the map does not do the job, then the person can always ask for help and direction from someone who lives locally in the city, who usually will be more than happy to help someone who is lost.

Combine Rewrite the paragraph above by deleting the unimportant details and combining the important ones into new sentences. Make the new paragraph concise and smooth.

Learning Outcome

Expand sentences.

LO7 Sentence Expanding

Sometimes a sentence does not say enough, or it is too general. When that happens, the sentence needs to be expanded. Sentence expanding simply means adding details. The best way to expand a sentence is to answer the 5 W's about the topic.

Original Sentence: My friend is odd.

Who is odd? my friend Jacob

What is odd about him? He has a collection of bottle caps.

Where are his bottle caps? in a set of boxes in his basement

When did he start collecting? about five years ago

Why did he start? He had a Guinness in Dublin and saved the cap.

Expanded Sentence: My friend Jacob is odd because he has a collection of bottle caps in a set of boxes in his basement.

Note: The expanded sentence does not use all of the answers to the 5 W's, but a second sentence could cover the other details.

He started the collection five years ago when he bought a Guinness in Dublin and saved the cap.

Listening & Speaking

Imagine each sentence-expanding activity on the facing page as a conversation you are having with a friend. Read the short sentence aloud and have a friend ask you the questions that follow. Then roll some of your answers into a single more informative sentence.

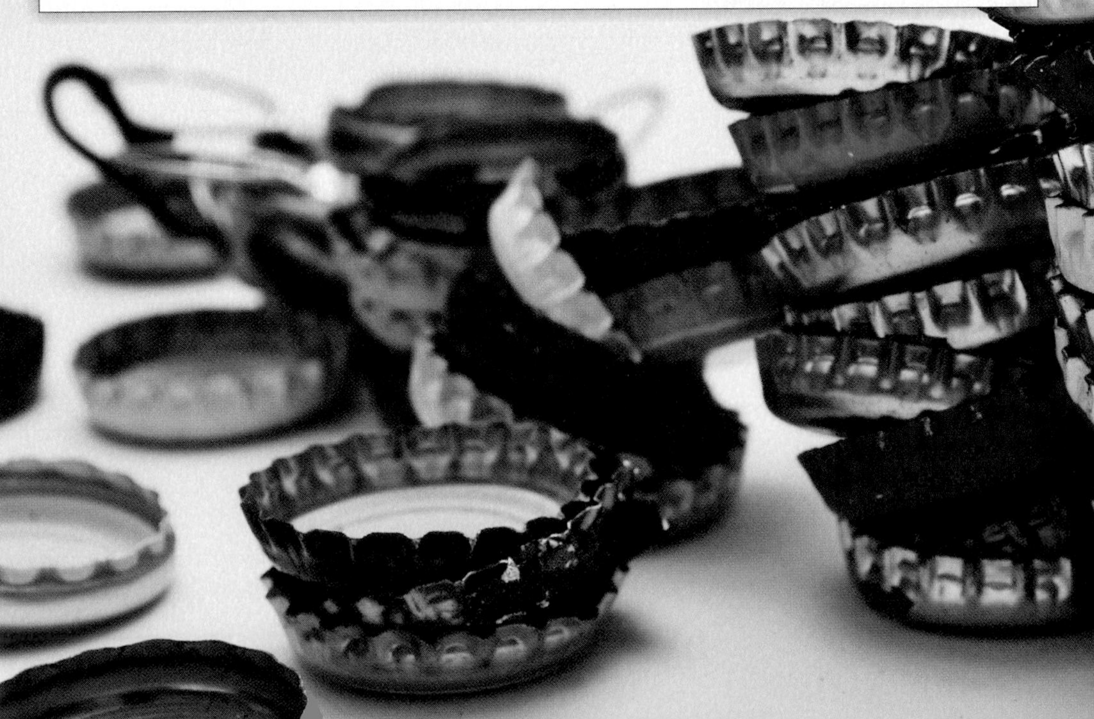

Expanding Sentences

Expand Expand the sentences below by answering the questions provided.

1. **Short Sentence:** My friend has a hobby.

   a. Who is your friend? ______

   b. What hobby does your friend have? ______

   c. Where does your friend do the hobby? ______

   d. When did your friend start? ______

   e. Why does your friend like it? ______

   Expanded Sentence: ______

2. **Short Sentence:** My friend has a job.

   a. Who is your friend? ______

   b. What job does your friend have? ______

   c. Where does your friend do the job? ______

   d. When did your friend start the job? ______

   e. Why does your friend do this job? ______

   Expanded Sentence: ______

Learning Outcome

Learning Outcome

Model professional sentences.

LO8 Sentence Modeling

Sentence modeling helps you see new ways to put sentences together. Modeling involves reading a well-written sentence and then writing a similar sentence by substituting words. Below are two example original sentences and the sentences modeled after them.

Original Sentence: We slid the boxcar door wide open at dawn to see a vast prairie, pale gold in the east, dark in the west.

—"On Running Away," John Keats

Modeled Sentence: I propped the tree-house hatch up at noon to see a small boy, pale in the corner, dark in the eyes.

Note: The new sentence doesn't *exactly* match the model. The writer made adjustments to make the sentence work.

Original Sentence: As the warm spring day lengthened, the young man grew increasingly restless, grumbling because there was not enough to eat, cursing the broken promises of the white men at Medicine Lodge.

—*Bury My Heart at Wounded Knee,* Dee Brown

Modeled Sentence: When the early October day ended, the old woman grew gradually more content, laughing because there was no more raking to do, recalling the easy grace of her young daughter at the ballet.

Note: In the sentence above, the writer chose words that had an opposite feeling from the ones in the original and created a passage with a very different impact. Notice, however, that the sentence still works and makes sense.

WAC

Instead of modeling sentences taken from literature, you can model well-constructed sentences from your academic discipline. When you find a great sentence in one of your books, try to craft a similar sentence. You'll be learning the way professionals write in your field of study.

Modeling Sentences

Model Create sentences that model the ones below.

1. Their greasy uncolored hair hung down, uncombed, with a grim finality.
—*I Know Why the Caged Bird Sings,* Maya Angelou

2. He stretched, looking straight up at the sun for a second.
—*Tiger, Tiger, Burning Bright,* Ron Koertge

3. The monster jigged and joggled, nodding its head, flopping all its prickles and plates.
—*The Moon's Revenge,* Joan Aiken

4. A thrifty homemaker, wife, mother of three, she also did all of her own cooking.
—"The Little Store," Eudora Welty

5. They'll honk nonstop for 10 minutes at a time, until the horns get tired and out of breath.
—"Canal Street," Ian Frazier

6. The hotel lobby was a dark, derelict room, narrow as a corridor, and seemingly without air.
—"Total Eclipse," Annie Dillard

7. My fingers a-tremble, I complied, smelling the fresh leather and finding an official-looking document inside.
—*Invisible Man,* Ralph Ellison

Learning Outcome

Revise a real-world document for sentence style.

LO9 Real-World Application

Expand Read the following cover letter, written to present a résumé for a job. Note how the writer uses a lot of short, say-nothing sentences that could refer to anyone. Then rewrite the letter below, expanding the sentences with details from your own life. Make the letter interesting, informative, and engaging by improving the sentence style and enriching the content.

Workplace

As you can see from this exercise, bland sentences can cost you a job, and great sentences can land you one.

Dear Mr. Dawson:

Do you need a good worker? I need a good employer. My education is good. I have work experience.

Many traits make me a good worker. I do well with many things.

Do you need a good worker? If so, please contact me.

I look forward to hearing from you.

Sincerely,

Dear Mr. Dawson:

"Men keep agreements when it is to the advantage of neither to break them."

—Solon

© Jamie Kingham/cultura/Corbis

20 Agreement

When people come to an agreement, they can begin to work together. Until an agreement is reached, the people most often work against each other, or perhaps have no working relationship at all.

The same goes for subjects and verbs. If the verb does not agree with the subject in number, both being either singular or plural, these two crucial sentence parts cannot work together. They fight each other, or even disconnect. And the same happens when pronouns and antecedents don't agree. Sentences break down.

This chapter helps you recognize and correct agreement errors. It also focuses on a few other pronoun problems. After you review the information and complete the exercises, you will be prepared to write well-connected sentences that work.

Learning Outcomes

LO1 Make subjects and verbs agree.

LO2 Make two subjects agree with verbs.

LO3 Practice agreement with *I* and *you.*

LO4 Practice agreement with indefinite pronouns.

LO5 Practice pronoun-antecedent agreement.

LO6 Correct other pronoun problems.

LO7 Check agreement in a real-world context.

What do you think?

What would happen if all agreements that have been made were suddenly broken?

Learning Outcome

Make subjects and verbs agree.

LO1 Subject-Verb Agreement

A verb must **agree in number** with the subject of the sentence. If the subject is singular, the verb must be singular. If the subject is plural, the verb must be plural.

singular subject + singular verb = agreement

The truck needs a tune-up.

plural subject + plural verb = agreement

The trucks need tune-ups.

Note how plural subjects often end in *s*, but plural verbs usually do not. Also note that only present-tense verbs and certain *be* verbs have separate singular and plural forms.

Present:	singular	plural	Past:	singular	plural
	walks	walk		walked	walked
	sees	see		saw	saw
	eats	eat		ate	ate
	is/am	are		was	were

To make most verbs singular, add just an *s.*

run—runs write—writes stay—stays

The verbs *do* and *go* are made singular by adding an *es.*

do—does go—goes

When a verb ends in *ch, sh, x,* or *z,* make it singular by adding *es:*

latch—latches wish—wishes fix—fixes buzz—buzzes

When a verb ends in a consonant followed by a *y,* change the *y* to *i* and add *es.*

try—tries fly—flies cry—cries quantify—quantifies

Insight

The "Say It" activity below will help you become familiar with the subject-verb agreement patterns in English. Practice it aloud, and for added practice, write the sentences as well.

Say It

Read the following sentences aloud, emphasizing the words in *italics.*

1. The alarm *rings.* The alarms *ring.* The dog *barks.* The dogs *bark.*
2. The man *is.* The men *are.* The woman *is.* The women *are.*
3. She *sits.* They *sit.* He *walks.* They *walk.*
4. The woman *tries.* The women *try.* The man *does.* The men *do.*
5. The door *latches.* The doors *latch.* The bee *buzzes.* The bees *buzz.*

Vocabulary

agree in number
match, as when a subject and verb are both singular, or when they are both plural

Correcting Basic Subject-Verb Agreement

Write In each sentence below, write the correct form of the verb in parentheses.

1. The people at the help desk __________ knowledgeable. (is)
2. They __________ more about computers than most. (know)
3. Any question __________ a quick, helpful answer. (receive)
4. One student __________ about the "any" key. (ask)
5. The instructions __________ to press the "any" key. (say)
6. One tech helper __________ the word "any" to space bars. (tape)
7. That sign __________ prevent many questions. (do)
8. The tech also __________ any computer that breaks down. (fix)
9. Or at least the tech __________ to fix any problems. (try)
10. Most users __________ glad they don't have to fix the computers. (is)

Speaking & Listening

After completing the sentences in the first activity, say them aloud, emphasizing the underlined verbs.

Correct Read the following paragraph. Correct any agreement errors you find by crossing out the incorrect verb and writing the correct verb above.

Those who study computer science has a challenging career. Since computer technology change so quickly, the things students learns when they is starting out will probably be outdated by the time they graduates. Memory capacity double every few years, and high-speed connections creates new possibilities. Innovations on the Web and in handheld devices drives change in all areas. One computer-science major confess, "Students doesn't have the luxury of being amazed by new technology. As soon as they hears about a new software or hardware development, they has to check it out and get on board—or they gets left behind."

Write For each plural verb below, write one sentence using the verb in its singular form.

1. do __________
2. go __________
3. wash __________
4. scratch __________
5. tax __________
6. dry __________

Learning Outcome

Make two subjects agree with verbs.

Test Taking

For more practice with compound subjects, see pages 214–215.

Vocabulary

compound subject
two or more subjects that share the same verb or verbs

LO2 Agreement with Two Subjects

Sentences with **compound subjects** have special rules to make sure that they agree.

Two or More Subjects

When a sentence has two or more subjects joined by *and,* the verb should be plural.

plural subject + plural verb = agreement

Bill and Sue try new hairstyles.

When a sentence has two or more subjects joined by *or, nor,* or *but also,* the verb should agree with the last subject.

© Rubberball/Corbis

singular subject + singular verb = agreement

Either Bill or Sue tries a new hairstyle.

Not only Bill but also Sue looks cool.

Say It

Read the following sentences aloud, emphasizing the words in *italics.*

1. The woman *and* man *talk.* The woman *or* man *talks.*
2. A mouse *and* gerbil *run.* A mouse *or* a gerbil *runs.*
3. Either Sarah *or* Steve *phones.* Neither Sarah *nor* Steve *phones.*
4. Not only Jim *but also* Patty *responds.*
5. A man, woman, *and* child *arrive.* A man, a woman, *or* a child *arrives.*

Fixing Agreement with Two Subjects

Write In each sentence below, write the correct form of the verb in parentheses.

1. The office manager and secretary __________ to multitask. (has)
2. The secretary or manager __________ as receptionist. (act)
3. Calls and faxes __________ every few minutes. (arrive)
4. Customer service and satisfaction __________ the keys to their jobs. (is)
5. Neither the secretary nor the manager __________ the rush. (mind)
6. Not only excitement but also challenge __________ with each call. (come)
7. Either the manager or the secretary __________ visitors as well. (greet)
8. A friendly smile and a polite word __________ the conversations. (smooth)
9. Praise or complaints __________ the same professional reply. (receive)
10. Not only the manager but also the secretary __________ voted employee of the month. (was)

Correct Read the following paragraph. Correct any agreement errors you find by crossing out the incorrect verb and writing the correct verb above.

Multitasking is the ability to do more than two things at a time. Talking on the phone and cooking dinner makes a person focus on both tasks at once. Multitaskers and nonmultitaskers disagrees about the value of doing more than one thing. Cooking, cleaning, and taking care of children is daily tasks for stay-at-home parents. Office workers and blue collar workers often focuses on one task at a time. Who gets more done? Multitaskers and nonmultitaskers sees it differently. Dinner, a clean house, and happy kids is the results of a multitasker's labor at home. A job done right and another job underway is the product of a nonmultitasker's attention at work. Both approaches succeeds. Not only the multitasker but also the nonmultitasker work efficiently and complete the task. The difference is perhaps not in the person but in the work.

Write Write a sentence with a compound subject joined by *and*. Write a sentence with a compound subject joined by *or*. Check subject-verb agreement.

Learning Outcome

Practice agreement with *I* and *you*.

LO3 Agreement with *I* and *You*

The pronouns *I* and *you* usually take plural verbs, even though they are singular.

plural verb

Correct: I sit here and think. You talk to me.

singular verb

Incorrect: I sits here and thinks. You talks to me.

Note: The pronoun *I* takes the singular verbs *am* and *was*. **Do not** use *I* with *be* or *is*.

Correct: I am glad. I was hoping to go. I am excited to see the show.

Incorrect: I are glad. I were hoping to go. I is excited to see the show.

Insight

The word *am* exists for one reason only, to go along with the word *I*. There is no other subject for the verb *am*. In academic or formal writing, *I* should never be used with *be* or *is*. Think of René Descartes saying, "I think, therefore I am."

Quick Guide

Using *am, is, are, was,* and *were*

	Singular	**Plural**
Present Tense	I *am* you *are* he *is* she *is* it *is*	we *are* you *are* they *are*
Past Tense	I *was* you *were* he *was* she *was* it *was*	we *were* you *were* they *were*

Say It

Read the following word groups aloud, emphasizing the words in *italics.*

1. I *walk* / You *walk* / She *walks* / They *walk*
2. I *drive* / You *drive* / He *drives* / They *drive*
3. I *do* / You *do* / He *does* / They *do*
4. I *am* / You *are* / She *is* / They *are*
5. I *was* / You *were* / He *was* / They *were*

Correcting Agreement with *I* and *You*

Write In each sentence below, write the correct forms of the verb in parentheses. (Do not change the tense.)

1. I __________ as hard as he __________ . (work)
2. You __________ as beautifully as she __________ . (sing)
3. The group __________ together, or you __________ alone. (decide)
4. My brother __________ guitar while I __________ piano. (play)
5. I __________ you if you __________ me. (forgive)
6. I __________ just as loudly as she __________ . (applaud)
7. I __________ tired, but he __________ tired, too. (is)
8. You __________ full of energy, and she __________ also. (is)
9. Yesterday, I __________ late, but you __________ late, too. (was)
10. You __________ my friend; I hope I __________ yours. (is)

Speaking & Listening

After completing the sentences in the first exercise, say them aloud, emphasizing the underlined verbs.

Correct Read the following paragraphs. Correct any agreement errors you find by crossing out the incorrect verb and writing the correct verb above.

I wants to thank you for such a wonderful day yesterday. I is still smiling to think about the art exhibit. You knows so much about the history of art, and you shares what you knows so willingly. You am my new favorite tour guide. I be happy to go back to the art institute any time you wants.

What were my favorite paintings? I were thrilled by the Impressionist paintings, especially the Monets and Manets. I weren't even sure there was a difference before yesterday. You was very gentle to point out they was two different people. I be glad to know that now.

Thank you again for the guided tour. You is generous with your time, and I is always interested to hear what you says about each artwork. Next time you is going, give me a call!

Write Write two sentences using "I" as the subject. Then write two more using "you" as the subject. Check your subject-verb agreement.

Learning Outcome

Practice agreement with indefinite pronouns.

LO4 Agreement with Singular Indefinite Pronouns

An **indefinite pronoun** is intentionally vague. Instead of referring to a specific person, place, or thing, it refers to something general or unknown.

"Everybody needs somebody to love."
—Solomon Burke

Singular Indefinite Pronouns

Singular indefinite pronouns take singular verbs:

Someone donates $10 a week.
No one knows who it is.
Everyone appreciates the generosity.

Note that indefinite pronouns that end in *one, body,* or *thing* are singular, just as these words themselves are singular. Just as you would write, "That thing is missing," so you would write "Something is missing." The words *one, each, either,* and *neither* can be tricky because they are often followed by a prepositional phrase that contains a plural noun. The verb should still be singular.

One of our roommates is generous.

Each of us wants to know who it is.

Remember that a compound subject joined with *and* needs a plural verb, and a compound subject joined with *or* needs a verb that matches the last subject.

Everybody and everything need to stay out of my way.
Something or someone prevents us from succeeding.

Singular

someone
somebody
something

anyone
anybody
anything

no one
nobody
nothing

everyone
everybody
everything

one
each
either
neither

Say It

Read the following word groups aloud, emphasizing the words in *italics.*

1. Someone *is* / Somebody *has* / Something *does*
2. Anyone *is* / Anybody *has* / Anything *does*
3. One of the books *is* / Each of the books *has* / Either of the books *does*

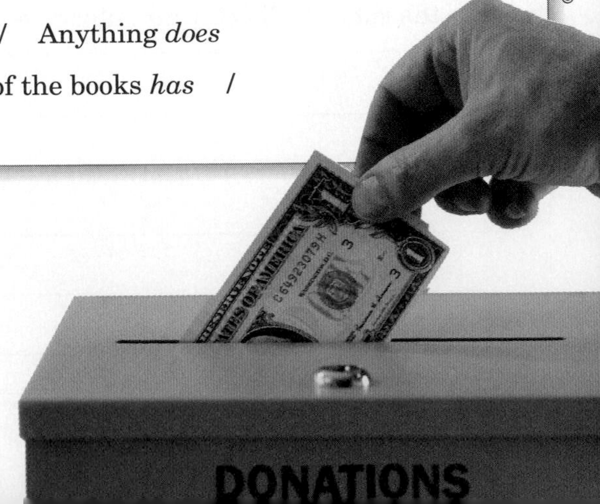

© Tetra Images/Corbis

Vocabulary

indefinite pronoun
a special type of pronoun that does not refer to a specific person or thing

Correcting Indefinite Pronoun Agreement I

Write In each sentence below, write the correct form of the verb in parentheses. (Do not change the tense.)

1. Someone ____________ a new muffler. (need)
2. Each of the cars ____________ repair. (need)
3. Something ____________ when I turn the ignition. (rattle)
4. Either of the garages ____________ good work. (do)
5. Neither of the options ____________ very affordable. (is)
6. Somebody ____________ to fix the tailgate. (have)
7. Nobody ____________ to drive a broken-down car. (want)
8. Nobody and nothing ____________ me from fixing the car. (deters)
9. Either of the repair jobs ____________ a fortune. (cost)
10. One of my paychecks ____________ each time I get repairs. (vanish)

Write Write sentences using each indefinite pronoun as a subject. Choose present-tense verbs and check subject-verb agreement.

1. Everyone ____
2. Each ____
3. No one ____
4. Anything ____
5. One ____
6. Either ____

Agreement with Other Indefinite Pronouns

Other indefinite pronouns are always plural, or have a singular or plural form, depending on how they are used.

Plural Indefinite Pronouns

Plural indefinite pronouns take plural verbs:

Both of us match the donation.
Many are wishing they did.

Plural

both
few
many
several

Singular or Plural Indefinite Pronouns

Some indefinite pronouns or quantity words are singular or plural. If the object of the preposition in the phrase following the pronoun is singular, the pronoun takes a singular verb; if the object is plural, the pronoun takes a plural verb.

Singular or Plural

all
any
half
part
most
none
some

All of the pizza is gone.
All of the pizzas are gone.

Notice the shift in meaning, depending on the prepositional phrase. "All of the pizza" means every last bit of a pizza is gone. "All of the pizzas" means each of the multiple pizzas is gone. Here is another startling difference:

Half of the mortgage is paid off.
Half of the mortgages are paid off.

In the first example, one mortgage is half paid off. In the second, out of a group of mortgages, half of them are fully paid off. What a difference one *s* can make!

Speaking & Listening

The "Say It" activity below will help you become familiar with subject-verb agreement patterns with indefinite pronouns.

Say It

Read the following word groups aloud, emphasizing the words in *italics.*

1. Both *are* / Few *have* / Many *do* / Several *were*
2. All of the budget *is* / Any of the budgets *are* / Half of the budget *does*
3. Part of the pie *is* / Most of the pies *are* / None of the foods *are* / Some of the food *is*

Correcting Indefinite Pronoun Agreement II

Write In each sentence below, write the correct forms of the verb in parentheses. (Do not change the tense.)

Speaking & Listening
After completing the sentences in the first exercise, say them aloud, emphasizing the underlined verbs.

1. Someone ____________ for others, but both of us ____________ for ourselves. (provide)
2. All of the book ____________ scary, but all of the scares ____________ fun. (was)
3. Some of my friends ____________ Facebook pages, and part of my Facebook page ____________ photos of friends. (have)
4. Everyone ____________ to be famous, but few ____________ to be followed day and night. (want)
5. One of my friends ____________ a Webcast show; several episodes ____________ in a row. (broadcast)
6. Either ____________ a valuable idea, and neither ____________ expensive. (is)
7. Few ____________ thought about the final exam, though all of the students ____________ reason to study. (has)
8. Of the competing bids, several ____________ desirable, but none of them ____________ affordable. (is)
9. Most of us ____________ the lions pace, though some of the lions ____________ us. (watch)
10. Half of the car ____________ submerged, and half of the spectators ____________ gasping. (was)

Write Write sentences using each indefinite pronoun as a subject. Choose present-tense verbs and check subject-verb agreement.

1. Several ____

____

2. Few ____

____

3. All ____

____

4. Most ____

____

5. Part ____

____

6. Both ____

____

Learning Outcome

Practice pronoun-antecedent agreement.

LO5 Pronoun-Antecedent Agreement

A pronoun must agree in **person**, **number**, and **gender** with its **antecedent**. (The antecedent is the word the pronoun replaces.)

The man went to lunch but forgot his lunch box.

antecedent (third person singular masculine) + **pronoun** (third person singular masculine) = **agreement**

Quick Guide

	Singular	Plural
First Person:	I, me (my, mine)	we, us (our, ours)
Second Person:	you (your, yours)	you (your, yours)
Third Person:		
masculine	he, him (his)	they, them (their, theirs)
feminine	she, her (her, hers)	they, them (their, theirs)
neuter	it (its)	they, them (their, theirs)

Workplace

In the workplace, it is important that you avoid sexist language, using masculine pronouns to refer to an antecedent that may be masculine or feminine. Either use alternate pronouns, such as "him or her" or make the antecedent plural and use a plural pronoun.

Two or More Antecedents

When two or more antecedents are joined by *and,* the pronoun should be plural.

Juan and Maria will do their dance.

When two or more singular antecedents are joined by *or, nor,* or *but also,* the pronoun or pronouns should be singular.

Juan or Maria will do his or her dance.

Not only Juan but also Maria presses his or her own costume.

Note: Avoid sexism when choosing pronouns that agree in number.

Sexist: Each student should bring his project.

Correct: Each student should bring her or his project.

Correct: Students should bring their projects.

Vocabulary

person
the person speaking (first person—*I, we*), the person being spoken to (second person—*you*), or the person being spoken about (third person—*he, she, it, they*)

number
singular or plural

gender
masculine, feminine, neuter, or indefinite

antecedent
the noun (or pronoun) that a pronoun refers to or replaces

Correcting Pronoun-Antecedent Agreement

Write In each sentence below, write the pronoun that agrees with the underlined word.

1. The cha-cha-cha began in Cuba, and __________ got its name from the shuffling sound of the dancers' feet.
2. In the 1950s, Monsieur Pierre traveled to Cuba, where __________ studied dance styles and from them created the ballroom rumba.
3. Pepe Sanchez is the father of the Cuban bolero, even though __________ was untrained as a musician and dancer.
4. The *paso doble* came from bullfight music, so __________ depicts the lead dancer as the bullfighter and the follower as the cape.
5. In the early twentieth century, Brazilians created the samba, and __________ danced three steps for each two-count measure.
6. The tango had __________ start in Argentina and Uruguay.
7. Stiff and stylized, the tango is performed with the man holding __________ arms in a rigid frame and the woman matching __________ steps to her partner's.
8. Salsa dancing combines other styles and blends __________ together like the ingredients in hot sauce.
9. Most of these styles require hip movements from side to side; __________ reflect a sensuous nature.
10. Northern European dancing, however, calls for straight hips and leaping, hopping movements; __________ may help the dancers stay warm.

Insight

Different languages treat gender differently. For example, Romance languages have masculine and feminine forms for nonliving things. In English, gender is reserved for people and animals.

Revise Rewrite each of the following sentences to avoid sexism.

1. Every dancer should put on his shoes.

____

____

2. Each dancer must keep track of her equipment.

____

____

3. One of the applicants will have his application accepted.

____

____

Learning Outcome

Correct other pronoun problems.

LO6 Other Pronoun Problems

Missing Antecedent

If no clear antecedent is provided, the reader doesn't know what or whom the pronoun refers to.

Confusing: In Wisconsin, they produce many types of cheese.
(Who does "they" refer to?)

Clear: In Wisconsin, cheese makers produce many types of cheese.

Vague Pronoun

If the pronoun could refer to two or more words, the passage is **ambiguous**.

Indefinite: Ben told his son to use his new surfboard.
(To whom does the pronoun "his" refer, Ben or Ben's son?)

Clumsy: Ben told his son to use Ben's new surfboard.

Clear: Ben lent his new surfboard to his son.

Double Subject

If a pronoun is used right after the subject, an error called a double subject occurs.

Incorrect: My grandmother, she is a great baker.

Correct: My grandmother is a great baker.

Incorrect Case

Personal pronouns can function as subjects, objects, or possessives. If the wrong case is used, an error occurs.

Incorrect: Them are the wrong size.

Correct: They are the wrong size.

The list below tells you which pronouns to use in each case.

Subject	Object	Possessive
I	me	my, mine
we	us	our, ours
you	you	your, yours
he	him	his
she	her	her, hers
it	it	its
they	them	their, theirs

Insight

Use *my* before the thing possessed and use *mine* afterward: *my cat,* but *that cat is mine.* Do the same with *our/ours, your/yours,* and *her/hers.*

Vocabulary

ambiguous
unclear, confusing

Correcting Other Pronoun Problems

Write In each blank below, write the correct pronoun from the choices in parentheses.

1. ________ want to give ________ some advice.
(I, me, my, mine) (you, your, yours)

2. ________ should watch ________ and learn what ________ does.
(you, your, yours) (he, him, his) (he, him, his)

3. ________ agreed to lend ________ that book of ________ .
(she, her, hers) (I, me, my, mine) (she, her, hers)

4. ________ grant ________ permission for ________ to go.
(I, me, my, mine) (I, me, my, mine) (she, her, hers)

5. ________ watched ________ dog do tricks for ________ .
(we, us, our, ours) (we, us, our, ours) (we, us, our, ours)

Revise Rewrite each sentence below, correcting the pronoun problems.

1. David and Jerry took his car to the shop.

____

____

2. Clare needed to work with Linda, but she had no time.

____

____

3. After driving all the way, it gave out.

____

____

4. When are they going to make an effective vaccine?

____

____

5. Bill and Sarah, they went to the movies.

____

____

6. Steve told Dave to bring his book.

____

____

Speaking & Listening

After completing the sentences in the first exercise, say them aloud, emphasizing the underlined verbs.

Learning Outcome

Check agreement in a real-world context.

LO7 Real-World Application

Correct In the letter below, correct the agreement errors. Use the correction marks to the left.

Correction Marks

 delete

 capitalize

 lowercase

 insert

 add comma

 add question mark

 add word

 add period

 spelling

 switch

Hope Services Child Development Center

2141 South Fifth Place, Seattle, WA 90761

414-555-1400 www.hopeserv.org

May 17, 2010

Mr. Donald Keebler

Keebler Electronics

466 Hanover Boulevard

Penticton, BC V2A 5S1

Dear Mr. Keebler:

Everyone at Hope Services want to thank you for helping us choose a sound system that fits both our needs and our budget. I is especially thankful for the way you worked around our schedule during installation.

We found that the system meets all their needs. Being able to adjust sound input and output for different uses in different rooms has been wonderful. The system help staff in the family room with play-based assessment, and team members are tuning in to different conversations as if they were in the room himself. As a result, children who might feel overwhelmed with too many people in the room relaxes and plays naturally. In addition, parents use the sound system to listen in on sessions in the therapy room as therapists model constructive one-on-one communication methods with children.

You does excellent work, Donald. I are happy to recommend your services to anyone needing sound equipment.

Yours friend,

Barbara Talbot

Barbara Talbot

Executive Director

jocicalek, 2010/used under license from www.shutterstock.com

"The verb is the heartthrob of the sentence. Without a verb, a group of words can never hope to be anything more than a fragment, a hopelessly incomplete sentence . . ."

—Karen Elizabeth Gordon

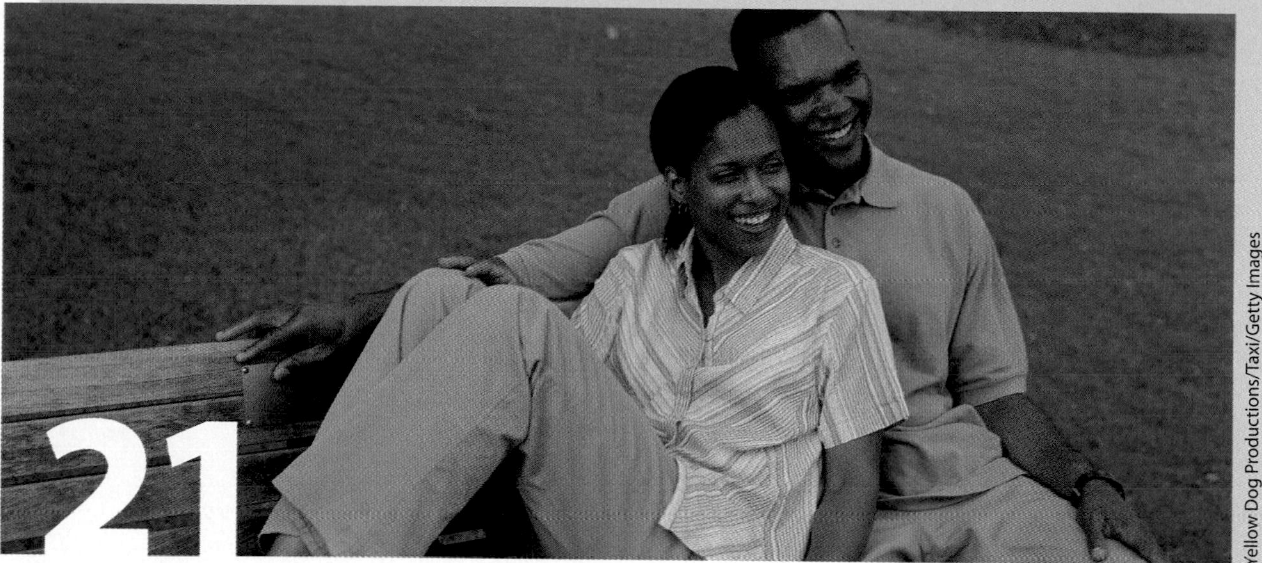

Yellow Dog Productions/Taxi/Getty Images

21 Sentence Fragments

What is a heartthrob? The meaning is literally there in the word. A heartthrob is something that makes one's heart throb—pound in desire and hope and love. The ancient philosopher Plato suggested that human beings were once connected and complete, but the gods became jealous and split people up. Afterward, we all sought our "better halves," and our hearts throbbed to be complete again.

A sentence fragment is in a similar position. By itself, the fragment is incomplete. It needs to be part of a whole sentence.

This chapter shows you how to make fragments into complete sentences. It's all about supplying what the fragment lacks.

Learning Outcomes

- LO1 Correct common fragments.
- LO2 Correct tricky fragments.
- LO3 Check for fragments in a real-world context.

What do you think?

Explain how the verb could be "the heartthrob of the sentence."

Learning Outcome

Correct common fragments.

Insight

In English, command sentences have an understood subject—*you*.

(*You*) Take my car.

Command sentences are not fragments because the subject is understood.

Zibedik, 2010/used under license from www.shutterstock.com

LO1 Common Fragments

In spoken conversation and informal writing, fragments occasionally occur and are understood. In formal writing however, fragments should be avoided.

Missing Parts

A sentence requires a subject and a predicate. If one or the other or both are missing, the sentence is a **fragment**. Such fragments can be fixed by supplying the missing part.

Fragment:	Went to the concert.
Fragment + Subject:	We went to the concert.
Fragment:	Everyone from Westville Community College.
Fragment + Predicate:	Everyone from Westville Community College may participate.
Fragment:	For the sake of student safety.
Fragment + Subject and Predicate:	The president set up a curfew for the sake of student safety.

Incomplete Thoughts

A sentence also must express a complete thought. Some fragments have a subject and a verb but do not express a complete thought. These fragments can be corrected by providing words that complete the thought.

Fragment:	The concert will include.
Completing Thought:	The concert will include an amazing light show.
Fragment:	If we arrive in time.
Completing Thought:	If we arrive in time, we'll get front-row seats.
Fragment:	That opened the concert.
Completing Thought:	I liked the band that opened the concert.

Say It

Read these fragments aloud. Then read each one again, but this time supply the necessary words to form a complete thought.

1. The student union building.
2. Where you can buy used books.
3. Walked to class every morning.
4. When the instructor is sick.
5. The cop was.

Vocabulary

fragment
a group of words that is missing a subject or a predicate (or both) or that does not express a complete thought

Fixing Common Fragments

Practice A Add words to correct each fragment below. Write the complete sentence on the lines provided.

1. Groceries for our special meal. ________________
2. While I made the pasta, Maya prepared. ________________
3. Finished everything within forty-five minutes. ________________
4. Easily, the best meal ever. ________________
5. Not everyone likes. ________________

Practice B The following paragraph contains numerous fragments. Either add what is missing or combine fragments with other sentences to make them complete. Use the correction marks to the right.

The kitchen truly needs a new coat of paint. Everyone who uses the kitchen. Should help out. Need lots of help. If you have next Saturday afternoon to spare, plan to paint. Ben and I will provide. We'll try to pick a color that goes with the cabinets. When we are finished. The kitchen will be more pleasant for everyone to use. However, we won't guarantee that the food will taste any better.

Correction Marks

- delete
- capitalize
- lowercase
- insert
- add comma
- add question mark
- add word
- add period
- spelling
- switch

Practice C On your own paper or orally, correct the following fragments by supplying the missing part.

1. The front hall of the dorm.
2. When I arrived.
3. Was filled with new students.
4. Worked hard all morning.
5. Which was more than most people had done.

Learning Outcome

Correct tricky fragments.

LO2 Tricky Fragments

Some fragments are more difficult to find and correct. They creep into our writing because they are often part of the way we talk.

Absolute Phrases

An **absolute phrase** looks like a sentence that is missing its helping verb. An absolute phrase can be made into a sentence by adding the helping verb or by connecting the phrase to a complete sentence.

Absolute Phrase (Fragment):	Our legs trembling from the hike.
Absolute Phrase + Helping Verb:	Our legs were trembling from the hike.
Absolute Phrase + Complete Sentence:	We collapsed on the couch, our legs trembling from the hike.

Insight

Some situations are formal—like a dress-up dance. Other situations are informal, like walking around the mall. English works the same way. When writing a formal assignment, you should use formal language. When writing to friends on the Internet, you may use informal language. (See page 5.)

Informal Fragments

Fragments that are commonly used in speech should be eliminated from formal writing. Avoid the following types of fragments unless you are writing dialogue.

Interjections:	Hey! Yeah!
Exclamations:	What a nuisance! How fun!
Greetings:	Hi, everybody. Good afternoon.
Questions:	How come? Why not? What?
Answers:	About three or four. As soon as possible.

Note: Sentences that begin with *Here* or *There* have a **delayed subject**, which appears after the verb. Other sentences (commands) have an **implied subject** (*you*). Such sentences are not fragments.

Delayed Subject:	Here are some crazy fans wearing wild hats.
Implied Subject:	Tackle him! Bring him down!

Vocabulary

absolute phrase
a group of words with a noun and a participle (a word ending in *ing* or *ed*) and the words that modify them

delayed subject
a subject that appears after the verb, as in a sentence that begins with *here* or *there* or a sentence that asks a question

implied subject
the word *you*, assumed to begin command sentences

Say It

Read these fragments aloud. Then read each one again, but this time supply the necessary words to form a complete thought.

1. Are three types of laptop computers.
2. Our instructor explaining the assignment.
3. About three in the morning.
4. Is my favorite Web site.
5. My friend working at a half-priced disk shop.

Fixing Tricky Fragments

Practice A Rewrite each tricky fragment below, making it a sentence.

1. Their hearts melting at the sight of the orphaned pets.

2. The dogs yelping hellos and wagging their tails.

3. Our cats and dogs chasing each other and playing together.

4. Are many benefits to pet ownership.

5. The vet's office teeming with a variety of pets.

Practice B The following paragraph contains a number of informal fragments. Identify and delete them. Reread the paragraphs and listen for the difference.

Both dogs and cats have long been companions to humans. Awesome! Dogs started off as wolves at the end of the last Ice Age. What then? Human hunters killed off wolves that tried to take their food, but a wolf that was neither afraid of humans nor aggressive toward them might be spared. Living alongside people meant wolves were beginning to be domesticated, or comfortable in a human environment.

Cats, however, came a bit later, when humans had become farmers. Yeah. Ancient "barn cats" were probably the first kind. They loved to eat the mice and rats that fed on stored grains, and farmers let them. Perfect! If kittens are handled by humans, they become tame. If they are not, they stay wild.

That's why dogs like walks and cats like to stay home. Dogs joined us when we were walking everywhere, and cats arrived when we were staying put. Yessir.

Learning Outcome

Check for fragments in a real-world context.

LO3 Real-World Application

Correct Correct any sentence fragments in this cover letter for a job application. Either add what is missing or combine the fragment with another sentence.

3041 45th Avenue
Lake City, WI 53000
November 14, 2010

Ms. Colleen Turner
Human Resource Director
Western Printing Company
100 Mound Avenue
Racine, WI 53001

Dear Ms. Turner:

In response to your advertisement in the *Racine Standard Press* on November 12, I am writing to apply for the position of Graphic Designer. Have worked as a designer for Alpha Publications in Brookfield, Wisconsin, for the past three years.

I worked with a team of talented designers to create business handbooks and workbooks, including the award-winning handbook *Write for Business.* Our team each product from early design ideas to preparation of the final disk. My special skills include coloring illustrations and incorporating graphics in page design.

My experience with design software packages includes. Adobe InDesign, Photoshop, and Illustrator. I also have basic knowledge of black-and-white photographic processes and digital print processes.

Enclosed is my résumé. Gives more information about my qualifications and training. I look forward to hearing from you and can be reached at (200) 555-6655 or at aposada@atz.com. Thank you for your consideration.

Sincerely,

Anna Posada

Anna Posada

Encl. résumé

Workplace

A cover letter filled with sentence fragments makes a bad impression on employers. To get the job, get help to make sure your letter is correct.

"If a comma is a yellow light and a period is a red light, the semicolon is a flashing red—one of those lights you drive through after a brief pause."

—Patricia T. O'Conner

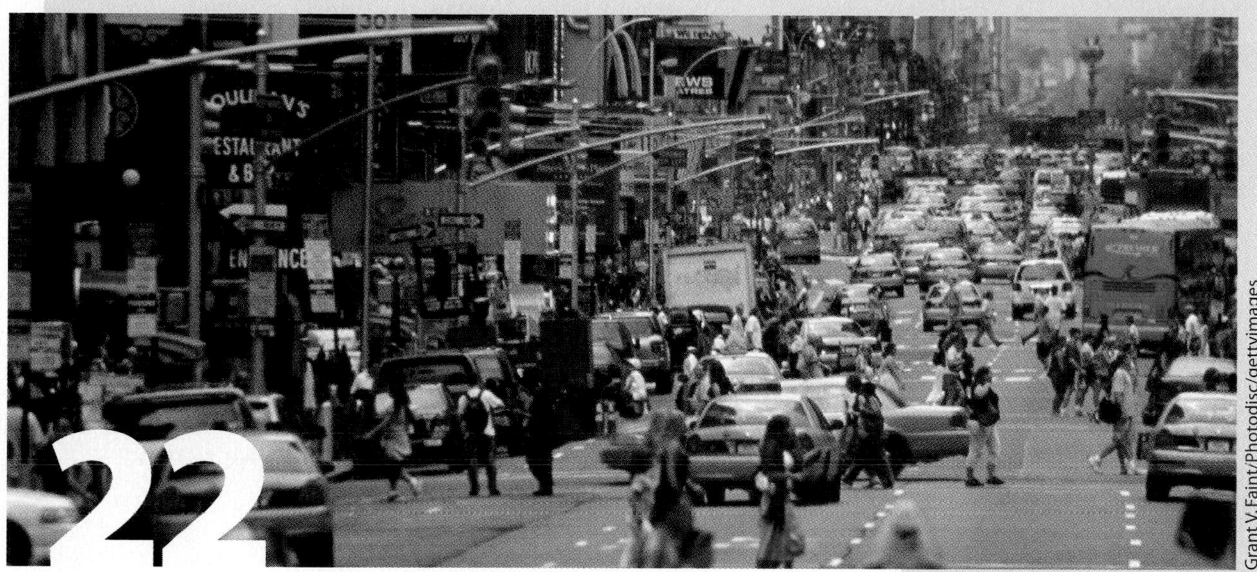
Grant V. Faint/Photodisc/gettyimages

22 Comma Splices, Run-Ons, and Ramblers

Let's face it: Some sentences cause problems. Don't worry, though; this chapter offers solutions. You'll not only learn to recognize comma splices, run-ons, and ramblers, but you also learn a number of strategies for fixing them. Once sentences are solid, your ideas come pouring out of them.

What do you think?

Do your sentences tend to ramble, or are they short and sweet? How do your sentences reflect who you are?

Learning Outcomes

- LO1 Correct comma splices.
- LO2 Correct run-on sentences.
- LO3 Fix rambling sentences.
- LO4 Correct comma splices and run-ons in a real-world context.

Learning Outcome

Correct comma splices.

LO1 Comma Splices

Comma splices occur when two sentences are connected with only a comma. A comma splice can be fixed by adding a coordinating conjunction (*and, but, or, nor, for, so, yet*) or a subordinating conjunction (*while, after, when,* and so on). The two sentences could also be joined by a semicolon (;) or separated by a period.

Comma Splice: The winners were announced, we were not mentioned.

Corrected by adding a coordinating conjunction:	The winners were announced, **but** we were not mentioned.
Corrected by adding a subordinating conjunction:	**When** the winners were announced, we were not mentioned.
Corrected by replacing the comma with a semicolon:	The winners were announced**;** we were not mentioned.

Comma Splice: Our instructor praised our efforts, he thought we deserved an award.

Corrected by adding a coordinating conjunction:	Our instructor praised our efforts, **and** he thought we deserved an award.
Corrected by adding a subordinating conjunction:	Our instructor praised our efforts **because** he thought we deserved an award.
Corrected by replacing the comma with a period:	Our instructor praised our efforts**.** He thought we deserved an award.

Insight

A comma is not strong enough to join sentences without a conjunction. A semicolon can join two closely related sentences. A period or question mark can separate the two sentences.

Say It

Read the following comma splices aloud. Then tell a classmate how you would correct each one.

1. Everyone owns at least one pair of tennis shoes, some people own many pairs of them.
2. Tennis shoes are also called sneakers, they are lightweight with rubber soles.
3. Tennis shoes are not used just for playing tennis, people use them for walking and for playing other sports.
4. Tennis shoes are very comfortable to wear, cheap ones wear out rather quickly.
5. Designer tennis shoes are quite fashionable, they are also very expensive.

Vocabulary

comma splice
a sentence error that occurs when two sentences are connected with only a comma

Correcting Comma Splices

Practice A Correct the following comma splices by adding a coordinating conjunction (*and, but, or, nor, for, so, yet*), a subordinating conjunction (*when, while, because,* and so on), or replacing the comma with a semicolon or period. Use the approach that makes the sentence read most smoothly. (The first one has been done for you.)

1. Contests are set up to have many participants, but very few actually win.
2. Businesses run contests to stir up buzz, they are trying to advertise.
3. The business gives away a few prizes, it brings in many names and addresses.
4. Most people enter a contest for one reason, they want the prize, of course.
5. A business should follow up with entrants, they provide a marketing opportunity.
6. Both Bill and I entered the contest, we both were disappointed.
7. Then we received discount coupons, we were happy to get them.
8. Winning is a long shot, there are other benefits to entering.
9. We each used our coupons, the discount was significant.
10. We're on the lookout for another contest, maybe we'll have better luck in the future.

Practice B Rewrite the following paragraph, correcting any comma splices that you find.

Braille is a system of communication used by the blind. It was developed by Louis Braille in 1824. The system uses combinations of small raised dots to create an alphabet, the dots are imprinted on paper and can be felt. A blind person reads the page by running his or her fingers across the dots. The basic unit is called a cell, a cell is two dots wide and three dots high. Numbers, punctuation marks, and written music can be expressed with this system. Braille has allowed the blind to read, it is truly a great invention.

Learning Outcome

Correct run-on sentences.

Insight

As you can see, run-ons and comma splices are very similar. As such, they can be corrected in the same basic ways.

LO2 Run-On Sentences

A **run-on sentence** occurs when two sentences are joined without punctuation or a connecting word. A run-on can be fixed by adding a comma and a conjunction or by inserting a semicolon or period between the two sentences.

Run-On: I was feeling lucky I was totally wrong.

Corrected by adding a comma and coordinating conjunction:	I was feeling lucky, but I was totally wrong.
Corrected by adding a subordinating conjunction and comma:	Although I was feeling lucky, I was totally wrong.
Corrected by inserting a semicolon:	I was feeling lucky; I was totally wrong.

Run-On: I signed up for the contest I had to write a story about **robotic** life.

Corrected by adding a comma and a coordinating conjunction:	I signed up for the contest, so I had to write a story about robotic life.
Corrected by adding a subordinating conjunction and a comma:	When I signed up for the contest, I had to write a story about robotic life.
Corrected by inserting a period:	I signed up for the contest. I had to write a story about robotic life.

Say It

Read the following run-ons aloud. Then be prepared to tell a classmate how you would correct each one.

1. The word robot was introduced in a play in 1920 the next use of the word was in 1941.
2. Robots are artificial helpers they do jobs unsuited for humans.
3. Robots are used in manufacturing they work cheaply and accurately.
4. Many robots are battery powered others run on compressed gases.
5. Scientists have developed SmartHand it works like a real hand.

Traits

Here's an additional way to correct a run-on sentence. Turn one of the sentences into a phrase and combine it with the other one. Number two could be combined in this way: *Robots are artificial helpers, doing jobs unsuited for humans.*

Vocabulary

run-on sentence
a sentence error that occurs when two sentences are joined without punctuation or a connecting word

robotic
related to robots

Correcting Run-On Sentences

Correct Correct the following run-on sentences. Use the approach that makes the sentence read most smoothly.

1. John McCarthy coined the term artificial intelligence this field deals with the intelligence of machines. ______________________________

____

2. Thinking machines first appeared in Greek myths they have been a common feature in fiction since the 1800s. ______________________________

____

3. True artificial intelligence could become a reality an electronic brain could be produced. ______________________________

____

4. Scientists had computers solving algebra word problems people knew these machines could do incredible things. ______________________________

____

5. Reports criticized the artificial intelligence movement funding for research stopped. ______________________________

____

6. Funding is again very strong today artificial intelligence plays an important role in the technology industry. ______________________________

____

7. Computers solve problems in one way human beings solve them in other ways. ______________________________

____

8. People acquire a great deal of basic knowledge it would not be so easy to build this knowledge into machines. ______________________________

____

Extend

Compare your answers with a classmate's. Did you both correct each sentence in the same way?

Rewrite Rewrite the following paragraph on your own paper, correcting any run-on sentences that you find.

Smart Cars look like little water bugs on the road. They are only about eight feet long they are less than five feet wide. You can fit two or three smart cars in a typical parking space. Smart Cars have been quite popular in Europe it remains to be seen how they will be received in the United States. By the way, the two co-stars in *Da Vinci Code* raced around Rome in one of these cars. Some versions of the Smart Car run on a three-cylinder engine they still can go from zero to 60 in about 15 seconds. They can get about 33 miles per gallon in the city and 41 miles per gallon on the highway.

Learning Outcome

Fix rambling sentences.

LO3 Rambling Sentences

A **rambling sentence** occurs when many ideas are strung together by linking words such as *and* or *but*. The result is an unfocused unit of writing that goes on and on. To correct a rambling sentence, break it into smaller units adding and cutting words as needed.

Rambling: When we first signed up for the contest, I had no thought that we would win, but then my brother started talking about how he would spend the money and he asked me if he could have my share of it, so we were counting on winning even though we really had no chance and as it turned out we of course didn't win.

Corrected: When we first signed up for the contest, I had no thought that we would win. Then my brother started talking about how he would spend the money. He even asked for my share. Soon, we were counting on winning even though we had no chance. As it turned out, we didn't win.

Say It

Read each following rambling sentence aloud. Afterward, circle all of the connecting words (*and, but, so*), and be prepared to suggest different ways to break each rambling idea into more manageable units.

1. I enjoyed touring the hospital and I would enjoy joining the nursing staff and I believe that my prior work experience will be an asset but I also know that I have a lot more to learn.
2. The electronics store claims to offer "one-stop shopping" and they can take care of all of a customer's computer needs and they have a fully trained staff to answer questions and solve problems so there is really no need to go anywhere else.

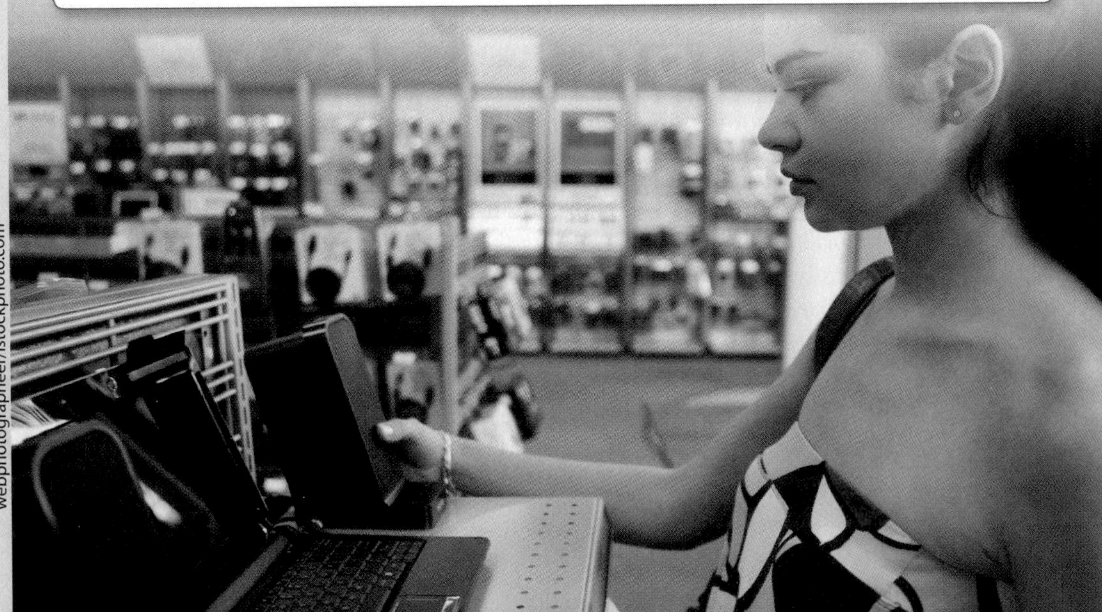

webphotographeer/istockphoto.com

Vocabulary

rambling sentence
a sentence error that occurs when a long series of separate ideas are connected by one *and, but,* or *so* after another

Correct Correct the following rambling sentences by dividing some of the ideas into separate sentences.

1. The cat entered silently through the window and next he jumped onto a chair and darted behind the curtain so he could hide from everyone and then he curled up and relaxed for awhile.

2. I went to the dentist yesterday and when I got there, I had to wait forever to see him and when he finally examined my teeth, he found two cavities and now I have to go back next week to get fillings and I don't want to go.

3. We use trampolines for entertainment but they were used for other purposes a long time ago and Eskimos once used a form of a trampoline made from skins to watch for whales and seals and I think that is a much better use of a trampoline than to just jump up and down on it so I wonder what practical way we can use them today.

Correct In the space provided below, write a rambling sentence or idea about a topic of your own choosing. Afterward, exchange your work with a classmate, and correct each other's rambling idea.

Extend

Share your corrections with a classmate. Did you change each rambling sentence in the same way?

Learning Outcome

Correct comma splices and run-ons in a real-world context.

LO4 Real-World Application

Correct Correct any comma splices or run-on sentences in the following sales letter.

Dale's **Garden Center**
405 Cherry Lane
Flower City, IL 53185

February 1, 2011

Dear Gateway College Student:

Did one of your science instructors ever tell you that plants can talk? Well, they can Dale's flowers speak the language of romance.

With Valentine's Day just two weeks away, let Dale's flowers give you the words to share with your sweetheart. Red roses share your love in the traditional way, a Southern Charm Bouquet says the same thing with a little more class. Or send "poetry" by choosing our Valentine Special in a porcelain vase!

Check out the enclosed selection guide then place your order by phoning 1-800-555-LEAF. If you call by February 13, we promise delivery of fresh flowers on Valentine's Day.

Let Dale's flowers help you start a conversation that could last a lifetime!

Sincerely,

Dale Brown

P.S. Long-distance romances are not a problem, we deliver flowers anywhere in the world.

Note:
An *ing* or *ed* phrase is called a participial phrase and serves as an adjective in a sentence. (See page 326 for more information.)

Extend Correct each of the following comma splices or run-on sentences by changing one of the following sentences into an *-ing* or *-ed* phrase and connecting it to the other sentence. The first one has been done for you.

1. Carnations are a very popular flower they show love and wonder.

   Carnations are a very popular flower, showing love and wonder.

2. The iris is an elegant flower, it is distinguished by its special blue color.

   ____

3. Orchids are tropical flowers they suggest delicate beauty.

   ____

4. Sunflowers follow the sun, they turn to face it as the day goes on.

   ____

"Another way to look at sentences is to see them as carriers of 'news.'"

—Scott Rice

Guzhevnikova Olga 2010/used under license from www.shutterstock.com

23 Additional Sentence Problems

Mathematics is full of problems. The whole point of math is to puzzle out a solution. And for each problem, there should be only one or, occasionally, a small set of right answers.

Writing is different. Sentences should not be full of problems. If a reader has to puzzle out the meaning of a sentence, the sentence *is* a problem. Sometimes a shift has occurred in person, tense, or voice. At other times, a modifier is misplaced or dangling. The result can be a sentence that confuses instead of communicates.

This chapter focuses on correcting these additional sentence problems. You'll find exercises for each type of problem as well as a real-world application.

Learning Outcomes

LO1 Correct misplaced and dangling modifiers.

LO2 Correct shifts in sentence construction.

LO3 Correct sentence problems in a real-world context.

What do you think?

How do sentence problems impact the sentence's ability to be a carrier of news?

Learning Outcome

Correct misplaced and dangling modifiers.

Insight

Avoid placing any adverb modifiers between a verb and its direct object.

Misplaced: *I will throw quickly the ball.*

Corrected: *I will quickly throw the ball.*

Also, do not separate two-word verbs with an adverb modifier.

Misplaced: *Please take immediately out the trash.*

Corrected: *Please immediately take out the trash.*

Vocabulary

dangling modifier
a modifying word, phrase, or clause that appears to modify the wrong word or a word that isn't in the sentence

illogical
without logic; senseless, false, or untrue

misplaced modifier
a modifying word, phrase, or clause that has been placed incorrectly in a sentence, often creating an amusing or illogical idea

LO1 Misplaced/Dangling Modifiers

Dangling Modifiers

A modifier is a word, phrase, or clause that functions as an adjective or adverb. When the modifier does not clearly modify another word in the sentence, it is called a **dangling modifier**. This error can be corrected by inserting the missing word and/or rewriting the sentence.

Dangling Modifier: After buckling the fancy red collar around his neck, my dog pranced proudly down the street. *(The dog could buckle his own collar?)*

Corrected: After I buckled the fancy red collar around his neck, my dog pranced proudly down the street.

Dangling Modifier: Trying desperately to chase a rabbit, I was pulled toward the bushes. *(The person was chasing the rabbit?)*

Corrected: Trying desperately to chase a rabbit, my dog pulled me toward the bushes.

Misplaced Modifiers

When a modifier is placed beside a word that it does not modify, the modifier is misplaced and often results in an amusing or **illogical** statement. A **misplaced modifier** can be corrected by moving it next to the word that it modifies.

Misplaced Modifier: The dog was diagnosed by the vet with mange. *(The vet has mange?)*

Corrected: The vet diagnosed the dog with mange.

Misplaced Modifier: The vet's assistant gave a chewable pill to the dog tasting like liver. *(The dog tastes like liver?)*

Corrected: The vet's assistant gave a chewable pill tasting like liver to the dog.

Say It

Read the following sentences aloud, noting the dangling or misplaced modifier in each one. Then tell a classmate how you would correct each error.

1. The new dog park makes good use of vacant property called Dog Heaven.
2. You will usually find an old basset hound running around the park with extremely stubby legs.
3. Though only five months old, my mother taught Marley to heel.
4. After running around for half an hour, I signaled Marley to stop.
5. One dog owner has worked with his golden lab to teach him to roll over for four weeks.

Correcting Dangling and Misplaced Modifiers

Rewrite Rewrite each of the sentences below, correcting the misplaced and dangling modifiers.

1. We saw a buck and a doe on the way to marriage counseling.

2. The car was reported stolen by the police.

3. We have new phones for hard-of-hearing people with loud ring tones.

4. Please present the proposal that is attached to Mr. Brumbly.

5. I drove with Jennie to the place where we live in a Buick.

6. I found some moldy cheese in the fridge that doesn't belong to me.

7. I bought a parrot for my brother named Squawky.

8. The doctor diagnosed me and referred me to a counselor with severe depression.

9. I gave the cashier my ID that works in the cafeteria.

10. I couldn't believe my sister would buy a cat who is allergic to fur.

Correct For each section, correct the placement of the adverb.

1. Provide promptly the form to Human Resources.

2. We will initiate immediately your new insurance.

3. Please fill carefully out the form.

Insight

When a modifier comes at the beginning of the sentence or the end of the sentence, make sure it modifies the word or phrase closest to it. Ask yourself, "Who or what is being described?"

Katrina Brown, 2010/used under license from www.shutterstock.com

Learning Outcome

Correct shifts in sentence construction.

LO2 Shifts in Sentences

Shift in Person

A **shift in person** is an error that occurs when first, second, and/or third person are improperly mixed in a sentence.

Shift in person: Once you feel better, you can do everything an individual loves to do. (The sentence improperly shifts from second person—*you*—to third person—*individual*.)

Corrected: Once you feel better, you can do everything you love to do.

Shift in Tense

A **shift in tense** is an error that occurs when more than one verb tense is improperly used in a sentence. (See pages 318–325 for more about tense.)

Shift in tense: I searched everywhere before I find my essay. (The sentence improperly shifts from past tense—*searched*—to present tense—*find*.)

Corrected: I searched everywhere before I found my essay.

Shift in Voice

A **shift in voice** is an error that occurs when active voice and passive voice are mixed in a sentence.

Shift in voice: As you search for your essay, your keys may also be found. (The sentence improperly shifts from active voice—*search*—to passive voice—*may be found*.)

Corrected: As you search for your essay, you may also find your keys.

Say It

Read the following sentences aloud, paying careful attention to the improper shift each one contains. Then tell a classmate how you would correct each error.

1. Margo drinks plenty of fluids and got plenty of rest.
2. Landon is running again and many new routes are being discovered by him.
3. When you are ready to work, a person can search for jobs online.
4. Charley served as a tutor in the writing lab and helps English language learners with their writing.
5. My mechanic replaced the front tires on my car and the radiator was flushed by him.

Vocabulary

shift in person
an error that occurs when first, second, and third person are improperly mixed in a sentence

shift in tense
an error that occurs when more than one verb tense is improperly used in a sentence

shift in voice
an error that occurs when active voice and passive voice are mixed in a sentence

Correcting Improper Shifts in Sentences

Rewrite Rewrite each sentence below, correcting any improper shifts in construction.

1. I jogged along the wooded path until I feel exhausted.

2. As we drove to the movie theater, favorite comedies had been discussed by us.

3. When you drop off my toolbox, can he or she also return my grill?

4. Cordero works for the city during the day, and school has been attended by him at night.

5. You should dress professionally for a person's job interview.

Correct Correct the improper shifts in person, tense, or voice in the following paragraph. Use the correction marks to the right when you make your changes.

When you think about today's technology, the first word that comes to mind was convenience. For instance, if you traveled before the creation of the Internet, printed maps were used by you. And if you were traveling out of state, a person needed to purchase other state maps from a gas station or convenience store. You would unfold each map and the best possible route was planned by you. Now you have access to digital maps, personal navigation systems, and Web sites to find your way. You probably enjoy the ease and speed of the new technology and thought the old methods are tiresome.

Correction Marks

- delete
- capitalize
- lowercase
- insert
- add comma
- add question mark
- add word
- add period
- spelling
- switch

Learning Outcome

Correct sentence problems in a real-world context.

LO3 Real-World Application

Correct Correct any dangling modifiers, misplaced modifiers, or shifts in construction in the following message. (Only one sentence is free of errors.) Use the correction marks to the left.

Correction Marks

 delete

d capitalize

D lowercase

∧ insert

add comma

add question mark

word add word

add period

 spelling

 switch

Home Builders

1650 Northwest Boulevard • St. Louis, MO 63124
314-555-9800 • FAX 314-555-9810 • www.homebuilders-stl.org

February 15, 2010

Philip Tranberg
1000 Ivy Street
St. Louis, MO 63450

Dear Philip:

You show a strong interest in Home Builders and the desire to provide people with affordable housing is expressed by you.

First review the enclosed list in Missouri of Home Builders affiliates. Each affiliate handles your own assignments and work groups. Then check the enclosed brochure for additional affiliates on Home Builders campus chapters. This brochure shows you how to join or start a campus chapter and explained service learning for academic credit. Ben Abramson, the Campus Outreach Coordinator, would love to talk with you, and can be contacted by you at the address printed on the brochure.

Again, thank you for your interest in providing affordable housing with Home Builders.

Sincerely,

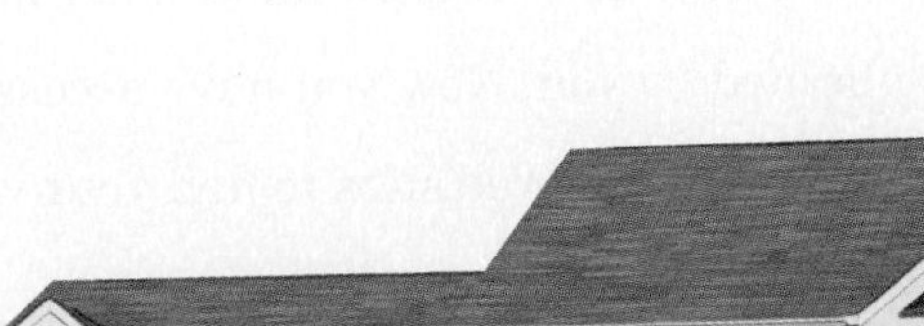

Matthew Osgoode

Enclosures

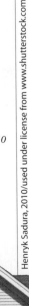

Henryk Sadura, 2010/used under license from www.shutterstock.com

Rewrite The sentences that follow come from *The Suspended Sentence* by Roscoe C. Born. Born found these sentences in newspaper and magazine articles, and each one contains a misplaced modifier. (Yes, even the professionals sometime make mistakes.) Working with a partner, rewrite each sentence to correct the error.

1. The Pistons' general manager wants a big guy who can bang in Tuesday's National Basketball Association draft.

2. Fiekens is to make a final decision on how the contractors, Vista and Michigan Disposal, Inc., can continue to haul Detroit sludge in a meeting next Monday with their lawyers.

3. Jessica W., 28, and Abernathy A., 26, both of Detroit, were charged with delivery of cocaine after the raid.

4. In 1935 he joined the embryonic [Count] Basie group and remained with what many consider the greatest jazz organization of all time until 1948.

Workplace

Journalists and publishers need to be especially careful to avoid mistakes in their writing. But errors in writing reflect badly on all professionals.

Write Write the first draft of a personal narrative (true story) in which you share a time when you misplaced or lost something important to you or to someone else. Here are some tips for adding interest to your story:

- Start right in the middle of the action.
- Build suspense to keep the reader's interest.
- Use dialogue.
- Use sensory details (what you heard, saw, felt, and so on).

Afterward, exchange your writing with a classmate. Read each other's narrative first for enjoyment and a second time to check it for the sentence errors discussed in this chapter.

Part 5 Word Workshops

"Mathematics, rightly viewed, possesses not only truth, but supreme beauty—a beauty cold and austere, like that of sculpture."

—Bertrand Russell

Noun

You have probably heard that a noun names a person, place, or thing. For example, the words *man* and *woman* are nouns. The words *Millennium Park* and *lakefront* also are nouns. And the words *sculpture* and *bean* are nouns as well.

But you may not know that nouns can also name ideas. The word *beauty* is a noun, for example, as are *artistry, mathematics,* and *awe.* You can't see these things, but they are real, and they change the world. At one point, this sculpture was only an idea in the mind of Anish Kapoor, who wanted to create a polished drop of mercury hovering above the ground. Years and $26 million dollars later, the "Cloud Gate" has become a real things—one of the most popular attractions along the Chicago lakefront.

This chapter helps you find the right nouns to name people, places, things, and ideas. You'll learn about the different classes of nouns, singular and plural nouns, count and noncount nouns, and noun markers. Last, you'll get to apply what you have learned in a real-world document.

What do you think?

Which do you most like to work with—people, places, things, or ideas? Why?

Learning Outcomes

- **LO1** Understand classes of nouns.
- **LO2** Use singular and plural nouns.
- **LO3** Form tricky plurals.
- **LO4** Use count and noncount nouns.
- **LO5** Use articles.
- **LO6** Use other noun markers.
- **LO7** Use nouns correctly in a real-world context.

Learning Outcome

Understand classes of nouns.

LO1 Classes of Nouns

All nouns are either *common* or *proper*. They can also be *individual* or *collective*, *concrete* or *abstract*.

Common or Proper Nouns

Common nouns name a general person, place, thing, or idea. They are not capitalized as names. **Proper nouns** name a specific person, place, thing, or idea, and they are capitalized as names.

	Common Nouns	Proper Nouns
Person:	rapper	P. Diddy
Place:	memorial	Vietnam Veterans Memorial
Thing:	car	Ford
Idea:	religion	Islam

Individual or Collective Nouns

Most nouns are **individual**: They refer to one person or thing. Other nouns are **collective**, referring most commonly to a group of people or animals.

	Individual Nouns	Collective Nouns
Person:	chairperson	committee
	quarterback	team
	tourist	crowd
	son	family
Animal:	bird	flock
	gnat	swarm
	lion	pride
	whale	pod
	fish	school

Concrete or Abstract

If a noun refers to something that can be seen, heard, smelled, tasted, or touched, it is a **concrete noun**. If a noun refers to something that can't be sensed, it is an **abstract noun**. Abstract nouns name ideas, conditions, or feelings.

Concrete Nouns	Abstract Nouns
sanctuary	Christianity
heart	love
skin	health

Vocabulary

common noun
noun referring to a general person, place, thing, or idea; not capitalized as a name

proper noun
noun referring to a specific person, place, thing, or idea; capitalized as a name

individual noun
noun referring to one person or thing

collective noun
noun referring to a group of people or animals

concrete noun
noun referring to something that can be sensed

abstract noun
noun referring to an idea, a condition, or a feeling—something that cannot be sensed

Using Different Classes of Nouns

Identify In each sentence below, identify the underlined nouns as common (C) or proper (P).

1. Waterfalls capture the imagination.
2. Niagara Falls is the most powerful set of falls in North America.
3. Niagara Falls is nearly 4,400 feet wide, but Victoria Falls is well over 5,500 feet wide.
4. Every second, 85,000 gallons of water rush over Niagara Falls.

Identify In each sentence below, identify the underlined nouns as individual (I) or collective (CL).

1. The tallest cascade is Angel Falls in Venezuela at 3,212 feet.
2. A team of explorers led by Ruth Robertson measured the height of Angel Falls in 1949.
3. In 1937, Jimmie Angel crash-landed on the falls; a crew had to bring the plane down.
4. The company that made *Up* drew inspiration for Paradise Falls from Angel Falls.

Identify In each sentence below, identify the underlined nouns as concrete (CT) or abstract (A).

1. Iguazu Falls is at the border of Argentina and Brazil.
2. Tourists gaze with wonder and amazement at 275 falls spread over 1.9 miles.
3. The largest fall, Devil's Throat, roars like a devil full of rage.
4. When Eleanor Roosevelt saw them, she said in awe, "Poor Niagara!"

Learning Outcome

Use singular and plural nouns.

LO2 Singular or Plural

The **number** of a noun indicates whether it is singular or plural. A **singular** noun refers to one person, place, thing, or idea. A **plural** noun refers to more than one person, place, thing or idea. For most words, the plural is formed by adding *s*. For nouns ending in *ch, s, sh, x,* or *z,* add an *es*.

	Most Nouns Add *s*		Nouns Ending in *ch, s, sh, x,* or *z* Add *es*	
	Singular	**Plural**	**Singular**	**Plural**
Person:	sister	sisters	coach	coaches
Place:	park	parks	church	churches
Thing:	spoon	spoons	kiss	kisses
Idea:	solution	solutions	wish	wishes

Same in Both Forms or Usually Plural

Some nouns are the same in both forms, and others are usually plural:

Same in Both Forms		Usually Plural	
Singular	**Plural**	**Plural**	
deer	deer	clothes	series
fish	fish	glasses	shears
moose	moose	pants	shorts
salmon	salmon	proceeds	species
sheep	sheep	savings	tongs
swine	swine	scissors	trousers

Insight

The irregular plurals from Old English are some of the oldest words in our language, so they are used very often. The irregular plurals from Latin are some of the newest, brought in through science. As such, they are used less often.

Irregular Plurals

Irregular plurals are formed by changing the words themselves. That is because the plural form comes from Old English or Latin.

From Old English		From Latin	
Singular	**Plural**	**Singular**	**Plural**
child	children	alumnus	alumni
foot	feet	axis	axes
goose	geese	crisis	crises
man	men	datum	data
mouse	mice	millennium	millennia
person	people	medium	media
tooth	teeth	nucleus	nuclei
woman	women	phenomenon	phenomena

Vocabulary

number
whether a word is singular or plural

singular
referring to one thing

plural
referring to more than one thing

irregular plural
a plural noun formed by changing the word rather than by adding *s*

Using Singular and Plural Nouns

Identify For each word, fill in the blank with either the singular or plural form, whichever is missing. If the word usually uses the plural form or is the same in both forms, write an X on the line.

1. boy	________
2. ________	girls
3. child	________
4. man	________
5. ________	women
6. deer	________
7. ________	clothes
8. ________	species
9. swine	________
10. axis	________
11. ________	teeth
12. ________	millennia
13. automobile	________
14. tree	________
15. ________	pants
16. ________	moose
17. phenomenon	________
18. crisis	________
19. ________	mice
20. ________	savings
21. ________	data
22. alumnus	________
23. goose	________
24. fish	________
25. ________	shears

Learning Outcome

Form tricky plurals.

LO3 Tricky Plurals

Some plural nouns are more challenging to form. Words ending in *y, f,* or *fe* and certain compound nouns require special consideration.

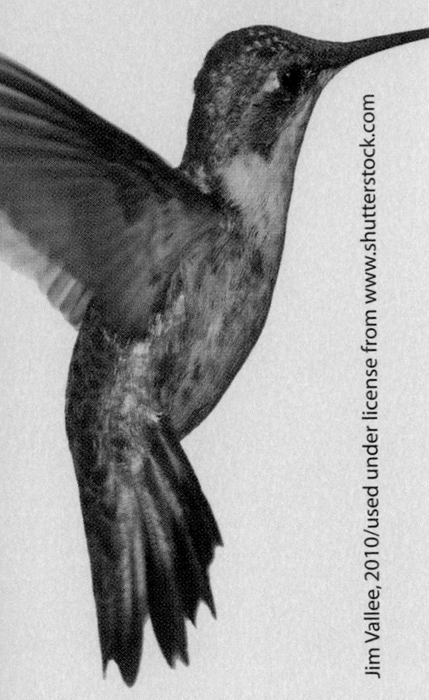

Jim Vallee, 2010/used under license from www.shutterstock.com

Nouns Ending in *y*

If a common noun ends in *y* after a consonant, change the *y* to *i* and add *es.* If the noun ends in *y* after a vowel, leave the *y* and add *s*.

y **After a Consonant**		***y*** **After a Vowel**	
Singular	**Plural**	**Singular**	**Plural**
fly	flies	bay	bays
lady	ladies	key	keys
penny	pennies	toy	toys
story	stories	tray	trays

Nouns Ending in *f* or *fe*

If a common noun ends in *f* or *fe,* change the *f* or *fe* to a *v* and add *es*—unless the *f* sound remains in the plural form. Then just add an *s.*

v **Sound in Plural**		***f*** **Sound in Plural**	
Singular	**Plural**	**Singular**	**Plural**
calf	calves	belief	beliefs
life	lives	chef	chefs
self	selves	proof	proofs
shelf	shelves	safe	safes

Compound Nouns

A **compound noun** is made up of two or more words that function together as a single noun. Whether the compound is hyphenated or not, make it plural by placing the *s* or *es* on the most important word in the compound.

Important Word First		**Important Word Last**	
Singular	**Plural**	**Singular**	**Plural**
editor in chief	editors in chief	bird-watcher	bird-watchers
mother-in-law	mothers-in-law	human being	human beings
professor emeritus	professors emeri-tus	test tube	test tubes
secretary of state	secretaries of state	well-wisher	well-wishers

Vocabulary

compound noun
noun made up of two or more words

Forming Tricky Plurals

Form Plurals For each word below, create the correct plural form.

1. ray ____________________
2. elf ____________________
3. high school ____________________
4. bunny ____________________
5. boy ____________________
6. leaf ____________________
7. reef ____________________
8. calf ____________________
9. guy ____________________
10. credit card ____________________
11. brother-in-law ____________________
12. day ____________________
13. patty ____________________
14. café ____________________
15. sister-in-law ____________________
16. fife ____________________
17. rear guard ____________________
18. jury ____________________
19. power of attorney ____________________
20. poppy ____________________

Form Plurals In the sentences below, correct the plural errors by circling them and writing the correct forms above.

1. I read two different storys about ladys that swallowed flys.
2. The toies on the shelfs belong to my stepchilds.
3. The cheves served salmon pattys with the soup of the days.
4. After a few daies, the daisys sprouted in front of the gardens apartment.
5. The secretary of states from both countrys discussed the treatys.
6. I saw mud puppys and rivers otter on my hike.
7. He gave me four pennys, which I divided between the two take-a-penny traies.
8. The keis for my carries-on are missing.
9. Why is "elfs" spelled one way and "dwarves" is spelled the other?
10. The crys of babys usually alert parents.

Learning Outcome

Use count and noncount nouns.

LO4 Count and Noncount Nouns

Some nouns name things that can be counted, and other nouns name things that cannot. Different rules apply to each type.

Count Nouns

Count nouns name things that can be counted—*pens, people, votes, cats,* and so forth. They can be singular or plural, and they can be preceded by numbers or articles (*a, an,* or *the*).

Singular	Plural
grape	grapes
dog	dogs
car	cars
idea	ideas

Insight

Many native English speakers aren't even aware of count and noncount nouns, though they use them correctly out of habit. Listen for their use of count and noncount nouns.

Noncount Nouns

Noncount nouns name things that cannot be counted. They are used in singular form, and they can be preceded by *the,* but not by *a* or *an*.

This semester, I'm taking **mathematics** and **biology** as well as **Spanish**.

Substances	Foods	Activities	Science	Languages	Abstractions
wood	water	reading	oxygen	Spanish	experience
cloth	milk	boating	weather	English	harm
ice	wine	smoking	heat	Mandarin	publicity
plastic	sugar	dancing	sunshine	Farsi	advice
wool	rice	swimming	electricity	Greek	happiness
steel	meat	soccer	lightning	Latin	health
aluminum	cheese	hockey	biology	French	joy
metal	flour	photography	history	Japanese	love
leather	pasta	writing	mathematics	Afrikaans	anger
porcelain	gravy	homework	economics	German	fame

Two-Way Nouns

Two-way nouns can function as count or noncount nouns, depending on their context.

Please set a **glass** in front of each place mat. (count noun)

The display case was made of tempered **glass**. (noncount noun)

Vocabulary

count noun
noun naming something that can be counted

noncount noun
noun naming something that cannot be counted

two-way noun
noun that can function as either a count or a noncount noun

Using Count and Noncount Nouns

Sort Read the list of nouns below and sort the words into columns of count and noncount nouns.

door	wool	vacation	happiness	sunshine
heat	tablecloth	wagon	photography	flour
swimming	cherry	French	ruler	tablespoon

Count Nouns	Noncount Nouns

Correct Read the following paragraph and correct the noun errors. Remember to delete articles or numbers in front of noncount nouns and to change verbs as needed. The first sentence has been corrected for you.

There are different activities for ~~four~~ different weather~~s~~. For days with sunshines, outdoor activities are best. Some people enjoy swimmings, others like boatings, and even more play soccers. For days in the spring or fall, quieter activities work well. Writing poetries or enjoying photographies are good pastimes, as well as dancings. During the winter, there are readings and homeworks to do. The key to happinesses is to enjoy whatever you are doing.

Correction Marks

- delete
- capitalize
- lowercase
- insert
- add comma
- add question mark
- add word
- add period
- spelling
- switch

Granite, 2010/used under license from www.shutterstock.com

Learning Outcome

Use articles.

LO5 Articles

Articles help you to know if a noun refers to a specific thing or to a general thing. There are two basic types of articles—definite and indefinite.

Definite Article

The **definite article** is the word *the*. It signals that the noun refers to one specific person, place, thing, or idea.

Get off the laptop.
(Get off a specific laptop.)

> **Note:** *The* can be used with most nouns, but usually not with proper nouns.

Incorrect: The Fluffy got off the laptop.

Correct: Fluffy got off the laptop.

"on my laptop... again" by Tanjila Ahmed, 2006/http://www.flickr.com/photos/...

Insight

If your heritage language does not use articles, pay close attention to the way native English speakers use *the* when referring to a specific thing. Note, however, that *the* is not usually used with proper nouns naming people or animals.

Indefinite Articles

The **indefinite articles** are the words *a* and *an*. They signal that the noun refers to a general person, place, thing, or idea. The word *a* is used before nouns that begin with consonant sounds, and the word *an* is used before nouns that begin with vowel sounds.

Chan needs a laptop.
(He'll take any laptop.)

> **Note:** Don't use *a* or *an* with plural count nouns or noncount nouns.

Incorrect: Pass me a cheese.

Correct: Pass me the cheese.

> **Note:** If a word begins with an *h* that is pronounced, use *a*. If the *h* is silent, use *an*.

Incorrect: It is a honor.

Correct: It is an honor.

Carla Gomez Monroy, OLPC CC-SA 3.0

Vocabulary

article
the most common type of noun marker (*a, an,* or *the*)

definite article
the word *the*, used to mark a noun that refers to a specific person, place, or thing

indefinite article
the words *a* or *an,* used to mark a noun that refers to a general person, place, or thing

Using Articles

Identify Add the appropriate indefinite article (*a* or *an*) to each of the words below. The first one has been done for you.

1. an	anthill	6. ______	ad	11. ______	euro
2. ______	pear	7. ______	heap	12. ______	honest man
3. ______	hog	8. ______	honor	13. ______	idea
4. ______	hour	9. ______	dolphin	14. ______	exaggeration
5. ______	apple	10. ______	egg	15. ______	handshake

Correct Either delete or replace any articles that are incorrectly used in the following paragraph. The first sentence has been done for you.

Scientists wonder whether a planet Neptune collided with the "super-Earth" when a solar system was forming. The Neptune emits much more radiation than the Uranus, though they are otherwise twins in a solar system. An extra radiation may be left over from this collision with the planet twice the size of an Earth. The Neptune's large moon, the Triton, rotates in an opposite direction to a planet's spin. That fact shows that a Triton was probably a moon of the super-Earth and was captured. If scientists are right, the Neptune holds another planet inside its gassy belly.

Correction Marks

- delete
- capitalize
- lowercase
- insert
- add comma
- add question mark
- add word
- add period
- spelling
- switch

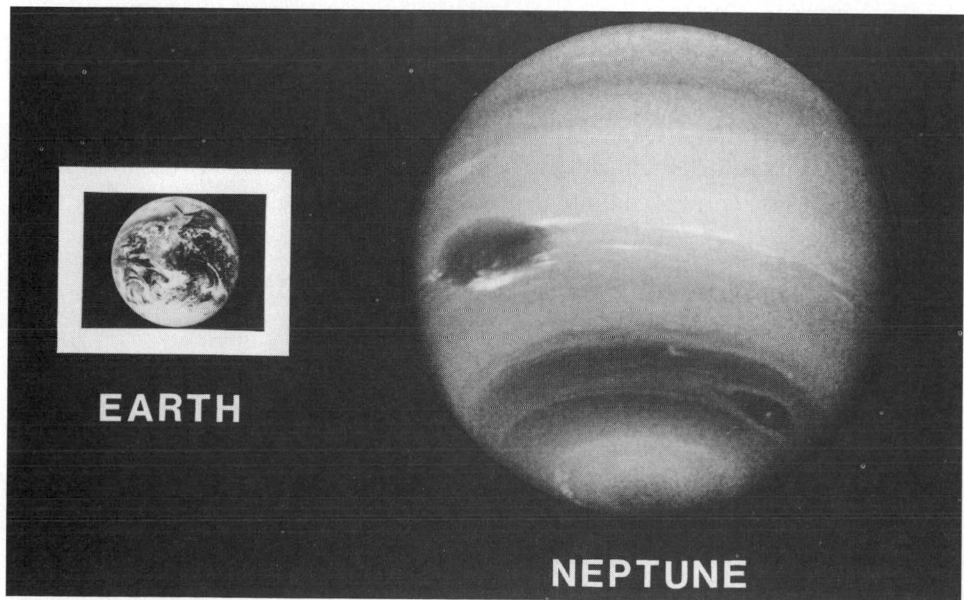

Courtesy S. Meszaros and Lunar and Planetary Institute.

Learning Outcome

Use other noun markers.

Traits

These noun markers show if a noun is owned, if it is very general, if it is very specific, or if it is numerous or plentiful.

Vocabulary

possessive adjective
the possessive form of a noun or pronoun, showing ownership of another noun

indefinite adjective
an indefinite pronoun (*many, much, some*) used as an adjective to mark a nonspecific noun

demonstrative adjective
a demonstrative pronoun (*this, that, those*) used as an adjective to mark a specific noun

quantifier
a modifier that tells *how many* or *how much*

LO6 Other Noun Markers

Other words help provide information about nouns.

Possessive Adjective

A **possessive adjective** is the possessive form of a noun or pronoun. Possessive adjectives can be formed by adding *'s* to singular nouns and *'* to plural nouns.

Dave's e-mail came back, but **Ellen's** didn't.

Milwaukee's harbor is usually calm.

The **Smiths'** house needs painting.

That is **my** car. That car is **mine**.

It's **your** book. The book is **yours**.

Possessive Pronouns

	Singular		Plural	
	Before	After	Before	After
First Person	my	mine	our	ours
Second Person	your	yours	your	yours
Third Person	his her its	his hers its	their their their	theirs theirs theirs

Note: One form of a possessive pronoun is used before the noun, and a different form is used after.

Indefinite Adjectives

An **indefinite adjective** signals that the noun it marks refers to a general person, place, thing, or idea. Some indefinite adjectives mark count nouns and others mark noncount nouns.

All people are welcome to join. **Much** celebrating will be done.

With Count Nouns	With Noncount Nouns	With Count or Noncount
each, either, every, few, many, neither, several	much	all, any, more, most, some

Demonstrative Adjectives

A **demonstrative adjective** marks a specific noun. The words *this* and *that* (singular) or *these* and *those* (plural) demonstrate exactly which one is meant.

These songs are by **that** artist. **This** song includes **those** lyrics.

Quantifiers

A **quantifier** tells *how many* or *how much* there is of something.

With Count Nouns	With Noncount Nouns	With Count or Noncount
each, several, a number of, both, nine, a couple of, every, many, a few	a bag of, a bowl of, a piece of, a little, much, a great deal of	no, not any, some, a lot of, lots of, plenty of, most, all

Using Noun Markers

Identify Circle the appropriate noun marker in parentheses for each sentence.

1. Please leave (*your, yours*) phone number after the beep.
2. Is this phone number (*your, yours*)?
3. How (*many, much*) students are allowed in the class?
4. The professor did not give us (*any, each*) homework.
5. I want to buy (*this, these*) shirts.
6. The resident assistant didn't like (*that, those*) idea.
7. After making the dough, we had (*several, a little*) flour left.
8. I liked (*a number of, much*) the suggestions.
9. The proposal was originally (*her, hers*).
10. Let's make sure to return (*their, theirs*) pillows.

Correct Delete and replace any incorrectly used noun markers in the following paragraph. The first two have been done for you.

What is ~~yours~~ *your* major? You probably have heard that ~~much~~ *many* times. But taking a little courses in one area does not mean it is yours major. Much students don't choose a major until theirs junior year. This students have to explore theirs options before making up theirs minds. Those delay isn't a problem. Those exploration is the point of undergraduate study. Until you know for sure a major is your, you should taste-test much fields. In mine junior year, I was told I would not graduate unless I picked mine major. I added up mine hours, and that total showed I was closest to English. Two weeks later, the head of the English Department called and said, "I thought we should meet since you are one of mine majors."

Correction Marks

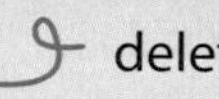 delete

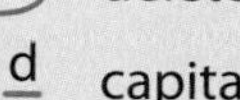 capitalize

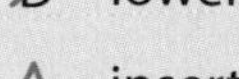 lowercase

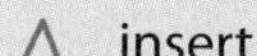 insert

add comma

add question mark

add word

add period

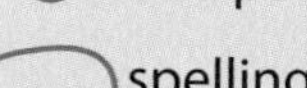 spelling

switch

Utemov Alexey, 2010/used under license from www.shutterstock.com

Learning Outcome

Use nouns correctly in a real-world context.

LO7 Real-World Application

Correct In the letter that follows, correct any errors with nouns, articles, or other noun markers. Use the correction marks to the left.

Dale's **Garden Center**
405 Cherry Lane
Flower City, IL 53185

February 1, 2010

Dear Student:

Did one of yours science professors ever tell you that plants can talk? Well, they can. Dale flowers speak a language of love to the womans or mans in your life.

If you're at an loss for words with valentine's day just two weeks away, let Dale's flowers give you the words. Red roses share yours love in the language of Romance. A Southern charm bouquet says it with class and a added touch of Magnolias. Or send poetries by choosing our Valentine's Day special in a porcelain vase!

Come browse our shelfs. Or check out the enclosed catalog and place yours order by phoning 1-800-555-LEAF. If you call by february 13, we guarantee delivery of fresh flowers on Valentine's Day. Order by Februaries 10, and you'll receive an 20 percent discount.

Let Dales' flowers help you start a conversation that could last a lifetime!

Sincerely,

Jerilynn Bostwick

Jerilynn Bostwick
Sales Manager

P.S. Is your a long-distance romance? Remember, we deliver flowers anywhere in the world through the telefloral network.

Correction Marks

- delete
- capitalize
- lowercase
- insert
- add comma
- add question mark
- add word
- add period
- spelling
- switch

Workplace

Note how the errors in nouns and noun markers make this letter less persuasive. Readers notice errors instead of hearing the persuasive pitch.

"The personal pronoun in English has three cases, the dominative, the objectionable, and the oppressive."
—Ambrose Bierce

Photo by Jay Bergesen

25 Pronoun

Mannequins are everywhere—trying to sell this dress or that shirt, trying to show you a suit or a pair of shorts. The reason mannequins are everywhere is that it would be too expensive and boring for real people to stand around all day showing off clothing.

Pronouns are like mannequins—they are stand-ins for nouns. Writing that has no pronouns quickly becomes overloaded with nouns, repetitive and hard to read. So a pronoun can take the noun's place.

This chapter will show you how to make sure your pronoun stand-ins work well.

Learning Outcomes

- LO1 Understand personal pronouns.
- LO2 Create pronoun-antecedent agreement.
- LO3 Correct other pronoun problems.
- LO4 Create agreement with indefinite pronouns.
- LO5 Use relative pronouns.
- LO6 Use other pronouns.
- LO7 Use pronouns correctly in a real-world context.

What do you think?

Have you ever confused a mannequin for a real person? What was the result?

Learning Outcome

Understand personal pronouns.

LO1 Personal Pronouns

A **pronoun** is a word that takes the place of a noun or another pronoun. The most common type of pronoun is the **personal pronoun**. Personal pronouns indicate whether the person is speaking, is being spoken to, or is being spoken about.

	Singular			Plural		
Person	**Nom.**	**Obj.**	**Poss.**	**Nom.**	**Obj.**	**Poss.**
First (speaking)	I	me	my/mine	we	us	our/ours
Second (spoken to)	you	you	your/yours	you	you	your/yours
Third (spoken about) masculine	he	him	his	they	them	their/theirs
feminine	she	her	her/hers	they	them	their/theirs
neuter	it	it	its	they	them	their/theirs

Nom.=nominative case / **Obj**=objective case / **Poss.**=possessive case

Case of Pronouns

The **case** of a personal pronoun indicates how it can be used.

- **Nominative** pronouns are used as the subjects of sentences or as subject complements (following the linking verbs *am, is, are, was, were, be, being,* or *been*).

  I was nominated, but the person selected was **she**.

- **Objective** pronouns are used as direct objects, indirect objects, or objects of prepositions.

  The professor lectured **them** about **it**.

- **Possessive** pronouns show ownership and function as adjectives.

  My notebook has fewer notes than **hers**.

Gender

Pronouns can be **masculine**, **feminine**, or **neuter**.

She helped **him** with **it**.

Say It

Read the following aloud.

1. *I* am / *You* are / *He* is / *She* is / *It* is / *We* are / *They* are
2. Help *me* / Help *you* / Help *him* / Help *her* / Help *it* / Help *us* / Help *them*
3. *My* book / *Your* book / *His* book / *Her* book / *Their* book
4. The book is *mine.* / The book is *yours.* / The book is *his.* / The book is *hers.* / The book is *theirs.*

Vocabulary

pronoun
a word that takes the place of a noun or other pronoun

personal pronoun
a pronoun that indicates whether the person is speaking, is spoken to, or is spoken about

case
whether a pronoun is used as a subject, an object, or a possessive

nominative
used as a subject or subject complement

objective
used as a direct object, an indirect object, or an object of a preposition

possessive
used to show ownership

masculine
male

feminine
female

neuter
neither male nor female

Using Personal Pronouns

Select For each sentence below, circle the correct personal pronoun in parentheses.

1. The dorm cafeteria is where *(I, me, my)* friends gather.
2. *(We, Us, Our)* talk about classes and also about each other.
3. I told Emily that I would help *(she, her, hers)* with her homework.
4. I have a heavy schedule, but not as heavy as *(she, her, hers) is*.
5. *(I, Me, My, Mine)* 18 credits require less work than *(she, her, hers)* 20.
6. Emily told *(I, me, my, mine)* that *(she, her, hers)* is free on Friday.
7. Kim and Jamie wanted to join *(we, us, our, ours)*.
8. Emily and *(I, me, my, mine)* told *(they, them, their, theirs)* to come.
9. Of course, Kim and Jamie need to bring *(they, them, their, theirs)* books.
10. We'll never forget *(we, us, our, ours)* afternoons in the cafeteria.

Correct In the following paragraph, correct the pronouns by crossing out the incorrect forms and writing the correct forms above.

I asked me sons if them would like to take a walk around Lake Geneva. Them asked how us could walk around the lake. I told they that a path goes all the way around the lake, and its is open to the public. My sons said that them wanted to go, but them wondered how far the walk was. Me told they that it was about 30 miles. They mouths dropped open. Them couldn't figure out what to say to I. My sons and me looked at each other. Then I said them needed to get theirs backpacks and shoes. They told me that I should get a life. But I convinced they, and us hiked all the way around Lake Geneva. When it was over, I wished I had listened to they. My legs hurt so much!

LO2 Pronoun-Antecedent Agreement

The **antecedent** is the word that a pronoun refers to or replaces. A pronoun must have the same person, number, and gender as the antecedent, which is called **pronoun-antecedent agreement**.

third-person (Linda) — singular feminine (hers)

Linda asked to borrow a pen but then found **hers**.

Agreement in Person

A pronoun needs to match its antecedent in **person** (first, second, or third).

third person (people) — second person (you)

Incorrect: If **people** look hard, **you** might find some good deals.
Correct: If **you** look hard, **you** might find some good deals.
Correct: If **people** look hard, **they** might find some good deals.

Agreement in Number

A pronoun needs to match its antecedent in **number** (singular or plural).

singular (student) — plural (their)

Incorrect: Each **student** should bring **their** assignment.
Correct: **Students** should bring **their** assignments.
Correct: Each **student** should bring **her** or **his** assignment.

Agreement in Gender

A pronoun needs to match its antecedent in **gender** (masculine, feminine, or neuter).

feminine (Janae) — masculine (his)

Incorrect: **Janae** will share **his** project.
Correct: **Janae** will share **her** project.

Say It

Speak the following words aloud.

1. First person: *I, me, my, mine; we, us, our, ours*
2. Second person: *you, your, yours*
3. Third person feminine: *she, her, hers; they, them, their, theirs*
4. Third person masculine: *he, him, his; they, them, their, theirs*
5. Third person neuter: *it, its; they, them, their, theirs*

Learning Outcome

Create pronoun-antecedent agreement.

Insight

Different languages use gender in different ways. English reserves gender for people and animals, though some languages use gender for nonliving things. Compare gender use in your heritage language with gender use in English, and note the differences.

Vocabulary

antecedent
the word that a pronoun refers to or replaces

pronoun-antecedent agreement
matching a pronoun to its antecedent in terms of person, number, and gender

person
whether the pronoun is speaking, being spoken to, or being spoken about

number
whether the pronoun is singular or plural

gender
whether the pronoun is masculine, feminine, or neuter

Correcting Agreement Errors

Correct Person Rewrite each sentence to correct the person error.

1. If both of you go to the job fair, they will probably find job opportunities.

2. We went to the fair last year, and they landed some good jobs.

3. If the graduates fill out applications, you may find jobs.

4. One considers the future when you attend the fair.

Correct Number Rewrite each sentence to correct the number error.

5. Each applicant should put down their name.

6. An employee will greet you, and they will interview you.

7. Applicants should supply his contact information.

8. Answer the interviewer unless they ask unfair questions.

Correct Gender Rewrite each sentence to correct the gender error.

9. If Lionel goes, she can drive others.

   he

10. Tawny said he was going.

    She

11. Ask David if she is planning to attend.

12. The hall is big, and she sits at a major intersection.

Learning Outcome

Correct other pronoun problems.

LO3 Other Pronoun Problems

Pronouns are very useful parts of speech, but if they are mishandled, they can cause problems.

Vague Pronoun

Do not use a pronoun that could refer to more than one antecedent.

Unclear: Lupe spoke to her roommate and **her** sister.
Clear: Lupe spoke to her roommate and **her roommate's** sister.

Missing Antecedent

Avoid using *it* or *they* without clear antecedents.

Unclear: **It** says in the tabloid that a donkey-boy was born.
Clear: The **tabloid** says that a donkey-boy was born.

Unclear: **They** have found one of the causes of arthritis.
Clear: **Scientists** have found one of the causes of arthritis.

Double Subjects

Do not place a pronoun right after the subject. Doing so creates an error called a **double subject**, which is not a standard construction.

Nonstandard: Kyle and Jules, **they** went to the movies.
Standard: Kyle and Jules went to the movies.

Usage Errors *(They're, You're, It's)*

Do not confuse possessive pronouns *(your, their, its)* with contractions *(you're, they're, it's)*. Remember that the contractions use apostrophes in place of missing letters.

Incorrect: Please place **you're** plastic bottles in **they're** recycling bin.
Correct: Please place **your** plastic bottles in **their** recycling bin.

Speaking & Listening

The pronoun problems on this page may not cause confusion in spoken English, which is assisted with gestures, body language, and other context cues. In written English, these problems can derail meaning. Watch for them and correct them in your writing.

Vocabulary

vague pronoun
using a pronoun that could refer to more than one antecedent

missing antecedent
using a pronoun that has no clear antecedent

double subject
error created by following a subject with a pronoun

usage error
using the wrong word (e.g., *they're* instead of *their*)

Correcting Other Pronoun Problems

Rewrite Rewrite each sentence to correct the pronoun-reference problems.

1. Raul asked his father and his friend to help him move.

   ____

2. It says in the article that three people are trapped.

   ____

3. They are proposing an amendment to the Constitution.

   ____

4. Shakira wants her sister and her friend to help.

   ____

5. It says in the news report that stocks are down.

   ____

6. They have a new cure for baldness.

   ____

Correct In the following paragraph, correct the pronoun errors. Use the correction marks to the right.

It says on the Internet that many major companies have pulled April Fool's Day pranks. They replaced the name "Google" with the name "Topeka," for one. It says also that a rare baby skeksis was born in a zoo, but it exists only in the film *The Dark Crystal*. One classical music station, it claimed that a British billionaire was sending a violinist to the moon in a special spaceship. It's console had a button to make the ship's cockpit sound like the Royal Albert Hall. They had a lot of fun with they're gags, but gullible people kept getting tripped up all day. It also claims that in the UK, Australia, and South Africa, the gags stop at noon, but they're citizens, they still get pranked by Americans all day.

Correction Marks

- delete
- capitalize
- lowercase
- insert
- add comma
- add question mark
- word — add word
- add period
- spelling
- switch

Learning Outcome

Create agreement with indefinite pronouns.

LO4 Indefinite Pronouns

An **indefinite pronoun** does not have an antecedent, and it does not refer to a specific person, place, thing, or idea. These pronouns pose unique issues with subject-verb and pronoun-antecedent agreement.

Singular Indefinite Pronouns

Some indefinite pronouns are singular. When they are used as subjects, they require a singular verb. As antecedents, they must be matched to singular pronouns.

each	anyone	anybody	anything
either	someone	somebody	something
neither	everyone	everybody	everything
another	no one	nobody	nothing
one			

Someone is supposed to empty the dishwasher.
No one has said **he** will do it.

Insight

For more practice with indefinite pronouns, see pages 252–255.

Plural Indefinite Pronouns

Some indefinite pronouns are plural. As subjects, they require a plural verb, and as antecedents, they require a plural pronoun.

both	few	several	many

A few of the housemates **leave** dirty dishes everywhere.
Several of their friends said **they** are fed up.

Singular or Plural Indefinite Pronouns

Some indefinite pronouns can be singular or plural, depending on the object of the preposition in the phrase that follows them.

all	any	most	none	some

All of the **pies were** eaten.
All of the **pie was** eaten.

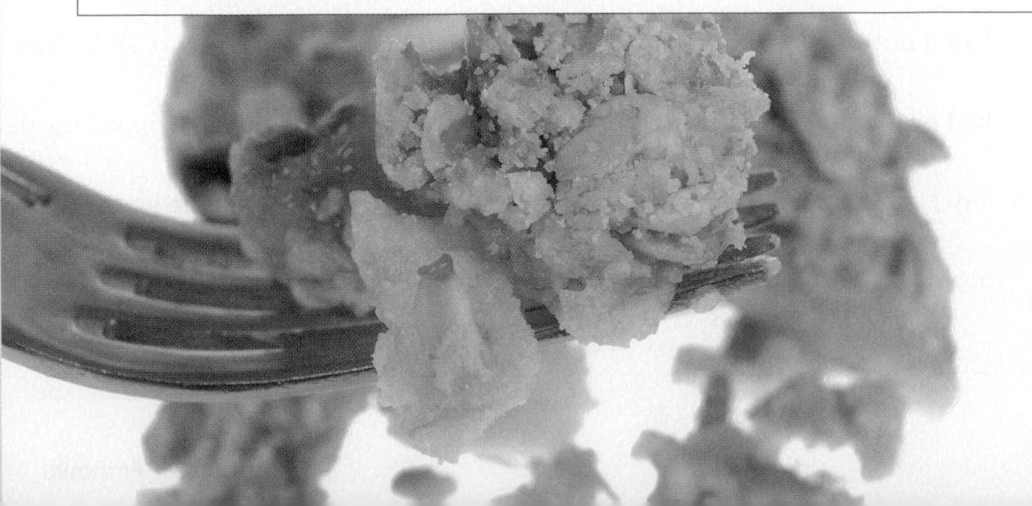

Vocabulary

indefinite pronoun
a pronoun that does not refer to a specific person, place, thing, or idea

Correcting Agreement

Correct Rewrite each sentence to correct the agreement errors. (Hint: the sentences are about a group of male roommates.)

1. Everyone needs to wash their own dishes.

2. No one are exempt.

3. Anyone not washing their dishes must wash everyone else's.

4. Nothing short of illness are an excuse.

5. Few is arguing with the new policy.

6. Several says it is about time.

7. Many expresses their appreciation.

8. For a week, all of the dishes has been washed.

9. Ted made sure all of his plates was washed and put away.

10. Most of the roommates agrees that this works.

11. Most of the morning are spent cleaning up.

12. None of the dishes is left lying about.

13. None of the food are left to eat either, since everybody have forgotten to go shopping.

Learning Outcome

Use relative pronouns.

Insight

For more practice with relative pronouns, see pages 222–223.

Vocabulary

relative pronoun
a pronoun that begins a relative clause, connecting it to a sentence

relative clause
a type of dependent clause that begins with a relative pronoun that is either the subject or the direct object of the clause

LO5 Relative Pronouns

A **relative pronoun** introduces a dependent clause and relates it to the rest of the sentence.

who	whom	which	whose
whoever	whomever	that	

relative clause: I would like to meet the man **who** invented the World Wide Web.

Who/Whoever and Whom/Whomever

Who, whoever, whom, and *whomever* refer to people. *Who* or *whoever* functions as the subject of the relative clause, while *whom* or *whomever* functions as the object of the clause.

relative clause: I would like to thank **whoever** chose the playlist for this party.

The person **whom** I thanked had terrific taste in music. (relative clause: whom I thanked)

Note: In the second **relative clause**, *whom* introduces the clause even though it is the direct object, not the subject (I thanked whom).

That and Which

That and *which* usually refer to things. When *that* introduces the clause, the clause **is not** set off with commas. When *which* introduces the clause, the clause **is** set off with commas.

relative clause: I read the book **that** told of Teddy Roosevelt's journey down the Amazon.

I enjoyed *The River of Doubt,* **which** was a $29 hardback. (relative clause: which was a $29 hardback.)

Note: In the first example, the *that* clause is restrictive, or essential to the meaning of the sentence. In the second example, the *which* clause is nonrestrictive, or unnecessary to the meaning of the sentence.

Whose

Whose shows ownership or connection.

relative clause: The mechanic **whose** hand got cut was fixing our car.

Note: Do not confuse *whose* with the contraction *who's* (who is).

Using Relative Pronouns

Select For each sentence, circle the correct relative pronoun.

1. Theo Jansen is an engineer and artist *(who, whom)* is creating new life.
2. He builds sculptures *(that, which)* harness the wind to walk.
3. Theo refers to his sculptures as animals, *(that, which)* is unusual for an engineer.
4. These animals are built of plastic pipe, *(that, which)* is inexpensive and strong.
5. Another engineer and artist *(who, whom)* Jansen admires is Leonardo da Vinci.
6. Theo's creations are on display for *(whoever, whomever)* is on the beach.
7. His most famous creation is the Strandbeest, *(that, which)* has wings on top.
8. The wings pump air into plastic bottles, *(that, which)* store it up.
9. The air powers "muscles" *(that, which)* are made of sliding tubes.
10. Muscles open taps that activate other muscles, *(that, which)* makes the beest walk.
11. Theo Jansen, *(who, whose)* creations are spellbinding, hopes these "animals" will roam on their own one day.
12. Theo feels that the boundary between art and engineering is only in our minds, *(that, which)* allows him to create such creatures.

Fabio Bruna from Flickr

Write On your own paper, write a relative clause for each of these relative pronouns:

1. who
2. whoever
3. whom
4. whomever
5. which
6. that
7. whose

Write a sentence including one of your clauses.

Learning Outcome

Use other pronouns.

LO6 Other Pronoun Types

Other types of pronouns have specific uses in your writing: asking questions, pointing to specific things, reflecting back on a noun (or pronoun), or intensifying a noun (or pronoun).

Interrogative Pronoun

An **interrogative pronoun** asks a question—*who, whose, whom, which, what.*

Who will help me make the salads? **What** is your favorite dressing?

Demonstrative Pronoun

A **demonstrative pronoun** points to a specific thing—*this, that, these, those.*

This is the best of times! **These** are wonderful days!

Reflexive Pronoun

A **reflexive pronoun** reflects back to the subject of a sentence or clause—*myself, ourselves, yourself, yourselves, himself, herself, itself, themselves.*

I e-mailed **myself** the file. You can send **yourself** the vacation photos.

Intensive Pronoun

An **intensive pronoun** emphasizes the noun or pronoun it refers to—*myself, ourselves, yourself, yourselves, himself, herself, itself, themselves.*

I **myself** will be there. You **yourself** will see me.

Reciprocal Pronoun

A **reciprocal pronoun** refers to two things in an equal way—*each other, one another.*

We should apologize to **each other**. We should love **one another**.

Say It

Speak the following words aloud.

1. Interrogative: *Who* is? / *Whose* is? / *Which* is? / *What* is? / *Whom* do you see?
2. Demonstrative: *This* is / *That* is / *These* are / *Those* are
3. Reflexive: I helped *myself.* / You helped *yourself.* / They helped *themselves*
4. Intensive: *I myself* / *You yourself* / *She herself* / *He himself* / *They themselves*
5. Reciprocal: *We helped each other.* / *We helped one another.*

Traits

To remember these terms, think of the words they came from: *Interrogate* means "ask questions," *demonstrate* means "point out," *reflect* means "show an image of," *intensify* means "make stronger," and *reciprocal* means "working together."

Vocabulary

interrogative pronoun
a pronoun that asks a question

demonstrative pronoun
a pronoun that points to a specific thing

reflexive pronoun
a pronoun that reflects back to the subject of a sentence or clause

intensive pronoun
a pronoun that emphasizes the noun or pronoun it refers to

reciprocal pronoun
a pronoun that refers to two things in an equal way

Using Other Types of Pronouns

Identify Indicate the type of each underlined pronoun: *interrogative, demonstrative, reflexive, intensive,* or *reciprocal.*

1. That is the reason we should fill the tank. ____________________
2. What should we use to pay for gas? ____________________
3. I myself expected you to bring money. ____________________
4. You should pat yourself on the back. ____________________
5. That is all the money you have? ____________________
6. The change itself won't be enough. ____________________
7. Who gets $1.73 worth of gas? ____________________
8. That won't get us far. ____________________
9. This is ridiculous. ____________________
10. What should we do? ____________________
11. I myself am prepared to push. ____________________
12. We should be ashamed of ourselves. ____________________
13. We shouldn't blame each other. ____________________
14. Let's help one another move this car. ____________________
15. Then let's get ourselves a soda. ____________________

Write Create a sentence using *myself* as a reflexive pronoun, and a second using *myself* as an intensive pronoun.

1. ____________________

2. ____________________

Learning Outcome

Use pronouns correctly in a real-world context.

LO7 Real-World Application

Correct In the letter that follows, correct any pronoun errors. Use the correction marks to the left.

Correction Marks

- delete
- capitalize
- lowercase
- insert
- add comma
- add question mark
- add word
- add period
- spelling
- switch

Workplace

In workplace documents, correct grammar is critical to creating a strong impression.

Rankin Technologies
401 South Manheim Road, Albany, NY 12236 ▪ Ph: 708.555.1980 ▪ Fax: 708.555.0056

April 28, 2010

Mr. Henry Danburn
Construction Manager
Titan Industrial Construction, Inc.
P.O. Box 2112
Phoenix, AZ 85009-3887

Dear Mr. Danburn:

Thank you for meeting with I last week at the National Convention in Las Vegas. I want to follow up on ours discussion of ways which Rankin Technologies could work with Titan Industrial Construction.

Enclosed is the information that your requested. I believe this material demonstrates what Rankin Technologies would be a solid match for yours projects in western Illinois.

You yourselves are the construction manager for the Arrow Mills renovation project in California. Rankin did the electrical installation on that project initially, and us would be very interested in working with you on the renovation. Someone whom is familiar with our work at Arrow Mills is Mike Knowlan. She is the plant manager and can be reached at 606-555-6328.

Us are excited about working with yous on any future projects, and on the Arrow Mills project in particular. Please call I with any questions (708-555-1980).

Sincerely,

James Gabriel

James Gabriel
Vice President
Enclosures 5

"I think I am a verb."
—R. Buckminster Fuller

Ipatov 2010/used under license by www.shutterstock.com

26 Verb

Of course, we call ourselves human beings, but a few people have suggested we should think of ourselves as human doings. They would argue that our actions define us more than who we are.

Whether you are a human being or a human doing, you are thinking of yourself as a verb. Verbs express states of being and actions (doing). They give a sentence energy, movement, and meaning. This chapter provides practice working with these amazing words.

Learning Outcomes

LO1 Understand and use verb classes.
LO2 Work with number and person.
LO3 Work with voice.
LO4 Form basic verb tenses.
LO5 Form progressive tense.
LO6 Form perfect tense.
LO7 Understand verbals.
LO8 Use verbals as objects.
LO9 Apply learning to real-world examples.

What do you think?

Are you a human being or a human doing? Why?

Learning Outcome

Understand and use verb classes.

LO1 Verb Classes

Verbs show action or states of being. Different classes of verbs do these jobs.

Action Verbs

Verbs that show action are called **action verbs**. Some action verbs are **transitive**, which means that they transfer action to a direct object.

Bill **clutches** the pillow.
(The verb *clutches* transfers action to the direct object *pillow*.)

Others are **intransitive**: They don't transfer action to a direct object.

Bill **sleeps**.
(The verb *sleeps* does not transfer action to a direct object.)

Linking Verbs

Verbs that link the subject to a noun, a pronoun, or an adjective are **linking verbs**. Predicates with linking verbs express a state of being.

Bill **is** a heavy sleeper.
(The linking verb *is* connects *Bill* to the noun *sleeper*.)

He **seems** weary.
(The linking verb *seems* connects *He* to the adjective *weary*.)

Linking Verbs

is	am	are	was	were	be	being	been	become
grow	feel	seem	look	smell	taste	sound	appear	remain

Note: The bottom-row words are linking verbs if they don't show action.

WAC

If you are mathematically minded, think of a linking verb as an equal sign. It indicates that the subject equals (or is similar to) what is in the predicate.

Helping Verbs

A verb that works with an action or linking verb is a **helping** (or auxiliary) verb. A helping verb helps the main verb form tense, mood, and voice.

Bill **has** slept till noon before, and today he **will be** sleeping even longer.
(The helping verb *has* works with the main verb *slept*; the helping verbs *will be* work with *sleeping*. Both form special tenses.)

Note: Helping verbs work with verbs ending in *ing* or in past tense form.

Helping Verbs

am	been	could	does	have	might	should	will
are	being	did	had	is	must	was	would
be	can	do	has	may	shall	were	

Vocabulary

action verb
word that expresses action

transitive verb
action verb that transfers action to a direct object

intransitive verb
action verb that does not transfer action to a direct object

linking verb
verb that connects the subject with a noun, a pronoun, or an adjective in the predicate

helping (auxiliary) verb
verb that works with a main verb to form some tenses, mood, and voice

Using Verb Classes

Identify/Write For each sentence below, identify the underlined verbs as transitive action verbs (T), intransitive action verbs (I), linking verbs (L), or helping verbs (H). Then write your own sentence using the same class of verb.

1. I need eight hours of sleep per night, but I often get only six.

2. This weekend, I will be getting even less sleep.

3. One of my favorite bands is playing in town.

4. They rock, and whenever I see a concert of theirs, I hardly sleep.

5. I am eager, but after the weekend, I will be worn out.

6. The problem with having too much fun on the weekend is the week after.

7. Maybe I should go to bed earlier so that I can store up sleep.

8. I feel awake now, but next week I will look weary.

Learning Outcome

Work with number and person.

LO2 Number and Person of Verb

Verbs reflect number (singular or plural) and person (first person, second person, or third person).

Number

The **number** of the verb indicates whether the subject is singular or plural. Note that most present tense singular verbs end in *s*, while most present tense plural verbs do not.

Singular: The Gettysburg Address **speaks** of those who "gave the last full measure of devotion."
Plural: Many historians **speak** of it as the greatest American speech.

Corbis Images by: Radius Images/Corbis

Person

The **person** of the verb indicates whether the subject is speaking, being spoken to, or being spoken about.

	Singular	Plural
First Person:	(I) am	(we) are
Second Person:	(you) are	(you) are
Third Person:	(she) is	(they) are

Note that the pronoun *I* takes a special form of the *be* verb—*am*.

Correct: I am excited about going to Gettysburg.
Incorrect: I is excited about going to Gettysburg.

The pronoun *I* also is paired with plural present tense verbs.

Correct: I want to go with you.
Incorrect: I wants to go with you.

In a similar way, the singular pronoun *you* takes the plural form of the *be* verb—*are, were*.

Correct: You are going to the Gettysburg National Military Park.
Incorrect: You is going to the Gettysburg National Military Park.

Correct: You were my first choice.
Incorrect: You was my first choice.

Vocabulary

number
singular or plural

person
whether the subject is speaking *(I, we)*, is being spoken to *(you)*, or is being spoken about *(he, she, it, they)*

Using Number and Person

Provide For each sentence below, provide the correct person and number of present tense *be* verb (*is, am, are*).

1. We ____________ interested in going to Gettysburg.
2. It ____________ a town in Pennsylvania where a great battle took place.
3. You ____________ welcome to come on the trip with us.
4. Little Round Top ____________ a hill where the fighting focused.
5. The Union troops ____________ memorialized in statues on the hill.
6. You ____________ standing on a piece of American history.
7. Pickett's Charge ____________ considered General Lee's greatest mistake.
8. Troops from both sides ____________ buried in the cemetery.
9. I ____________ eager to see where Lincoln gave the Gettysburg Address.
10. We ____________ hoping to spend two days in Gettysburg.

Rewrite Rewrite each sentence below to fix the errors in the number and person of the verb.

1. I listens as the tour guide describe the last day of battle.

   ____

2. Rifle shots hails down on the Confederate soldiers.

   ____

3. General Pickett order them to charge Little Round Top.

   ____

4. Flying lead kill many Southern soldiers.

   ____

5. The Union troops repels the charge and wins the day.

   ____

6. President Lincoln deliver the Gettysburg Address.

   ____

Learning Outcome

Work with voice.

LO3 Voice of the Verb

The **voice** of the verb indicates whether the subject is acting or being acted upon.

Voice

An **active voice** means that the subject is acting. A **passive voice** means that the subject is acted on.

Active: The usher **led** us to our seats.
Passive: We **were led** by the usher to our seats.

	Active Voice		**Passive Voice**	
	Singular	**Plural**	**Singular**	**Plural**
Present Tense	I see you see he/she/it sees	we see you see they see	I am seen you are seen he/she/it is seen	we are seen you are seen they are seen
Past Tense	I saw you saw he saw	we saw you saw they saw	I was seen you were seen it was seen	we were seen you were seen they were seen
Future Tense	I will see you will see he will see	we will see you will see they will see	I will be seen you will be seen it will be seen	we will be seen you will be seen they will be seen
Present Perfect Tense	I have seen you have seen he has seen	we have seen you have seen they have seen	I have been seen you have been seen it has been seen	we have been seen you have been seen they have been seen
Past Perfect Tense	I had seen you had seen he had seen	we had seen you had seen they had seen	I had been seen you had been seen it had been seen	we had been seen you had been seen they had been seen
Future Perfect Tense	I will have seen you will have seen he will have seen	we will have seen you will have seen they will have seen	I will have been seen you will have been seen it will have been seen	we will have been seen you will have been seen they will have been seen

Active voice is preferred for most writing because it is direct and energetic.

Active: We gave the band a standing ovation.
Passive: The band was given a standing ovation by us.

Passive voice is preferred when the focus is on the receiver of the action or when the subject is unknown.

Passive: A rose was thrown onstage.
Active: Someone threw a rose onstage.

Matthieu Spohn/PhotoAlto/Corbis

Workplace

In workplace writing, use active voice for most messages. Use passive voice to deliver bad news.

Vocabulary

voice
active or passive

active voice
voice created when the subject is performing the action of the verb

passive voice
voice created when the subject is receiving the action of the verb

Using Voice of a Verb

Rewrite Read each passive sentence below and rewrite it to be active. Think about who or what is performing the action and make that the subject. The first one is done for you.

1. The concert was attended by 3,000 fans.
   Three thousand fans attended the concert.
2. A good time was had by everyone.
3. The ten greatest hits of the band were played by them.
4. Three concert T-shirts were bought by my friends and me.
5. The opening acts were tolerated by the crowd.
6. The air was electrified by the appearance of the main act.
7. I was not disappointed by their performance.
8. My short friend's view was blocked by a tall guy.
9. The guy was asked by my friend to switch seats.
10. Every new song was cheered by the crowd.

Write Using the chart on the facing page, write a sentence for each situation below.

1. (a present tense singular active sentence)
2. (a past tense plural passive sentence)

LO4 Present and Future Tense Verbs

Learning Outcome

Form basic verb tenses.

Basic verb tenses tell whether action happens in the past, in the present, or in the future.

Present Tense

Present tense verbs indicate that action is happening right now.

A cruise ship **arrives** in Cabo San Lucas, Mexico.

Present tense verbs also can indicate that action happens routinely or continually.

Every day, ships **drop** anchor outside of the harbor.

Present Tense in Academic Writing

Use present tense verbs to describe current conditions.

Cabo San Lucas **makes** most of its income through tourism.

Use present tense verbs also to discuss the ideas in literature or to use historical quotations in a modern context. This use is called the "historical present," which allows writers to continue speaking.

Some **say** that those who see Cabo do not truly see Mexico, or as G. K. Chesterton **writes**, "The traveler sees what he sees; the tourist sees what he has come to see."

Note: It is important to write a paragraph or an essay in one tense. Avoid shifting needlessly from tense to tense as you write. (See also page 278.)

WAC

Look at writing in your field of study. Is most writing done in present tense or past tense? When writing in your field, use the tense that is most expected.

Future Tense

Future tense verbs indicate that action will happen later on.

Cruise ships **will visit** Cabo San Lucas for many years to come.

Vocabulary

present tense
verb tense indicating that action is happening now

future tense
verb tense indicating that action will happen later

Using Present and Future Verb Tenses

Write For each sentence below, fill in the blank with the present tense form of the verb indicated in parentheses.

1. Many visitors ______________ in Cabo's warm waters. (snorkeled)
2. White, sandy beaches ______________ many swimmers. (attracted)
3. Parasailors ______________ overhead from parachutes. (flew)
4. Waves ______________ if winds are strong. (picked up)
5. Boats ______________ people from cruise ships to shore. (ran)

Change Cross out and replace the verbs in the following paragraph, making them all present tense.

We went to Lover's Beach in Cabo San Lucas. The beach was very busy. About a third of the people sunbathed, a third scuba dived, and a third just splashed in the waves. The waves were large because the wind was strong. We swam all afternoon until the water taxi returned for us. The day we spent in Cabo San Lucas was one of our favorite days of the trip.

Write Write a sentence of your own, using each word below in the form indicated in parentheses.

1. enjoy (present) ______________
2. swim (future) ______________
3. realize (present) ______________
4. complete (future) ______________

Past Tense Verbs

Past tense verbs indicate that action happened in the past.

When referring to his campaign in England, Julius Caesar **reported**, "I **came**. I **saw**. I **conquered**."

Forming Past Tense

Most verbs form the past tense by adding *ed*. If the word ends in a silent *e*, drop the *e* before adding *ed*.

help → help**ed**
look → look**ed**

love → lov**ed**
hope → hop**ed**

If the word ends in a consonant preceded by a single vowel and the last syllable is stressed, double the final consonant before adding *ed*.

stop → stop**ped**
plan → plan**ned**

occur → occur**red**
refer → refer**red**

If the word ends in a *y* preceded by a consonant, change the *y* to *i* before adding *ed*.

study → stud**ied**
worry → worr**ied**

hurry → hurr**ied**
carry → carr**ied**

Irregular Verbs

Some of the most commonly used verbs form the past tense by changing the verb itself. See the chart below:

Present	Past	Present	Past	Present	Past
am	was, were	fly	flew	see	saw
become	became	forget	forgot	shake	shook
begin	began	freeze	froze	shine	shone
blow	blew	get	got	show	showed
break	broke	give	gave	shrink	shrank
bring	brought	go	went	sing	sang
buy	bought	grow	grew	sink	sank
catch	caught	hang	hung	sit	sat
choose	chose	have	had	sleep	slept
come	came	hear	heard	speak	spoke
dig	dug	hide	hid	stand	stood
do	did	keep	kept	steal	stole
draw	drew	know	knew	swim	swam
drink	drank	lead	led	swing	swung
drive	drove	pay	paid	take	took
eat	ate	prove	proved	teach	taught
fall	fell	ride	rode	tear	tore
feel	felt	ring	rang	throw	threw
fight	fought	rise	rose	wear	wore
find	found	run	ran	write	wrote

Insight

Note that the irregular verbs at the bottom of the page are some of the oldest verbs in the English language. That's why they are irregular. Even so, they are used quite often because they describe the everyday tasks that English speakers have been doing for more than a thousand years.

Vocabulary

past tense
verb tense indicating that action happened previously

Using Past Tense Verbs

Write For each verb, write the correct past tense form.

1. give ____________
2. shop ____________
3. trick ____________
4. type ____________
5. teach ____________
6. cry ____________
7. sing ____________
8. soap ____________
9. cap ____________
10. cope ____________
11. try ____________
12. fly ____________
13. think ____________
14. grip ____________
15. gripe ____________
16. pour ____________
17. swing ____________
18. slip ____________
19. reply ____________
20. tip ____________

Edit Make changes to the following paragraph, converting it from present tense to past tense. Use the correction marks to the right.

During my junior year of high school, I become a lifeguard at a campground pool. I think it is a cushy job, sitting poolside all summer. However, this pool hosts many day camps, meaning hundreds of little kids with little supervision. I quickly discover that the other guards and I are the supervision. It is hard to yell at kids all day, but it is more dangerous to stay silent. They run on the deck or dive into shallow water or jump into deep water when they don't know how to swim. Worse yet, families come, and when their kids do the same things and I yell, parents tell me their kids can run on deck if they want. Facing down adults at sixteen isn't easy. Still, my brother's summer job is mowing lawns at the same campground. When he walks by, drenched in sweat, my job sitting in my lifeguard chair suddenly seems cushy.

Correction Marks

- delete
- capitalize
- lowercase
- insert
- add comma
- add question mark
- add word
- add period
- spelling
- switch

LO5 Progressive Tense Verbs

The basic tenses of past, present, and future tell when action takes place. The progressive tense or aspect tells that action is ongoing.

Progressive Tense

Progressive tense indicates that action is ongoing. Progressive tense is formed by using a helping verb along with the *ing* form of the main verb.

> Scientists **are studying** the growth of human populations.

There are past, present, and future progressive tenses. Each uses a helping verb in the appropriate tense.

> In 1804, one billion people **were sharing** the globe.
>
> Currently, about seven billion people **are living** on Earth.
>
> In 2040, about nine billion people **will be calling** this planet home.

Forming Progressive Tenses

Past:	was/were	+	main verb	+	ing
Present:	am/is/are	+	main verb	+	ing
Future:	will be	+	main verb	+	ing

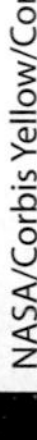

Learning Outcome

Form progressive tense.

Insight

Avoid using progressive tense with the following:

- Verbs that express thoughts, attitudes, and desires: *know, understand, want, prefer*
- Verbs that describe appearances: *seem, resemble*
- Verbs that indicate possession: *belong, have, own, possess*
- Verbs that signify inclusion: *contain, hold*

  I ***know*** *your name*, not *I* ***am knowing*** *your name.*

Vocabulary

progressive tense
verb tense that expresses ongoing action

Using Progressive Tense

Form Rewrite each sentence three times, changing the tenses as requested in parentheses.

Epidemics drop populations, but vaccination leads to upswings.

1. (present progressive) ______________________________

2. (past progressive) ______________________________

3. (future progressive) ______________________________

Though food production grows by addition, population grows by multiplication.

4. (present progressive) ______________________________

5. (past progressive) ______________________________

6. (future progressive) ______________________________

Improved public-health programs led to lower mortality rates.

7. (present progressive) ______________________________

8. (past progressive) ______________________________

9. (future progressive) ______________________________

Learning Outcome

Form perfect tense.

LO6 Perfect Tense Verbs

The perfect tense tells that action is not ongoing, but is finished, whether in the past, present, or future.

Perfect Tense

Perfect tense indicates that action is completed. Perfect tense is formed by using a helping verb along with the past tense form of the main verb.

An estimated 110 billion people **have lived** on earth.

There are past, present, and future perfect tenses. These tenses are formed by using helping verbs in past, present, and future tenses.

By 1804, the world population **had reached** one billion.
We **have added** another billion people in the last 13 years.
In 13 more years, we **will have welcomed** another billion.

Forming Perfect Tense

Past:	had	+	past tense main verb
Present:	has/have	+	past tense main verb
Future:	will have	+	past tense main verb

Perfect Tense with Irregular Verbs

To form perfect tense with irregular verbs, use the past participle form instead of the past tense form. Here are the past participles of common irregular verbs.

Present	Past Part.	Present	Past Part.	Present	Past Part.
am, be	been	fly	flown	see	seen
become	become	forget	forgotten	shake	shaken
begin	begun	freeze	frozen	shine	shone
blow	blown	get	gotten	show	shown
break	broken	give	given	shrink	shrunk
bring	brought	go	gone	sing	sung
buy	bought	grow	grown	sink	sunk
catch	caught	hang	hung	sit	sat
choose	chosen	have	had	sleep	slept
come	come	hear	heard	speak	spoken
dig	dug	hide	hidden	stand	stood
do	done	keep	kept	steal	stolen
draw	drawn	know	known	swim	swum
drink	drunk	lead	led	swing	swung
drive	driven	pay	paid	take	taken
eat	eaten	prove	proven	teach	taught
fall	fallen	ride	ridden	tear	torn
feel	felt	ring	rung	throw	thrown
fight	fought	rise	risen	wear	worn
find	found	run	run	write	written

Insight

For the simple past tense form of these irregular verbs, see page 320.

Vocabulary

perfect tense
verb tense that expresses completed action

Using Perfect Tense

Form Rewrite each sentence three times, changing the tenses as requested in parentheses.

According to scientists, the earth circles the sun over 4.5 billion times.

1. (past perfect) ______________________________

2. (present perfect) ______________________________

3. (future perfect) ______________________________

The sun lives half of its lifetime.

4. (past perfect) ______________________________

5. (present perfect) ______________________________

6. (future perfect) ______________________________

Two stars within our galaxy go supernova.

7. (past perfect) ______________________________

8. (present perfect) ______________________________

9. (future perfect) ______________________________

Learning Outcome

Understand verbals.

LO7 Verbals

A **verbal** is formed from a verb but functions as a noun, an adjective, or an adverb. Each type of verbal—gerund, participle, and infinitive—can appear alone or can begin a **verbal phrase**.

Gerund

A **gerund** is formed from a verb ending in *ing,* and it functions as a noun.

Swimming is my favorite pastime. (subject)

I love **swimming**. (direct object)

A **gerund phrase** begins with the gerund and includes any objects and modifiers.

Swimming laps at the pool builds endurance. (subject)

I prefer **swimming laps in pools rather than in lakes**. (direct object)

Participle

A **participle** is formed from a verb ending in *ing* or *ed,* and it functions as an adjective.

Excited, I received my lifesaving certification! (*excited* modifies *I*)

What an **exciting** day! (*exciting* modifies *day*)

A **participial phrase** begins with the participle and includes any objects and modifiers.

Exciting the crowd of young swimmers, I said we were diving today.

Infinitive

An **infinitive** is formed from *to* and a present-tense verb, and it functions as a noun, an adjective, or an adverb.

To teach is a noble profession. (noun)

This is an important point **to remember**. (adjective)

Students must pay attention **to understand**. (adverb)

An **infinitive phrase** begins with an infinitive and includes any objects or modifiers.

I plan lessons **to teach an easy progression of swimming skills**.

Vocabulary

verbal
gerund, participle, or infinitive; a construction formed from a verb but functioning as a noun, an adjective, or an adverb

verbal phrase
phrase beginning with a gerund, a participle, or an infinitive

gerund
verbal ending in *ing* and functioning as a noun

gerund phrase
phrase beginning with a gerund and including objects and modifiers

participle
verbal ending in *ing* or *ed* and functioning as an adjective

participial phrase
phrase beginning with a participle and including objects and modifiers

infinitive
verbal beginning with *to* and functioning as a noun, an adjective, or an adverb

infinitive phrase
phrase beginning with an infinitive and including objects and modifiers

Using Verbals

Identify Identify each underlined verbal by circling the correct choice in parentheses. (gerund, participle, infinitive).

1. Jogging is another excellent exercise. (gerund, participle, infinitive)
2. You should plan to jog three times a week. (gerund, participle, infinitive)
3. Jogging with friends, you can also be social. (gerund, participle, infinitive)
4. Try to wear good shoes. (gerund, participle, infinitive)
5. Avoiding joint injury is important. (gerund, participle, infinitive)
6. Toned through exercise, your body will look better. (gerund, participle, infinitive)

Form Complete each sentence below by supplying the type of verbal requested in parentheses.

1. The exercise I would choose is ______________________________. (gerund)
2. ______________________________, I would lose weight. (participle)
3. ______________________________ is a good toning exercise. (infinitive)
4. I would also like to try ______________________________. (gerund)
5. When exercising, remember ______________________________. (infinitive)
6. ______________________________, I'll be in great shape. (participle)

Write For each verbal phrase below, write a sentence that correctly uses it.

1. to lift weights ______________________________

   ____
2. preparing myself for a marathon ______________________________

   ____
3. filled with anticipation ______________________________

   ____

Learning Outcome

Use verbals as objects.

LO8 Verbals as Objects

Though both infinitives and gerunds can function as nouns, they can't be used interchangeably as direct objects. Some verbs take infinitives and not gerunds. Other verbs take only gerunds and not infinitives.

Gerunds as Objects

Verbs that express facts are followed by **gerunds**.

admit	deny	enjoy	miss	recommend
avoid	discuss	finish	quit	regret
consider	dislike	imagine	recall	

I enjoy **playing** cards.
not I enjoy to play cards.

I imagine **winning** a poker tournament.
not I imagine to win a poker tournament.

Infinitives as Objects

Verbs that express intention, hopes, and desires are followed by **infinitives**.

agree	demand	hope	prepare	volunteer
appear	deserve	intend	promise	want
attempt	endeavor	need	refuse	wish
consent	fail	offer	seem	
decide	hesitate	plan	tend	

I attempt **to win** every hand.
not I attempt winning every hand.

I need **to get** a better poker face.
not I need getting a better poker face.

Gerunds or Infinitives as Objects

Some verbs can be followed by either a gerund or an infinitive.

begin	hate	love	remember	stop
continue	like	prefer	start	try

I love **to play** poker.
or I love **playing** poker.

Vocabulary

gerund
verbal ending in *ing* and functioning as a noun

infinitive
verbal beginning with *to* and functioning as a noun, an adjective, or an adverb

Using Verbals as Objects

Select For each sentence below, circle the appropriate verbal in parentheses.

1. I enjoy (to play, playing) canasta.
2. We should promise (to play, playing) canasta this weekend.
3. In canasta, you need (to get, getting) seven-card melds.
4. You and a partner endeavor (to meld, melding) suits.
5. You and your partner can discuss (to go, going) out.
6. The rules demand (to keep, keeping) other table talk down.
7. I recall (to win, winning) three hands in a row.
8. If you lose a hand, you'll regret (to have, having) wild cards.
9. If you fail (to use, using) a wild card, it costs.
10. You'll dislike (to get, getting) penalized 50 points.

Write For each verb below, write your own sentence using the verb and following it with a gerund or an infinitive, as appropriate.

1. deny ______________________________

____

2. promise ______________________________

____

3. refuse ______________________________

____

4. consider ______________________________

____

5. recommend ______________________________

____

6. avoid ______________________________

____

Learning Outcome

Apply learning to real-world examples.

LO9 Real-World Application

Revise Rewrite the following paragraph, changing passive verbs to active verbs. (See page 316.)

Your request to send all the sales reps to the Adobe training seminar in Cincinnati was reviewed by me. Your idea that this training would help your staff is agreed to by me. Our training budget was reviewed by me to see if the seminar could be afforded by us.

Revise In the following paragraph, change future perfect verbs into past perfect verbs by crossing out helping verbs and writing new helping verbs. (See page 312.)

We will have used a large portion of our budget to upgrade design software for the engineering staff. In addition, we will have made prior commitments to train office staff in August. As a result, we will not have reserved enough money to send all sales reps to Cincinnati.

Revise In the following paragraph, correct misused verbals by crossing out the gerund or infinitive and replacing it with the correct verbal form. (See page 328.)

I want exploring other solutions with you. Do you recommend to send two reps who then could train others? I recall to do that in previous situations. I admit to agree that this isn't the optimal course, but I hope doing something.

"We do our best that we know how at the moment, and if it doesn't turn out, we modify it."
—Franklin Delano Roosevelt

Photo by Jenny Solecki

27 Adjective and Adverb

All right, so you have a car. Lots of people have cars. It's a vintage Volkswagen beetle? Nice. And it's decked out with custom paint, toys, barrettes, and words like "smile," "laugh," and "let flow"? You call it your "crazy, lovey, hippy, dippy, vintage buggy"? Wow, do *you* have a car!

The owner of the car above has totally modified it and then has used strings of modifying words and phrases to describe it. That's what adjectives and adverbs do. They add color, texture, shape, size, and many more vivid details to each picture. Remember, though, that too many modifiers can overload a sentence—much as bric-a-brac can overwhelm a car.

Learning Outcomes

LO1 Understand adjective basics.
LO2 Put adjectives in order.
LO3 Use adjectivals.
LO4 Understand adverb basics.
LO5 Place adverbs well.
LO6 Use adverbials.
LO7 Apply adjectives and adverbs in real-world contexts.

What do you think?

How would you describe a car you wish you had?

Learning Outcome

Understand adjective basics.

Speaking & Listening

Read the first example sentence aloud. Then read it without the adjectives. Note how adjectives add spice to the description. Like spice, though, adjectives should be used sparingly, to "season" nouns, not to overwhelm them.

Vocabulary

adjective
word that modifies a noun or pronoun

articles
the adjectives *a, an,* and *the*

predicate adjective
adjective that appears after a linking verb and describes the subject

positive adjective
word that modifies a noun or pronoun without comparing it

comparative adjective
word that modifies a noun or pronoun by comparing it to something else

superlative adjective
word that modifies a noun or pronoun by comparing it to two or more things

LO1 Adjective Basics

An **adjective** is a word that modifies a noun or pronoun. Even **articles** such as *a, an,* and *the* are adjectives, because they indicate whether you mean a general or specific thing. Adjectives answer these basic questions: *which, what kind of, how many / how much?*

Adjectives often appear before the word they modify.

You have **a cute, fluffy** dog.

A **predicate adjective** appears after the noun it modifies and is linked to the word by a linking verb.

Your dog is **cute** and **fluffy**.

Proper adjectives come from proper nouns and are capitalized.

He is a **Yorkshire** terrier.

Forms of Adjectives

Adjectives come in three forms: positive, comparative, and superlative.

- **Positive adjectives** describe one thing without making any comparisons.

Keats is a **friendly** dog.

- **Comparative adjectives** compare the thing to something else.

Keats is **friendlier** than our cat, Yeats.

- **Superlative adjectives** compare the thing to two or more other things

He is the **friendliest** dog you will ever meet.

Note: For one- and two-syllable words, create the comparative form by adding *er*, and create the superlative form by added *est*. For words of three syllables or more, use *more* (or *less*) for comparatives and *most* (or *least*) for superlatives. Also note that *good* and *bad* have special superlative forms:

Positive	Comparative	Superlative
good	better	best
bad	worse	worst
big	bigger	biggest
happy	happier	happiest
wonderful	more wonderful	most wonderful

Using the Forms of Adjectives

Identify/Write In each sentence below, identify the underlined adjectives as positive (P), comparative (C), or superlative (S). Then write a new sentence about a different topic, but use the same adjectives.

1. We once had a beautiful collie with a long, shiny coat.

2. She was smarter than our last dog, perhaps the smartest pet we've ever owned.

3. She thought she was the alpha female and my wife was the beta female.

4. My wife became even more unhappy when the dog tore up her best couch.

5. My wife was happiest on the day we gave the dog to a farmer.

Correct Read the paragraph below and correct adjective errors, using the correction marks to the right. The first one has been done for you.

Did you know there is an Intelligence test for dogs? It includes Various tasks to check the dog's Adaptive intelligence or problem-solving ability. The most smartest dogs can quickly find a treat under one of three buckets, get a treat from under a piece of furniture, find its Favorite spot after a room is rearranged, and gets a towel off its head. In tests, border collies, poodles, and german shepherds have tested as the most smartest, and afghan hounds, british bulldogs, and chow chows tested at the most low end. Even if they aren't the intelligentest, these dogs might still be the most cuddliest.

Correction Marks

- delete
- capitalize
- lowercase
- insert
- add comma
- add question mark
- add word
- add period
- spelling
- switch

Learning Outcome

Put adjectives in order.

LO2 Adjective Order

Adjectives aren't all created equally. Native English speakers use a specific order when putting multiple adjectives before a noun, and all speakers of English can benefit from understanding this order.

Begin with . . .

1. articles	a, an, the
demonstrative adjectives	that, this, these, those
possessives	my, our, her, their, Kayla's

Then position adjectives that tell . . .

2. time	first, second, next, last
3. how many	three, few, some, many
4. value	important, prized, fine
5. size	giant, puny, hulking
6. shape	spiky, blocky, square
7. condition	clean, tattered, repaired
8. age	old, new, classic
9. color	blue, scarlet, salmon
10. nationality	French, Chinese, Cuban
11. religion	Baptist, Buddhist, Hindu
12. material	cloth, stone, wood, bronze

Finally place . . .

13. nouns used as adjectives	baby [seat], frog [legs]

Example:

that gorgeous old French shrimp boat
(**1** + **7** + **8** + **10** + **13** + **noun**)

Insight

As the introduction indicates, native English speakers use this order unconsciously because it sounds right to them. If you put adjectives in a different order, a native English speaker might say, "That's not how anybody says it." One way to avoid this issue is to avoid stacking multiple adjectives before nouns.

Note: Avoid using too many adjectives before a noun. An article and one or two adjectives are usually enough. More adjectives may overload the noun.

Too many:	my last three spiky old blue Cuban coral souvenirs
Effective:	my last three coral souvenirs

Placing Adjectives in Order

Order Rearrange each set of adjectives and articles so that they are in the correct order. The first one has been done for you.

1. purple rectangular this
this rectangular purple ______ carton

2. your Mexican beautiful
______ guitar

3. wooden worn-out many
______ blocks

4. precious the Islamic
______ mosaic

5. traditional several Russian
______ dolls

6. stone chess Doug's
______ pieces

7. pen French my
______ pal

8. broken-down that old
______ sedan

9. felt his pin-striped
______ fedora

10. old the mossy
______ temple

11. original three piano
______ pieces

12. first real our
______ vacation

Learning Outcome

Use adjectivals.

LO3 Adjective Questions and Adjectivals

Adjectives answer four basic questions: *which, what kind of, how many / how much?*

	Children
Which?	those children
What kind of?	smiling Indian children
How many/how much?	many children

those many smiling Indian children

Photo by McKay Savage

Insight

Instead of trying to memorize the names of different types of phrases and clauses, just remember the adjective questions. Turn them into a cheer—*which, what kind of, how many/ how much?*

Adjectivals

A single word that answers one of these questions is called an adjective. If a phrase or clause answers one of these questions, it is an **adjectival** phrase or clause.

	Children
Which?	children who were waiting to vote
What kind of?	children wanting to get photographed

Wanting to get photographed, the children **who were waiting to vote** crowded my camera.

The following types of phrases and clauses can be adjectivals:

Prepositional phrase:	from the school
Participial phrase:	standing in a line
Adjective clause:	who greeted me warmly

Vocabulary

adjectival
phrase or clause that answers one of the adjective questions and modifies a noun or pronoun

prepositional phrase
phrase that starts with a preposition and includes an object and modifiers

participial phrase
phrase beginning with a participle (*ing* or *ed* form of verb) plus objects and modifiers; used as an adjective

adjective clause
clause beginning with a relative pronoun and including a verb, but not able to stand alone; functioning as an adjective

Say It

Partner with a classmate. One of you should say the noun, and the other should ask the adjective questions. Then the first person should answer each question with adjectives or adjectivals.

1. **mini-vans**
   Which mini-vans?
   What kind of mini-vans?
   How many mini-vans?

2. **shampoo**
   Which shampoo?
   What kind of shampoo?
   How much shampoo

Using Adjectives and Adjectivals

Answer/Write For each word, answer the adjective questions using adjectives and adjectivals. Then write a sentence using two or more of your answers.

1. Cats

Which cats? ______

What kind of cats? ______

How many cats? ______

Sentence: ______

2. Hobbies

Which hobbies? ______

What kind of hobbies? ______

How many hobbies? ______

Sentence: ______

3. Plans

Which plans? ______

What kind of plans? ______

How many plans? ______

Sentence: ______

Learning Outcome

Understand adverb basics.

LO4 Adverb Basics

An **adverb** modifies a verb, a **verbal**, an adjective, an adverb, or a whole sentence. An adverb answers five basic questions: *how, when, where, why, to what degree, how often / how long.*

AYAKOVLEV.COM shutterstock

He danced **boldly**.
(*Boldly* modifies the verb *danced.*)

He leaped **very high.**
(*Very* modifies the adverb *high*, which modifies *leaped.*)

Apparently, he has had dance training.
(*Apparently* modifies the whole sentence.)

Note: Most adverbs end in *ly*. Some can be written with or without the *ly*, but when in doubt, use the *ly* form.

loud → loud**ly** tight → tight**ly** deep → deep**ly**

Insight

In the United States, intensifying adverbs such as *very* and *really* are used sparingly. Also, in academic writing, it is considered better to find a precise, vivid verb than to prop up an imprecise verb with an adverb.

Forms of Adverbs

Adverbs have three forms: positive, comparative, and superlative.

- **Positive adverbs** describe without comparing.

He danced **skillfully**.

- **Comparative adverbs** (*er, more,* or *less*) describe by comparing with one other action.

He danced **more skillfully** than his brother.

- **Superlative adverbs** (*est, most,* or *least*) describe by comparing with more than one action.

He danced **most skillfully** of any of those trying out.

Note: Some adjectives change form to create comparative or superlative forms.

well → better → best badly → worse → worst

Vocabulary

adverb
word that modifies a verb, a verbal, an adjective, an adverb, or a whole sentence

verbal
word formed from a verb but functioning as a noun, an adjective, or an adverb

positive adverb
adverb that modifies without comparing

comparative adverb
adverb that modifies by comparing with one other thing

superlative adverb
adverb that modifies by comparing to two or more things

Using the Forms of Adverbs

Provide In each sentence below, provide the correct form of the adverb in parentheses—positive, comparative, or superlative.

1. I like to dance ______________________ (fast).
2. I dance ______________________ (fast) than any of my friends.
3. My moves are the ______________________ (fast) of anyone on the floor.
4. My brother moves ______________________ (well) for an older guy.
5. He certainly dances ______________________ (well) than my father.
6. But I dance ______________________ (well) in my family.
7. I ask the band to play the song ______________________ (quickly).
8. They sometimes play it ______________________ (quickly) than I intended.
9. A thrash band played ______________________ (quickly) of any band I've heard.
10. That's when I danced ______________________ (badly) in my whole life.

Choose In each sentence, circle the correct word in parentheses. If the word modifies a noun or pronoun, choose the adjective form (*good, bad*). If the word modifies a verb, a verbal, an adjective, or an adverb, choose the adverb form (*well, badly.*)

1. I hope this turns out to be a (good, well) movie.
2. Even if the actors do (good, well), the plot might not be (good, well).
3. I don't want to spend (good, well) money on a (bad, badly) movie.
4. I wanted to see this movie (bad, badly).
5. Every time Richard comes along, he behaves (bad, badly).
6. If I tell him to straighten up, he takes it (bad, badly).
7. That guy has a (bad, badly) attitude.
8. I have done (good, well) not to invite him.
9. The movie was (good, well) acted.
10. Its plot was (good, well).

Learning Outcome

Place adverbs well.

LO5 Placement of Adverbs

Adverbs should be placed in different places in sentences, depending on their use.

How Adverbs

Adverbs that tell *how* can appear anywhere except between a verb and a direct object.

Furiously we paddled the raft.
We **furiously** paddled the raft.
We paddled the raft **furiously**.

not We paddled furiously the raft.

When Adverbs

Adverbs that tell *when* should go at the beginning or end of the sentence.

We ran the white water **yesterday**. **Today** we'll tackle the course again.

"The road to hell is paved with adverbs."
—Stephen King

Where Adverbs

Adverbs that tell where should follow the verb they modify, but should not come between the verb and the direct object. (**Note:** Prepositional phrases often function as *where* adverbs.)

The raft shot **downstream** and plunged **over a waterfall**.
Our guide shouted instructions **from the back of the boat**.

not Our guide shouted from the back of the boat instructions.

To What Degree Adverbs

Adverbs that tell *to what degree* go right before the adverb they modify.

I learned **very** quickly to hang on tight.

How Often Adverbs

Adverbs that tell *how often* should go right before an action verb, even if the verb has a helping verb.

I **often** dreamed about going white-water rafting.
Before that trip, I had **never** gotten to go.

Placing Adverbs Well

Place For each sentence below, insert the adverb (in parentheses) in the most appropriate position. The first one has been done for you.

1. The instructor often reminded us to stay alert. (often)
2. He began our training by explaining the equipment. (thoroughly)
3. We got our paddles and helmets. (next)
4. The instructor was careful about safety. (very)
5. We took our positions. (in the raft)
6. The rapids chattered all around us. (soon)
7. We went over challenging rapids. (often)
8. No one fell out. (fortunately)
9. I would recommend that guide. (highly)
10. I hope to go rafting again. (someday)

Revise In the paragraph below, use the transpose mark (∩∪) to move adverbs that incorrectly come between a verb and a direct object.

Adrenaline junkies seek often thrills by putting themselves in danger. Dangerous situations trigger usually the release of adrenaline. Adrenaline is a hormone that causes typically the heart rate to increase. It triggers also the fight-or-flight response. Adrenaline junkies enjoy very much this feeling and seek often it out through high-risk activities. They try frequently skydiving or bungee jumping. Some use repeatedly white-water rafting to get their thrills.

Learning Outcome

Use adverbials.

LO6 Adverb Questions and Adverbials

Adverbs answer six basic questions: *how, when, where, why, to what degree,* and *how often*.

Photo by Kevin Tostado

	They bounced.
How?	bounced joyously
When?	bounced yesterday
Where?	bounced around
Why?	bounced spontaneously
To what degree?	extremely joyously
How often?	bounced repeatedly

Yesterday, they **repeatedly, spontaneously,** and **extremely joyously** bounced **around.**

Note: Avoid this sort of adverb overload in your sentences.

Adverbials

Often, the adverb questions are answered by **adverbial** phrases and clauses, which answer the same six questions.

Insight

The adverb questions can be memorized by turning them into a cheer: *how, when, where, why, to what degree, how often!*

	They bounced.
How?	bounced doing the splits
When?	bounced during the Fun Day Festival
Where?	bounced in the inflatable castle
Why?	bounced because they had been studying too much
To what degree?	bounced until they got sick
How often?	bounced throughout the afternoon

Because they had been studying too much, they bounced **in the inflatable castle throughout the afternoon until they got sick.**

Note: Again, avoid this sort of adverbial overload in your sentences.

The following types of phrases and clauses can be adverbials:

Prepositional phrase:	in the inflatable castle
Participial phrase:	doing the splits
Dependent clause:	because they had been studying too much

Vocabulary

adverbial
phrase or clause that answers one of the adverb questions

Using Adverbials

Answer/Write For each sentence, answer the adverb questions using adverbs and adverbials. Then write a sentence using three or more of your answers.

1. **They ran.**

How did they run? ______________________

When did they run? ______________________

Where did they run? ______________________

Why did they run? ______________________

To what degree did they run? ______________________

How often did they run? ______________________

Sentence: ______________________

____

____

____

2. **They laughed.**

How did they laugh? ______________________

When did they laugh? ______________________

Where did they laugh? ______________________

Why did they laugh? ______________________

To what degree did they laugh? ______________________

How often did they laugh? ______________________

Sentence: ______________________

____

____

____

Learning Outcome

Apply adjectives and adverbs in real-world contexts.

LO7 Real-World Application

Correct In the following document, correct the use of adjectives and adverbs. Use the correction marks to the left.

Correction Marks

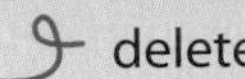 delete

d̳ capitalize

Ø lowercase

∧ insert

∧ add comma

? ∧ add question mark

word ∧ add word

⊙ add period

◯ spelling

∾ switch

1500 West Ridge Avenue
Tacoma, WA 98466

January 6, 2011

Ms. Karen Bledsoe
Blixen Furniture
1430 North Bel Air Drive
Tacoma, WA 98466-6970

Dear Ms. Bledsoe:

We miss you! Verdant Landscaping has been scheduled not to care for your grounds since fall 2008. You were a valued customer. Did our service fall short in some way? Whatever prompted you to make a change, we would like to discuss ways we could serve you gooder.

During the past year, Verdant has added important these new three services: A full-time landscape architect helps happily you improve your grounds with flower beds, hardy shrubs, and blooming trees. A tree surgeon can give at a moment's notice you help with diseased or damaged trees. And our lawn crews offer now mulching services. We provide the most good service and value at the most good price!

I'd like to call next week you to discuss whatever concerns you may have, and to offer you a 10 percent discount on a lawn-service new agreement. I can answer at that time any questions you may have about our new services as they are described in the enclosed brochure.

Sincere,

Stephen Bates

Stephen Bates
Customer Service

Enclosure

Workplace

Note the effect of adjectives and adverbs on voice. Errors make the writer sound odd, but careful use can create energy and interest.

"Take hold lightly; let go lightly.
This is one of the great secrets of felicity in love."
—Spanish Proverb

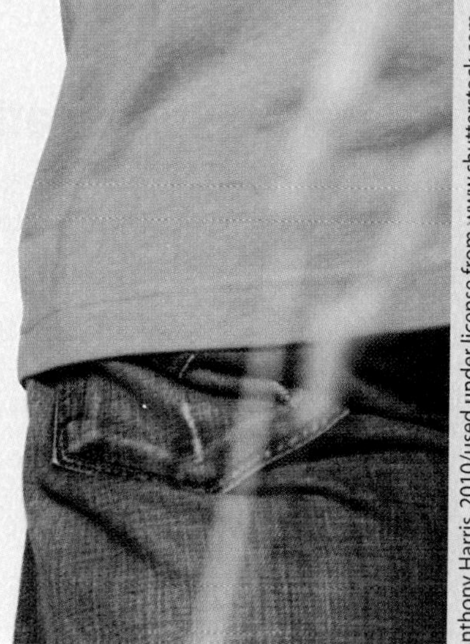

Anthony Harris, 2010/used under license from www.shutterstock.com

28 Conjunction and Preposition

Every relationship is different. A boyfriend and girlfriend will probably be equals, but a mother and daughter probably won't be. In fact, the daughter may be legally classified as a dependent.

Ideas have relationships, too. Sometimes ideas are equal—you can tell by the conjunction that connects them. At other times, one idea depends on another. There are conjunctions for that situation, too. And when words form a special relationship, prepositions are there to connect them.

Conjunctions and prepositions make connections in your writing and help your ideas relate to each other. This chapter shows how.

Learning Outcomes

LO1 Use coordinating and correlative conjunctions.

LO2 Use subordinating conjunctions.

LO3 Understand common prepositions.

LO4 Use *by, at, on,* and *in.*

LO5 Use conjunctions and prepositions in real-world documents.

What do you think?

What kind of relationship does the photo suggest?

Learning Outcome

Use coordinating and correlative conjunctions.

LO1 Coordinating and Correlative Conjunctions

A **conjunction** is a word or word group that joins parts of a sentence—words, phrases, or clauses.

Coordinating Conjunctions

A **coordinating conjunction** joins grammatically equal parts—a word to a word, a phrase to a phrase, or a clause to a clause. (A clause is basically a sentence.)

Andresr, 2010/used under license from www.shutterstock.com

Coordinating Conjunctions

and	but	or	nor	for	so	yet

Equal importance: A coordinating conjunction shows that the two things joined are of equal importance.

Ted and Jana like rhythm and blues.
(*And* joins words in an equal way.)

I have R&B songs on my iPod and on CDs.
(*And* joins the phrases *on my iPod* and *on CDs*.)

I want to download more, but I lost my USB cord.
(*But* joins the two clauses, with a comma after the first.)

Items in a series: A coordinating conjunction can also join more than two equal things in a series.

Ted, Jana, and I are planning to attend an R&B festival.
(*And* joins *Ted, Jana,* and *I*. A comma follows each word except the last.)

We will drive to the fest, check out the acts, and buy our tickets.
(*And* joins three parts of a compound verb.)

Correlative Conjunctions

Correlative conjunctions consist of a coordinating conjunction paired with another word. They also join equal grammatical parts: word to word, phrase to phrase, or clause to clause.

Correlative Conjunctions

either/or	neither/nor	whether/or	both/and	not only/but also

Stressing equality: Correlative conjunctions stress the equality of parts.

I like not only rock but also classical.
(*Not only / but also* stresses the equality of *rock* and *classical*.)

Either I will become a musician, or I will be a recording technician.
(*Either / or* joins the two clauses, with a comma after the first.)

Vocabulary

conjunction
word or word group that joins parts of a sentence

coordinating conjunction
conjunction that joins grammatically equal components

correlative conjunction
pair of conjunctions that stress the equality of the parts that are joined

Using Coordinating and Correlative Conjunctions

Correct In each sentence below, circle the best coordinating conjunction in parentheses.

1. I should buy an MP3 player (but, for, or) an iPod.
2. Kelly, Eli, (and, nor, yet) I sometimes share music.
3. We have different tastes, (or, so, yet) we get to hear a variety.
4. Kelly likes hip hop, (nor, but, for) I like Latin music.
5. Eli likes classic rock, (but, yet, so) he shares '70s bands.
6. Each week, Kelly, Eli, (and, but, or) I meet to talk about music.
7. We want to broaden our tastes, (and, or, yet) we don't like everything we hear.
8. I like rhythm, Kelly likes words, (and, nor, so) Eli likes melodies.
9. Ask us for recommendations, (and, for, so) we are committed fans.
10. We'll tell you what we like, (but, nor, for) you have to choose for yourself.

Write Create sentences of your own, using a coordinating conjunction (*and, but, or, nor, for, so, yet*) as requested in each.

1. joining two words: ______________________________

____

2. joining two phrases: ______________________________

____

3. creating a series: ______________________________

____

4. joining two clauses (place a comma after the first clause, before the conjunction): ______________________________

____

____

____

Write Create a sentence using a pair of correlative conjunctions:

____

____

____

Traits

When two ideas correlate, they work together. They co-relate. Thinking in this way can help you remember the term *correlative conjunctions.*

Learning Outcome

Use subordinating conjunctions.

LO2 Subordinating Conjunctions

A **subordinating conjunction** is a word or word group that connects two clauses of different importance. (A clause is basically a sentence.)

Subordinating Conjunctions

after	as long as	if	so that	till	whenever
although	because	in order that	than	unless	where
as	before	provided that	that	until	whereas
as if	even though	since	though	when	while

Subordinate clause: The subordinating conjunction comes at the beginning of the less-important clause, making it subordinate (it can't stand on its own). The **subordinate clause** can come before or after the more important clause (the **independent clause**).

I go out to eat. I like to order Mexican food.
(two clauses)

Whenever I go out to eat, I like to order Mexican food.
(*Whenever* introduces the subordinate clause, which is followed by a comma.)

I like to order Mexican food whenever I go out to eat.
(If the subordinate clause comes second, a comma usually isn't needed.)

Special relationship: A subordinating conjunction shows a special relationship between ideas. Here are the relationships that subordinating conjunctions show:

Time	after, as, before, since, till, until, when, whenever, while
Cause	as, as long as, because, before, if, in order that, provided that, since, so that, that, till, until, when, whenever
Contrast	although, as if, even though, though, unless, whereas

Whenever Mexican food is on the menu, I will order it.
(time)

I order it extra spicy because I love to feel the burn.
(cause)

Even though I ask for extra heat, I often still have to add hot sauce.
(contrast)

Traits

In the military, a *subordinate* is someone who takes orders from a superior. Think of a subordinate clause as one that takes orders from the main clause.

Vocabulary

subordinating conjunction
word or word group that connects clauses of different importance

subordinate clause
word group that begins with a subordinating conjunction and has a subject and verb but can't stand alone as a sentence

independent clause
group of words with a subject and verb and that expresses a complete thought; it can stand alone as a sentence

Using Subordinating Conjunctions

Write Fill in the blank in each sentence with an appropriate subordinating conjunction. Then circle what type of relationship it shows.

1. ______________________ we washed the car, I got sprayed many times.
   (time, cause, contrast)
2. Car washing is work ______________________ it feels like play.
   (time, cause, contrast)
3. ______________________ the hoses go on, a splash fight is inevitable.
   (time, cause, contrast)
4. I usually don't start the fight ______________________ I'm willing to join in.
   (time, cause, contrast)
5. ______________________ people can't resist sudsy buckets, the fight begins.
   (time, cause, contrast)
6. The car may not get clean ______________________ the people do.
   (time, cause, contrast)
7. ______________________ I first get sprayed, I yell in shock.
   (time, cause, contrast)
8. ______________________ I get used to it, all bets are off.
   (time, cause, contrast)
9. I can be pretty ruthless ______________________ I have a hose in hand.
   (time, cause, contrast)
10. ______________________ people have such fun, not much washing gets done.
    (time, cause, contrast)

Write Create three of your own sentences, one for each type of relationship.

1. time: ______________________

____

____

2. cause: ______________________

____

____

3. contrast: ______________________

____

____

Understand common prepositions.

LO3 Common Prepositions

A **preposition** is a word or word group that shows a relationship between a noun or pronoun and another word. Here are common prepositions:

Prepositions

aboard	back of	except for	near to	round
about	because of	excepting	notwithstanding	save
above	before	for	of	since
according to	behind	from	off	subsequent to
across	below	from among	on	through
across from	beneath	from between	on account of	throughout
after	beside	from under	on behalf of	'til
against	besides	in	onto	to
along	between	in addition to	on top of	together with
alongside	beyond	in behalf of	opposite	toward
alongside of	but	in front of	out	under
along with	by	in place of	out of	underneath
amid	by means of	in regard to	outside	until
among	concerning	inside	outside of	unto
apart from	considering	inside of	over	up
around	despite	in spite of	over to	upon
as far as	down	instead of	owing to	up to
aside from	down from	into	past	with
at	during	like	prior to	within
away from	except	near	regarding	without

Speaking & Listening

A prepositional phrase can help break up a string of adjectives. Instead of writing "the old, blue-awninged store," you can write "the old store with the blue awning." Read sentences aloud to find stacked-up adjectives and use prepositional phrases to create a better flow.

Prepositional Phrases

A **prepositional phrase** starts with a preposition and includes an object of the preposition (a noun or pronoun) and any modifiers. A prepositional phrase functions as an adjective or adverb.

The store at the corner advertises in the newspaper.
(*At the corner* modifies *store,* and *in the newspaper* modifies *advertises.*)

Hand me the keys on the rack by the side of the door.
(*On the rack* modifies *keys; by the side* modifies *rack; of the door* modifies *side.*)

Vocabulary

preposition
word or word group that creates a relationship between a noun or pronoun and another word

prepositional phrase
phrase that starts with a preposition, includes an object of the preposition (noun or pronoun) and any modifiers; and functions as an adjective or adverb

Using Common Prepositions

Create In each sentence, fill in the blanks with prepositional phrases. Create them from the prepositions on page 350 and nouns or pronouns of your own choosing. Be creative!

1. This morning, I drove ______________________________.
2. Another driver ______________________________ honked loudly.
3. I was so startled, I swerved ______________________________.
4. The other driver swerved ______________________________.
5. We both had looks of shock ______________________________.
6. I accelerated ______________________________.
7. My car shot ______________________________.
8. Next thing I knew, I was ______________________________.
9. The incident ______________________________ was a lesson.
10. The lesson was never to drive ______________________________.

Model Read each sentence below and write another sentence modeled on it. Note how the writer uses prepositional phrases to create specific effects.

1. The boat went through the rapids, down a bowl, into the air, and over the falls.

____

____

2. I don't want to talk at you, but to you—but with you.

____

____

3. After days of arguing and hours of negotiation, the Senate compromised.

____

____

4. Go through the back door, up the stairs, past the security guard, and into the party.

____

____

Learning Outcome

Use *by, at, on,* and *in.*

LO4 *By, At, On,* and *In*

Prepositions often show the physical position of things—above, below, beside, around, and so on. Four specific prepositions show position but also get a lot of other use in English.

by the shore
at sunset
on June 23
on the ocean
in a sailboat

Photo by Lauri Väin

Uses for *By, At, On,* and *In*

By means "beside" or "up to a certain place or time."

by the shed, by the road
by midnight, by April 15

At refers to a specific place or time.

at the corner, at the station
at 4:35 p.m., at noon

On refers to a surface, a day or date, or an electronic medium.

on the desk, on the cover
on June 9, on Tuesday
on the disk, on TV, on the computer

In refers to an enclosed space; a geographical location; an hour, month, or year; or a print medium.

in the drawer, in the room
in Seattle, in Britain
in an hour, in May, in 2012
in the book, in the newspaper

Insight

Native English speakers follow these rules without thinking about them. Listen to the way native English speakers use *by, at, on,* and *in,* and practice their use until it seems second-nature.

Say It

Team up with a partner. Have the first person read one of the words below, and have the second person use it in a prepositional phrase beginning with *by, at, on,* or *in.* The first person should check if the form is correct. (Some have more than one correct answer.) Then you should switch roles.

1. the living room
2. October 9
3. 11:15 a.m.
4. the cell phone
5. the edge
6. Chicago
7. the table
8. the restaurant
9. sunrise
10. the magazine

Using *By, At, On,* and *In*

Provide In each sentence, circle the correct preposition in parentheses.

1. Please arrive (by, on, in) 11:55 p.m. because we will leave promptly (at, on, in) noon.
2. Make sure your carry-on fits (by, at, on, in) the overhead compartment or (by, at, on, in) the foot well in front of you.
3. I looked for a science article (by, at, on, in) the journal but could find only one (by, at, on, in) the Internet.
4. Though we sat (by, at, on, in) the waiting room, we weren't called (by, on, in) 3:15 p.m. for our appointment.
5. Four people standing (by, at, in) the corner reported a fire (at, on, in) a nearby garbage can.
6. (By, At, On, In) July 20, 1969, Neil Armstrong stepped (by, at, on, in) the surface of the moon.
7. I will meet you (by, at, on) the restaurant for our dinner reservation (by, at, on, in) 8:00 p.m.
8. Please place your check (by, at, on, in) the envelope, seal it, and write the following address (by, at, on, in) the envelope.
9. A parrot sat (by, at, on, in) the pirate's shoulder and looked me (by, at, on, in) the eye.
10. The song goes, "Under the boardwalk, down (by, at, on, in) the sea, (by, at, on, in) a blanket with my baby is where I'll be."

Write Write a sentence that uses all four of these prepositions in phrases: *by, at, on, in.*

Learning Outcome

Use conjunctions and prepositions in real-world documents.

LO7 Real-World Application

Revise Read the following e-mail, noting how choppy it sounds because all of the sentences are short. Connect some of the sentences using a coordinating conjunction and a comma, and connect others using a subordinating conjunction. You can also change other words as needed. (Use the correction symbols to the left.) Reread the e-mail to make sure it sounds smooth.

Coordinating Conjunctions

and	but	or	nor
for	so	yet	

Subordinating Conjunctions

after	as long as	if	so that	till	whenever
although	because	in order that	than	unless	where
as	before	provided that	that	until	whereas
as if	even though	since	though	when	while

Correction Marks

delete

capitalize

lowercase

insert

add comma

add question mark

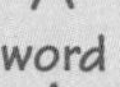

add word

add period

spelling

switch

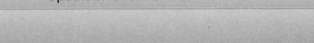

Update on Book Revision

From: mwilliams@bramfeldpub.com

To: ESleightner@bramfeldpub.com

Subject: Update on Book Revision

Dear Ed:

Thank you for writing about the revision. It is going well. It should be complete in two weeks. I have finished most chapters. I have addressed the main points. It is easy to forget to apply a change throughout. I will read the whole book to watch for changes.

Some of the graphics are still rough. I will need to finalize them. The maps for the inside covers are drawn. They need to be professionally inked.

The permissions requests are still pending. I have gotten permissions for three of the five excerpts. The fee for using the material was reasonable. If the fees for the other two are not, I will replace them.

I will wrap up the revision in two weeks. You can plan to start editing then.

Thanks,

Maurice Williams
Author

Correct Read the following party invitation, noting the incorrect use of the prepositions *by, at, on,* and *in*. (See page 352.) Correct the errors by deleting the prepositions and replacing them. Use the correction marks on the facing page.

Workplace

Correct use of *by, at, on,* and *in* will mark you as a writer comfortable with English.

Rankin Technology Annual Picnic

Send Attach Format

From: Josiah Warren

To: Rankin Staff

Subject: Rankin Technology Annual Picnic

Dear Staff:

It's time for the Rankin Technology Annual Picnic!

Who? All employees and their families

What? Should come have fun, eat corn by the cob, and burgers cooked in the grill!

Where? On Lakeside Park, on the main pavilion.

When? At Wednesday, July 18, starting on noon and finishing in 6 p.m.

Why? We're celebrating another year on Rankin Technologies!

The day is full of fun, including a watermelon-seed-spitting contest in 1:00 p.m., a water-balloon toss on 2:00 p.m., and a karaoke sing-along on the main pavilion in 3:00 p.m. Of course, there will be plenty of burgers and hot dogs in every plate, and lots of soda on every glass.

Please RSVP at July 12 to let us know how many people from your family will be on the park for the picnic.

We look forward to having fun with everyone in Wednesday, July 18.

Sincerely,

Josiah Warren
Human Resources

Part 6 Punctuation and Mechanics Workshops

"The writer who neglects punctuation, or
mispunctuates, is liable to be misunderstood"
—Edgar Allan Poe

29 Comma

Commas divide sentences into smaller sections so that they may be read more easily and more precisely. Of all the punctuation marks, commas are used most frequently—and oftentimes incorrectly.

This chapter will guide you in the conventional use of commas. Understanding correct comma usage is an important step in becoming a college-level writer.

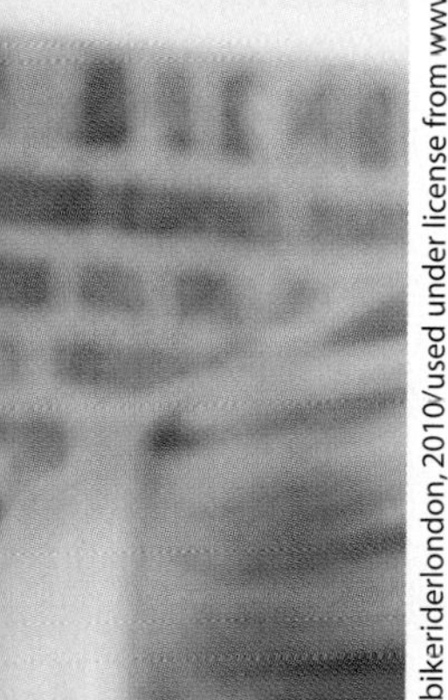

What do you think?

Commas are said to be the most important form of punctuation. Why do you think this might be true? Explain.

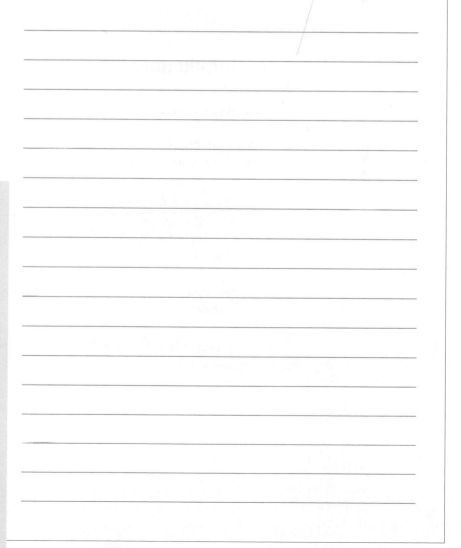

Learning Outcomes

LO1 Use commas in compound sentences.

LO2 Use commas with introductory words and equal adjectives.

LO3 Use commas between items in a series.

LO4 Use commas with appositives and nonrestrictive modifiers.

LO5 Use commas in real-world writing.

Learning Outcome

Use commas in compound sentences.

Traits

Make sure to use both a comma and a coordinating conjunction in a compound sentence, or you will create a comma splice or a run-on. For more information, see pages 268–271.

LO1 In Compound Sentences and After Introductory Clauses

The following principles will guide the conventional use of commas in your writing.

In Compound Sentences

Use a comma before the coordinating conjunction *(and, but, or, nor, for, yet, so)* in a compound sentence.

Heath Ledger completed his brilliant portrayal as the Joker in *The Dark Knight*, **but** he died before the film was released.

Note: Do not confuse a compound verb with a compound sentence.

Ledger's Joker became instantly iconic and won him the Oscar for best supporting actor. (compound verb)

His death resulted from the abuse of prescription drugs**,** but it was ruled an accident. (compound sentence)

After Introductory Clauses

Use a comma after most introductory clauses.

Although Charlemagne was a great patron of learning, he never learned to write properly. (adverb dependent clause)

When the clause follows the independent clause and is not essential to the meaning of the sentence, use a comma. This comma use generally applies to clauses beginning with *even though, although, while,* or some other conjunction expressing a contrast.

Charlemagne never learned to write properly**, even though he continued to practice**.

Note: A comma is *not* used if the dependent clause following the independent clause is needed.

Correcting Comma Errors

Correct For each sentence below, add a comma (^,) before the coordinating conjunction *(and, but, or, nor, for, so, yet)* if the clause on each side could stand alone as a sentence. Write "correct" if the conjunction separates word groups that can't stand alone.

1. I was sick of sitting around on the couch so I drove over to the driving range. __________
2. Her cell phone rang but she decided against answering it. __________
3. Maria downloaded some new music and imported it on her iPod. __________
4. I wanted to finish my assignment but I couldn't turn away from the *House* marathon. __________
5. Should I put a down payment on a new car or should I save my money for a new apartment? __________
6. Kelly is studying frog populations in the rain forest and she hopes to publish her work. __________
7. Ryan wanted to make a new style of chili but he lost the recipe. __________
8. Trisha was looking forward to the baseball game but it got rained out. __________

Correct For each sentence below, add a comma after any introductory clauses. If no comma is needed, write "correct" next to the sentence.

1. While Becca prefers grilled salmon Mia's favorite food is sushi. __________
2. Although the water conditions were perfect I couldn't catch a wave to save my life. __________
3. Perhaps I should rethink my major because I don't enjoy the classes. __________
4. Even though the Cubs haven't won a World Series since 1901 I still cheer for them. __________
5. While *American Idol* is popular in America *Britain's Got Talent* is the craze in England. __________

Learning Outcome

Use commas with introductory words and equal adjectives.

LO2 With Introductory Words and Equal Adjectives

After Introductory Phrases

Use a comma after introductory phrases.

In spite of his friend's prodding, Jared decided to stay home and study.

A comma is usually omitted if the phrase follows an independent clause.

Jared decided to stay home and study **in spite of his friend's prodding.**

You may omit a comma after a short (four or fewer words) introductory phrase unless it is needed to ensure clarity.

At 10:30 p.m. he would quit and go to sleep.

Speaking & Listening

Try the strategies below by speaking the words aloud. If it sounds strange to switch the order of the adjectives or to insert an *and* between them, do not separate them with a comma.

To Separate Adjectives

Use commas to separate adjectives that equally modify the same noun. Notice in the examples below that no comma separates the last adjective from the noun.

You should exercise regularly and follow a **sensible, healthful** diet.
A good diet is one that includes lots of **high-protein, low-fat** foods.

To Determine Equal Modifiers

To determine whether adjectives modify a noun equally, use these two tests.

1. Reverse the order of the adjectives; if the sentence is clear, the adjectives modify equally. (In the example below, *hot* and *crowded* can be reversed, but *and* does not make sense between *short* and *coffee*.)

   Matt was tired of working in the **hot, crowded** lab and decided to take a **short coffee** break.

2. Insert *and* between the adjectives; if the sentence reads well, use a comma when *and* is omitted. (The word *and* can be inserted between *hot* and *crowded,* but *and* does not make sense between *short* and *coffee*.)

Correcting Comma Errors

Correct For each sentence below, insert a comma after the introductory phrase if it is needed. If no comma is needed, write "correct" next to the sentence.

1. Before you can receive your diploma you will need to pay your unpaid parking tickets. __________
2. At Central Perk Ross, Rachel, and the gang sipped coffee and exchanged barbs. __________
3. In accordance with state law Hanna decided against sending a text message while driving on the interstate. __________
4. On the other hand pursuing the wrong type of adrenaline high can be destructive. __________
5. After handing in her paper Eva felt a great wave of relief. __________
6. Eva felt a great wave of relief after handing in her paper. __________
7. Based on his primary research Andy came up with a preliminary hypothesis. __________
8. To save a few dollars Stephanie rode her bike to work. __________

Correct For each sentence below, determine whether or not a comma is needed to separate the adjectives that modify the same noun. Add any needed commas (^,). Write "no" next to the sentence if a comma is not needed.

1. The **long difficult** exam took a lot out of me. __________
2. Last night I went to a **fun graduation** party. __________
3. A good concert includes many **memorable hair-raising** moments. __________
4. A **thoughtful considerate** friend goes an extra mile to make you smile. __________
5. I could really use a **relaxing back** massage. __________
6. When dressing for skiing, consider wearing a **thick well-insulated** jacket. __________

Learning Outcome

Use commas between items in a series.

LO3 Between Items in a Series and Other Uses

Between Items in Series

Use commas to separate individual words, phrases, or clauses in a series. (A series contains at least three items.)

> Many college students must balance studying with **taking care of a family, working a job, getting exercise, and finding time to relax**.

Do not use commas when all the items in a series are connected with *or, nor,* or *and*.

> Hmm . . . should I study **or** do laundry **or** go out?

To Set Off Transitional Expressions

Traits

Do not use a comma before an indirect quotation.

Incorrect: My roommate said**,** that she doesn't understand the notes I took.

Correct: My roommate said that she doesn't understand the notes I took.

Use a comma to set off conjunctive adverbs and transitional phrases.

> Handwriting is not**, as a matter of fact,** easy to improve upon later in life**; however,** it can be done if you are determined enough.

If a transitional expression blends smoothly with the rest of the sentence, it does not need to be set off.

> If you are **in fact** coming**,** I'll see you there.

To Set Off Dialogue

Use commas to set off the words of the speaker from the rest of the sentence.

> **"Never be afraid to ask for help,"** advised Ms. Kane
>
> **"With the evidence that we now have,"** Professor Thom said**, "many scientists believe there could be life on Mars."**

To Enclose Explanatory Words

Use commas to enclose an explanatory word or phrase.

> Time management**, according to many professionals,** is an important skill that should be taught in college.

Correcting Comma Errors

Correct Indicate where commas are needed in the following sentences.

1. I'm looking forward to graduation summer vacation and moving into a new apartment.
2. A new strain of virus according to biologists could cause future outbreaks of poultry disease.
3. "To confine our attention to terrestrial matters would be to limit the human spirit" said Stephen Hawking.
4. I need you to pick up two jars of peanut butter, a half-gallon of skim milk and snacks for the party.
5. I enjoy live music; however I don't like big crowds.
6. "With all the advancements in technology" Sara said, "you'd think we would have invented a quicker toaster by now."
7. Eighty percent of states as a matter of fact are in financial trouble.
8. We can meet up at either the library the student union or memorial hall.
9. The difference between perseverance and obstinacy according to Henry Ward Beecher is that one comes from strong will, and the other from a strong won't.
10. Chicago, Detroit and Indianapolis are the most-populated cities in the Midwest.

Correct Indicate where commas are needed in the following paragraph.

The Erie Canal is a man-made waterway that connects the Atlantic Ocean to Lake Erie. It was the first transportation system to connect the eastern seaboard and the Great Lakes was faster than carts pulled by animals and significantly cut transportation time. "The opening of the Erie Canal to New York in 1825 stimulated other cities on the Atlantic seaboard to put themselves into closer commercial touch with the West" said John Moody. Since the 1990s the canal is mostly home to recreational traffic; however some cargo is still transported down the waterway.

Learning Outcome

Use commas with appositives and nonrestrictive modifiers.

LO4 With Appositives and Other Word Groups

To Set Off Some Appositives

A specific kind of explanatory word or phrase called an **appositive** identifies or renames a preceding noun or pronoun.

Albert Einstein**, the famous mathematician and physicist,** developed the theory of relativity.

Do not use commas if the appositive is important to the basic meaning of the sentence.

The famous physicist **Albert Einstein** developed the theory of relativity.

Traits

Do not use commas to set off necessary clauses and phrases, which add information that the reader needs to understand the sentence.

Example: Only the professors **who run at noon** use the locker rooms in Swain Hall to shower. (necessary clause)

With Some Clauses and Phrases

Use commas to enclose phrases or clauses that add information that is not necessary to the basic meaning of the sentence. For example, if the clause or phrase (in **boldface**) were left out of the two examples below, the meaning of the sentences would remain clear. Therefore, commas are used to set off the information.

The locker rooms in Swain Hall**, which were painted and updated last summer,** give professors a place to shower. (nonrestrictive clause)

Work-study programs**, offered on many campuses,** give students the opportunity to earn tuition money. (nonrestrictive phrase)

Using "That" or "Which"

Use *that* to introduce necessary clauses; use *which* to introduce unnecessary clauses.

Campus jobs **that are funded by the university** are awarded to students only. (necessary)

The cafeteria**, which is run by an independent contractor,** can hire nonstudents. (unnecessary)

Vocabulary

appositive
a noun or noun phrase that renames another noun right beside it

Correcting Comma Errors

Correct Indicate where commas are needed in the following sentences. If no commas are needed, write "correct" next to the sentence.

1. John D. Rockefeller the famous American philanthropist and oil executive is sometimes referred to as the richest person in history. ____________

2. The new library which is scheduled to open in July will include three different computer labs. ____________

3. The renowned trumpeter Louis Armstrong sang the song "What a Wonderful World." ____________

4. Kansas City along with Memphis, Tennessee is known for its delicious barbecue. ____________

5. Judge Sonya Sotomayer the first Hispanic Supreme Court justice was confirmed into office in 2009. ____________

6. The book *The Notebook* which was later adapted into a movie was written by Nicolas Sparks. ____________

Write The following sentences contain clauses using *that*. Rewrite the sentences with clauses using *which,* and insert commas correctly. You may need to reword some parts.

1. The road construction that delayed traffic yesterday should be completed by the end of the week.

____

____

2. The homework that Dr. Grant assigned yesterday will consume the next two weeks of my life.

____

____

3. The earplugs that we bought before the race made the deafening noise more bearable.

____

____

LO5 Real-World Application

Learning Outcome

Use commas in real-world writing.

Correct Indicate where commas are needed in the following e-mail message.

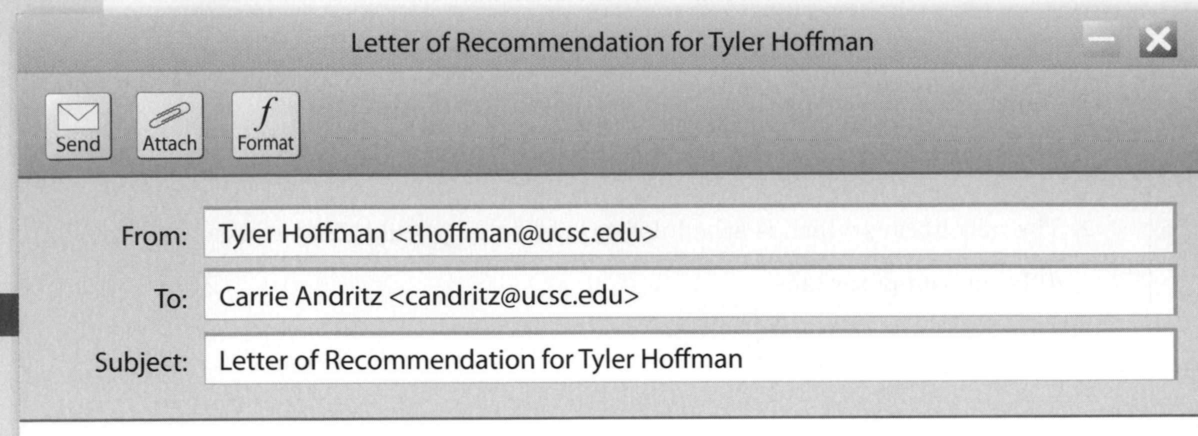

Letter of Recommendation for Tyler Hoffman
Send
Attach
Format
From: Tyler Hoffman <thoffman@ucsc.edu>
To: Carrie Andritz <candritz@ucsc.edu>
Subject: Letter of Recommendation for Tyler Hoffman

Dear Professor Andritz:

I enjoyed meeting with you today to discuss my letter of recommendation. You know the quality of my academic work my qualities as a person and my potential for working in the marketing industry.

As my professor for Marketing 303 and Economics 401 you have witnessed my hardworking nature. As my adviser you know my career plans and should have a good sense of whether I have the qualities needed to succeed in the fast-paced competitive marketing industry.

Please send your letter to Craig Emmons human resources director at FastTech by April 14. If you have any questions please call me at (324) 472-3489.

Sincerely,

Tyler Hoffman

Correction Marks

- delete
- capitalize
- lowercase
- insert
- add comma
- add question mark
- add word
- add period
- spelling
- switch

Workplace

Correct comma use is critical for clear business communication.

"If the English language made any sense, a catastrophe would be an apostrophe with fur."
—Doug Larson

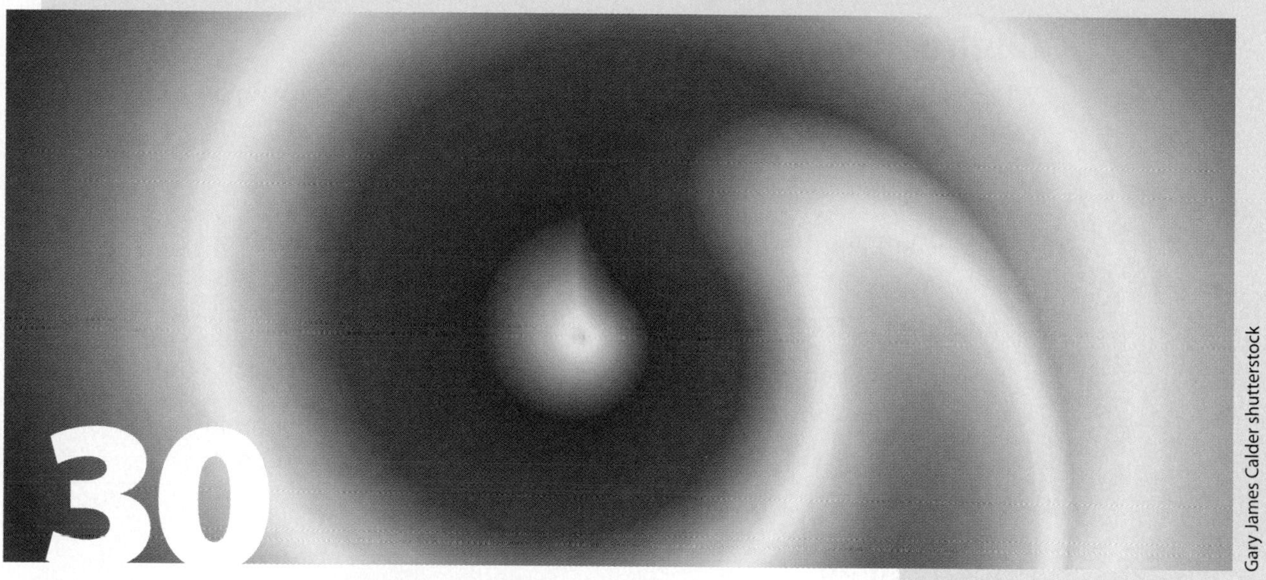

Gary James Calder shutterstock

30 Apostrophe

You may be surprised to discover that the words *catastrophe* and *apostrophe* have something in common. Both come from the Greek word for "turn." An apostrophe simply turns *away*, but a catastrophe *over*turns.

Sometimes the use of apostrophes becomes a catastrophe. Apostrophes shouldn't be used to form plurals of words. Their main use is to form possessives and contractions. The rules and activities in this chapter will help you understand their usage and avoid an apostrophe catastrophe.

Learning Outcomes

LO1 Use apostrophes for contractions and possessives.

LO2 Apply apostrophes in real-world documents.

What do you think?

Why do you think *apostrophe* comes from the word "to turn away?"

Learning Outcome

Use apostrophes for contractions and possessives.

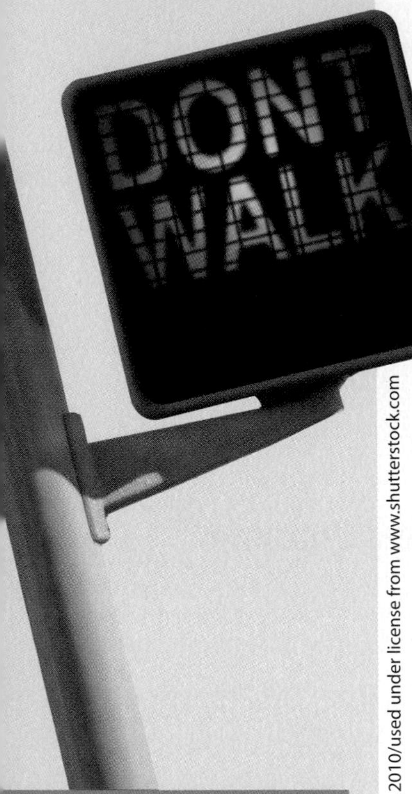

Binkski, 2010/used under license from www.shutterstock.com

Insight

Pronoun possessives *do not use* apostrophes: *its, whose, hers, his, ours*

Vocabulary

contraction
word formed by joining two words, leaving out one or more letters (indicated by an apostrophe)

LO1 Contractions and Possessives

Apostrophes are used primarily to show that a letter or number has been left out, or that a noun is possessive.

Contractions

When one or more letters is left out of a word, use an apostrophe to form the **contraction**.

don't (*o* is left out)	he'd (*woul* is left out)	would've (*ha* is left out)

Missing Characters

Use an apostrophe to signal when one or more characters are left out.

class of '16 (*20* is left out)	rock 'n' roll (*a* and *d* are left out)	good mornin' (*g* is left out)

Possessives

Form possessives of singular nouns by adding an apostrophe and an *s*.

Sharla's pen	the man's coat	*The Pilgrim's Progress*

Singular Noun Ending In *s* (One Syllable)

Form the possessive by adding an apostrophe and an *s*.

the boss's idea	the lass's purse	the bass's teeth

Singular Noun Ending In *s* (Two Or More Syllables)

Form the possessive by adding an apostrophe and an *s*—or by adding just an apostrophe.

Kansas's plains *or* Kansas' plains

Plural Noun Ending In *s*

Form the possessive by adding just an apostrophe.

the bosses' preference	the Smiths' home

Note: The word before the apostrophe is the owner.

the girl's ball (*girl* is the owner)	the girls' ball (*girls* are the owners)

Plural Noun Not Ending In *s*

Form the possessive by adding an apostrophe and an *s*.

the children's toys	the women's room

Forming Contractions and Possessives

Write For each contraction below, write the words that formed the contraction. For each set of words, write the contraction that would be formed.

1. they're ____________________
2. you've ____________________
3. Charlie is ____________________
4. wouldn't ____________________
5. we have ____________________
6. have not ____________________
7. I would ____________________
8. I had ____________________
9. won't ____________________
10. will not ____________________

Rewrite Rework the following sentences, replacing the "of" phrases with possessives using apostrophes.

1. The idea of my friend is a good one.

   ____

2. I found the flyer of the orchestra.

   ____

3. The foundation of the government is democracy.

   ____

4. He washed the jerseys of the team.

   ____

5. I went to the house of the Kings.

   ____

6. The plan of the managers worked well.

   ____

7. I like the classic albums of Kiss.

   ____

8. I graded the assignment of Ross.

   ____

9. The pastries of the chef were delicious.

   ____

10. The books of the children covered the floor.

   ____

Learning Outcome

Apply apostrophes in real-world documents.

LO2 Real-World Application

Correct The following letter sounds too informal because it contains too many contractions. Cross out contractions and replace them with full forms of the words. Also, correct any errors with apostrophes. Use the correction marks to the left.

Correction Marks

- delete
- capitalize
- lowercase
- insert
- add comma
- add question mark
- add word
- add period
- spelling
- switch

5821 North Fairheights Road
Milsap, CA 94218
Ph: 567-555-1908

June 1, 2011

Account: 4879003

Mr. Robert Burnside, Controller
Circuit Electronic's Company
4900 Gorham Road
Mountain View, CA 94040-1093

Dear Mr. Burnside:

This letter's a reminder that your account's past due (presently 60 days).

As of today, we haven't yet received your payment of $1,806.00, originally due March 31. I've enclosed the March 1 invoice. It's for the mitered flange's that you ordered January 10 and that we shipped January 28.

You've been a valued customer, Mr. Burnside, and Hanford appreciate's your business. We've enclosed a postage-paid envelope for your convenience.

If there's a problem, please call (567-555-1908, ext. 227) or e-mail me (marta@hanford.comm). As alway's, we look forward to serving you.

Sincerely,

Marta Ramones

Marta Ramones'
Billing Department

Enclosures 2

"The right word may be effective, but no word was ever as effective as a rightly timed pause."
—Mark Twain

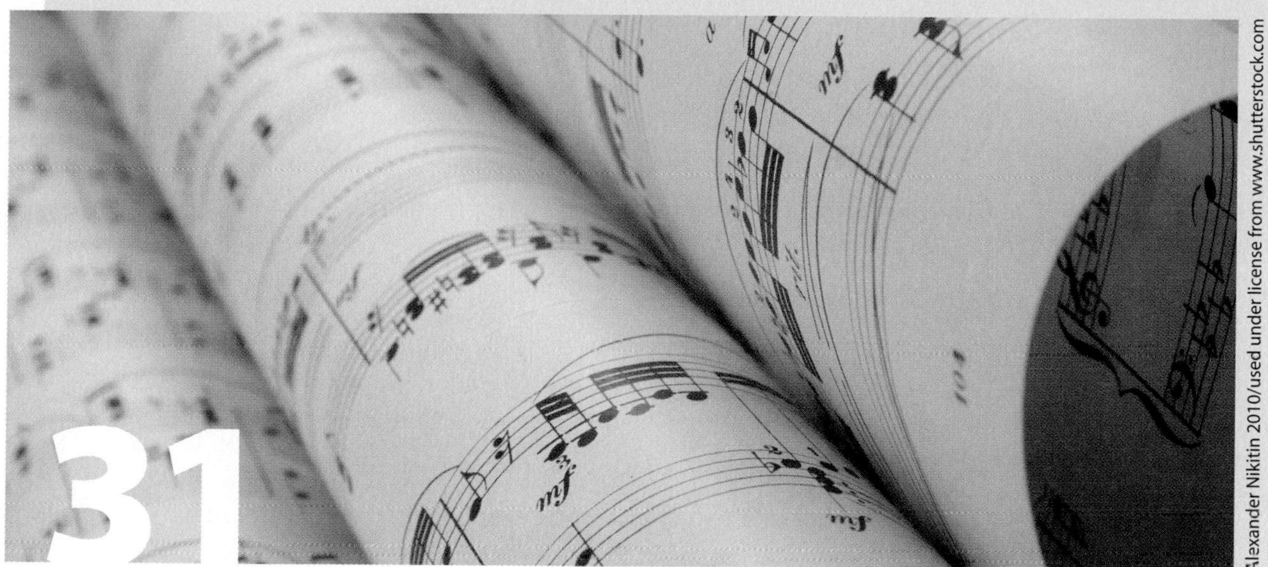
Alexander Nikitin 2010/used under license from www.shutterstock.com

31 Semicolon, Colon, Hyphen, Dash

Music notation contains notes and rests. The notes carry the melody and harmony. The rests punctuate sound with silence, giving rhythm. Whole, half, quarter, eighth, dotted eighth—there are different lengths of rest for different effects.

You can think of punctuation as rests in writing. They come in different lengths, from the period (sometimes called a full stop), through semicolons, colons, hyphens, and dashes. These marks help readers know which pieces of information belong together and which should be separated by pauses. In so doing, they help create rhythm in writing. This chapter shows how.

Learning Outcomes

LO1 Use semicolons and colons correctly.

LO2 Understand hyphen use.

LO3 Use dashes well.

LO4 Apply punctuation in real-world documents.

What do you think?

What would music sound like without rests? How about words without punctuation?

Learning Outcome

Use semicolons and colons correctly.

LO1 Semicolons and Colons

Semicolons and colons have specific uses in writing.

Semicolon

A **semicolon** is a sort of soft period. Use the semicolon to join two sentences that are closely related.

The job market is improving**;** it's time to apply again.

Before a Conjunctive Adverb

Often, the second sentence will begin with a conjunctive adverb *(also, besides, however, instead, then, therefore)*, which signals the relationship between the sentences. Place a semicolon before the conjunctive adverb, and place a comma after it.

I looked for work for two months**;** however, the market is better now.

With Series

Use a semicolon to separates items in a series if any of the items already include commas.

I should check online ads, headhunting services, and position announcements**;** compile a list of job openings**;** create a résumé, an e-résumé, and a cover letter**;** and apply, requesting an interview.

WAC

In addition to the colon uses listed below, a colon is often used in academic writing to separate the main title of a paper from its subtitle.

Colon

The main use of a **colon** is to provide an example or a list. Write an introduction as a complete sentence, place the colon, and then provide the example or list.

I've forgotten one other possibility**:** social networking.

I'll plan to use the following**:** LinkedIn, Twitter, and Facebook.

After Salutations

In business documents, use a colon after **salutations** and in memo headings.

Dear Mr. Ortez**:** To**:** Lynne Jones

Times and Ratios

Use a colon to separate hours, minutes, and seconds. Also use a colon between the numbers in a ratio.

7**:**35 p.m. 6**:**15 a.m. The student-teacher ratio is 30**:**1

Vocabulary

semicolon
punctuation mark (;) that connects sentences and separates items in some series

colon
punctuation mark (:) that introduces an example or a list and has other special uses

salutation
the formal greeting in a letter; the line starting with "Dear"

Using Semicolons and Colons

Correct Add semicolons (^;) and commas (^,) as needed in the sentences below.

1. Searching for a job is nerve-wracking however it's also about possibilities.
2. Don't think about rejections think about where you could be working.
3. Each résumé you send is a fishing line then you wait for a nibble.
4. Put out dozens of lines also give yourself time.
5. Make sure that you have a strong résumé e-résumé and cover letter that you consult social networks local newspapers and friends and that you keep your spirits up.
6. It doesn't cost much to send out résumés therefore send out many.
7. Job searching can feel lonely and frustrating rely on friends and family to help you through.
8. Ask people if you can use them as references don't provide the list of references until requested.
9. When you interview, wear professional clothing show up at the right place at the right time and armed with any information you need and be confident.
10. Try to enjoy the process it is the gateway to your future.

Correct Add colons (^:)where needed in the sentences below.

1. Use your social resources contacts, references, and organizations.
2. Call for an appointment between 9 00 a.m. and 4 00 p.m.
3. Remember a response rate of 1 10 is good for résumés submitted.
4. Politely start your cover letter with a salutation "Dear Mrs. Baker."
5. For an interview, remember these three keys Be punctual, be polite, and be professional.
6. Here's one last piece of advice Be yourself.

Learning Outcome

Understand hyphen use.

WAC

The directions below for dividing words at the ends of lines date back to the time of typewriters, when it was difficult to guess whether a word would fit on a line. Now, in most disciplines, it is best to disable hyphenation in your word-processing program.

Vocabulary

hyphen
short, horizontal line (-) that joins words to words, numbers, or letters

compound noun
noun made of two or more words, often hyphenated or spelled closed

compound adjective
adjective made of two or more words, hyphenated before the noun but not afterward

compound numbers
two-word numbers from twenty-one to ninety-nine

LO2 Hyphens

A **hyphen** joins words to each other or to numbers or letters.

Compound Nouns

Use hyphens to create **compound nouns:**

city-state fail-safe fact-check one-liner mother-in-law

Compound Adjectives

Use hyphens to create **compound adjectives** that appear before the noun. If the adjective appears after, it usually is not hyphenated:

peer-reviewed article	an article that was peer reviewed
ready-made solution	a solution that is ready made

Note: Don't hyphenate a compound made up with an *-ly* adverb and an adjective or one that ends with a single letter.

newly acquired songs (*-ly* adverb) grade B plywood (ending with a letter)

Compound Numbers

Use hyphens for **compound numbers** from twenty-one to ninety-nine. Also use hyphens for numbers in a fraction and other number compounds.

twenty-two fifty-fifty three-quarters seven thirty-seconds

With Letters

Use a hyphen to join a letter to a word that follows it.

L-bracket U-shaped T-shirt O-ring G-rated x-ray

With Common Elements

Use hyphens to show word parts that are shared by two or more words.

We offer low-, middle-, and high-coverage plans.

To Divide Words at the Ends of Lines:

1. Divide a compound word between its basic units: *attorney-at-law,* not *at-tor-ney-at-law.*
2. When a vowel is a syllable by itself, divide the word after the vowel: *ori-gin,* not *or-igin.*
3. Divide at the prefix or suffix: *bi-lateral,* not *bilat-eral.*

Do Not Divide:

1. Never divide a word so that it is difficult to recognize.
2. Never divide a one-syllable word: *filed, trains, rough.*
3. Avoid dividing a word of five letters or fewer: *final, today, radar.*
4. Never leave a single letter at the end of a line: *omit-ted,* not *o-mitted.*
5. Never divide contractions or abbreviations: *couldn't,* not *could-n't.*
6. Avoid dividing a number written as a figure: *42,300,000,* not *42,300-000.*
7. Avoid dividing the last word in a paragraph.
8. Avoid ending two consecutive lines with a hyphen.

Using Hyphens

Correct Add hyphens (‸) to the following sentences as needed.

1. The secretary treasurer recorded the vote as four five.
2. We had to x ray twenty one people today.
3. Cut each board at seven and three sixteenths inches.
4. The statistics on low , middle , and high income households are ready.
5. A double insulated wire should be used for high voltage applications.
6. This application is high voltage so the wire should be double insulated.
7. The x axis shows months and the y axis shows dollar amounts.
8. The tax rate table shows I should pay twenty eight cents.
9. My mother in law thinks I am quite a fine son in law.
10. The L bracket measured eleven sixteenths by twenty seven thirty seconds.

Divide Use the guidelines for word division to decide where each word can be broken. (Write the word with hyphen at possible breaks.) If a word cannot be broken, write "NB" for "no break."

1. operate ____________________
2. anticipate ____________________
3. newsstand ____________________
4. sister-in-law ____________________
5. billed ____________________
6. avoid ____________________
7. helpfully ____________________
8. bilateral ____________________
9. staple ____________________
10. 5,345,000 ____________________

Learning Outcome

Use dashes well.

WAC

In most academic writing, use dashes sparingly. If they are overused, they loose their emphasis.

Vocabulary

dash
long horizontal line that separates words, creating emphasis

LO3 Dashes

Unlike the hyphen, the **dash** does more to separate words than to join them together. A dash is indicated by two hyphens with no spacing before or after. Most word-processing programs convert two hyphens into a dash.

For Emphasis

Use a dash instead of a colon if you want to emphasize a word, phrase, clause, or series.

Ice cream—it's what life is about.

I love two things about ice cream—making it and eating it.

Ice cream is my favorite dessert—cold, sweet, and flavorful.

To Set Off a Series

Use a dash to set off a series of items.

Rocky road, moose tracks, and chocolate-chip cookie dough—these are my favorite flavors.

Neapolitan ice cream—chocolate, strawberry, and vanilla—is my sister's favorite.

With Nonessential Elements

Use a dash to set off explanations, examples, and definitions, especially when these elements already include commas.

Ice milk—which, as you might guess, is made of milk instead of cream—provides a light alternative.

To Show Interrupted Speech

Use a dash to show that a speaker has been interrupted or has started and stopped while speaking.

"Could you help me crank this—"

"I've got to get more salt before—"

"It'll freeze up if you don't—Just give me a hand, please."

Photo by Ivan Ahlert

Using Dashes

Correct In the sentences below, add a dash ($\overline{\wedge}$) where needed.

1. Which dessert would you prefer brownies, apple pie, or ice cream?
2. I love the triple brownie surprise a brownie with vanilla and chocolate ice cream covered in hot fudge.
3. Ice cream it's what's for dinner.
4. "Could I have a taste of " "You want to try some of " "I want to try um could I try the pistachio?"
5. Bananas, ice cream, peanuts, and fudge these are the ingredients of a banana-split sundae.
6. Making ice cream at home takes a long time and a lot of muscle!
7. An electric ice-cream maker which replaced arm power with a cranking motor makes the job easier but less fun.
8. Nothing tastes better than the first taste of freshly made ice cream nothing except perhaps the next taste.
9. Don't eat too quickly brain-freeze.
10. A danger of ice cream I'll risk it every time.

Correct Write your own sentence, correctly using dashes for each of the situations indicated below:

1. For emphasis: ______________________________

____

____

2. To set off a series: ______________________________

____

____

3. With nonessential elements: ______________________________

____

____

Learning Outcome

Apply punctuation in real-world documents.

LO4 Real-World Application

Correct In the following e-mail message, insert semicolons (‸;), colons (‸:), hyphens (‸-), and dashes (‸—) where necessary. (Clearly distinguish short hyphens from long dashes.)

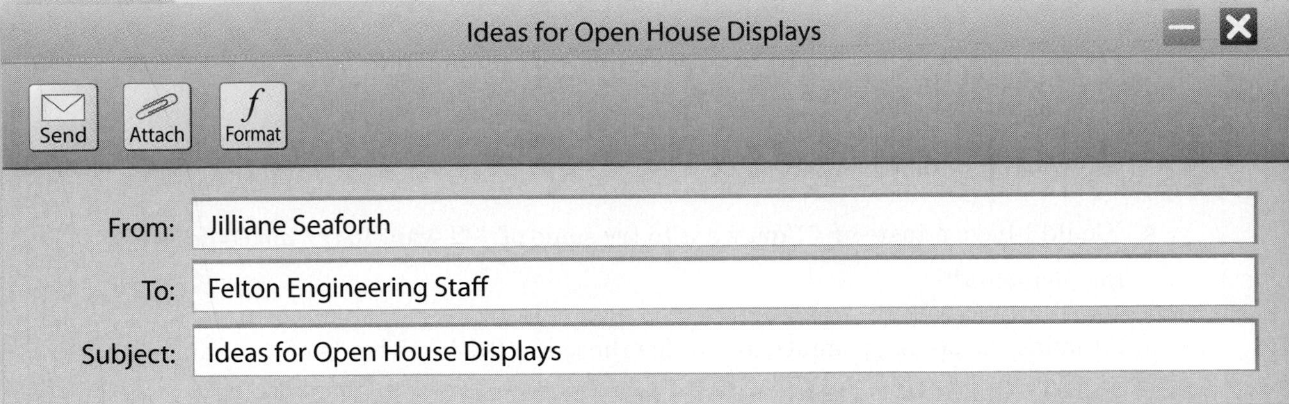

Ideas for Open House Displays

Send Attach Format

From: Jilliane Seaforth

To: Felton Engineering Staff

Subject: Ideas for Open House Displays

Hello, all:

September 1 that's the big open house we will celebrate our new location. To help visitors understand what Felton Engineering does, I plan to set up displays heater designs, product applications, and aerospace technology.

Please help me by doing the following looking for blueprints, sketches, small models, and prototypes that illustrate what we do identifying items that would interest visitors and setting them aside as you pack.

Then please respond to this e-mail with the following your name, the name of the product, the product number, and the type of display materials that you have.

Please respond no later than August 22. I will handle the other arrangements pick up your materials, set up the displays, and return the materials to you after the open house. Innovation it's what drives Felton Engineering!

Thanks,

Jilliane Seaforth

"A fine quotation is a diamond on the finger of a man of wit, and a pebble in the hand of a fool."

—Joseph Roux

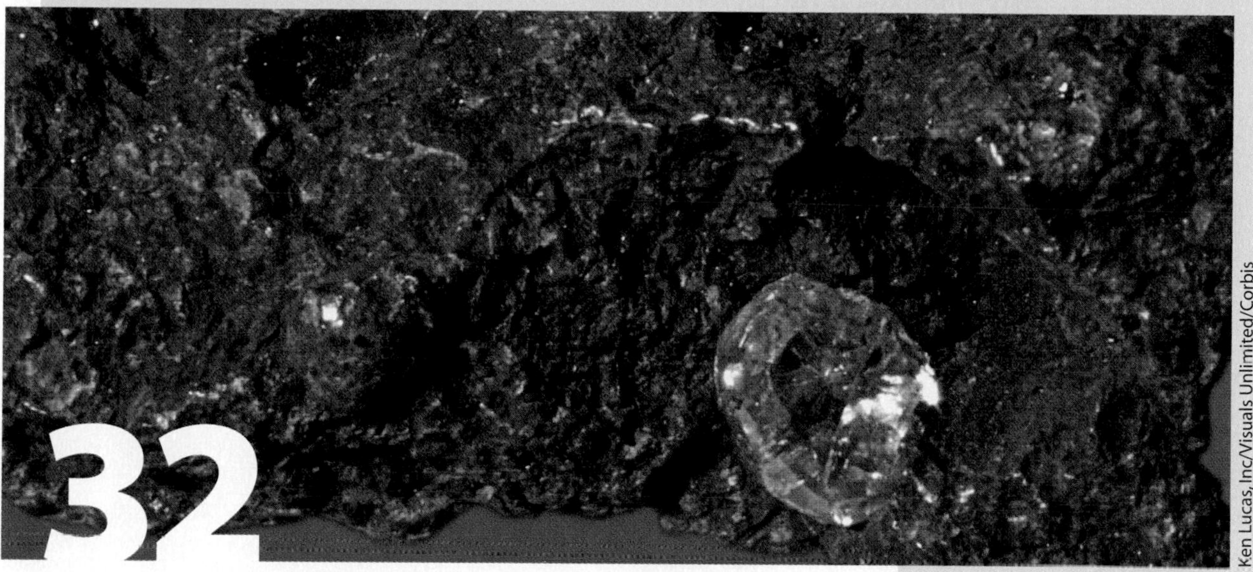

Ken Lucas, Inc/Visuals Unlimited/Corbis

32 Quotation Marks and Italics

Much of the time, language flows from us as naturally as breathing. We think; we speak; someone hears and responds—all without consciously thinking about the words.

Sometimes, however, we have need to note a word as a word, to call attention to a phrase in a special sense, to use an apt or time-honored quotation from someone else, or to mark the title of a work. In such cases, quotation marks and italics allow us to indicate this special use of language.

Learning Outcomes

LO1 Understand the use of quotation marks.

LO2 Understand the use of italics.

LO3 Apply quotation marks and italics in a real-world document.

What do you think?

Study the image and quotation. What makes the gemstones in the photo valuable? In what way does this relate to the Joseph Roux quotation?

Learning Outcome

Understand the use of quotation marks.

LO1 Quotation Marks

To Punctuate Titles (Smaller Works)

Use quotation marks to enclose the titles of smaller works, including speeches, short stories, songs, poems, episodes of audio or video programs, chapters or sections of books, unpublished works, and articles from magazines, journals, newspapers, or encyclopedias. (For other titles, see page 382.)

Speech:	"The Cause Endures"
Song:	"Head Like a Hole"
Short Story:	"Dark They Were, and Golden Eyed"
Magazine Article:	"The Moral Life of Babies"
Chapter in a Book:	"Queen Mab"
Television Episode:	"The Girl Who Was Death"
Encyclopedia Article:	"Cetacean"

Insight

In British English, a single quotation mark is used instead of double quotation marks. Also, British English has different rules for using other punctuation with quotation marks. When writing in a U.S. setting, use the rules on this page.

Placement of Periods and Commas

When quoted words end in a period or comma, always place that punctuation inside the quotation marks.

"If you want to catch the train," Grace said, "you must leave now."

Placement of Semicolons and Colons

When a quotation is followed by a semicolon or colon, always place that punctuation outside the quotation marks.

I finally read "Heart of Darkness"; it is amazingly well written!

Placement of Exclamation Points and Question Marks

If an exclamation point or a question mark is part of the quotation, place it inside the quotation marks. Otherwise, place it outside.

Marcello asked me, "Are you going to the Dodge Poetry Festival**?**" What could I reply except, "Yes, indeed"**?**

For Special Words

Quotation marks can be used (1) to show that a word is being referred to as the word itself; (2) to indicate that it is jargon, slang, or a coined term; or (3) to show that it is used in an ironic or sarcastic sense.

(1) Somehow, the term "cool" has survived decades.
(2) The band has a "wicked awesome" sound.
(3) I would describe the taste of this casserole as "swampy."

Using Quotation Marks

Correct In the following sentences, insert quotation marks (“ ”) where needed.

1. Kamala loves to listen to the song I Take Time, over and over and over.
2. Ray Bradbury's short story A Sound of Thunder has been republished many times.
3. Fast Company published an article today called How Google Wave Got Its Groove Back.
4. Angelo told Arlena, I have a guy who can fix that fender.
5. Arlena asked, How much will it cost me?
6. Was she thinking, This car is driving me into bankruptcy?
7. This is the message of the article Tracking the Science of Commitment: Couples that enhance one another have an easier time remaining committed.
8. I love the article Tall Tales About Being Short; it challenged my preconceptions about the effect of height on a person's life.
9. How many examples of the word aardvark can you find on this page?
10. Is anyone else here tired of hearing about his bling bling?

Write Write a sentence that indicates the actual meaning of each sentence below.

1. Hoyt's great Dane “skipped” across the floor and “settled” its bulk across his lap.

   ____

   ____

2. Our baked goods are always “fresh.”

   ____

   ____

3. And so began another “wonderful” day of marching through a “fairyland” of bugs.

   ____

   ____

Learning Outcome

Understand the use of italics.

WAC

As you write research reports in different classes, find out which style your discipline uses for reporting titles of larger and smaller works.

LO2 Italics

To Punctuate Titles (Larger Works)

Use italics to indicate the titles of larger works, including newspapers, magazines, journals, pamphlets, books, plays, films, radio and television programs, movies, ballets, operas, long musical compositions, CD's, DVD's, software programs, and legal cases, as well as the names of ships, trains, aircraft, and spacecraft. (For other titles, see page 380.)

Magazine: *Wired*
Play: *Night of the Iguana*
Film: *Bladerunner*
Book: *Moby Dick*
Newspaper: *Washington Post*
Journal: *Journal of Sound & Vibration*
Software Program: *Paint Shop Pro*
Television Program: *The Prisoner*

For a Word, Letter, or Number Referred to as Itself

Use italics (or quotation marks—see page 380) to show that a word, letter, or number is being referred to as itself. If a definition follows a word used in this way, place that definition in quotation marks.

The word *tornado* comes to English from the Spanish *tronar*, which means "to thunder."

I can't read your writing; is this supposed to be a *P* or an *R*?

For Foreign Words

Use italics to indicate a word that is being borrowed from a foreign language.

Je ne sais pas is a French phrase that many English speakers use as a fancy way of saying "I don't know what."

For Technical Terms

Use italics to introduce a technical term for the first time in a piece of writing. After that, the term may be used without italics.

The heart's *sternocostal* surface—facing toward the joining of sternum and ribs—holds the heart's primary natural pacemaker. If this sternocostal node fails, a lower, secondary node can function in its place.

Note: If a technical term is being used within an organization or a field of study where it is common, it may be used without italics even the first time in a piece of writing.

Using Italics

Correct In the following sentences, underline words that should be in italics.

1. I almost couldn't finish Stephenie Meyer's second book, New Moon, because of its deep emotion.
2. What is your favorite part of the movie Avatar?
3. The Spanish say duende to describe a transcendent, creative passion.
4. Was the aircraft carrier Enterprise named after the vessel from the Star Trek series or the other way around?
5. You might use the term bonhomie to describe our relationship.
6. One thing I love about the MS Word program is its "Track Changes" feature.
7. In this course, we will use the term noetics as an indication of deep-felt self-awareness, beyond mere consciousness.
8. How am I supposed to compete at Scrabble when all I have is an X and a 7.
9. Wait, that's not a 7; it's an L.
10. That, ladies and gentleman, is what we in show business call a finale!

Write Write three sentences, each demonstrating your understanding of one or more rules for using italics.

1. ____

____

____

____

2. ____

____

____

____

3. ____

____

____

____

Learning Outcome

Apply quotation marks and italics in a real-world document.

LO3 Real-World Application

Practice In the following business letter, underline any words that should be italicized and add quotation marks (“ ”) where needed.

Brideshead Publishing
1012 Broadway
New York, New York 10011

May 13, 2010

Neva Konen
4004 W. Obleness Parkway
Hollenshead, New Hampshire 03305

Dear Neva Konen:

Thank you for your recent novel submission entitled A Time of Dimly Perceived Wonders, which I read with great interest. The setting is richly portrayed, and the main characters are at the same time both mysterious and familiar, conveying a certain je ne sais quas about themselves. For example, although his words land strangely on my ear, still I am overwhelmed with feelings of kinship for Anibal when he cries out, I could've et ‘em up right there 'n' then! Similarly, when at the end Kandis softly croons the words of Come One, Come All, to the Family Reunion, I feel I'm being called home myself, although I've never actually seen the Appalachians.

While I greatly enjoyed the novel, and it would certainly receive an A in my Creative Writing Seminar at Midtown College, I do have a few concerns. For one thing, the title seems long and somewhat vague; I'd recommend Foggy Mountain Memories, instead. Also, it seems unnecessary to print the full text of Abraham Lincoln's Gettysburg Address and Martin Luther King, Jr.'s, I Have a Dream speech in the chapter entitled A Few Words of Hope. Modern readers are certainly familiar with both speeches. It should be enough to merely include a few phrases, such as Four score and seven years ago, and Let freedom ring from Lookout Mountain of Tennessee.

If you are willing to accept changes such as these, I believe we can work together to make your novel a commercial success. Please review the enclosed contract and return it to me at your earliest convenience.

Sincerely,

Christene Kaley

Christene Kaley
Assistant Editor
Brideshead Publishing

Workplace

Note how improperly punctuated titles can lead to confusion in business writing. Correct punctuation makes for clear communication.

"Words, once they are printed, have a life of their own."
—Carol Burnett

Dariusz Sas, 2010/used under license from www.shutterstock.com

33 Capitalization

By now you know writing requires correct capitalization. You know that every first word in a sentence should be capitalized and so should all proper nouns and proper adjectives. But what are the special uses of capitalization? And why are some nouns capitalized in one instance but not another?

This chapter will guide you in the conventional use of capital letters in writing. Throughout the section, examples demonstrate correct capitalization and serve as a handy reference during editing and proofreading.

Learning Outcomes

LO1 Understand basic capitalization rules.

LO2 Understand advanced capitalization rules.

LO3 Understand capitalization of titles, organizations, abbreviations, and letters.

LO4 Understand capitalization of names, courses, and Web terms.

LO5 Apply capitalization in real-world documents.

What do you think?

What does a word that is capitalized reveal to you? What does incorrect capitalization reveal about a writer?

Learning Outcome

Understand basic capitalization rules.

Insight

Different languages use capitalization differently. For example, German capitalizes not just proper nouns but all nouns. Compare and contrast capitalization styles between your heritage language and English.

LO1 Basic Capitalization

All first words, proper nouns, and proper adjectives must be capitalized. The following guidelines and examples will help explain these rules.

Proper Nouns and Adjectives

Capitalize all proper nouns and all proper adjectives (adjectives derived from proper nouns). The chart below provides a quick overview of capitalization.

Quick Guide: Capitalization at a Glance

Days of the week	**Saturday, Sunday, Tuesday**
Months	**March, August, December**
Holidays, holy days	**Christmas, Hanukah, President's Day**
Periods, events in history	**the Renaissance, Middle Ages**
Special events	**Tate Memorial Dedication Ceremony**
Political parties	**Republican Party, Green Party**
Official documents	**Bill of Rights**
Trade names	**Frisbee disc, Heinz ketchup**
Formal epithets	**Alexander the Great**
Official titles	**Vice-President Al Gore, Senator Davis**
Official state nicknames	**the Garden State, the Beaver State**
Planets, heavenly bodies	**Earth, Mars, the Milky Way**
Continents	**Asia, Australia, Europe**
Countries	**France, Brazil, Japan, Pakistan**
States, provinces	**Montana, Nebraska, Alberta, Ontario**
Cities, towns, villages	**Portland, Brookfield, Broad Ripple**
Streets, roads, highways	**Rodeo Drive, Route 66, Interstate 55**
Sections of the United States and the world	**the West Coast, the Middle East**
Landforms	**Appalachian Mountains, Kalahari Desert**
Bodies of water	**Lake Erie, Tiber River, Atlantic Ocean**
Public areas	**Central Park, Rocky Mountain National Park**

First Words

Capitalize the first word in every sentence and the first word in a full-sentence direct quotation.

> **Preparing** for the final exam will help you get a good grade.
>
> Shawna asked, "**Does** anyone want to study with me at the coffee house?"

Correcting Capitalization

Practice A In each sentence below, place capitalization marks (≡) under any letters that should be capitalized.

1. Singer jack johnson finds musical inspiration in his hometown of oahu, hawaii.
2. Hawaii is the only state made up entirely of islands and is located in the pacific ocean.
3. Known as the aloha state, it's home to the hawaii volcanoes national park.
4. Another national park, the U.S.S. *arizona* memorial, is dedicated to the navy members who were lost during the attack on pearl harbor.
5. On december, 7, 1941, the United States naval base at pearl harbor, Hawaii, was attacked by japan.
6. The attack triggered the united states' entry in world war II.
7. President franklin d. roosevelt declared December 7 as "a day that will live in infamy."
8. Hawaii's beautiful beaches and tropical temperatures attract tourists from the midwest to the far east.

Practice B Read the following paragraph. Place capitalization marks (≡) under any letters that should be capitalized in proper nouns, adjectives, or first words.

My favorite holiday is thanksgiving. every november family members from illinois, indiana, and Michigan travel to my parents' house to celebrate the best thursday of the year. While Mom and my aunts work on the dressing and mashed potatoes, my cousins and I watch football on the fox network. it has long been a tradition for the Detroit lions to play a home game every thanksgiving. By the time the game is finished, the food is ready and the feast is on. Turkey, gravy, and green-bean casserole—you can't beat thanksgiving.

Learning Outcome

Understand advanced capitalization rules.

LO2 Advanced Capitalization

Sentences in Parentheses

Capitalize the first word in a sentence that is enclosed in parentheses if that sentence is not combined within another complete sentence.

My favorite designer is hosting a fashion show for her new collection. (**Now** I just need a ticket.)

Note: Do *not* capitalize a sentence that is enclosed in parentheses and is located in the middle of another sentence.

Rachel's cousin (his name is Carl) can't make it tonight.

Sentences Following Colons

Capitalize a complete sentence that follows a colon when that sentence is a formal statement, a quotation, or a sentence that you want to emphasize.

I would like to paraphrase Patrick Henry: Give me chocolate or give me death.

Salutation and Complimentary Closing

In a letter, capitalize the first and all major words of the salutation. Capitalize only the first word of the complimentary closing.

Dear Dr. Howard: **Sincerely** yours,

Sections of the Country

Words that indicate sections of the country are proper nouns and should be capitalized; words that simply indicate directions are not proper nouns.

I'm thinking about moving to the **West Coast**. *(section of country)*

I'm thinking about driving **west** to California. *(direction)*

Insight

Do not capitalize words used to indicate direction or position.

Turn **south** at the stop sign. *(South refers to direction.)*

The **South** is known for its great Cajun food. *(South refers to a region of the country.)*

Languages, Ethnic Groups, Nationalities, and Religions

Capitalize languages, ethnic groups, nationalities, religions, Supreme Beings, and holy books.

African **Navajo** **Islam** **God** **Allah**
Jehovah **the Koran** **Exodus** **the Bible**

Correcting Capitalization

Practice A In each sentence below, place capitalization marks (≡) under any letters that should be capitalized.

1. The midwest region of the United States is made up of 12 states.
2. The bible and the koran are considered holy books.
3. The navajo indians of the southwest have significant populations in an area known as the Four Corners (arizona, new mexico, utah, and Colorado).
4. Mark Twain once said this about adversity: "it's not the size of the dog in the fight; it's the size of the fight in the dog."
5. My brother Phil is starting college today. (my mom finally has the house to herself.)
6. I'm a proud member of the latino community in Miami.
7. In Quebec, Canada, many citizens speak both english and french.

Practice B Read the following paragraph. Place capitalization marks (≡) under any letters that should be capitalized.

I ate the best seafood of my life at a new england restaurant. The small, coastal restaurant in Massachusetts features fresh seafood from the atlantic ocean. I ordered the maine lobster, and I have one impression: it was awesome. If you have never tried fresh lobster before, I highly recommend it. You won't be disappointed. (now I need to figure out when I can go back.)

Practice C Place capitalization marks (≡) under any letters that should be capitalized.

tomorrow hanukah wednesday bank frisbee

u.s. bank flying disc russia tree

Learning Outcome

Understand capitalization of titles, organizations, abbreviations, and letters.

WAC

Note that the American Psychological Association has a different style for capitalizing the titles of smaller works. Be sure you know the style required for a specific class.

LO3 Other Capitalization Rules I

Titles

Capitalize the first word of a title, the last word, and every word in between except articles *(a, an, the)*, short prepositions, *to* in an infinitive, and coordinating conjunctions. Follow this rule for titles of books, newspapers, magazines, poems, plays, songs, articles, films, works of art, and stories.

The Curious Case *of* ***Benjamin Button***	***New York Times***
"**Cry Me** a **River**"	"**Cashing** in on **Kids**"
A Midsummer Night's Dream	***The Da Vinci Code***

Organizations

Capitalize the name of an organization or a team and its members.

American Indian Movement	**Democratic Party**
Lance Armstrong Foundation	**Indiana Pacers**
Susan G. Komen for the **Cure**	**Boston Red Sox**

Abbreviations

Capitalize abbreviations of titles and organizations.

M.D. **Ph.D.** **NAACP** **C.E.** **B.C.E.** **GPA**

Letters

Capitalize letters used to indicate a form or shape.

U-turn **I-beam** **V-shaped** **T-shirt**

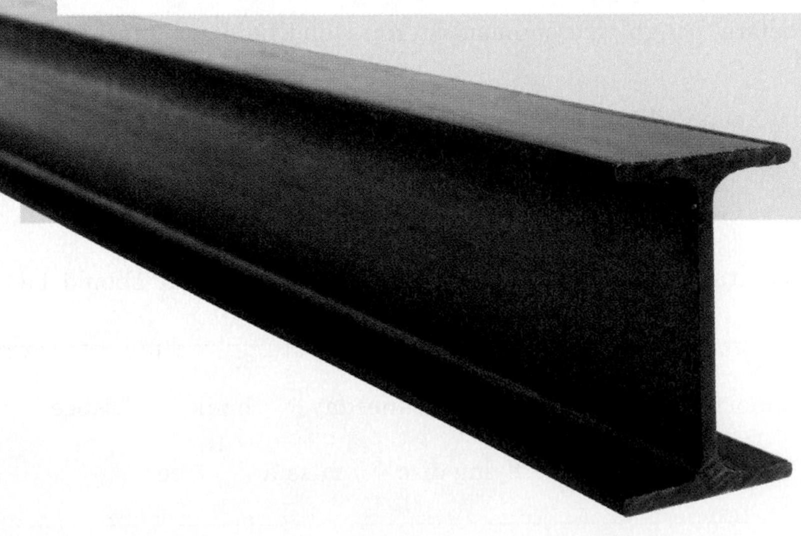

Correcting Capitalization

Practice A In each sentence below, place capitalization marks (≡) under any letters that should be capitalized.

1. I'm stopping by the gas station to pick up the sunday *Chicago tribune*.
2. The Los Angeles lakers play in the staples center.
3. At the next stoplight, you will need to take a u-turn.
4. My favorite author is Malcolm Gladwell, who wrote the best-sellers *blink* and *The tipping point*.
5. How many times have you heard the song "I got a feeling" by the Black-eyed peas?
6. The American cancer society raises money for cancer research.
7. I was happy to improve my gpa from 3.1 to 3.4 last semester.
8. Where did you buy that Seattle mariners t-shirt?
9. The doctor charted the growth of the tumor using an s-curve.
10. The man read a copy of *gq* magazine in New York City's central park.
11. Jill was promoted to chief operating officer (ceo) this july.

Practice B Read the paragraph below, placing capitalization marks (≡) under letters that should be capitalized.

On our way to the Kansas city royals game, my friend Ted and I got in an argument over our favorite music. He likes coldplay, while I prefer radiohead. His favorite song is "Vida la viva." My favorite is "Fake plastic trees." But as we argued about the merits of each band, we completely missed our exit to the stadium. Ted suggested we perform a u-turn. Instead, I used my gps to find a new route. Luckily, we made it to the ballpark in time to grab a hot dog and coke before the opening pitch.

Learning Outcome

Understand capitalization of names, courses, and Web terms.

Insight

Do not capitalize common nouns and titles that appear near, but are not part of, a proper noun.

Chancellor John Bohm . . . (Chancellor *is part of the name.)*

John Bohm, our chancellor, . . . (Chancellor *appears near, but is not part of the proper noun.)*

LO4 Other Capitalization Rules II

Words Used as Names

Capitalize words like *father, mother, uncle, senator,* and *professor* only when they are parts of titles that include a personal name or when they are substitutes for proper nouns (especially in direct address).

Hello, **Senator** Feingold. (*Senator* is part of the name.)

It's good to meet you, **Senator.** (*Senator* is a substitute for the name.)

Our **senator** is an environmentalist.

Who was your chemistry **professor** last quarter?

I had **Professor Williams** for Chemistry 101.

Good morning, **Professor.**

Note: To test whether a word is being substituted for a proper noun, simply read the sentence with a proper noun in place of the word. If the proper noun fits in the sentence, the word being tested should be capitalized. Usually the word is not capitalized if it follows a possessive—*my, his, our, your,* and so on.

Did **Dad** (Brad) pack the stereo in the trailer?
(*Brad* works in the sentence.)

Did your **dad** (Brad) pack the stereo in the trailer?
(*Brad* does not work in the sentence; the word *dad* follows the *your*.)

Titles of Courses

Words such as *technology, history,* and *science* are proper nouns when they are included in the titles of specific courses; they are common nouns when they name a field of study.

Who teaches **Art History 202**?
(title of a specific course)

Professor Bunker loves teaching **history**.
(a field of study)

Internet and E-Mail

The words *Internet* and *World Wide Web* are capitalized because they are considered proper nouns. When your writing includes a Web address (URL), capitalize any letters that the site's owner does (on printed materials or on the site itself).

When doing research on the **Internet**, be sure to record each site's **Web** address (URL) and each contact's **e-mail** address.

Correcting Capitalization

Practice A In each sentence below, place capitalization marks (≡) under any words that should be capitalized.

1. I met mayor Greg Ballard by chance today at the daily brew coffee shop.
2. When I was a freshman, I studied the history of roman art in art history 101.
3. Ever since I gained wireless access to the internet, I've spent hours each day on YouTube.
4. Let's hope dad can make it in time for our tee time.
5. In a speech to his constituents, congressman Paul Ryan called for fiscal responsibility.
6. My favorite class this semester is advanced forensics 332 with dr. Charles Wendell, a well-known professor.
7. My uncle Brad has no clue how to navigate the world wide web.
8. Elizabeth attended the Wayne State University senior Banquet.
9. In searching for exercise routines, Jack bookmarked a web address (url) for *men's health* magazine.
10. You will need to contact commissioner Sheffield for permission.

Practice B Read the paragraph below, placing capitalization marks (≡) under any words or letters that should be capitalized.

Before Steve Jobs became ceo of apple Inc. and the brainchild behind Macintosh, he attended high school in the San Francisco bay Area, a region that is famously known as silicon valley. Jobs enrolled at Reed College in portland, Oregon, but dropped out after the first semester to return home to co-create apple. At the same time, other tech innovators flooded the area to create companies such as Hewlett-packard and Intel. It is also here where internet giants google and Yahoo! were founded. Today Silicon valley remains a region of technological innovation.

Learning Outcome

Apply capitalization in real-world documents.

LO5 Real-World Application

Correct In the following basic letter, place capitalization marks (≡) under letters that should be capitalized. If a letter is capitalized and shouldn't be put a lowercase editing mark (/) through the letter.

Ball State university Volunteer Center
7711 S. Hampton drive
Muncie, IN 47302
July, 5 2010

Mr. Ryan Orlovich
Muncie parks Department
1800 Grant Street
Muncie, IN 47302

Dear superintendent Orlovich:

Last Saturday, the Ball State volunteer center committee met to discuss new volunteer opportunities for the upcoming semester. We are interested in putting together a service event at big oak park for the incoming Freshmen.

We would like to get in contact with someone from your department to set up a time and date for the event. We would prefer the event to take place between thursday, August 23, and Sunday, August 26. Also, we hope to design t-shirts for the volunteers and were wondering if your office knew of any sponsors who might be interested in funding this expenditure.

When you have time, please contact me by phone at 317-555-3980 or E-mail at ehenderson@bs23u.edu. (you may also e-mail the office at bsuvolunteerism@bs23u.edu.)

Yours Truly,

Liz Henderson

Liz Henderson

BSU Volunteer President

Workplace

Proper capitalization in a business document not only reflects well on the writer, but also shows respect for the names of readers and businesses.

Special Challenge Write a sentence that includes a colon followed by another sentence you want to emphasize. (See page 388).

Sally Student

Prof. Quine

Eng. 82.7877

August 2, 2010

Abuse: An Equal Opportunity Dealer

In the selection "Forever Sorry," Sheila Sampson describes the years she spent in an abusive marriage. Sampson details many instances when she begged her husband's forgiveness for things she never did so that she could avoid being physically assaulted by him. She was often unsuccessful. In fact, Sampson's husband was so abusive that she finally realized that her only recourse was to seek protection at a local shelter for abused women. Looking back, she remembers the first words she uttered to the shelter staff member who greeted her on that cold night: "I'm sorry, but I need help" (96). Sampson observes that, "particularly for women, the worst mark of abuse is left on the ego to the extent that we are forever apologizing" (97). I disagree: I believe that abuse has similar emotional impact on both men and women.

According to the American Family Association (AFA), "In 1979, nearly twenty percent of Americans reported having been abused by a family member—usually by a parent or a spouse" (199). The AFA reports that the number increased to thirty percent in 1997 (201)....

Comment [CQ1]: Sally's paper is formatted in Times New Roman 12-point font (black). Her paper's margins are all set at one inch. In addition, Sally's paper is double spaced.

Comment [CQ2]: Sally's title is concise, relevant, and correctly capitalized.

Comment [CQ3]: The first line of each paragraph is indented .5 inches.

Sally's first paragraph is the essay's introduction. Sally has worked hard to interest the reader in the paper by introducing her topic early in the introduction. Sally has also saved her thesis statement (one-sentence statement of position) until the end of the introduction.

Comment [CQ4]: Sally's paper demonstrates the correct use of MLA documentation both in-text (parenthetical) and, later, through a Works Cited page.

Comment [CQ5]: This is Sally's thesis statement.

Comment [CQ6]: Sally does a good job of transitioning from one paragraph to the next.

Works Cited

American Family Association. *The Effects of Familial Abuse.* New York: Random, 2007. Print.

Sampson, Sheila. "Forever Sorry." *An Anthology of Modern Essays.*. Ed. Ben Rafoth. Portsmouth, NH: Hellick, 2000. 96-98. Print.

Comment [CQ7]: Here are the two sources Sally cited (mentioned) in her paper. Note that the entries are double-spaced. Note that the second entry runs onto a second line, which, in turn, is indented .5 inches.

CHAPTER 10

What Is Plagiarism and When Would I Be Cheating on My Paper?

- *What is plagiarism?*
- *How can I recognize the different kinds of plagiarism and cheating?*
- *How can I avoid plagiarism?*

TIPS IN THIS CHAPTER

- Definition of plagiarism
- Types of plagiarism and cheating
- Facts

What Is Plagiarism?

Plagiarism is the intellectual theft of someone else's ideas and words. When you plagiarize, you are taking someone else's work and attempting to pass it off as your own. This seems straightforward enough, but when you are writing a research paper you may find yourself saying: "All the information I have collected is new to me. How can I tell what is unique enough that it must be cited?" If you are in doubt, ask yourself the following: Are these words unique to this author? Have I seen this idea anywhere else? Have I really put this into my own words?

☞ *HELPING HAND* If you are tempted to plagiarize, consider this: Your professor is not stupid; you will rarely be able to fool her. The reasons? (1) The books and articles you use for your research, and from which you might consider plagiarizing, contain more sophisticated analyses than the average student can produce. As a result, she'll have no trouble spotting material taken from a published article. (2) Your professor reads many more books and articles than most students do, so she might very well recognize the original source immediately. If she does not, she can contact friends in the field who can probably point her in the right direction. (3) Your professor knows how to use Internet search engines as well as her students; she can find the same paper you can. Many colleges now subscribe to plagiarism-fighting databases where thousands, perhaps millions, of papers once offered for sale on the Internet are stored for cross-checking against suspected plagiarism cases.

How Can I Recognize the Different Kinds of Plagiarism and Cheating?

Plagiarism comes in all sizes and colors, sometimes blatant and sometimes more subtle. Several different types of plagiarism are described below.

Word-for-Word Transcription This example is the easiest to define. Plagiarism rules are very explicit on this point. It is forbidden to copy someone else's work, word for word, and present it as your own. If only one sentence in the paper contains a word-for-word transcription, the paper is plagiarized. Word-for-word transcriptions must be placed within quotation marks and the source cited.

Unique Terms Authors often invent their own terms to make a given point. These invented words or phrases are often combinations of two words or a merger of an English word and a foreign one. Sometimes, the word has been given a new definition by the author. Frequently, the word or combination will be contained within quotes. If you do not see this term in another article or book, you can assume that it is unique to the author. You must cite the source of any such terms.

Paraphrasing A common misconception is that if you change a few words in a text, the text is now your own. This is not true.

- If you copy the same basic sentence structure as the original text, you are plagiarizing, regardless of how many nouns and verbs you change.
- If you present your evidence in the same order as the original text, you are plagiarizing.

In other words, if you retain the same stylistic and analytical framework of the original text, you are plagiarizing.

Despite these potential pitfalls, paraphrasing can be part of your paper. You may begin a section of paraphrasing by saying something like, "Author X states . . . " or "To paraphrase author X's work . . . " and then provide a citation at the end of the section.

☞ *HELPING HAND* The best way to avoid crossing the line into plagiarism is to work solely from your own notes and your own interpretations of the data and not directly from the book.

Papers on the Web Thousands of websites selling and giving away prewritten papers have been created in the past decade. Without any doubt, it is plagiarism to copy or buy a paper from the Internet and present it as your own work.

Papers Written by Your Friends Fraternities, sororities, campus organizations, and your own friends often keep old papers on file.

Copying these papers represents plagiarism because you did not do the work and the words are not your own.

Papers You Wrote for Another Class Many students have an interest in a particular topic or region of the world and so they take a number of courses covering it. As a result, students may find themselves writing papers on similar subjects. You are cheating if you submit a paper to more than one class.

Citing Works You Have Never Read or Data You Haven't Collected The following group of offenses are loosely connected and constitute cheating.

- Padding your bibliography with materials you have never read.
- Changing the results of your data to better fit your thesis.
- Citing a source you did not actually consult.

☞ *HELPING HAND* If you're not sure if a piece of information should be cited, ask the professor. If the professor isn't available, err on the side of caution and cite the source. It's always better to use too many citations than too few.

How Can I Avoid Plagiarism?

Several options for avoiding plagiarism are available to you. Some of these options are described below.

1. Conduct sufficient research to have an understanding of what material is unique to a particular author and what information is not. This sounds like a heavy burden, but this is the goal of a research paper—to find enough information to present your case and to prove your thesis.

With each source you find, you'll have a better understanding about what information is unique to a particular author. If you do a shoddy research job, your paper will not be good, even if you don't plagiarize.

2. Never write your paper with a book or an article open in your lap or propped up on the desk. Always take notes while reading your sources, placing the ideas and facts into your own words. Only exact quotes should be written word for word and, in those cases, you should place quotes around the passage and indicate the source of the quotation. If you try to take a shortcut and highlight your sources with a marker, you're setting the stage for plagiarism later. It's much too tempting to use the original author's words if the book is right in front of you. If you write out notes in your own words from the very beginning, you're working from your own statements, not the original author's.

When you start to write the paper, place all the original sources (the books, the articles, whatever you've used) away from the computer or your writing pad. You should work only from your notes. At this point, your job is to write sentences and paragraphs that best present your analysis of the various pieces of information you've compiled. You are now reworking and rewriting your notes, not the original author's.

3. Don't copy and paste information from the Web. The procedure for copying text from a Web page and pasting it into a document is so easy that you may be tempted to do so. ***This is plagiarism.*** Students cannot take a section of someone else's work and pass it in to a professor as their own. Plagiarism rules apply to the Web as stringently as they do to traditional sources found in books, journals, and magazines. Quotes and pieces of information may be taken from Web pages but the sources must be properly identified in the paper.

This information is so important that it needs to be repeated: ***Do not be lulled by how easy it is to get information from the Web; copying and pasting someone else's words constitutes plagiarism.***

The Web should be considered a tool for research, just as a book or a magazine has always been. The Web offers thousands of newspapers, analyses, and critiques that can add to the quality of a student's paper; but only as the stepping-stones to a good paper, not as the body of that paper.

☞ *HELPING HAND* Professors have access to the same websites as the students. This means that professors can easily surf the Web and find the sources when they suspect plagiarism has occurred.

After reading about all these problems, you may be asking yourself, when can I use the copy and paste function on the Web? Since the Web can be considered a source for research, it is acceptable to copy and paste small pieces of text from the Web into a document of research notes. Next to the text, the URL of the Web page, the writer of the text (if identifiable on the page), and the date the text was obtained should all be included. In the final paper, the text must then be cited in a footnote or endnote to identify it as someone else's words and ideas.

☞ HELPING HAND If you do not heed the advice offered in this chapter, your professor and your school administration will bring you before an academic conduct board. Every school in the country has a clearly stated plagiarism policy that may differ slightly from the wording presented in this book but that covers the same general issues. The punishments for plagiarism include probation, suspension, and expulsion from the college or university.

RECAP

This chapter illustrated the many types of plagiarism so that you can avoid the pitfalls they present. Plagiarism is a serious offense because stealing intellectual property is the same as stealing a stereo. School is a time for you to learn how to think and how to write. If you steal the work of others, you're destroying the benefits of your own school experience.

Index

A

B

C

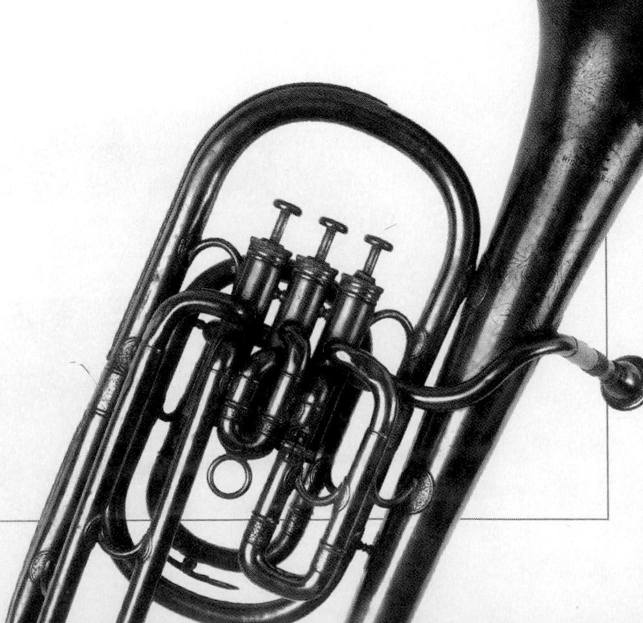

D

E

F

G

H

I

J

K

L

M

N

O

P

DONT
WALK

S

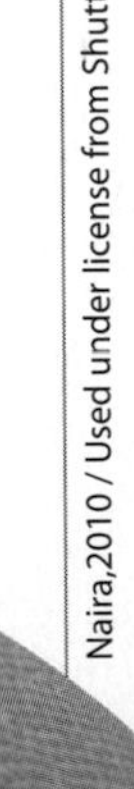
Naira,2010 / Used under license from Shutterstock.com

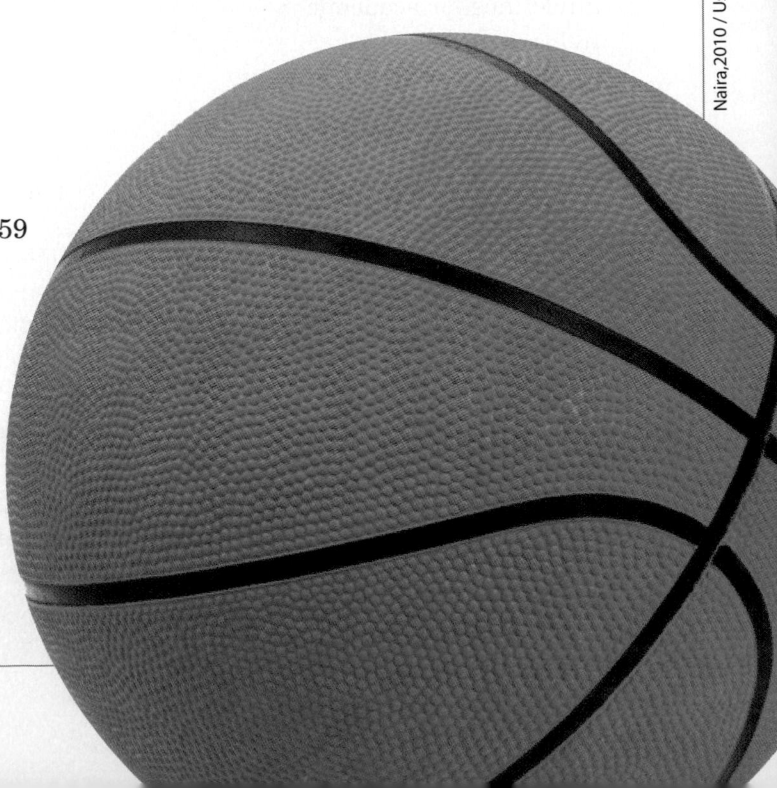

T

U

V

W

X

Y

Z

Reading-Writing Connection

Writing and reading are your two essential tools of learning. You gain new information by reading, and you understand this information more fully by writing about it. In addition, reading and writing stimulate your thinking, and being a college student is all about good thinking—about understanding causes and effects, about making comparisons, and about forming logical arguments.

1. Think of **writing** as . . .
   - a learning tool, helping you sort out your thoughts about new information, and
   - a way to share what you have learned in paragraphs and essays.

You are writing for yourself when you use writing as a learning tool; you are writing for an audience (instructors, classmates) when you are writing to share what you've learned.

2. Think of **reading** as a number of related tasks:
   - previewing the assignment,
   - writing and thinking about the text as you read, and
   - summarizing what you have learned after the reading.

If you own the book or are working with a copy, consider annotating the text (making comments on the pages) as you read.

Stimulates thinking and learning

Assess Demonstrate your understanding of the writing and reading connection by answering these two questions.

1. How is writing a learning tool?

____

____

2. How is effective, active reading more than simply following the words on the page?

____

____

Reflect Which skill challenges you more, reading or writing? Why?

____

____

____

Linking Writing and Reading Assignments

Three common strategies can help you carry out your writing and reading assignments: (1) using the STRAP strategy, (2) using the traits of writing, and (3) using graphic organizers.

1. The **STRAP strategy** consists of a series of questions to answer before you start a reading or writing assignment.

For Writing Assignments		For Reading Assignments
What specific topic should I write about?	**Subject**	What specific topic does the reading address?
What form of writing *(essay, article)* will I use?	**Type**	What form *(essay, text chapter, article)* does the reading take?
What position *(student, citizen, employee)* should I assume?	**Role**	What position *(student, responder, concerned individual)* does the writer assume?
Who is the intended reader?	**Audience**	Who is the intended reader?
What is the goal *(to inform, to persuade)* of the writing?	**Purpose**	What is the goal of the material?

2. The **traits of writing** identify the important features in reading and writing assignments. Use the traits to analyze each type of assignment.
   - Ideas (*The main points and details in a text*)
   - Organization (*The overall structure of the material*)
   - Voice (*The text's personality—how the writer speaks to the reader*)
   - Word Choice (*The writer's use of words and phrases*)
   - Sentence Fluency (*The flow of sentences*)
   - Conventions (*The correctness of the language*)
   - Design (*The appearance of the text*)

3. **Graphic organizers** chart the key points you collect for writing assignments and the key points you find in reading assignments.

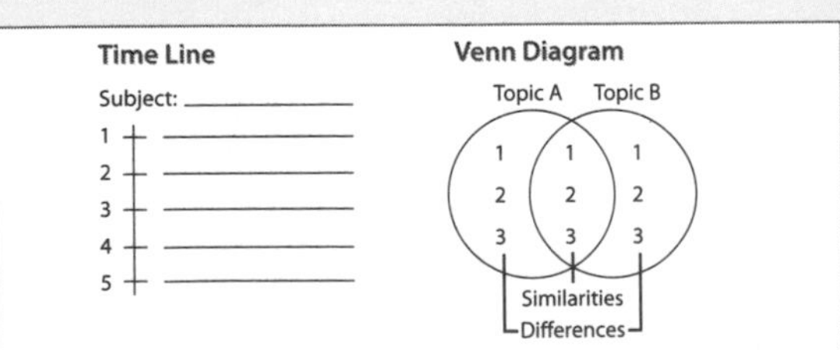

Reflect Which of these strategies would prove most helpful to you? Why?

The Writing Process

Writing is a process. It is very difficult to write a great paragraph or essay all at once. The process makes writing easy by breaking the job into five steps:

Process	Activities
Prewriting	Start the process by (1) selecting a topic to write about, (2) collecting details about it, and (3) finding your focus, the main idea or thesis.
Writing	Then write your first draft, using your prewriting plan as a general guide. Writing a first draft allows you to connect your thoughts about your topic.
Revising	Carefully review your first draft and have a classmate review it as well. Change any parts that could be clearer and more complete.
Editing	Edit your revised writing by checking for style, grammar, punctuation, and spelling errors.
Publishing	During the final step, prepare your writing to share with your instructor, your peers, or another audience.

Assess Demonstrate your understanding of the writing process by matching the steps in the process with the activities that are appropriate to each step.

1. Prewriting
2. Writing
3. Revising
4. Editing
5. Publishing

- Correcting errors in punctuation and spelling
- Posting your work online or sharing it with your instructor or family members
- Deciding what you want to write about and gathering details about it
- Asking a classmate to read your work and help you figure out the best way to fix it
- Creating a first draft and letting your planning guide the way

Reflect Which part of the writing process is most challenging to you? Why?

A "Recursive" Process

The writing process might not go in a straight line. You might be in the middle of writing when you realize you need to gather more details. After a classmate reviews your work, you might need to rewrite parts. The chart below shows how you can move back and forth in the process as you need.

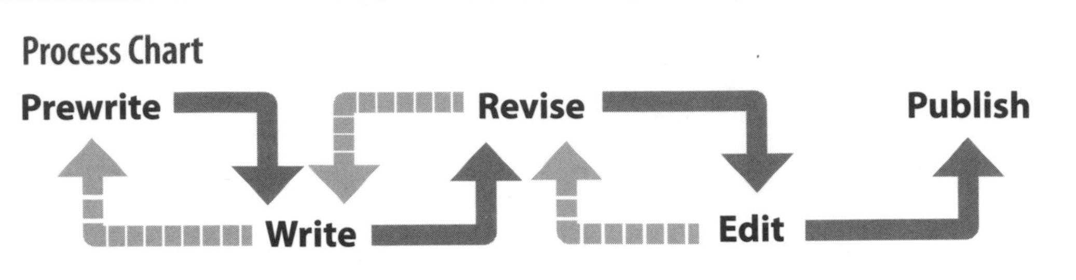

Assess For each situation below, tell which step you would move to in the writing process and why.

1. You are editing an essay when you realize that you need a stronger ending. What do you do now?

   ___

   ___

2. You are supposed to write a paragraph for a class assignment, but you can't think of what to write about. What do you do now?

   ___

   ___

3. A classmate has read your first draft and says you need to add some more interesting and exciting details. What do you do now?

   ___

   ___

4. You have posted your writing online, and people love it so much that they want you to write more about the same topic. What do you do now?

   ___

   ___

Reflect If you can always go backward and forward in the writing process, how do you know when you are "done"?

___

___

The Traits of Effective Writing

What elements make up good writing? The seven traits below provide criteria for effective writing in all forms and subject areas.

Traits	Description
Strong Ideas	Good writing contains plenty of good information (ideas and details), and all of the information holds the reader's interest.
Logical Organization	Effective writing has a clear overall structure—with a beginning, a middle, and an ending. Transitions link the ideas.
Fitting Voice	In the best writing, you can hear the writer's voice—his or her own unique way of saying things. Voice shows that the writer cares about the subject.
Well-Chosen Words	In strong writing, nouns and verbs are specific and clear, and the modifiers add important information.
Smooth Sentences	The sentences in good writing flow smoothly from one to the next. They carry the meaning of the essay or article.
Correct Copy	Strong writing is easy to read because it follows the conventions or rules of the language.
Appropriate Design	In the best academic writing, the design follows the guidelines established by the instructor or school.

Assess Demonstrate your understanding of the traits of effective writing by matching the traits with the activity that would most improve each trait.

1. Strong Ideas	■ Rearranging details into a better order
2. Logical Organization	■ Doing further research for more interesting details
3. Fitting Voice	■ Making a paragraph sound as if you were explaining something to a friend
4. Well-Chosen Words	■ Replacing a general verb with a more specific verb
5. Smooth Sentences	■ Fixing an error in subject-verb agreement
6. Correct Copy	■ Double checking to see if you need to include a cover page for your essay
7. Appropriate Design	■ Making sure your sentences don't sound too choppy

Reflect Which of the seven traits of effective writing is your greatest strength? Which one do you need to most work on?

Traits Across the Writing Spectrum

The writing traits help you write and read in any subject area. Each writing discipline has its own ideas and organizational structures that you should learn. And whether you are writing an informal blog entry or a comparison-contrast essay, strong words, smooth sentences, correctness, and effective design will make your writing stronger.

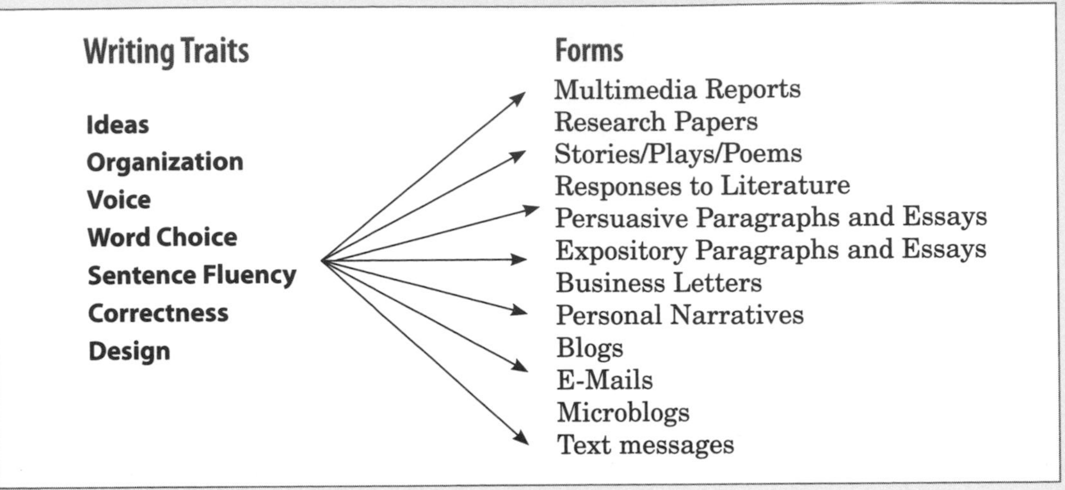

Assess For each situation below, tell which trait you would work on to improve your writing and why.

1. Your initial draft has a lot of good ideas but they seem out of order. What trait or traits could you improve upon?

   ____

   ____

2. A reader points out your new blog entry sounds too formal and doesn't show off your personality. What trait or traits could you improve upon?

   ____

   ____

3. A number of spelling and grammar errors make your e-mail message difficult to understand. What trait or traits could you improve upon?

   ____

   ____

Reflect How can the traits help you analyze your writing and reading?

____

____

Paragraph Patterns

The structure of your paragraphs and essays will depend on a clear topic sentence or thesis. Use the following formula:

Forming a Thesis

A specific topic	+	A particular feeling, feature, or part	=	An effective thesis statement or topic sentence

Once you identify a thesis, you'll need to decide how to organize information that supports it. You have many patterns of organization to choose from.

Patterns of Organization

- Use **chronological order** (time) when you are sharing a personal experience, telling how something happened, or explaining how to do something.
- Use **spatial order** (location) for descriptions, arranging information from left to right, top to bottom, from the edge to the center, and so on.
- Use **order of importance** when you are taking a stand or arguing for or against something. Either arrange your reasons from most important to least important or the other way around.
- Use **deductive organization** if you want to follow your thesis statement with basic information—supporting reasons, examples, and facts.
- Use **inductive organization** when you want to present specific details first and conclude with your thesis statement.
- Use **compare-contrast organization** when you want to show how one topic is different from and similar to another one.

Assess Demonstrate your understanding of the patterns of organization by choosing an appropriate method of organization for the example thesis statement. Briefly explain your choice.

Thesis Statement: *The view from the mountaintop was like nothing I'd ever seen before.*

Method of Organization: ____________________

Explain: ____________________

____

Reflect What is the difference between inductive and deductive organization? Which method do you prefer? Why?

____

____

Forming a Meaningful Whole

Forming a meaningful whole for a paragraph means including a topic sentence, body sentences, and a closing sentence. For an essay, it means including an opening paragraph (with a thesis statement), multiple supporting paragraphs, and a closing paragraph.

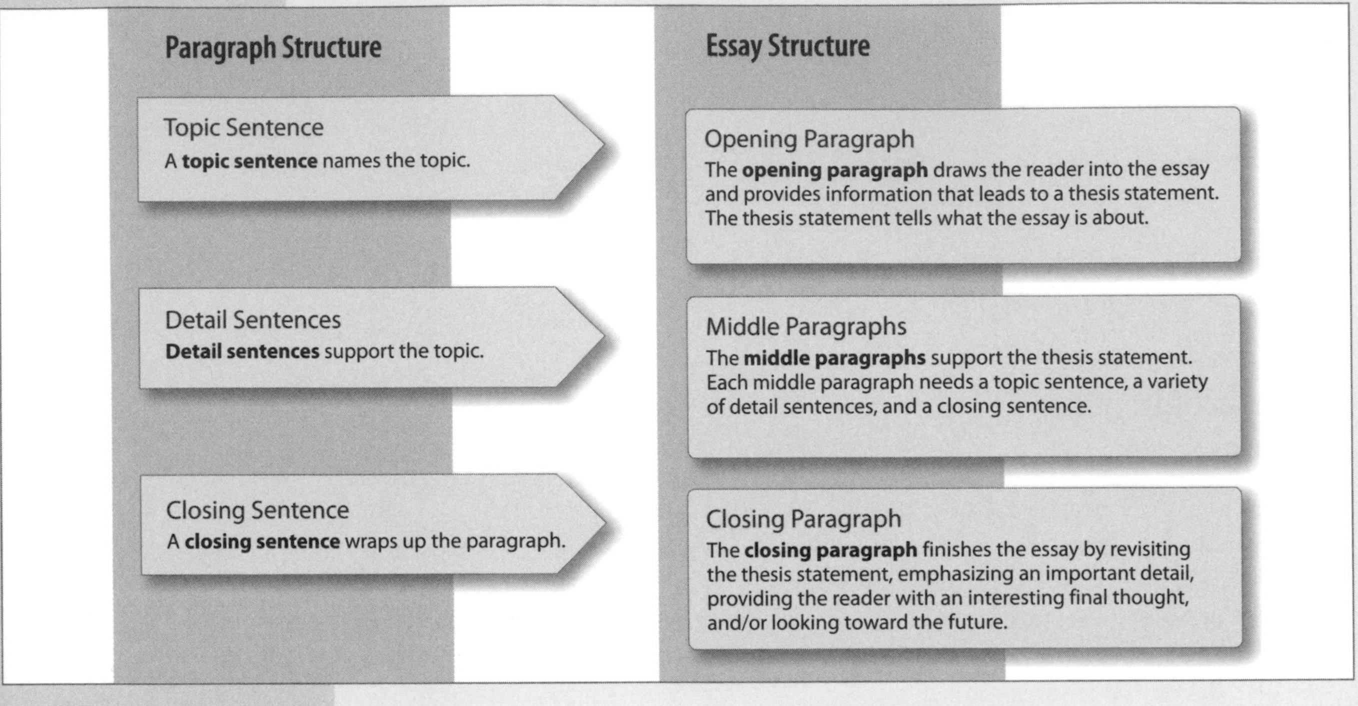

Paragraph Structure
Topic Sentence
A topic sentence names the topic.
Detail Sentences
Detail sentences support the topic.
Closing Sentence
A closing sentence wraps up the paragraph.
Essay Structure
Opening Paragraph
The opening paragraph draws the reader into the essay and provides information that leads to a thesis statement. The thesis statement tells what the essay is about.
Middle Paragraphs
The middle paragraphs support the thesis statement. Each middle paragraph needs a topic sentence, a variety of detail sentences, and a closing sentence.
Closing Paragraph
The closing paragraph finishes the essay by revisiting the thesis statement, emphasizing an important detail, providing the reader with an interesting final thought, and/or looking toward the future.

Assess Study the following writing sample. Put a plus (+) next to the sample if it forms a meaningful whole; put a minus (-) next to the sample if it doesn't. Explain what is missing if you label a sample with a minus.

____ Air travel is both amazing and frustrating, and not necessarily in that order. My air travel experience from Boston back to my hometown in rural Illinois last weekend demonstrates this point. In one sense, the convenience of the trip was extraordinary. To think I flew from Massachusetts Bay in Boston, to Newark, NJ (where I saw the Statue of Liberty outside my window), to Rockford, IL in under four hours is mind blowing. But the plane rides were less than spectacular. In fact, they were downright miserable.

Explanation: ______________________________

____

Reflect How do the structure of paragraphs and essays relate to each other?

____

____

Simple Sentences

A simple sentence consists of a subject and a verb and expresses a complete thought. The subject names what the sentence is about, and the verb says what the subject does or is. A direct object can receive the action of the verb.

Subject + Verb	**Subject + Verb + Direct Object**
Roger works.	He builds homes.

Compound Sentences

A compound sentence consists of two simple sentences joined with a comma and a coordinating conjunction (*and, but, or, nor, for, so, yet*). (The sentences can also be joined with a semicolon.)

Simple Sentence + , CC + Simple Sentence

Roger works**, for** he builds homes.

Complex Sentences

A complex sentence consists of two simple sentences joined with a subordinating conjunction. The subordinating conjunction makes one sentence depend on the other.

Dependent Clause + Simple Sentence

When Roger works, he builds homes.

Simple Sentence + Dependent Clause

Roger works whenever he builds homes.

Subordinating Conjunctions	
after	since
although	so that
as	that
as if	though
as long as	unless
because	until
before	when
even though	whenever
given that	where
if	whereas
in order that	while
provided that	

Assess Join the following simple sentences first as a compound sentence and then as a complex sentence.

Roger also builds boats. He is a novice at boat building.

Compound sentence: ______________________________

____

Complex sentence: ______________________________

____

Reflect Coordinating conjunctions connect sentences in an equal way, and subordinating conjunctions join sentences in an unequal way. Explain.

Avoiding Fragments

A sentence must have a subject and verb and must express a complete thought. Otherwise, the group of words is a sentence fragment. You can fix a fragment by supplying the part it is missing.

Fragment Missing a Subject		**Sentence With a Subject**
Works all summer.	→	Roger works all summer.
Fragment Missing a Verb		**Sentence With a Verb**
His construction company.	→	His construction company thrives.
Fragment Missing a Subject and Verb		**Sentence With a Subject and Verb**
With three projects.	→	They are busy with three projects.
Fragment Missing a Complete Thought		**Sentence With a Complete Thought**
When they work.	→	When they work, the company thrives.

Avoiding Run-On Sentences and Comma Splices

When joining two simple sentences to make a compound sentence, make sure to use both a comma and a coordinating conjunction. If you leave out both, you have a run-on, and if you leave out the conjunction, you have a comma splice.

Run-On Missing Both		**Compound Sentence Joined Correctly**
Roger works hard he is tired.	→	Roger works hard, and he is tired.
Comma Splice Missing Conjunction		**Compound Sentence Joined Correctly**
Roger works hard, he is tired.	→	Roger works hard, and he is tired.

Assess Correct each fragment, run-on, or comma splice below.

1. The Roger Davies Construction Company. ______________________________

____

2. Built the convention center. ______________________________

____

3. On time and on budget. ______________________________

____

4. Roger runs the company he has 12 employees. ______________________________

____

Reflect Why are complete, correct sentences more important in writing than in speaking?

Varying Lengths and Beginnings

If all your sentences are the same, your writing will sound repetitive and dull. You can create interest by using different lengths of sentences and beginning them in different ways.

Sentence Lengths

Here are the three basic sentence lengths and their best uses:

Medium sentences (10–20 words): Use medium sentences to express most ideas.

When I saw the advertisement online, I wrote my résumé and cover letter and sent them in.

Long sentences (over 20 words): Use long sentences to express complex ideas.

After waiting anxiously to hear from the employer, I received a call requesting an interview, went in to meet the department manager, toured the facility, and completed a test.

Short sentences (under 10 words): Use short sentences to make a point.

I got the job!

Sentence Beginnings

Instead of starting each sentence with the subject, start some sentences with a transition word, phrase, or clause.

Transition Word

However, I won't start work until July.

Transition Phrase

With all the arrangements, I won't start work until July.

Transition Clause

Though I am eager to begin, I won't start work until July.

Assess Write each type of sentence requested below.

1. Write a medium sentence about applying for school. ______________________________

____

2. Write a long sentence about the process of applying. ______________________________

____

3. Write a short sentence about the result of applying. ______________________________

____

Reflect What transition word, phrase, or clause could you use to start a sentence above?

Varying Kinds of Sentences

Some sentences make statements. Others ask questions. Still others express strong emotion, give commands, or show how one condition depends on another. Here are the different kinds of sentences and their best uses.

Statements provide information about the subject. Use them most often.

I was one of 25 applicants for the job.

Questions ask for information about the subject. Use them to engage the reader.

What made me stand out from the other applicants?

Exclamations express strong emotion. Use them sparingly in academic writing.

I had the best attitude!

Commands tell the reader what to do. (They have an implied subject—*you.*) Use them to call the reader to act.

Show a positive attitude when you interview.

Conditional sentences show that one situation depends on another.

If you have a good attitude and résumé, then the interviewer will notice.

Assess Write each kind of sentence requested below.

1. Write a statement about finding a job. ______________________________

____

2. Write a question about finding a job. ______________________________

____

3. Write an exclamation about finding a job. ______________________________

____

4. Write a command about finding a job. ______________________________

____

5. Write a conditional (if/then) about finding a job. ______________________________

____

Reflect How do different kinds of sentences reflect different kinds of thinking?

____

____

Combining Sentences

Sometimes sentences are short and choppy and should be combined to improve the flow of thought. Use the following strategies.

Coordination

When two sentences share equal ideas, combine them using a comma and a coordinating conjunction (*and, but, or, nor, for, so, yet*). To combine three or more sentences, create a series, using a comma between each sentence and a coordinating conjunction before the last.

Two sentences: I'm a nursing major. My roommate studies business.
Combined: I'm a nursing major, but my roommate studies business.

Three sentences: I'll heal you. She'll bill you. Mark will drive you home.
Combined: I'll heal you, she'll bill you, and Mark will drive you home.

Subordination

When one sentence is less important than another, combine them using a subordinating conjunction. Place the subordinating conjunction before the less-important sentence, creating a dependent clause. If the dependent clause comes first, put a comma after it.

Two sentences: Mark drives a taxi. He hopes to be an actor.
Combined: Though Mark drives a taxi, he hopes to be an actor.
Combined: Mark drives a taxi though he hopes to be an actor.

Subordinating Conjunctions	
after	since
although	so that
as	that
as if	though
as long as	unless
because	until
before	when
even though	whenever
given that	where
if	whereas
in order that	while
provided that	

Assess Combine each pair of sentences as indicated.

Mark has appeared on stage. He has done more work backstage.

1. Coordinate ______________________________

____

2. Subordinate ______________________________

____

Acting is a tough career. Mark has talent and drive.

3. Coordinate ______________________________

____

4. Subordinate ______________________________

____

Combining by Moving and Deleting

Sometimes sentences sound repetitive and should be combined to be more concise. Combine such sentences by moving the key bits of information and deleting the rest.

Repetitive sentences:	I plan to be a nurse. I want to work in a hospital.
Combined sentences:	I plan to be a nurse in a hospital.

Expanding Sentences

Some sentences provide little information and should be expanded. Expand a sentence by answering the 5 W's and H about the sentence and then adding some of your answers to the sentence.

Say-nothing sentence:	She works there.
Who works there?	my friend Stacy
What does she do?	She's a pediatrics nurse.
Where does she work?	at Lakeside Memorial Hospital
When does she work?	She works nights.
Why does she work?	to support her son
How does she work?	cheerfully
Expanded sentence:	My friend Stacy cheerfully works nights as a pediatrics nurse at Lakeside Memorial Hospital.

Assess Combine the sentences in 1 and 2 by moving and deleting. Expand sentence 3 by answering the 5 W's and H about it.

1. Stacy's work supports her son. Her work also supports her husband. ______________________

____

2. Her husband works days. He works at a canning plant. ______________________

____

3. Her friend helps out.

Who helps out? ______________________

What does the friend do? ______________________

Where? ______________________

When? ______________________

Why? ______________________

How? ______________________

Expanded sentence: ______________________

____

____

Noun

A common noun refers to a general person, place, thing, or idea, and a proper noun refers to a specific person, place, thing, or idea. Proper nouns are capitalized.

	Common Nouns	Proper Nouns
Person:	politician	Barack Obama
Place:	park	Yellowstone
Thing:	marker	Sharpie
Idea:	religion	Hinduism

Pronoun

There are different personal pronouns to indicate whether a person is speaking (*I, me, my, us, we*), is being spoken to (*you, your*), or is being spoken about (*he, she, they, them*).

	Singular			Plural		
Person	**Nom.**	**Obj.**	**Poss.**	**Nom.**	**Obj.**	**Poss.**
First (speaking)	I	me	my/mine	we	us	our/ours
Second (spoken to)	you	you	your/yours	you	you	your/yours
Third (spoken about) masculine	he	him	his	they	them	their/theirs
feminine	she	her	her/hers	they	them	their/theirs
neuter	it	it	its	they	them	their/theirs

Verb

Verbs show number (singular or plural), voice (active or passive), and tense (present, past, and future).

	Active Voice		Passive Voice	
	Singular	**Plural**	**Singular**	**Plural**
Present Tense	I see you see he/she/it sees	we see you see they see	I am seen you are seen he/she/it is seen	we are seen you are seen they are seen
Past Tense	I saw you saw he saw	we saw you saw they saw	I was seen you were seen it was seen	we were seen you were seen they were seen
Future Tense	I will see you will see he will see	we will see you will see they will see	I will be seen you will be seen it will be seen	we will be seen you will be seen they will be seen
Present Perfect Tense	I have seen you have seen he has seen	we have seen you have seen they have seen	I have been seen you have been seen it has been seen	we have been seen you have been seen they have been seen
Past Perfect Tense	I had seen you had seen he had seen	we had seen you had seen they had seen	I had been seen you had been seen it had been seen	we had been seen you had been seen they had been seen
Future Perfect Tense	I will have seen you will have seen he will have seen	we will have seen you will have seen they will have seen	I will have been seen you will have been seen it will have been seen	we will have been seen you will have been seen they will have been seen

Adjective and Adverb

Adjectives modify nouns, and adverbs modify verbs, adjectives, or other adverbs. Each type of modifier answers a different set of questions.

Adjective Questions	Adverb Questions
Which?	How?
What kind of?	When?
How many/how much?	Where?
	Why?
	To what degree?
	How often/how long?

Conjunction

Conjunctions join ideas, showing their relationship. Coordinating conjunctions join ideas in an equal way. Correlative conjunctions stress the equality of the ideas. Subordinating conjunctions show that one idea depends on another.

Coordinating Conjunctions

and but or nor for so yet

Correlative Conjunctions

either/or neither/nor whether/or both/and not only/but also

Subordinating Conjunctions

after	as long as	if	so that	unless	where
although	because	in order that	that	until	whereas
as	before	provided that	though	when	while
as if	even though	since	till	whenever	

Preposition

Prepositions create a special relationship between a noun or pronoun and another word or phrase in the sentence. A prepositional phrase starts with a preposition (such as *by, at, on, in*), includes an object (a noun or pronoun), and functions as an adjective or adverb, answering one of the questions above.

Assess Write examples of the parts of speech requested.

1. Nouns: common ______________________ proper ______________________
2. Pronouns: first person ____________ second person ____________ third person ____________
3. Verbs: present ______________ past ______________ future ______________
4. Adjective ______________________ adverb ______________________
5. Conjunction: coordinating ______________________ subordinating ______________________
6. Conjunction: correlative ______________________ / ______________________
7. Preposition ______________________ prepositional phrase ______________________